Organizational 00/01
Behavior

First Edition

EDITOR

Dr. Fred H. Maidment
Park College

Dr. Fred Maidment is associate professor and department chair of the Department of Business Education at Park College. He received a bachelor's degree from New York University in 1970 and a master's degree from Bernard M. Baruch College of the City University of New York. In 1983 he received a doctorate from the University of South Carolina. His research interests include training and development in industry. He resides in Kansas City, Missouri, with his wife and children.

Dushkin/McGraw-Hill
Sluice Dock, Guilford, Connecticut 06437

Visit us on the Internet
http://www.dushkin.com/annualeditions/

Credits

1. Introduction to Organizational Behavior
Unit photo—TRW.
2. Individual Behavior
Unit photo—TRW.
3. Social and Group Process
Unit photo—Digital Stock.
4. Organizational Systems
Unit photo—New York Stock Exchange.
5. Organizational Change and Development
Unit photo—© 1999 by PhotoDisc.

Copyright

Cataloging in Publication Data
Main entry under title: Annual Editions: Organizational behavior. 2000/2001.
    1. Business enterprises. 2. Employee motivation. 3. Business ethics. I. Maidment, Fred., comp.
II. Title: Organizational behavior.
ISBN 0–07–233376–6   658'.16   ISSN 1525–3600

First Edition

Printed in the United States of America   1234567890BAHBAH543210   Printed on Recycled Paper

Editors/Advisory Board

Staff

To the Reader

In publishing ANNUAL EDITIONS we recognize the enormous role played by the magazines, newspapers, and journals of the public press in providing current, first-rate educational information in a broad spectrum of interest areas. Many of these articles are appropriate for students, researchers, and professionals seeking accurate, current material to help bridge the gap between principles and theories and the real world. These articles, however, become more useful for study when those of lasting value are carefully collected, organized, indexed, and reproduced in a low-cost format, which provides easy and permanent access when the material is needed. That is the role played by ANNUAL EDITIONS.

New to ANNUAL EDITIONS is the inclusion of related World Wide Web sites. These sites have been selected by our editorial staff to represent some of the best resources found on the World Wide Web today. Through our carefully developed topic guide, we have linked these Web resources to the articles covered in this ANNUAL EDITIONS reader. We think that you will find this volume useful, and we hope that you will take a moment to visit us on the Web at *http://www.dushkin.com* to tell us what you think.

This first of edition of *Annual Editions: Organizational Behavior* is a compilation of some of the most current research and articles in the field. Articles have been selected from a wide variety of sources, including *The Harvard Business Review, Organizational Dynamics, The Academy of Management Journal,* and *The Futurist.* We think you will find this collection to be a useful source of current instructional materials in organizational behavior.

Annual Editions: Organizational Behavior contains a number of features designed to make the book easy to use. These include a *table of contents* with abstracts that summarize each article, a *topic guide* for locating articles on specific subjects, and *World Wide Web* sites that can be used to further explore topics that are addressed in the essays. These sites are cross-referenced by number in the topic guide and can be hot-linked through the *Annual Editions* home page: *http://www.dushkin.com/annualeditions/.* The volume is organized into five units, each dealing with specific interrelated topics in organizational behavior. The overviews at the beginning of each section provide the reader with the necessary background information that allows the reader to place the selections in the context of the book. Also, at the end of each section are short exercises for use in the instructional setting that are designed to illustrate selected topics from the section.

This is the first edition of *Annual Editions: Organizational Behavior,* and we hope that it will be the first in a long line of books addressing the most current developments in the field. This collection, we believe, provides the reader with the most current selection of readings available on the subject. To help us with the revision of this volume, we would like your help. Please take a few minutes to complete the *article rating form* in the back of the volume. Anything can be improved, and your comments will be important to the process.

Fred Maidment
Editor

Contents

A. ORGANIZATIONAL BEHAVIOR IN CONTEXT

B. EMPLOYER–EMPLOYEE RELATIONS

UNIT 1

Introduction to Organizational Behavior

Five articles in this section review
the organizational paradigms
and development of industry.
Also considered are the relations
of the individual in the workplace.

The concepts in bold italics are developed in the article. For further expansion please refer to the Topic Guide and the Index.

UNIT 2

Individual Behavior

In this section, eight selections examine diversity in the workforce, organizational policies, ethical issues, motivation, and mentoring programs.

The concepts in bold italics are developed in the article. For further expansion please refer to the Topic Guide and the Index.

UNIT 3

Social and Group Process

Seven articles discuss how
groups interact with regard to
networking, establishing
relationships, communication,
negotiation, and team dynamics.

UNIT 4

Organizational Systems

Ten articles in this section examine
the dynamics of organizational
designs, external influences on the
organization, training, the impact
of women on the workplace, the
significance of human resources, and
the importance of commitment.

The concepts in bold italics are developed in the article. For further expansion please refer to the Topic Guide and the Index.

The concepts in bold italics are developed in the article. For further expansion please refer to the Topic Guide and the Index.

UNIT 5

Organizational Change and Development

In this section, five selections
examine the importance of
developing a learning organization, merger integration,
and the importance
of stress management.

The concepts in bold italics are developed in the article. For further expansion please refer to the Topic Guide and the Index.

The concepts in bold italics are developed in the article. For further expansion please refer to the Topic Guide and the Index.

This topic guide suggests how the selections and World Wide Web sites found in the next section of this book relate to topics of traditional concern to organizational behavior students and professionals. It is useful for locating interrelated articles and Web sites for reading and research. The guide is arranged alphabetically according to topic.

The relevant Web sites, which are numbered and annotated on pages 4 and 5, are easily identified by the Web icon (◎) under the topic articles. By linking the articles and the Web sites by topic, this ANNUAL EDITIONS reader becomes a powerful learning and research tool.

TOPIC AREA	TREATED IN	TOPIC AREA	TREATED IN
Communication	2. New Agenda for Organization Development 3. New Loyalty: Grasp It. Earn It. 4. *Trust*, an Asset in Any Field 5. Organizational Cynicism 9. Measuring the Effectiveness of Recognition Programs 11. Guide Lines 12. Will Your Culture Support KM? 14. Networks within Networks 15. Managing Staff Relationships 16. Organizational Rules on Communicating 18. Interest Alignment and Coalitions 19. Keeping Team Conflict Alive 20. Inter- and Intracultural Negotiations 22. Beyond the Org Chart 27. New Keys to Employee Performance and Productivity 29. Building Heart and Soul 31. Toward a Learning Organization 32. Integrating Corporate Culture 33. Building Teams across Borders 35. Desperately Seeking Synergy ◎ *1, 2, 5, 6, 7, 16, 17, 18, 19, 20, 21, 22, 23*		29. Building Heart and Soul 33. Building Teams across Borders 35. Desperately Seeking Synergy ◎ *1, 2, 5, 6, 9, 16, 17, 18, 19, 20, 21, 22*
Diversity	1. Shifting Paradigms 3. New Loyalty: Grasp It. Earn It. 6. Building a Rainbow 7. Why Diversity Matters 13. Managing Oneself 14. Networks within Networks 18. Interest Alignment and Coalitions 20. Inter- and Intracultural Negotiations 25. Feminization of the Workforce 32. Integrating Corporate Culture from International M&As 33. Building Teams across Borders 35. Desperately Seeking Synergy ◎ *2, 4, 9, 10, 11, 12, 14, 15, 34*	**Human Resources**	2. New Agenda for Organization Development 5. Organizational Cynicism 6. Building a Rainbow 7. Why Diversity Matters 9. Measuring the Effectivness of Recognition Programs 11. Guide Lines 13. Managing Oneself 24. There Is No Future for the Workplace 25. Feminization of the Workforce 26. Making Work Meaningful: Secrets of the Future-Focused Corporation 27. New Keys to Employee Performance and Productivity 28. What Do CEO's Want from HR? 29. Building Heart and Soul 30. Cultural Change Is the Work/Life Solution 32. Integrating Corporate Culture 34. Cutting-Edge Stressbusters ◎ *1, 2, 3, 4, 5, 6, 8, 9, 10, 11, 12, 14, 15, 20, 22, 24, 25, 26, 27, 29, 32*
Group Behavior	1. Shifting Paradigm 2. New Agenda for Organization Development 3. New Loyalty: Grasp It. Earn It. 5. Organizational Cynicism 6. Building a Rainbow 7. Why Diversity Matters 9. Measuring the Effectivensss of Recognition Programs 12. Will Your Culture Support KM? 13. Managing Oneself 14. Networks within Networks 15. Managing Staff Relationships 16. Organizational Rules on Communicating 18. Interest Alignment and Coalitions 20. Inter- and Intracultural Negotiations 22. Beyond the Org Chart	**Leadership**	1. Shifting Paradigms 2. New Agenda for Organization Development 3. New Loyalty: Grasp It. Earn It. 4. *Trust*, an Asset in Any Field 5. Organizational Cynicism 12. Will Your Culture Support KM? 17. What Makes a Leader? 21. Shape of the New Corporation 22. Beyond the Org Chart 23. Future That Has Already Happened 24. There Is No Future for the Workplace 28. What Do CEO's Want from HR? 31. Toward a Learning Organization 35. Desperately Seeking Synergy ◎ *5, 6, 17, 18, 20, 28, 29, 30, 31, 33*
		Morale	1. Shifting Paradigms 2. New Agenda for Organization Development 3. New Loyalty: Grasp It. Earn It. 4. *Trust*, An Asset in Any Field 5. Organizational Cynicism 7. Why Diversity Matters 8. Walking the Tightrope, Balancing Risks and Gains 9. Measuring the Effectivness of Recognition Programs

● AE: Organizational Behavior

The following World Wide Web sites have been carefully researched and selected to support the articles found in this reader. If you are interested in learning more about specific topics found in this book, these Web sites are a good place to start. The sites are cross-referenced by number and appear in the topic guide on the previous two pages. Also, you can link to these Web sites through our DUSHKIN ONLINE support site at *http://www.dushkin.com/online/*.

The following sites were available at the time of publication. Visit our Web site—we update DUSHKIN ONLINE regularly to reflect any changes.

General Sources

1. American Psychological Association
http://www.apa.org/books/homepage.html
Search this site to find references and discussion of important workplace issues for the 1990s and beyond, including restructuring and revitalization of businesses.

2. Human Resource Professional's Gateway to the Internet
http://www.hrisolutions.com/index2.html
Eric Wilson's site is rich with information about human resources management and links easily to additional Web sources.

3. HVL HR Internet Resources
http://www.hvl.net/hr_res.htm
This site covers topics that range from Benefits to Salary Information, to Recruiting and Training.

4. Voice of the Shuttle
http://humanitas.ucsb.edu/shuttle/commerce.html
Information on many subjects includes Restructuring, Reengineering, Downsizing, Flattening; Outsourcing; Human Resources Management; Labor Relations; Learning Organizations; The Team Concept; and Diversity Management.

Introduction to Organizational Behavior

5. Center for Organizational Theory (COT)
http://socrates.berkeley.edu/~iir/cot/cot.html
COT was founded in 1995 at the Institute of Industrial Relations at the University of California, Berkeley. Its major research project centers on the demography of corporations and industries and organizational processes.

6. Industrial-Organizational Psychology Resource Center
http://www.cs.ius.indiana.edu/LZ/PMCCARTH/web_docs/homepage.htm
Dr. Patrick McCarthy's site is for new students and experienced professionals alike. Both will find many valuable resources here, including documents and information on numerous industrial-organizational psychology topics of interest.

7. Monograph: Trust within the Organization
http://www.psc-cfp.gc.ca/prcb/mono1-e.htm
This monograph from the Public Service Commission of Canada concludes that trust is an essential element of effective change management and organizational success.

8. Society for Human Resource Management (SHRM) HR Links
http://www.shrm.org/hrlinks/
Here is a very complete collection of links, that includes topics such as Diversity, Flexible Work Arrangements, International HR, and Management Practices. From this starting point, explore other aspects of SHRM also.

Individual Behavior

9. American Civil Liberties Organization (ACLU)
http://www.aclu.org/issues/worker/campaign.html
The ACLU provides this interesting page on workplace rights in "Campaign for Fairness in the Workplace." Briefing papers on workplace issues cover issues of lifestyle discrimination, workplace drug testing, and electronic monitoring.

10. Career Magazine: Diversity in the Workplace
http://www.careermag.com/newsarts/diversity/fed.html
This keynote address by David Clark of Federated Department Stores offers seven indicators of an employer's genuine commitment to diversity.

11. Diversity in the Workforce
http://www.consciouschoice.com/issues/cc083/workdiv.html
This article by Lisa Stewart appeared in the magazine *Conscious Choice* and provides interesting reading on the issue of diversity in the workplace.

12. Diversity in Workforce Produces Bottom Line Benefits
http://www.villagelife.org/news/archives/diversity.html
Melissa Lauber's short article following the $176 million discrimination settlement with Texaco is presented here. Related Web sites are also available at this site.

13. Knowledge Management and Organizational Learning
http://www.brint.com/OrgLrng.htm
BRINT, the BizTech Network provides this exhaustive site that covers definitions, discussions, and data mining, and it presents unlimited resources on organizational learning and learning organizations, and out-of-box thinking.

14. Report on Workforce Diversity
http://www.fs.fed.us/land/fire/difference.htm
At this site, an update and revitalization of Fire and Aviation Management's efforts to improve workforce diversity is available. The report offers key recommendations for revitalizing the human resource specialist's position that can be adapted by other companies.

15. Workforce Diversity Plan for ORNL
http://www.ornl.gov/HR_ORNL/WFD/plan_pub.htm
Oak Ridge National Laboratory's (ORNL) report concerns diversity leadership in order to achieve mission success "in a rapidly changing scientific business and political environment through the unique strengths of our employees, community, and business partners."

Social and Group Process

16. IIR Library Site Map
http://socrates.berkeley.edu/~iir/sitemap.html
This site map of the Institute of Industrial Relations at the University of California, Berkeley, points out research planned by the Center for Culture, Organization, and Politics, the Center for Organization and Human Resource Effectiveness, and the Center for Work, Technology, and Society.

17. Journal of Organizational Behavior: Aims and Scope
http://www.interscience.wiley.com/jpages/0894-3796/aims.html
The Journal of Organizational Behavior reports on the growing research in organization behavior fields throughout the world. Topics include motivation, work performance, job design, quality of work life, training, leadership, and many more.

18. Organizational Behavior and Human Decision Processes
http://www.apnet.com/www/journal/ob.htm
Research areas presented by this journal include group structure and communication, individual and group decision processes, judgment and choice behavior, leadership, and task performance and motivation.

19. Teams, Teambuilding, and Teamwork
http://www.organizedchange.com/teamhome.htm
Here is a source for articles on teams that are accessible on the Internet. Titles include "Improving Cross-Functional Teamwork" and "Nailing Jelly to a Tree: Self-Directed Work Teams," among many others.

Organizational Systems

20. Center for Organization and Human Resource Effectiveneess
http://socrates.berkeley.edu/~iir/cohre/cohre.html
From this COHRE page navigate to Brief Policy Papers, Research in Progress, and a Virtual Library. The Center is dedicated to "anticipating and creating new responses to a continuously changing business environment."

21. Global Business Network (GBN)
http://www.gbn.org/home.html
Committed to perceiving the present in order to anticipate the future and better manage strategic responses, the GBN's activities and services are designed to think collaboratively about the business environment. GBN originates scenario planning and offers help with the process online.

22. Human Resources—Corporate Culture
http://www.auxillium.com/culture.htm
This site offers a short and interesting paper on corporate culture. It includes the Hofstede Cultural Orientation Model, which classifies cultures based on where they fall on five continuums.

23. Organizational Development
http://home.navisoft.com/hrmbasics/orgdev.htm
The Human Resource Basics home page includes an excellent list of Web sites and discussion lists.

Organizational Change and Development

24. AHN.COM: Researchers Link Job Strain, Hypertension
http://www.ahn.com/Health_News_Nov/112398A.htm
Among the interesting research pieces available at this America's Health Network site is this one on stress.

25. APA HelpCenter: Get the Facts: Psychology at Work: Stress in the Workplace
http://helping.apa.org/work/stress5.html
This selection is adapted from *The Stress Solution* by Lyle Miller and Alma Dell Smith, and it is offered by the American Psychological Association.

26. Canadian Institute of Stress
http://www.stresscanada.org/wman.html
In this selection, which focuses on "corporate vitality," you are invited to evaluate "How Fit for Change" any particular workforce is when compared to 100 North American workplaces. Learn about change management programs here.

27. Employer-Employee.com: Preventing and Curing Employee Burnout
http://www.employer-employee.com/Burnout.html
This article offers suggestions for how to tell whether an employee problem is burnout and, if so, how to deal with it.

28. Organisation and Management Theory
http://www.nbs.ntu.ac.uk/staff/lyerj/list/hromt.htm
This part of Ray Lye's list of Human Resource Management Resources on the Internet includes links to Learning Organisation, Research at Harvard Business School, Human Change by Design, Learning and Change, and Organisations.

29. Organizational Behavior Resources
http://www.graceland.edu/~dungan/org-be/resources_org-be.html
Andy Dungan keeps this Internet list on organizational behavior and human resource management research resources at Graceland College. Links include organizational behavior sources, an essay on corporate culture, material on organizational development, and a site on quality management principles.

30. Organized Change Consultancy
http://www.organizedchange.com/framesetindex.htm
This selection from an international consulting and training firm includes a useful miniquiz for evaluating companies, many articles, and a topical index.

31. Researching Organisational Change and Learning
http://www.nova.edu/ssss/QR/QR2-4/rhodes.html
Carl Rhodes's paper offers a qualitative narrative approach to organizational change and learning.

32. Simple Stress-Busters Relieve Burnout
http://www.ncci.com/html/ncfoj2.htm
Bill Hager discusses how an enlightened employer can reduce workers' compensation costs by following 10 actions to relieve employee stress.

33. Six Management Concepts
http://www.timesystem.com/timesystem/methods/book/default.htm
This book, published on the Web, examines the contemporary concepts of benchmarking, networking, business process reengineering, organizational learning, core competence, and empowerment.

34. Studies in Cultures, Organizations, and Societies
http://www.ucalgary.ca/~cancomm/studies.html
A scholarly forum for critical debate on the culture and symbolism of everyday life in organizations can be acessed here.

We highly recommend that you review our Web site for expanded information and our other product lines. We are continually updating and adding links to our Web site in order to offer you the most usable and useful information that will support and expand the value of your Annual Editions. You can reach us at: *http://www.dushkin.com/annualeditions/*.

www.dushkin.com/online/

Unit 1

Unit Selections

Organizational Behavior in Context

1. **Shifting Paradigms: From Newton to Chaos,** Toby J. Tetenbaum
2. **The New Agenda for Organization Development,** W. Warner Burke

Employer-Employee Relations

3. **The New Loyalty: Grasp It. Earn It. Keep It.,** Jennifer Laabs
4. ***Trust,* an Asset in Any Field,** Roger C. Mayer
5. **Organizational Cynicism,** James W. Dean, Jr., Pamela Brandes, and Ravi Dharwadkar

EXERCISE 1: What Participation? Have Them "Vote with Their Feet"! Barbara H. Holmes

Key Points to Consider

❖ People are the primary asset of any organization. Name several other forms of competitive advantage in the marketplace.

❖ What is the value of trust in the organization? Between employees? Between the employee and the employer?

❖ In a changing world where order is becoming chaos, how can organizations deal with change?

❖ How can companies and employees deal with the changes in the social contract between employer and employee?

 **Links** www.dushkin.com/online/

5. **Center for Organizational Theory (COT)**
   http://socrates.berkeley.edu/~iir/cot/cot.html
6. **Industrial-Organizational Psychology Resource Center**
   http://www.cs.ius.indiana.edu/LZ/PMCCARTH/ web_docs/homepage.htm
7. **Monograph: Trust within the Organization**
   http://www.psc-cfp.gc.ca/prcb/mono1-e.htm
8. **Society for Human Resource Management (SHRM) HR Links**
   http://www.shrm.org/hrlinks/

These sites are annotated on pages 4 and 5.

Organizations are made up of people—not machines, balance sheets, or buildings. For an organization to be successful in today's highly competitive global environment, it must rely on its people.

For most organizations, competitive advantage founded on technology is often transitory at best and deceptive at worst, especially as the pace of technological change quickens and today's cutting edge technology becomes tomorrow's obsolete equipment.

Organizations themselves must recognize that they are bound to change over time, if for no other reason than the fact that their personnel will change over time. It bears repeating that a corporation is a collection of individuals with different and varied talents, all seeking to achieve success in their daily lives, which includes their role in the company.

The only thing that is certain for any organization today is that things are changing. In the past, most organizations and people viewed the world in a sort of linear context. This view of the world can be traced back to one of the first modern scientists, Isaac Newton. One of the great minds to grace the world's stage, Newton developed the intellectual basis for most of the world's scientific and intellectual development for the past 400 years. That linear approach no longer necessarily applies. Just as Newton's physics was replaced by Albert Einstein's, because it was inadequate to explain what scientists were observing in the real world, so the linear explanation of reality is about to be replaced. It is no accident that a recent business best-seller by Tom Peters was entitled *Thriving on Chaos* (Park Avenue Press, 1999). The old idea of "if X then Y" is obsolete. Now the new paradigm amounts to "if X, then who knows what will follow."

The question in organizational behavior is how to deal with these rapid and unpredictable changes in the organization, and, of course, in society as a whole. Personal, internal values and ethics are the only true source of guidance possible in an environment marked by chaos. There is no great guiding beacon of light that can be used to navigate the world of work, no lighthouse of knowledge or techniques that can magically transform chaos into order. As the article "The New Agenda for Organizational Development," points out, only people who are true to their own set of values can have an impact on their organizations.

This change in the organizational environment has led to a great deal of change on the part of employees who are simply responding to and trying to make some sense out of what is essentially a chaotic world. People simply do not work for an organization for 40 years anymore and get a gold watch at the end of their working lives. Employees are no longer loyal to the organization in the old sense because the organization is no longer loyal to them. In the current environment, employees are trying to develop and prepare themselves at all times for what is likely to happen next. They will remain loyal if they perceive that it is in their interest to remain with the organization. Otherwise, they will move on. The challenge for organizations who are seeking to retain their best employees is how to take advantage of "The New Loyalty: Grasp It. Earn It. Keep It." (See article 3).

Perhaps the single greatest loss for organizations in their relations with their employees has been trust. During this era of downsizing, rightsizing, reengineering, and RIF's (reduction in force), trust has been lost in many organizations. When whole departments and divisions are simply eliminated in a frenzy of cost cutting, the employees, both those discharged and those retained, can only conclude that their individual efforts, successes, accomplishments, and concerns are of little or no consequence to the organization. The only thing that the company cares about is the short-term bottom line. "*Trust,* an Asset in Any Field" (see article 4), is thrown to the winds, and employees are left to fend for themselves.

As the twenty-first century begins, the American economy has the lowest unemployment rate in over 20 years, and the lowest employment rate among industrialized nations. Jobs are plentiful and often go begging because there are not enough qualified people to fill them. Wages are up and unemployment is down, but many employees are in a bad mood. Griping, lawsuits, and even violence are increasing because there is a gap between what organizations say and what they do. Many organizations may "talk the talk" but seem unable to "walk the walk" when the time comes. These unfulfilled expectations and promises on the part of the organization create an atmosphere of distrust. Putting the right spin on something has become more important than dealing with it in a straightforward manner. Firings become "reengineering," and layoffs, "rightsizing." Black becomes white in an almost Orwellian attempt at what amounts to "doublespeak."

These conditions have led to a new era of cynicism (see "Organizational Cynicism") that is infecting many parts of American society. People have learned that all is not as it seems and that organizations will quickly turn on people. They have been treated with disrespect and an obvious attitude that implies that they do not matter. They have learned that their best efforts are often not appreciated; that loyalty, based on the old, unspoken contract between the employees and the employer, is a thing of the past; and that their value to the organization is often measured in ways over which they have no control.

Employees and their organizations must learn to be more flexible and responsive to a changing and chaotic environment that guarantees nothing, but that will reward those willing to take advantage of the opportunities presented to them.

Shifting Paradigms:
From Newton to Chaos

Chaos theory shows us a world far more complex and unpredictable than Newton's physics can explain. Can we apply the theory to organizations?

Toby J. Tetenbaum

Chaos often breeds life,
When order breeds havoc.

—Henry Brooks Adams

Chaos theory and its spin-off, complexity theory, argue that relationships in complex systems, like organizations, are non-linear, made up of interconnections and branching choices that produce unintended consequences and render the universe unpredictable. Can this theory, now widely discussed in the scientific community, provide a new, more accurate lens for viewing organizations? Or is it something useful for physicists, with no application to management?

Various commentators have suggested that this new paradigm can be useful in dealing with current and future change in organizations. Using this lens, however, presents an unprecedented challenge for change agents in all types of organizations. The new realities differ dramatically from the past.

THE TRADITIONAL WORLD OF NEWTON

Newtonian science, the underpinning of civilization from the 1700s to the present, is rooted in physics and mathematics—rule-bound disciplines that require data "up front"

in order to operate. The core of the paradigm, the laws of motion, suggests that the world is a well-behaved machine. It offers the promise of a law-abiding and predictable universe, a belief strengthened by the notion that relationships between cause and effect are simple, clear, and linear. The "if X . . . , then Y" view of the world prevailed for two centuries, delighting scientists whose ultimate goal was to predict and control.

When we entered the industrial era, the lens of Newtonian science led us to look at organizational success in terms of maintaining a stable system. If nature or crisis upset this state, the leader's role was to reestablish equilibrium. Not to do so constituted failure. With stability as the sign of success, the paradigm implied that order should be imposed from above (leading to top-down, command-and-control leadership) and structures should be designed to support the decision makers (leading to bureaucracies and hierarchies). The reigning organizational model, scientific management, was wholly consistent with ensuring regularity, predictability, and efficiency.

When the future is viewed as predictable, organizations do well to send their top leaders off on a retreat where they can envision a future state and develop a long-range plan for realizing that vision. The leaders have various planning models at their disposal, some of which have been used effectively for years;

however, it may well be that their success has been more serendipitous than purposeful, a function of relatively quiescent times. But as the speed of change increases and as the complexities of life and of the workplace expand, the assumptions underlying models such as these, as well as traditional views of organizations and their leadership, will no longer tolerate violation. They rely too heavily on a belief in linearity and predictability.

Toby J. Tetenbaum founded Toby Tetenbaum and Associates, a consulting firm specializing in organizational behavior. Her clients include Exxon, Ciba-Geigy, Automatic Data Processing (ADP), United Water Resources, Conde Nast Publications, The New York Times Broadcasting Company, Guardian Insurance, Fidelity Investments, Fuji, TIAA-CREF, Merrill Lynch, and many colleges and universities.

Dr. Tetenbaum has designed and implemented programs and interventions in areas of management development, strategic planning, developing corporate culture, and managing change. She has created and implemented program evaluations and conducted qualitative research studies in organizations. She has also conducted workshops and seminars in various areas of organizational behavior, including leadership, interpersonal communication, managing and changing behavior, group dynamics and team building, and managing conflict.

Dr. Tetenbaum received her doctorate from New York University in educational psychology with a specialization in social psychology and research methodologies. Her post-doctoral studies at Harvard University focused on the interface between organizational behavior and management. A licensed psychologist, she has been a professor at Fordham University for 20 years where she initiated and directs the human resource education masters degree program. She has conducted research and published extensively in national and international journals.

THE NEW, NONLINEAR WORLD OF WORK

The shift from an industrial to information age has altered the nature of the workplace, the worker, and the work. Industrial era workers were located primarily in urban factories where they engaged in routine work, often on an assembly line. They worked a specific shift, punched a time clock, and performed tasks under close supervision. A "good" worker was one who was reliable and passive, capable of modest manual dexterity.

In contrast, thanks to modern technology, information era workers can be located anywhere and can conduct much of their work anytime. A telecommuter can be with his or her children after school and make up the work in the evening after the children are in bed. The prized worker is one who learns quickly and continuously, who works collaboratively, and who is comfortable in an environment of experimentation and risk. The new knowledge workers perform their work largely without supervision, and those who are engaged in collaborative efforts do so as members of self-managed teams.

It would seem obvious that these two worlds cannot operate effectively under the same set of guiding principles.

Characteristics of the 21st Century

As we enter the new millennium, the differences with the past are exacerbated by the context in which organizations operate. Organizations must now contend with six primary characteristics:

1 **Technology.** The infomedia industries (computers, communications, and consumer electronics) are capitalized at $3 trillion. It is not surprising, therefore, that whereas there were only 50,000 computers 20 years ago, that many are now installed daily. In 1994, 2.2 million people were on the World Wide Web. One year later, there were 6.6 million. Almost 20 million people own cellular phones and/or carry pagers. The new technologies increase efficiency, productivity, speed of production, and consumer power.

2 **Globalization.** Today everyone is interconnected in the flow of information, money, or goods. Between 1987 and 1992, the market value of U.S. investment abroad rose 35 percent to $776 billion. In 1994 alone, Americans bought $663 billion overseas. Foreign investment in the U.S. more than doubled between 1987 and 1992 to $692 billion. It is clear that our interdependencies are increasing.

3 Competition. Globalization and technology have led businesses to compete fiercely for market share. American icons such as the Eastman Kodak Company are finding their market share eroding on their home front. Japanese-owned Fuji, with newly built plants on American soil, has continually grabbed business from Kodak in both color film and photographic paper. The once proud auto industry has suffered as well. In 1950, America had 76 percent of the world's motor vehicle production. In 1995, our share had fallen to 25 percent.

4 Change. Today's changes are discontinuous and happening at a geometric rate. Organizations must be sufficiently agile to be instantly reconfigurable to meet new demands. The disequilibrium created is unprecedented in our history.

5 Speed. In 1946, the first computer, ENIAC, was capable of calculating 5,000 basic arithmetic operations per second, which was thought to be astounding. Today's 486 microprocessor, already being eclipsed by the Pentium chip, is capable of handling 54 million instructions per second. This incredible increase in technological speed is matched in business (product life cycles are measured in months not years) and in people's lives (most of us feel we are running as fast as we can merely to stay in place).

6 Complexity and Paradox. All of these factors contribute to the complex nature of our current existence, a situation reflected in the eruption of paradoxes that confront us. (See Exhibit 1 for examples of current organizational paradoxes.) Charles Handy predicts that paradoxes will be ubiquitous in the new millennium and will present a significant challenge to managers. As Gareth Morgan notes:

The management of organizations, of society, and of personal life ultimately involves the management of contradiction. . . .The choice that individuals and societies ultimately have before them is thus really a choice about the kind of contradiction that is to shape the pattern of daily life.

The conflicting choices or conditions that are the essence of paradox make most people uncomfortable, enveloping them in the ambiguity that attends the perceived need to choose between seeming bipolar opposites. It is human nature to prefer, to seek out, and even to expect certainty. Paradoxes threaten that world order. A common way to handle this unpleasant state is to "fix" on one polarity and to see the world as "either/or" rather than to reconcile the two polarities with "both/and" thinking.

Nowhere is this more prevalent than in managers' choice of order to the exclusion of disorder. While this option served them well in the 20th century industrial era, continuation of that practice will be a disservice in the 21st century. Tom Peters captured the essence of the situation a decade ago when he observed that we'd spent the past 40 years teaching people to create order out of chaos, but would have to spend the next 10 years teaching people to create chaos out of order. In fact, we have spent so much time teaching our organizations to be systematized and orderly that now they can't respond to the fast-changing environment.

CHAOS: THE NEW PARADIGM

Tom Peters did not use the term "chaos" gratuitously. He was on the cutting edge of a new order. The Newtonian vision of an orderly universe no longer exists.

The new world is full of unintended consequences and counterintuitive outcomes. In such a world, the map to the future cannot be drawn in advance. We cannot know enough to set forth a meaningful vision or to plan productively. In fact, engaging in such activities in the belief that we can predict the future and, to a degree, control it, is probably both illusory and dangerous, in that it allows a false and potentially debilitating sense of security.

The focus of chaos is the web of feedback loops present in every system. In some systems, the feedback loops are linear; in others, nonlinear. Business organizations, because they are made up of people and, hence, are highly complex, are nonlinear feedback systems. Feedback loops can be negative, pro-

---

EXHIBIT 1

PARADOXES FOR LEADERS AND ORGANIZATIONS IN THE 21ST CENTURY

Long-term and short-term	Independence and interdependence
Plan and experiment	People and productivity
Revenue growth and cost containment	Empowerment and accountability
Lower costs and increase quality	People skills and technical skills
Centralize and decentralize	Conflict and consensus
Product and process	Compete and cooperate
Creativity and efficiency	Stability and change
Core competency and diversification	Incremental and quantum
Specialist and generalist	Predictability and unpredictability
Entrepreneur and team player	Simplicity and complexity
Lead and follow	Intention and chance
Manager and leader	Regularity and irregularity
Take charge and everyone's a leader	Order and disorder

---

ducing stable equilibrium, or positive, producing unstable equilibrium. At their border, these two contradictory forces, operating simultaneously, pull the system in opposite directions. Scientists have discovered that, at this border area, where chaos lies, feedback autonomously flips between positive and negative, generating patterns that are neither stable nor unstable, but rather a paradoxical combination of both.

Chaos as Order

For the non-scientist, the term "chaos" conjures up images of a birthday party for 20 four-year-olds, or an airport terminal when runways have closed down in a blizzard, or a shopping mall on Christmas Eve. These images lead us to see chaos as synonymous with confusion, disarray, and pandemonium.

Scientists have learned that chaos is none of these. Rather, chaos describes a complex, unpredictable, and orderly disorder in which patterns of behavior unfold in *irregular but similar* forms. Consider, for example the regular irregularity of snowflakes: an always-recognizable six-sided figure, but each snowflake unique.

Similarly, every human is different, but we know one when we see one. Ralph Stacey calls this "bounded equilibrium" and Dee Hock, futurist and founder of Visa, calls it "chaordic," a combination of chaos plus order. As Hock puts it, "In chaordic systems, order emerges. Structure evolves. Life is a recognizable pattern within infinite diversity."

Chaos as a Self-Organizing Entity

Hock's words "emerges" and "evolves" are highly significant and at the core of chaos theory. In fact, they are what make chaos theory so intriguing: While irregular and unpredictable, the patterns that emerge from chaos have a "hidden" recognizable form. Chaos is actually constrained by the rules that govern it. If we can identify the rules, we can forecast the conditions under which the chaotic behavior will occur.

Waldrop describes research conducted by Craig Reynolds in 1987 in a nuclear physics lab in Los Alamos, New Mexico. Reynolds simulated bird-flocking behavior, having bird-like objects called "boids" fly together in a flock following only three rules: (1) fly in the direction of other objects, (2) try to match velocity with neighboring boids, and (3) avoid bumping into things. He found that the boids, forced to break apart to avoid an obstacle, soon regrouped into a new formation even though nothing about their programming told them to display this collective behavior. This demonstrates the essence of chaos theory; namely, that simple agents obeying simple rules can interact to create elaborate and unexpected behaviors.

Geographical economic development provides a real life example of this paradox of rules and randomness. How did Silicon Valley come into being? Its existence can be attributed largely to the intersection of distinguished research centers at Stanford and the University of California at Berkeley and the availability of skilled labor. While Silicon Valley is unique, other high-tech economic areas have emerged in Austin, Texas, the Triangle Research Center of North Carolina, and Route 128 outside Boston. Their emergence shares a commonality with Silicon Valley; namely, that they, too, arose in areas providing excellent educational institutions and skilled labor. Thus, while these centers differ from one another, clear patterns can be detected: The availability of advanced technology attracts electronics manufacturers which, in turn, attracts component suppliers and support companies.

The "rules" or common features in these patterns of geographical economic development would seem to suggest that they can be deliberately created, yet when governments attempt to artificially create these geographic concentrations, they often fail. One reason for this is that chaos is self-organizing. No individual was in charge of creating a high-tech industry. Silicon Valley "emerged." It is a prime example of how spontaneous self-organizing systems produce extraordinary outcomes out of chaos.

The global marketplace is another self-organizing system. No one is in charge of the market, yet considerable coherence emerges from millions of independent, but connected, decisions. The Internet is yet another example. No one is in charge of this mammoth entity, which is still in the process of evolving.

Margaret Wheatley explains the self-organizing concept in simple terms: "Life seeks order in a disorderly way . . . mess upon mess until something workable emerges." Whereas a Newtonian view of the world imposes structure on an organization from above, the biological model, represented by chaos theory, views the organization as a living, self-organizing system; complex and self-adaptive. It suggests that if you set a group of people in motion, each one following the right set of three or four simple rules, then, like the "boids" in Reynolds' study, they will spontaneously self-organize into something complex and unexpected.

Self-Organization and Emergent Change in Companies

Visa is an example of a self-organizing company. It has grown 10,000% since 1970 and is a trillion dollar business serving over half a billion people. It consists of 20,000 financial institutions operating in more than 200 countries and territories and has a staff of about 3,000 in 21 offices on four continents.

Despite its size and growth, you don't know where it's located, how it's operated, or who owns it. That's because Visa is decentralized, non-hierarchical, evolving, self-organizing, and self-regulating. Founded by Dee Hock, it is a chaordic system conceived as an organization solely on the basis of purpose and principle. Its structure evolved from them. Hock is a prime proponent of chaordic organizations and argues that the way organizations should develop is to imagine the world as it ought to be and behave accordingly.

Chaos theory is potentially threatening to organizations, particularly to those that are large and traditional, owing to the risk involved in the concept of self-organization. The concept has a prime audience, however, in the newer, smaller entrepreneurial companies whose workforces are made up of 20- and 30-year-olds who have little investment in traditional ways of doing things.

One such organization is Sony's PlayStation, a unit that had virtually no sales just three years ago. This year, PlayStation will generate worldwide revenues of more than $5 billion on gross retail sales of $9 billion. Almost everyone on the management team at PlayStation is in their 30s. Their entire day is spent managing the paradoxes of chaos and order as they juggle creativity and experimentation along with control and efficiency. In an industry that must push the envelope to survive, they live in a constant stream of tensions: balancing work with play, creativity with competition, complacency with outrageousness. The tempo in the industry is so rapid that people are assigned to new teams in readiness for a new project before they even know what that project will be. Teams are kept in constant motion, which is the essence of managing in chaos.

Motorola provides an example of a large American business that did not deliberately set out to apply the chaordic model to its organizational change (as Visa did), yet engaged in emergent change. The illustration is instructive regarding the problems change agents will face in managing the transition from the Newtonian to the Chaotic model of change in well-established organizations.

In 1983, Motorola's CEO, Bob Galvin, recognized that, despite experiencing 15 percent growth, the company faced a serious threat from foreign competition. At the biennial meeting of the company's top officers, rather than issue a directive, Galvin threw out a seemingly spontaneous challenge: renew the organization.

The officers, accustomed to specific, well-defined statements of need, goals, and plans, waited for Galvin to flesh out his ideas. When he didn't, they were baffled. Largely because they were unsure of what Galvin was proposing, they were unable to respond in their usual manner of efficiently carrying out their leader's wishes. They dealt with their confusion and anxiety by denying the need for change.

Throughout that year and into the next, managers struggled without a road map. Galvin's follow-up memo to the biennial meeting did not spell out specific actions to be taken or results to be achieved. Even a document produced late in 1984 by a Policy Committee (which included Galvin) raised more questions than it gave answers. Through it all, Galvin refused to provide a silver bullet solution.

Finally, when senior managers were asked to identify projects in their own business units and to report back on their plans and their results, progress was made. At long last, managers stopped agonizing over what Galvin wanted and began to act, to experiment, to accelerate the development and work of teams and projects. Suddenly, product development took less time and money than before. Galvin's challenge... indistinct and radical, providing neither vision nor means nor ends ... produced emergent change.

BUILDING A CHAORDIC ORGANIZATION

Few companies have the temerity to embrace the emergent paradigm to the degree that Visa and Motorola have. Rather than immerse the entire organization in the messiness attending a full acceptance of chaos theory, they are proceeding cautiously, building a *readiness* to engage in the new order, designing and erecting one or more dimensions of a culture of chaos.

1 Knowledge and Information Sharing. Knowledge is one of the primary preconditions for emergent change. Companies that want to prepare themselves to become chaordic organizations must rely on the collective intelligence of their people to create a desired future. Knowledge and information sharing go hand-in-glove. The traditional practice of hoarding knowledge in order to enhance one's personal power is not only unacceptable in the new order, it will backfire. In the chaordic organization, power accrues to those who become a source of knowledge by sharing what they know. The concept of collective intelligence presupposes system-wide sharing of information so internal barriers, such as those that prevent cross-functional learning, must be eradicated. Hewlett-Packard deals with this issue by having an award called "Not Invented Here." It is an honor bestowed on a division that implements the most ideas from other divisions in the company.

One company that understands the importance of the knowledge element of emergent change is Buckman Laboratories International, a specialty chemicals company in Memphis, Tennessee. Buckman, the CEO of this privately held company, developed a global knowledge transfer network, called K'Netix, which makes a steady flow of information accessible to everyone in the company worldwide. Answers to problems or questions can come from anyone anywhere in the world, including Buchman himself. To ensure knowledge reciprocity and sharing of information, the company offers incentives and rewards to its best knowledge sharers.

2 Innovation and Creativity. Along with knowledge and information, emergent change requires innovation and creativity. These characteristics require an organizational culture in which rules are meant to be broken and assumptions are continually being tested. They call for an environment that supports experimentation, risk-taking, and failure, and views trial-and-error as a viable process.

Companies are beginning to acknowledge that many of their successes attributed to brilliant foresight were, in fact, the result of trying lots of different things and keeping what worked. 3M, for example, began as a mining company and its evolution into the tape business was totally serendipitous. The derivation of 3M's Post-it Notes is a classic tale of accidental success. Similarly, Johnson & Johnson did not deliberately set out to enter the baby-powder market. As the story goes, a director of research sent a packet of talc to a physician who complained that patients were developing a skin irritation from the company's plaster. The director began sending talc with various products and soon customers began to buy the talc separately. Today, 44 percent of the company's revenues come from baby powder.

3 **Teamwork and Project Orientation.** Knowledge growth, information sharing, creativity, and innovation thrive best in small groups where people can interact freely. A few people with new ideas and creative thoughts is not sufficient for institutional learning unless they are encouraged to interact with others.

Therefore, to prepare the organization for emergent change, companies need to delayer and decentralize, to organize work around tasks performed in teams and project task forces, and then ensure that these teams and project groupings are flexible enough to form, change, and dissolve, as needed. High-tech companies are always shifting jobs to areas that have higher potential payoffs. Their work groups need to be sufficiently agile to continually reorganize. Intel, for example, uses temporary teams drawn from a range of disciplines, constantly forming around specific business issues or projects. It's a task-oriented company where the organization is more like a web of teams and projects than a clearly defined vertical hierarchy.

Another example is 3M, a company synonymous with innovation. One way that the company achieves its goal of having 15 percent of its revenue come from new products is by providing its managers with the latitude to move from one business unit or laboratory to another without bureaucratic obstruction. Project groups, operating with little constraint from the formal organization, come together to accomplish a task and disband when their work is completed. There's lots of self-organization and self-design without the need for formal coordination. Similarly, 3M researchers who cannot get funding for their ideas within their own center or lab are encouraged to search out other centers and labs.

The flexibility of work arrangements, the emphasis on ideas rather than structures, and the clear signal that it is better to share ideas rather than reinvent them, frees people to focus on their imagination and creativity, thus making 3M one of the most successful companies in the world and one that is close to being a chaordic organization.

4 **Diversity.** The secret to productive and creative project groupings is diversity. Homogeneous groups tend to produce homogeneous ideas. Executives talking with other executives rarely produces a diversity of opinion. To achieve a high level of creative thought, it is necessary to bring together diverse groups of people: people with different levels of expertise (including representatives of non-business disciplines), employees at all levels of the organization (representing a variety of ages, experiences, and backgrounds), people outside of the organization (customers, suppliers), and, above all, people representing a broad spectrum of ideas.

At Skandia, the Swedish financial services company, CEO Leif Edvinsson wanted to reach the future faster, so he created Skandia Future Centers with five elite Future Teams. These are based on a model he calls "3G": a mix of three generations ranging from their 20s to 60s as well as a variety of functional roles, organizational experiences, and cultural backgrounds. Edvinsson believes discussions among diverse groups advance learning faster than traditional groups.

For original thinking, the diverse mix should include the company's mavericks. Every company has them, but they often must struggle against company orthodoxy. Having their ideas dismissed out of hand leaves them so frustrated that they either stop participating or leave the company altogether. Arie De Geuss, reporting on a study of companies that survived one hundred years or more, found that one of the four traits they held in common was a tolerance of new ideas. Clearly, companies that crossed a century's worth of changes could not control their world; therefore, they learned to tolerate ideas and activities at the margin.

Honoring the contributions of everyone, including mavericks, requires a high tolerance for conflict. Levi-Strauss and Company is an example of an organization that believes people need to be allowed to challenge ideas, no matter where they originate. To foster dissension, the company hangs whiteboards in the halls and encourages people to anonymously contribute their criticisms of what is wrong with the company's plans. Managers hang bulletin boards at meetings for people who prefer to post anonymous comments rather than make them publicly.

At 3M, new recruits actually take a course with their supervisors on risk-taking in which they are explicitly taught to be willing to defy their supervisors. They are told stories of victories won despite the boss's opposition. Chaordic organizations are, by definition, conflictual, but the very tension that produces conflict also produces genuinely creative, fruitful ideas.

5 **Strong Core Values.** To enable individuals and small groups to pursue the learning and innovation that leads to self-organizing behavior, they must be allowed autonomy. But autonomy cannot be allowed to dissolve into anarchy. There must be some grounding entity that unites the independent participants and their efforts.

Traditionally, that entity was managerial control. In chaordic organizations, it is core values or, as was noted earlier, what Dee Hock refers to as purpose and principle. Collins and Porras, in their study of visionary companies, describe values as a bonding glue that keep a fluid organization from evolving beyond recognition. Values allow for coordination without control and for experimentation and adaptation without lawlessness. A value system creates a sense of purpose; the organization knows what it is about and can invest focused attention despite seemingly random behavior.

Boeing's ideology, for example, revolves around its commitment to push the envelope of technology and to take risks and accept challenges to do this. 3M's values center on innovation and the desire to solve real human problems with truly original ideas. At Sony, the focus is on being a pioneer in doing the impossible and experiencing the joy that comes from advancing and applying technol-ogy. Despite the complexity and chaotic nature of the environment and the messy state of the emergent change, it is the company's core ideology or values that can provide its direction and purpose.

THE ROLE OF THE MANAGER

Precisely how chaos and complexity theories will shape the work world isn't clear, nor are there many examples of emergent change to guide those responsible for managing on the edge of chaos. Nevertheless, five essential ingredients of the 21st century manager's role are apparent.

1 **Manage the Transition.** The most important role managers have *at this time* is to lead people through the transition from the industrial era to the information era, from the world of Newton to the world of Chaos. William Bridges defines transition as "the *psychological* process people go through to come to terms with the new situation" [italics added].

That process begins with letting go of the past and coming to terms with what is being lost. Today's workers are being asked to trade their comfortable, safe, stable, and predictable work world for one that is unstable, unpredictable, and highly ambiguous. Traditional workers are accustomed to carrying out decisions made by higher authorities, being told the end result and how to get there, and relying on tried-and-true knowledge and skills that have served them well in the past.

With the new order, however, they are being called upon to identify and solve problems, make decisions, experiment, generate perpetual novelty, and continually learn new skills and behaviors.

Their world has turned topsy-turvey. Managers need to help people understand the reasons behind these dramatic changes and generate a sense of urgency about the need to move forward in a different manner. To do this, they must be specific regarding the attitudinal and behavioral changes that are necessary, communicate consistently and often, expect and accept people's negative reactions, and reward their positive efforts.

2 **Build Resilience.** As the speed, volume, and complexity of change accelerate, workers, mental and physical stamina are worn down. Reeling from multiple downsizings, organizational restructurings, mergers and acquisitions, and programmatic initiatives over the past two decades, many of them feel incapable of gearing up for yet another assault on their energies. Feeling out of control, they have reached what Alvin Toffler termed "future shock." But much as they long for "the good 'ol days," they are destined to be disappointed. Chaos theory and emergent change tell us that ability to adapt and to absorb *even more change* is what lies ahead. Therefore, an important role for managers is to help people increase their resilience; that is, their capacity to bounce back no matter how intense the speed or complexity of the changes.

Daryl Conner argues that major change occurs when people have significant disruption in their expectations. When people can anticipate and prepare for the change, they respond better, in part, because they feel more in control. Negative reactions and dysfunctional responses come from being surprised, feeling unprepared and out of control.

Reaction to change is largely a function of perception and managers can build resilience by helping people adjust their expectations. Managers need to help workers understand the new realities; namely, that there is no going back, that change is the order of the day, and that we may never feel "in control" again. They need to explain the nature of chaos and emergent change, emphasizing the lack of predictability and stability along with the principle of "order in disorder."

But at the same time, managers need to ensure that people have the skills they need so they can feel equipped to meet the challenges ahead. Never before has training been so important to the workforce and to organizations. Motorola, with one of the best training programs in the country, pushes employees to continually redefine themselves and how they do their jobs, requiring each employee to attend a minimum of 40 hours of training annually. Motorola University, begun in 1987, delivered 123,000 hours of training by 1991 with 6,800 people participating in courses. One estimate is that 300 to 400 companies now have their own versions of corporate universities or learning centers.

3 **Destabilize the System.** In the industrial era, we viewed a successful organization as one that operates as close to equilibrium as possible. But a model that places stability at its core serves to restrict managers to strategies of repetition and imitation. As such, it is dysfunctional for a world that has become increasingly complex and competitive and in which organizations literally live or die on the basis of their ability to innovate.

Therefore, managers need to assume the important role of creating an environment that elicits, supports, and nurtures creativity by deliberately upsetting the status quo, escalating some changes while damping others, and seeking a chaordic state or a state of bounded instability.

One way to destabilize the system is to keep it in a state of tension. Tension is a necessary ingredient of creativity, but it will take particular skill on the part of managers to keep the tension level at a point where it generates dynamic imagination without exceeding people's ability to handle the stress engendered.

Another way to destabilize the system is to deliberately seek disconfirmation of our beliefs. A secret of success in the new order, according to Intel's CEO, Andrew Grove, is to continually try to prove yourself wrong, to challenge your thinking, to find flaws in your own mental models, to continually experiment and test every possible alternative.

To voluntarily annihilate one's ideas, however, is not as ego-satisfying as having them confirmed, so managers need to maintain constant vigil to ensure that the process of disconfirmation becomes a natural, acceptable mode of problem solving. They can do this by modeling an openness to the testing of their own ideas, by rewarding those who raise tough questions, and by playing devil's advocate when consensus is achieved too readily and without debate.

4 **Manage Order and Disorder, the Present and the Future.** The self-organizing principle of chaos theory might lead one to conclude that managers are superfluous. On the contrary, they have a critical role in providing the balance between the need for order and the imperative to change. They are responsible for seeing to it that the organization engages in enough innovation to keep it competitive yet enough stability to prevent its dissolving into total disarray.

This paradox, which is really a constellation of paradoxes consisting of regularity and irregularity, simplicity and complexity, predictability and unpredictability, and stability and instability, calls for tremendous agility on the part of managers. In the old order, with its either/or thinking, managers merely pursued one end of each continuum, but today, with both/and thinking required, they will have to juggle both ends.

One approach to the conundrum is to apply order, regularity, predictability, and stability to the daily business and disorder, irregularity, unpredictability, and instability to future change. Ken Blanchard suggests having people in the organization on two teams: a Present Team, focused on today, and a Future Team, focused on tomorrow.

Further, Blanchard argues that people are naturally suited to one or the other. He points to Michael Eisner, CEO of Disney, as a natural visionary, and the late Frank Wells, Disney's former President and COO, as a natural implementor. Where Eisner preferred to innovate, Wells preferred to redesign systems to support the new directions Eisner charted. By allowing managers to function in a capacity suited to their preferred mode of operation, Blanchard's model might well provide a means for easing the anxiety and tension that the paradox creates for many workers. Both the organization and the workers get their needs met.

5 **Create and Maintain a Learning Organization.** Learning is the *sine qua non* of an information/knowledge age and central to the self-organizing activities from which new systems emerge. Thus, a major role of managers in chaordic organizations will be to create the means by which everyone can be involved in continuous learning.

This should not be difficult since there is always potential for learning in the everyday problems and opportunities workers confront. Learning and doing are synchronous so workers can learn in real time, but only if learning is made an explicit organizational value and only if there is time put aside for reflection on what worked, what didn't, and why. When learning is an accidental byproduct of activity rather than a central core process, it is neither sustainable nor does it get integrated into the business.

To create and maintain a genuine learning organization, managers need to establish an environment supportive of and conducive to learning. If experimentation, risk-taking, and trial-and-error modes of problem solving are to compete with the overused rational, analytic modes, then the culture must tolerate failure, refrain from placing blame, and reinforce nontraditional thinking. If truly innovative ideas are a primary goal, then the culture must tolerate conflict, people "pushing back," public testing of one another's assumptions, and healthy debate around diverse ideas. If the organization wants to capitalize on its collective human capital, then the culture must tolerate a messy structure in which project groups form, reconstitute themselves, or disband as needed.

These five roles, critical for managers to enact if their companies are to enter the 21st century as chaordic organizations capable of engaging in emergent change, call for leaders who, themselves, understand and accept the assumptions of chaos and complexity theories. These invaluable agents of future change seek neither stability nor predictability, developing a comfort level that tolerates disequilibrium. They know that messiness and ambiguity are part of the process of self-organization and self-emergence and that, rather than attempt to manage it through command-and-control, their role is to support it through allocation of resources and the design of an appropriate culture. They recognize the futility of attempting to draw a map of the future in advance, appreciating the fact that, when the waters are uncharted, their destination can only be discovered through the actual process in real time; that the map can only get drawn as they go along.

To be a successful manager in the 21st century and to enact the five roles enumerated above calls for a new mental model of manager, one suited to a world of chaos. Those who retain their Newtonian world view will find themselves leading their organizations into oblivion.

IS CHAOS THE NEXT ORGANIZATIONAL PARADIGM?

Let's return to the question posed at the beginning of this article. Can chaos theory provide us with useful methods and metaphors for understanding the world of work? Does it lend itself to the self-organization of people in companies? Is there utility to chaos and complexity theory which could add to, or even supplant, the Newtonian order? Or is chaos theory the current darling of scientists with no application to organizations or management?

So far, complexity theory has been applied successfully to operational problems. At both GM and Deere & Co., complexity-based computer systems were used to develop programs for manufacturing. These models solved operational problems better than previously used linear techniques, saving the companies time and money.

To date, chaos and complexity theories have not been applied to human systems, although self-directed teams represent a small version of self-organization. The recent shift to team- and project-based processes in many organizations demonstrates the fact that groups of workers will, if given the chance, find ways to accomplish a task.

Top consulting firms, including Coopers and Lybrand, McKinsey, and Ernst & Young, sent people to the Sante Fe Institute (SFI), the heart of exploration into chaos theory, to find ways to use chaos and complexity theories in their consulting practice. While direct application has not yet occurred, Ernst & Young was so taken with the possibilities of this new paradigm that the firm ran a three-day symposium, "Embracing Complexity," and mailed 15,000 copies of Kaufman's *At Home in the Universe* to its clients.

The next steps in the application of chaos theory, and its off-shoot complexity theory, involve developing lifelike simulations followed by testing the theory in real time on actual human problems. Chaos theory may not be a viable model for understanding organizations as yet, but it is an intriguing way to think about the world.

SELECTED BIBLIOGRAPHY

For current data and thought-provoking forecasting data, see *The Futurist* and *Outlook '97* published by the World Future Society.

For more on the role of paradoxes and their ubiquity in the coming years, see C. Handy, *The Age of Paradox* (Cambridge, MA: Harvard Business School Press, 1994) and R. Farson, *Management of the Absurd: Paradoxes of Leadership* (New York: Simon & Schuster, 1994).

Some of the clearest writing on chaos and complexity theories can be found in S. Kaufman, *At Home in the Universe* (New York: Oxford University Press, 1995); Kevin Kelly's *Out of Control: The Rise of Biological Civilization* (Reading, MA: Addison-Wesley, 1994); and M. Waldrop, *Complexity* (New York: Simon & Schuster, 1993).

Books that provide an understanding of chaos theory and its application to organizations and management include: R. Stacey, *Managing the Unknowable: Strategic Boundaries Between Order and Chaos in Organizations* (San Francisco, CA: Jossey-Bass, 1992); M. Wheatley, *Leadership as Science: Learning About Organizations from an Orderly Universe* (San Francisco, CA: Berrett-Koehler, 1994); and M. Wheatley and M. Kellner-Rogers, *A Simpler Way* (San Francisco, CA: Berrett-Koehler, 1996).

One of the best sources of information about cutting-edge companies functioning on the border of chaos is *Fast Company* magazine. A brief history of the origins of Visa and a biography of its founder, Dee Hock, for example, can be found in the October-November 1996 issue. Buchman Laboratories was described in the June-July 1996 issue and Sony's PlayStation in the August-September 1997 issue.

The quote from William Bridges is taken from *Managing Transitions: Making the Most of Change* (Reading, MA: Addison-Wesley, 1991).

If organization development practitioners want to sleep better at night, they need to live the basic values of their profession, challenge actions they know are immoral, and play a more expansive role in improving organizational life.

The New Agenda for Organization Development

W. WARNER BURKE

Founded on a value base circa 1960 that emanated from the human relations movement, in general, and the sensitivity training (T group) movement, in particular, organization development (OD) has always operated within a framework of humanistic and ethical concerns for people. Although not all practitioners would agree on the specific values that guide the field, most would concur that OD has tended to emphasize such concerns as:

Human development—It is worthwhile for people in organizations to have opportunities for personal learning and for growth toward a full realization of their individual potentials.

Fairness—It is important that people in organizations are treated equitably without discrimination and with dignity.

Openness—It is imperative that communication in organizations be conducted with forthrightness, honesty, and integrity.

Choice—It is critical that people in organizations are free from coercion and the arbitrary use of authority.

Balance of autonomy and constraint—It is significant that people in organizations have autonomy and freedom to perform their work responsibilities as they see fit, yet execute these responsibilities within reasonable organizational constraints. The OD practitioner's responsibility is to see that these two forces—autonomy and constraint—are in balance.

While this list may fall short of expressing the value system that guides OD, it likely comes close. The problem we face today is not so much agreeing on the specifics, but rather living the values we do espouse.

A number of senior practitioners in OD, i.e., those with 20 or more years of experience, believe that the profession has lost its way—that its values are no longer sufficiently honored, much less practiced, and that the unrelenting emphasis on the bottom line has taken over. Moreover, such management techniques—fads, if you will—as reengineering and downsizing have taken the country by storm, hurt people, and violated the values associated with OD. In the meantime, OD practitioners have stood on the sidelines and watched—or themselves become victims. Regardless of how valid these observations may be, it does seem true that OD has lost some of its power, its presence, and perhaps its perspective.

The purpose of this paper, then, is to address some of these issues, first by examining what we know about the efficacy of reengineering and downsizing and, second, by articulating a current and future agenda for OD practitioners with respect to these techniques. Reengineering and downsizing were selected for examination as opposed to, say, total quality management (TQM), because the former represent a greater challenge to the practice of OD—they more directly impact the field's underlying values.

To be clear about the direction of this paper: It begins by examining reengineering and downsizing to determine the OD practitioner's agenda vis-à-vis these two interventions, but it does not leave it at that. The overriding purpose is to propose a deeper agenda for OD and to consider six additional intervention domains—community, the employer-employee social contract, employability, trust, culture clash, and corporate power.

REENGINEERING, DOWNSIZING, AND ORGANIZATION DEVELOPMENT

To begin, let's review what is known about the efficacy of reengineering and downsizing and, for each, ask if the technique should even continue to be used. Answering these questions allows us to focus on the implications for OD practitioners, i.e., the agenda.

Reengineering—Does It Work?

Even though reengineering as we know it today (similar practices were previously labeled "business process redesign") has been in evidence for about a decade, we do not as yet have enough research to draw sound conclusions about its validity. Part of the problem is

> *W. Warner Burke* is professor of psychology and education, and chair, Department of Organization and Leadership at Teachers College, Columbia University, where he has been since 1979. He earlier served as professor and chair of the Department of Management at Clark University, executive director of the Organization Development Network, and an executive for eight years at the NTL Institute for Applied Behavioral Science. He was the editor of *Organizational Dynamics* (1978–1985) and the charter editor of the *Academy of Management Executive* (1986–1989). He has served on the Board of Governors of both the Academy of Management and the American Society for Training and Development. He was awarded NASA's Public Service Medal, and the American Society for Training and Development's Distinguished Contribution to Human Resources Development Award, and the Organization Development Professional Practice Award for Excellence. He is a Diplomate in industrial/organizational psychology, American Board of Professional Psychology, and has published over 90 articles and 13 books. For over 30 years he has been an organization consultant and is currently consulting with organizations in financial services, health, broadcasting, federal government, and education. He holds a Ph.D. in social psychology from the University of Texas, Austin.

that reengineering has taken on the trappings of a fad—a rapid surge in popularity in the early 1990s, fueled by Michael Hammer and J. Champy's book on the subject, which rode the best-seller list for months. Organizations rapidly initiated reengineering projects; then, faced with disappointing early results, abandoned the effort just as quickly. Likely, the results would have been better had companies stayed with the ship longer. Most of the evidence so far (much of it anecdotal) builds a case for a low success rate. Some recent evidence provides encouragement, but the jury is still out.

Reengineering—Should It Be Done?

There's nothing inherently wrong with the idea. To consider a set of workplace activities and processes at their most basic levels in an effort to improve the activities, eliminate them altogether, and/or add new procedures and processes can be highly beneficial. Like so many other organizational change ideas, the problems come with implementation.

Typically, these problems arise for several reasons. Rather than fine-tune work processes, reengineering has focused on a radical redesign of work—a reinvention of how tasks get done. By emphasizing the details of specific procedures, the designers lose sight of the bigger picture—how changes at the work unit level will affect the larger business or organizational unit. In addition, reengineering has frequently been associated with downsizing and therefore vehemently resisted by many organizational members, much to Michael Hammer's dismay.

The Agenda for the OD Practitioner

If reengineering is a passing fad, why bother to set an agenda? There are two answers to this.

First, much of what is involved in reengineering is not new. Its roots can be traced to Frederick Taylor, and before that, to the very foundation of industrial engineering. This discipline, after all, has been around for 90 years. Its fundamentals are basic to any and all work organizations and, moreover, are not likely to pass from the scene. Other labels for the practice may come into vogue, just as "reengineering" superseded "work redesign," but the knowledge of how to redesign work processes, even radically, will remain useful.

Second, reengineering means change, and there is much to be said for starting with a clean slate and redesigning work for the good of workers and the organization. It should even be alluring for OD practitioners. Moreover, OD practitioners are in a position to contribute. In their study of 20 organizations involved in reengineering (at least three of these achieving successful implementations), Gene Hall, Jim Rosenthal, and Judy Wade identified six crucial organizational elements, or depth levers as they call them, that must be the focus of change if reengineering is really going to work: roles and responsibilities, organizational structure, measurements and incentives, shared values, skills, and information technology.

With the possible exception of the last item, OD practitioners provide (or should provide) ballast for all these levers and thus play a key role in any reengineering effort. And by being organizationally focused (as opposed to working exclusively with certain individuals and selected work processes), the OD practitioner can be highly useful in keeping the larger business or organizational units, and their intricate relationships, in mind. To the extent that OD ignores or, even worse, challenges reengineering, it loses an important opportunity to make an impact and to be true to its values.

Downsizing—Does It Work?

The short answer is "no." The amazing fact about downsizing is that, in most cases, the action produces the opposite of what is intended. Consider, for example, cost reduction—a primary goal for most downsizing plans. Although this may occur in the short run, a longer term scenario usually shows either no cost reduction or, in a number of instances, actual cost increases.

Another typical goal, productivity improvement, proves equally elusive. The evidence shows either no improvement or even a deterioration in productivity!

To add to the evidence, research by R. E. Cole found nine additional organizational problems resulting from downsizing: loss of personal relationships between employees and customers, increases in rules and procedures (therefore adding to bureaucracy), and loss of a common organizational culture, to name three. And a study of over 200 organizations by Kim Cameron and his colleagues added a dozen other problems to Cole's list.

The toll taken on individuals is immense. For a flavor of the consequences on individual and family lives, see the recent *New York Times*

Special Report: The Downsizing of America and David M. Noer's book, *Healing the Wounds*. The pictures painted are not pretty. In fact, our American experience with downsizing is similar to cancer; practically every family we know has been touched.

The history of downsizing, now 16 or so years in the making, has left its legacy. The American workplace will never be quite the same.

Downsizing—Should It Be Done?

We might well ask if there is ever any justification for downsizing. The short answer is maybe.

We know that most large organizations employ people with "non jobs" and continue to support useless if not downright wasteful activities. There is some evidence that when downsizing is done carefully it can have positive consequences. Poor outcomes result from poor implementation and a lack of supporting activities such as counseling, training, severance packages, and outplacement. The way downsizing is carried out seems to be more important than the decision itself. Also, downsizing is more likely to be associated with positive outcomes when it works as part of an overall strategic plan.

Regardless of the potential for positive results, many would argue that downsizing is harmful to the economy, devastating to both its victims and the corporate survivors, and plainly and simply immoral. But not everyone would so argue.

In a carefully crafted and balanced article in *The New Yorker*, John Cassidy points to evidence supporting a net gain over the past decade in American jobs rather than a loss. He refers to two important reports, one by Joseph Stiglitz, chairman of the Council of Economic Advisors, the other by Princeton economics professor Henry Farber. These two reports independently concur that downsizing has not had the dire consequences on our economy and the country as a whole that the popular press and other anecdotal writings would lead us to believe.

Cassidy points out that these reports "should permit a more dispassionate discussion of downsizing." He goes on to emphasize that downsizing is real, that there are victims, and that these victims should not be ignored. Furthermore, layoffs and downsizing have been with us a long time, as our economy ebbs and flows. Ask any blue collar worker.

The two reports by Stiglitz and Farber on which Cassidy relies suggest "that what is really new about the downsizing phenomenon is not its absolute scale as much as its impact on the upper echelons of society. An increasing number of its victims are middle-aged, educated, and affluent." Labor Department statistics show that while displacement has indeed occurred, there has been little change in overall job stability in the United States. Job loss, then, while serious (just ask a recent victim), does not appear to be any more serious today than 10 or 15 years ago.

And to quote Cassidy one last time: "The ability of the United States economy to create jobs at a rate matching its rapid population growth distinguishes it sharply from many other industrial economies, especially those in Europe.... While American commentators worry about downsizing, the talk in Paris and Berlin is about how best to mimic American job creation."

So perhaps what we are experiencing is not "the downsizing of America" (the title of *The New York Times* book) but the "job shifting of America." And maybe we are not losing our middle class, but rather our middle class is changing its work affiliations, from the bulk employed by large corporations—each person for an entire career—to a more dispersed and diverse group of Americans. This group may include more people than before working in small to mid-size companies (many starting their own enterprises), more working in non-profit organizations, and some living off their severance packages or working in temporary situations until they discover what they want to do next with their lives.

The Downsizing Agenda for the OD Practitioner

It's tempting for the OD practitioner to want absolutely nothing to do with downsizing. After all, downsizing hurts people, and the act itself can border on (if not blatantly constitute) immorality.

Yet, if OD practitioners are employed by or contracted to work with an organization, are they not obligated to help? If they are capable of providing help, are they not obligated to do so? Isn't this provision to help a value of higher priority than avoiding involvement in a situation where people may be hurt, if not treated immorally?

These queries beg the question of what we mean by *help*. For the good of the organization and its individual members, consultative help may mean confrontation, questioning, and challenging.

Let's consider downsizing from a different point of view, namely, why so many executives stick to their decision to reduce headcount in the face of so much negative evidence regarding the outcomes. William McKinley, Carol M. Sanchez, and Allen G. Schick provide insights on this issue. Building on institutional theory from sociology and simplifying the language, they cite three social forces that support an executive's downsizing rationale: "constraining," "cloning," and "learning."

Constraining forces pressure executives to conform to what is the "right thing" to do at a particular time. Although previously associated with decline, a negative force, downsizing is now seen as "the right step." Large organizations mean bureaucracy, rigidity, and resistance to change. Today's fashion is to be lean, mean, and nimble, and thus more competitive. To capture the essence of this social force, the authors refer to a *Fortune* article in which the writer stated that "The chiefs of America's biggest companies seem caught in the grip of what might be called wee-ness envy—my company's workforce is smaller than yours.

Organizational cloning can take a number of forms; for example, mimicking other organizations with respect to such management techniques as TQM, reengineering, self-directed groups and, of course, downsizing. Cloning is particularly prominent within industries, each company wanting to mimic what the best in its field is doing. And when executives want to measure how well their cloning process is going, they call it benchmarking.

Learning occurs via educational institutions and conferences sponsored by professional associations, as well as by finding "lessons" in the actions of apparently successful peers at other companies. Academic courses in cost accounting, for example, teach (at least by implication) that downsizing is an efficient form of doing business. And when one CEO sees another turn companies around with a "slash and burn" strategy (e.g., Albert J. Dunlap, previously at Scott Paper and now at Sunbeam), there is a temptation to duplicate the practice.

McKinley et al. go on to identify four conditions that enhance the power of these social pressures for downsizing: (1) dependence,

(2) ambiguous standards, (3) uncertain core technologies, and (4) frequent corporate interaction patterns. In other words, the more dependent a company is on other organizations for resources, especially when those other organizations are dominant partners, the greater the ambiguity regarding what should be proper performance. Also, the greater the uncertainty about what a company's core technologies are, and the more interactive a company is with its constituents and competitors, the more susceptible that company is to conformity, cloning, and learning. And the more likely to downsize, if that is what others are doing.

The point, then, is as follows: When an OD practitioner's client is contemplating downsizing, the intervention of choice is to test the wisdom of such a decision. Testing the degree to which the potential decision seems to be a response to the social forces that McKinley et al. define (and within the context of their four conditions that enhance the power of these forces) would be highly appropriate—because this testing, or intervention, would be grounded in relevant theory and would confront forces to which the client may be oblivious.

There are other reasons for challenging a potential act of downsizing. Consider, for example, the consequences in terms of organizational memory loss and erosion of valued skills and experience. Service companies are highly susceptible to such loss. An example:

One insurance group, having slimmed its claims department, found itself settling larger claims both too swiftly and too generously. Belatedly, the group discovered that it had sacked a handful of long-term employees who had created an informal—but highly effective—way to screen claims. The company was eventually forced to reinstate them.

Moreover, there are alternative models to follow. For example, Sara Lee, under the leadership of its CEO, John Bryan, seems to compete quite well in a tough business and to do so globally without laying off hundreds or thousands of people when times are tough. Sara Lee takes pride in being socially responsible, a good corporate citizen.

For corporate leaders, perhaps the model regarding downsizing is Bill Flynn, the former CEO, now chairman, of Mutual of America. Mr. Flynn stated at an annual employee meeting that if the company ever had to institute a corporate layoff policy, it would not be because someone in the mail room had made a mistake. Rather, it would be because he had made a mistake—and he would put his name first on the layoff list. Not surprisingly, Flynn's statement earned him the trust of the employees attending that meeting.

OD practitioners have a twofold role to play in the downsizing arena. First, to challenge a potential downsizing decision by asking "why" and to test for the impact of social forces. This includes searching for other ways to control and reduce costs and to become a key player in implementing those alternatives. Second, if other options have been thoroughly explored and downsizing is the only remaining choice, to push for dignity, humane treatment, and ultimate fairness in how the victims and survivors are dealt with.

THE OD PRACTITIONER'S DEEPER AGENDA

Rather than become obsessed with reengineering and downsizing, it is more important that practitioners understand and become involved with issues that are deeper, longer lasting, and more critical to the bigger picture. Six issues in particular merit attention.

Community

Each summer, we conduct a two-week conference for public school superintendents at Teachers College, Columbia University. Participants come from all pockets and corners of the United States—large, medium, and small districts from urban, suburban, and rural areas. My colleague, Professor Tom Sobol, runs the program. In his summary report of the 1996 summer conference, the following paragraph was a jolt:

> It's not easy being a public school superintendent these days, so cataloging their mutual problems was easy: lack of money, too many conflicting public demands, public hostility, uncertain tenure. But surprisingly, once these matters were acknowledged, they were not what superintendents wanted to spend time on. The problem that gripped their attention was the decline of community in America—the role of the public school in creating and sustaining that community.

I suspect that the assessment is accurate. Downsizing may hurt victims much more today than a few decades ago when communities were stronger. Support now comes from professionals (e.g., outplacement counselors), not so much from friends and neighbors.

More of the burden is placed on one's family, and some families have not survived the ordeal. Moreover, downsizing has hit the white collar worker harder and, compared with a layoff of hourly wage earners, is more permanent. And white collar workers have no labor union for support, to help serve in the community's role of providing sustenance.

This lack of community is not likely to change anytime soon. As a culture, we Americans are clearly an independent lot. This independence seems to have become more pronounced in recent years, in part because of two trends. One is an apparent increase in self-orientation, the "what's in it for me?" syndrome. Christopher Lasch has written about the syndrome in his 1978 book, *The Culture of Narcissism*. Similarly, a national survey by Donald L. Kanter and Philip H. Mirvis identified what they subsequently labeled "the cynical Americans"—a group that made up 43 percent of those surveyed. Consider, also, that 58 percent of the survey respondents agreed or strongly agreed with this statement, "People pretend to care more about one another than they really do."

A second trend, growing stronger as technology marches onward, is that for daily living, we literally do not need other people as much as in the past. We can live alone quite comfortably, thank you, especially in large urban areas. We can have almost anything—from a mattress to pizza—delivered. And with Blockbuster Video, who needs friends for entertainment? Besides, we have the Internet.

There are, no doubt, other trends that help explain the decline in community—crime, geographical dispersion of family members, and less personal time, to name a few. Suffice it to say, the superintendents are probably right.

Agenda for the OD Practitioner: Organizational effectiveness depends on interactions and interrelationships among employees at all levels. The OD practitioner plays a significant role by bringing people together. This means initiating and arguing for, if not calling and conducting meetings themselves—not just facilitating them. This means, especially, promoting activities such as cross-functional teams and helping self-directed groups to actually self-direct.

Is it not true that the lack of community in society carries over into the organization? Also, employees today are incredibly busy just keeping up with their individual tasks and responsibilities. They spend considerably more time with a computer terminal (with troublesome software and poor interactive systems) than with people. They are reluctant to get together; they have too much to do. By promoting community via small and large group meetings, the OD practitioner helps with organizational effectiveness and also improves individuals' quality of worklife.

The Employer-Employee Social Contract

We know that the relationship between employer and employee has changed. Company loyalty—especially in large corporations—is a thing of the past. True, in small and family-owned businesses, loyalty may still be strong. But with the pervasiveness of downsizing, and with the message that one can no longer expect a lifetime career with a single employer ringing clear, the weakening of the bond between the organization and its employees comes as no surprise.

In fact, a recent study by Chip Walker and Elissa Moses shows that a "self-navigation" subculture has emerged in America, representing about 26 percent of those sampled, half of them being under the age of 35. Members of this group hold strongly to the value "I must take care of myself." They tend to reject tradition and conformity and are more likely to start their own businesses.

The self-navigators, however, are not the majority. A far larger number of workers would prefer to stay with their companies, if possible, yet feel insecure about the prospects. The popular press continues to report that in spite of low unemployment and a strong economy, people continue to express an unease about the security of practically any workplace. Even the Federal government (e.g., NASA) and employee-owned companies have downsized.

In addition to doing away with loyalty, downsizing has affected another aspect of the employer-employee social contract. A new work relationship falling under the banner of "rent an employee" has recently emerged. The so-called contract worker has been around for a long time, but many of the new contracts return former employees to their old jobs, some as consultants, others as employees of temp agencies or leasing companies. Approximately 20 percent of those who were victims of downsizing fall into this category, another version of the changing employer-employee relationship in which the two parties feel less obligation to one another. As *The New York Times* reported,

> Not having careers to advance, some praise the liberation from enervating office politics, and from the stress of competing for raises and promotions. They talk of a greater flexibility to work when they please. But their altered status cuts at their self-esteem. They are sometimes shunned by co-workers. They are often less effective than they had been. Many find themselves no longer going the extra mile to get a job done or acquire a new skill.

This new arrangement is attractive to companies because they can immediately place experienced workers into their former jobs, sidestepping the need for training. But these workers are not likely to be as motivated as before. Consequently, productivity suffers. If the rental employee trend continues, productivity will be adversely affected nation-wide.

While most of these "rental" workers reported that they enjoyed their increased freedom, they regretted the loss of pension and health benefits. Although portability is not fully in place as yet, it looks as though employees will be able to carry these benefits from one employer to another sometime in the near future. This kind of portability should help bolster their feeling of security. But rental employees will have to find other means for their benefits.

Agenda for the OD Practitioner: The agenda for the OD practitioner in this domain concerns at least the following:

1. *Expectations.* The greater an employee's ambiguity regarding the employer's expectations related to role and task responsibilities, the more likely the employee is going to experience feelings of job insecurity, if not reduced motivation. OD practitioners can help by cajoling and coaching managers to be clear with their people about goals, objectives, and task requirements and about what they as managers want.

2. *Performance Feedback.* The absence of feedback also contributes to insecurity and reduced motivation. Again, urging and coaching managers to provide feedback to their people will help clarify employees' understanding of their social contract with the organization.

3. *Reward Systems.* If employers want to keep their above-average performers but cannot guarantee long-term employment, then they must make it worthwhile for these employees to stay with the organization. OD practitioners can help with the development and sustainability of a true pay-for-performance system. What discourages employees is a reward system that (a) does not base pay appropriately on the level of work and/or skills required, and (b) provides incentives based on some seemingly arbitrary process.

Employability

A recent opinion survey of bank employees, conducted by our organization, revealed very clear attitudes concerning training and development. These employees, the survey showed, want opportunities for training and development and are very likely to take advantage of these. Consider this in the context of the "employability clause" many companies are adding to the social contract, along the lines of "if we have to let you go some time in the future, we will ensure that you are employable." If these bank employees are representative, they intend to hold their employer to that promise.

Whether employees work for a large bank, General Motors, or for a variety of companies as contract labor, they need to think of themselves as self-employed in the sense that they are in charge of their own careers. As Edward E. Lawler III recently put it:

> . . . individuals must be able to develop marketable skills, assess and compare their skill levels with those of others, and manage their own careers.

In other words, few employers today and in the future are going to take responsibility for career management.

Agenda for the OD Practitioner: The employability arena is, of course, all about career development, but not exactly as we have known it in the past. Rather, it is about one's career per se, as a professional, as a specialist, as an expert, regardless of organizational affiliation. The OD practitioner's job is to help individuals understand more clearly what they (a) are good at, i.e, their unique set of skills and talents; (b) want in their work life, e.g., one career, multiple careers, etc.; and (c) feel about the balance of work and other activities in life, e.g., family, hobbies, community service, etc.

It would behoove us as OD practitioners to revisit such sources as Edgar Schein's writings on career anchors; J. Kotter, V. Faux, and C. McArthur on self-assessment and one's career; Herb Shepherd's life planning exercise; Morgan McCall, Michael Lombardo, and Ann Morrison's "lessons of experience"; and Warren Bennis's "invented life." In addition, we can help individuals by being knowledgeable about continuing education and distance learning opportunities as well as the broad array of training and development programs.

Trust

In a consultant's private interviews with employees, sooner rather than later, the subject of trust (or more accurately, distrust) is likely to surface. This topic rarely appeared in my interviews a dozen or more years ago. Today, the issue seems pervasive. Why? While there are multiple reasons, three stand out: (1) the widening gap between "haves" and "have nots," (2) a diminished congruence between words and deeds, and (3) a lack of openness.

1. As we know, there is an increasing disparity between the wealthy and the poor in our society. Corporations clearly contribute to this: the disparity between a CEO's compensation and the average worker's has, in some instances, reached the incredible ratio of 140 to 1 in the United States. This gap remains regardless of the CEO's or the organization's performance. And with a merger or acquisition, the CEO and others at the top become multimillionaires while the rank and file continue to worry about their jobs, pensions, and health insurance. In time, the tremendous wage gap may begin to deflate, but the damage to trust has been done.

2. Not unrelated is another gap that I hear about time and again in my consulting interviews—the difference between what managers and executives say and what they do. We Americans cannot abide hypocrisy.

On this issue, Warren Bennis refers to the special case of empowerment, that is, executives espousing empowerment on the one hand and downsizing on the other. He puts it this way:

> ...empowerment is an increasingly Orwellian term, not simply a lie, but an infuriating inversion of the truth. A demoralizing sense of powerlessness is what many jobholders are feeling (as they worry about being downsized) ... How can you have workplace empowerment in the absence of trust? ... Empowerment and restructuring are on a collision course. It's impossible for a company to reengineer and empower at the same time, even though many firms are attempting it.

3. And, finally, distrust comes from a lack of openness. Executives rarely believe that it is wise to tell employees anything about an impending change until they have all the facts in hand and their ducks in a row. Yet I have never encountered an organization where executives are accurate in their assessment of what employees know. Invariably, employees know more than executives think they do. So, when executives delay or communicate in an ambiguous manner, they breed distrust.

Agenda for the OD Practitioner: The trust issue is fundamental. Trust, after all, is an outcome, a result of certain behaviors. But the prime behavioral precursor to trust is openness, and openness is one of the fundamental values guiding OD. We practitioners must espouse and push for openness in the organization(s) we serve. We might begin by modeling the behavior ourselves. And, of course, coach and provide feedback for executives on this dimension of their behavior.

Culture Clash

Attempts to integrate very distinct organizational cultures as part of a merger or acquisition is not uncommon today and will become even more prevalent in the future. Even though the merging companies may be in the same business, the difference in their respective cultures can be remarkable. Putting the two cultures together is a monumental task and will take years, not mere months.

A merger or acquisition provides an obvious example of the cultural issue. Not so obvious is, say, outsourcing, often a result of downsizing or some other form of restructuring. The outsourced unit is not a formal member of the organizational family, but the relationship has to be nurtured and managed nevertheless. And the relationship is not dramatically different from the partnering dynamics of a strategic alliance or joint venture.

The ability to recognize and manage the effects of cultural differences constitutes a strategic advantage in today's environment. Culture influences the negotiation process, management in general, performance monitoring and control, and work and information-sharing norms. Cultural differences can be assets or liabilities, depending on the strategic goals for the interorganizational relationship. Cultural characteristics should therefore be considered as important determinants of relationship viability when assessing the potential partner's compatibility.

Several revealing insights on this subject emerged from a recent interview with a group of seven senior bank executives. The executives had been through a merger some 18 months earlier and were about to enter a second, considerably larger and more complicated merger. I asked what they had learned from their previous experience that, when applied, would make this upcoming merger more effective. The following is a synopsis:

1. First and foremost, they stressed the importance of having a vision of what the merged bank should be. This emphasis is similar to what social psychologists refer to as a superordinate goal, that is, a goal that can only be achieved through the cooperation of the two parties.

2. People in the merged organization need to understand the "why" behind the vision— the rationale for the merger and how individual action supports and contributes to a realization of the vision.

3. Related to the previous point, they talked about the importance of employee communications, especially being open and truthful with all employees. For example, if people are going to be forced to leave the firm and find jobs elsewhere, the sooner they can be told, the better.

4. Establishing relationships with one's merged partners beyond the workplace is helpful: for example, having lunch together, going to a ballgame together, etc.

5. The executives believed that having a few off-site meetings together early in the process to work on critical issues was highly useful. Getting together on neutral territory and away from the daily grind of their respective offices expedited the communication and decision-making processes.

6. These executives also believed that proximity was key. Being in separate geographical locations was detrimental to a successful merger, they maintained.

7. Also key was rapid decision making, particularly in the early days of a merger. These executives believed that "getting on" with the new organization as rapidly as possible, even though some corrections might have to made later, was more important because people needed clarity and structure to begin the long and arduous process of making the merger work.

8. Again on the theme of openness, these executives stated that in order for them to gain the respect of their people in the merged organization, they had to "walk the talk," that

is, say what they mean, mean what they say, and be highly congruent in word and deed.

9. Most importantly, the executives stressed that the customer must not be forgotten. Prior to and in the midst of a merger, everyone becomes insular, discussing in great detail the new organization and forgetting the business, especially the customer.

This list of nine principles comes from these executives' collective experiences and does not constitute research. Yet in the arena of interorganizational relations, practice continues to outpace research. It is therefore sensible that lessons from experiences such as these should guide both practice and research about interorganizational relations.

Agenda for the OD Practitioner: Instead of focusing on organizational culture change as I advocated back in 1982, the work of OD should now emphasize the interrelationships of cultures. To some extent, this is an extension of our diversity work at the interpersonal and group level. But at the same time it is different, in that culture, from an organizational perspective, is related more to general systems theory, social psychology, and organizational sociology than to interpersonal psychodynamics and the dynamics within and across small groups.

I do not mean to advocate an either/or scenario here—either culture change or emphasis on cultural interrelationships. Rather, there needs to be a different theoretical perspective and consequently a difference in certain action steps. For example, an early step in a merger is putting together two, usually different, compensation systems. This requires expertise of a different order from what an OD practitioner would normally bring to the table, although the OD person could contribute by helping participants become aware of the assumptions and values that underlie the two systems.

Back to the main point. The agenda for the OD practitioner is *inter*, working in between persons and systems. OD skills that need to be honed, therefore, include negotiation, mediation, conflict management, and conflict resolution. Add to this a good dose of understanding about organizational cultures for good measure. Increasing our knowledge about cross-cultural dynamics, general systems theory, and organizational psychology and sociology would help as well.

EXHIBIT 1
SUMMARY OF ORGANIZATIONAL CONSULTING ISSUES AND THE OD PRACTITIONER'S AGENDA

Organizational Consulting Issue	OD Practitioner's Agenda
Reengineering	Focus on specific change targets that are critical to the success of a reengineering effort, e.g., roles and responsibilities, the larger systemic picture, etc.
Downsizing	Confront reasons for decision and test for constraining, cloning, or learning forces; push for humane treatment, dignity, and fairness.
Community	Bring people together; initiate meetings, not just facilitate them.
Employer-Employee Social Contract	Seek clarity regarding task expectations and goals/objectives; help to provide feedback for employees; promote reward system based on merit and perhaps pay for performance.
Employability	Foster career development by helping people to understand what they (a) are good at, (b) want in their work, and (c) desire concerning balance of work and other aspects of life. Review career development literature and related sources.
Trust	Espouse and live the value of openness; provide coaching and feedback for executives regarding the congruence of their words and actions.
Culture Clash	Place emphasis on the interrelationships of cultures and consult in the domain of "in-between-ness."
Corporate Power	Read the two books by Korten and Estes, and think about the implications for OD work and feel the values that are confronted.

Corporate Power

My final agenda item is simply to call attention to two important books: David Korten's *When Corporations Rule the World* and Ralph Estes's *Tyranny of the Bottom Line.* Our agenda here is to read these books and to think about values. Our actions, whatever they may be, will come later. My urging at this stage is to read, think, and feel.

With strong credentials and considerable documentation, Korten contends that global corporations are becoming more powerful than nation states and, therefore, are not sufficiently monitored or regulated. Driven predominantly by financial goals, global corporations contribute significantly to (1) widening the gap between the haves and have-nots throughout the world, (2) destroying the middle class, and (3) weakening local economies. With all the hype about globalization, Korten's perspective is sobering. Not everyone agrees with Korten, particularly global executives—see, for example, a book by a former global company execu-

tive, Henry Wendt, titled *Global Embrace: Corporate Challenges in a Transnational World.* In any case, as you read Korten's book, think about where you stand vis-à-vis the issues he raises, especially if you work with a global corporation.

Even those who have not as yet read Estes's book can predict much of its content—corporations being driven by short-term profits and working to please stockholders more than customers and certainly more than employees. Estes makes these points and more. He addresses the fundamental purpose of a corporation, raises the question of who controls the corporation and, of course, discusses accountability. Again, not all would agree with Estes. But he raises the right questions—important questions for us to consider and . . . use in determining our own position.

It is equally important, as we read Estes, to clarify for ourselves what the primary causal factors are for a positive bottom line—what organizational behaviors contribute to profitability, which hinder. Our job is to determine the antecedents, then decide which ones we should get behind, which ones to fight against.

This final agenda, then, is one that confronts our values. My purpose has been to raise awareness. Joining a picket line, a march on Washington, DC, or storming the gates of a global corporation *is* your business.

Exhibit 1 provides a summary of the eight organizational consulting issues that have been covered, plus brief statements of the OD practitioner's agenda.

THE TAO OF OD

There are at least two primary criteria for a professional practice. One is to have a theoretical basis for the practice and the other is to act within the bounds of a set of ethics.

The way for OD is in place. It is more a matter of owning the theories and values of OD and, with strong commitment, putting them into practice. As we say to our clients: "If you own the decision, you're likely to implement it."

And, finally, back to the purpose of this paper, that is, to argue in favor of a deeper agenda for OD. In an attempt to be relevant to "real" business issues, such as downsizing, we have neglected many of the fundamental values of our field, values that are integral to community, the organization-individual interface, the development of people, trust, interorganizational relations, especially concerning cross-cultural dynamics, and how power is addressed and exercised.

It is time—indeed, past time—for OD practitioners to challenge issues and actions that we know to be wrong, to run counter to the very foundation of our field, and to cause us to wake up in the middle of the night and question ourselves.

SELECTED BIBLIOGRAPHY

This paper is based on a presentation given for the combined preconference on "Restructuring, Reengineering, and Downsizing: A Crossroads for Society" and "The Bottom Line: Defining Our Values for the Future" at the Annual Conference of the Organization Development Network, Orlando, Florida, October 5, 1996. I am grateful to Billie Alban, Dennis Gallagher, Len Goodstein, Dick Powell, and Lisa Tolliver for their feedback on an earlier draft of this paper.

The wave of reengineering began with M. Hammer and J. Champy's book, *Reengineering the Corporation: A Manifesto for Business Revolution* (New York: HarperBusiness, 1993). Some case examples of successful and unsuccessful reengineering have been described by G. Hall, J. Rosenthal and J. Wade in a 1993 Harvard Business Review (Vol. 71, No. 6, pp. 119–131) article, "How to Make Reengineering Really Work," but more comprehensive reviews have been provided by Kim Cameron, "Techniques for Making Organizations Effective," a chapter in D. Druckman, J. E. Singer, and H. P. van Cott (eds.) *Enhancing Organizational Performance* (Washington, DC: National Academy Press, 1997) and by J. P. Womack and D. T. Jones in their 1996 book, *Lean Thinking* (New York: Simon & Schuster). *The Economist* article recording Michael Hammer's defense of reengineering was in the November 5, 1994 issue on page 70.

For articles showing the ill effects on productivity as a result of downsizing, see A. Bennett, "Downsizing Doesn't Necessarily Bring an Upswing in Corporate Profitability," *The Wall Street Journal,* June 6, 1991, pp. B1, B4; R. E. Cole, "Learning From Learning Theory: Implications for Quality Improvements of Turnover, Use of Contingent Works, and Job Rotation Policies," *Quality Management Journal,* 1993, Vol. 1, pp. 9–25; and R. Henkoff, "Getting Beyond Downsizing," *Fortune,* Jan. 10, 1994, pp. 58–64. Kim Cameron's work concerning downsizing is published in a number of sources; the one referred to in this paper is K. S. Cameron, S. J. Freeman, and A. K. Mishra, "Best Practices in White-collar Downsizing: Managing Contradictions," *Academy of Management Executive,* 1991, Vol. 5, No. 3, pp. 57–73. For a current and more extensive coverage, see his chapter in the Druckman et al. book referred to above. And for yet another review, see Wayne Casio's article, "Downsizing: What Do We Know? What Have We Learned?" *Academy of Management Executive,* 1993, Vol. 7. No. 1, pp. 95–104. For publications about the effect of downsizing on individuals, victims, and survivors, see the 1996 book, *New York Times Special Report: The Downsizing of America* (New York: Times Books, Random House), and David M. Noer's book, *Healing the Wounds: Overcoming the Trauma of Layoffs and Revitalizing Downsized Corporations* (San Francisco: Jossey-Bass, 1993). For a recent article claiming that downsizing is not over, see L. Uchitelle's piece in *The New York Times,*

"Despite Drop, Rate of Layoffs Remains High," August 23, 1996, pp. 1, D2.

Studies showing the importance of *how* downsizing is implemented and demonstrating the possibility of some positive outcomes include S. W. J. Kozlowski, G. T. Chao, E. M. Smith, and J. Hedlund, "Organizational Downsizing: Strategies, Intervention, and Research Implications," *International Review of Industrial & Organizational Psychology,* 1993, Vol. 8; J. Brockner, S. Grover, T. Reed, R. DeWitt, and M. O'Malley, "Survivors' Reactions to Layoffs: We Get By With a Little Help From Our Friends," *Administrative Science Quarterly,* 1987, Vol. 32, pp. 526–554; G. D. Bruton, J. K. Keels, and C. L. Shook, "Downsizing the Firm: Answering the Strategic Questions," *Academy of Management Executive,* 1996, Vol. 10, No. 2, pp. 38–45; and Cameron's chapter in Druckman et al. (see above). *The New Yorker* article by J. Cassidy was in the April 22, 1996 issue, pp. 51–55.

For information on the ebb and flow of the American middle class, at least from an economics perspective, see the article by E. Kacapyr, "Are You Middle Class?" *American Demographics,* 1996, Vol. 18. No. 10, pp. 30–35.

The W. McKinley, C. M. Sanchez, and A. G. Schick article is "Organizational Downsizing; Constraining, Cloning, Learning," *Academy of Management Executive,* 1995, Vol. 9, No. 3, pp. 32–42. The "wee-ness envy" article is by L. S. Richman in the September 20, 1993 issue (pp. 54–56) of *Fortune* and entitled, "When Will the Layoffs End?"

The articles about the downsized insurance group and the CEO of Sara Lee are both from *The Economist:* the former "Fire and Forget," April 20, 1996, p. 51, and the latter "The Cecil Rhodes of Chocolate-Chip Cookies: How to Be a Good Corporate Citizen in a World of Globalized Markets," May 25, 1996, p. 74. The anecdote about Bill Flynn comes from an article by the current CEO of Mutual of America—T. J. Moran, "What Leaders Owe," *Leader to Leader,* 1996, Vol. 1, No. 2, pp. 15–17.

The "me-syndrome" was expounded in Christopher Lasch's book, *The Culture of Narcissism: American Life in an Age of Diminishing Expectations* (New York: Norton, 1978), and the cynical Americans in the D. L. Kanter and P. H. Mirvis book, *The Cynical Americans: Living and Working in an Age of Discontent and Disillusion* (San Francisco: Jossey-Bass, 1989).

The "age of self-navigation" study is by C. Walker and E. Moses and reported in *American Demographics,* 1996, Vol. 18, No. 9, pp. 36–

42. For an article about downsizing in employee-owned companies see L. Uchitelle, "Downsizing Comes to Employee-Owned America," *The New York Times,* July 7, 1996, p. E3. Also by Uchitelle is *The New York Times* article about rental employees, "More Downsized Workers Are Returning as Rentals," December 8, 1996, pp. 1, 34.

Ed Lawler's thinking and advice about career self-management can be found in his latest book, E. E. Lawler III, *From the Ground Up: Six Principles for Building the New Logic Corporation* (San Francisco: Jossey-Bass, 1996, Chapter 12). And sources for OD practitioners regarding careers and career development include E. H. Schein's *Career Dynamics: Matching Individual and Organizational Needs* (Reading, MA: Addison-Wesley, 1978); the book by J. Kotter, V. Faux, and C. McArthur, *Self-Assessment and Career Development* (Englewood Cliffs, NJ: Prentice-Hall, 1978); a description of Herb Shepherd's life-planning exercise can be found in Chapter 13 of W. L. French and C. H. Bell, Jr., *Organization Development: Behavioral Science Interventions for Organizational Improvement,* 5th Ed. (Englewood Cliffs, NJ: Prentice-Hall, 1995); "lessons of experience" is recorded in the book by M. W. McCall, M. M. Lombardo, and A. M. Morrison, *The Lessons of Experience: How Successful Executives Develop on the Job* (Lexington, MA: Lexington Books, 1988); and the "invented life" is W. G. Bennis's *An Invented Life: Reflections on Leadership and Change* (Reading, MA: Addison-Wesley, 1993).

The quote from Warren Bennis about empowerment comes from an article in the February 20, 1996 *Los Angeles Times.*

With respect to interorganizational relations and culture clash, see W. W. Burke and N. W. Biggart, "Interorganizational Relations," in D. Druckman, J. E. Singer, and H. P. Van Cott (eds.) *Enhancing Organizational Performance* (Washington, DC: National Academy Press, 1997). In 1982 in W. W. Burke, *Organization Development: Practices and Principles* (Boston: Little, Brown) I argued that OD practitioners should focus on culture change.

With respect to corporate power, see D. C. Korten, *When Corporations Rule the World* (West Hartford, CT: Kumarian Press, and San Francisco: Berrett-Koehler, 1995) and R. Estes, *Tyranny and the Bottom Line: Why Corporations Make Good People Do Bad Things* (San Francisco: Berrett-Koehler, 1996). A counter-argument is provided by H. Wendt's *Global Embrace: Corporate Challenges in a Transnational World* (New York: HarperBusiness, 1993).

The New Loyalty:

Grasp it.
Earn it.
Keep it.

The old brand of employee loyalty is dead.
In its place is a commitment that demands
more give-and-take from employers.
Here's what's driving it.

By Jennifer Laabs

The gold watch—it used to be the ultimate goal for the American worker. It was bestowed on the most loyal of employees at the end of a long career and was coveted by all. But today's worker has changed dramatically from the days of the 1950s "organization man." These days, you'd be hard-pressed to find a worker who'd be loyal to your firm for a decade, let alone a lifetime.

But how has today's worker changed exactly? What's the pulse on employee commitment these days? It's not as bad as you might think. Although there's been much said about the death of worker loyalty (see "New Employment Rules Are Thwarting Employee Commitment" WORK-FORCE, August 1996), employees are generally more satisfied with their jobs now than they were only three years ago in 1995 (72 percent are happy now vs. 58 per-

cent then)—according to Boston-based Towers Perrin's "1997 Workplace Index" study. Towers Perrin is an international management consulting firm that tracked the attitudes of 3,300 employees in 1995 and 2,500 employees in 1997, who were working in U.S. companies with at least 500 employees.

However, the newest survey on the pulse of employee commitment shows that employee loyalty actually took a slight dip (2.2 points) again between 1997 and 1998, according to the Workforce Commitment Index™, a national measure of employee loyalty that's part of the 1998 America @ Works℠ study conducted by Aon Consulting Worldwide Inc., an HR consulting firm based in Chicago. Aon's study included data from 1,800 U.S. workers in organizations of 20 employees or more.

Workers have seen the light.

These types of ups and downs are to be expected. After all, the American workforce—131-million strong—has been through a lot over the past years, leaving many employees feeling disenfranchised. "Society in general walks around on a daily basis ever ready to utter the words, 'Screw you!'" says Carrie Pierce, a former cosmetic company VP who quit her job last year because of extreme

---

Jennifer Laabs is the associate managing editor at WORK-FORCE. Research for this series was also provided by Deb McCusker, president of McCusker & Associates, based in Plaistow, New Hampshire, and Ilene Wolfman, group vice president of the Davis Companies based in Marlborough, Massachusetts. E-mail laabsj@workforcemag.com to comment.

disloyalty on her employer's part. "I was tired of feeling like a prostitute and working with others that felt the same way," says Pierce. For her, loyalty died when her employer betrayed her.

And while it's difficult to nail down exactly when the old style of employee commitment died for most American workers (it has been slowly decaying over the past few decades), everyone agrees that the layoffs, rightsizings, re-organizations, mergers and acquisitions of the mid-'90s were the final dagger to the heart of the old employee contract.

Through it all, employers, for the most part, took the attitude that those who were left should just be glad to have jobs. Those workers left warming the seats were, after all, the "chosen" few. Even five years ago, many U.S. managers still saw employees as disposable commodities. They hadn't yet realized how important those employees were going to be to future business. Now those same managers are being forced to admit they were wrong. In the Information Age, employees have become companies' biggest assets, and perhaps the only sustainable source of competitive advantage to push corporate and employment growth—growth that is picking up steam.

Although the layoffs haven't stopped completely, job creation is far outpacing jobs eliminated. "Companies announced plans to cut 332,665 jobs during the first eight months of this year," says John Challenger, executive vice president of Challenger, Gray and Christmas, an international outplacement firm based in Chicago. But more than 1.5 million new jobs were created in the same period, according to the U.S. Labor Department.

"Only three years ago, people were still coming out of the trauma of the layoff era," says Stephen M. Bookbinder, a principal with Towers Perrin and author of both his firm's employee commitment studies. "Remember, the height of the layoffs came in '92 and '93-and in '95 there were still a lot of residual effects." Most workers have now gotten used to the reality that there's no job security.

Because of this, you'd expect workers to be bitter and withdrawn. "But when you look at the data, American workers—for the most part—aren't bitter and they aren't cynical," says David L. Stum, president of The Loyalty

These Kids Today: Commitment Just Ain't What It Used to Be—with Good Reason

Many managers say Generation Xers (the post-baby boomer generation born between 1965 and 1977, comprising 52 million Americans), and Generation Y (those who come after Xers—born between 1978 and 2003) aren't committed to their companies, and that the younger kids are only in it for themselves. But it depends on how you look at it. According to the "1997 Workforce Commitment Index" study by Chicago-based Aon Consulting Worldwide Inc., Gen Xers do show high levels of commitment to their companies.

"It may seem like Xers don't want to pay their dues, but this is what makes Xers so amenable to the kind of day-to-day value-adding relationship most employers want from their employees," says Bruce Tulgan, author of several books focusing on Generation X, and the founder of Rainmaker Thinking Inc., a New Haven, Connecticut-based research, training and consulting form. "Of course, Xers think, learn and communicate differently from those of other generations, but this is also what makes Xers so comfortable with information and technology." And that's a highly needed skill in today's information society.

"Organizations ought to stop beating their chests about this and ask why new employees don't have that same loyalty and commitment older workers had and what their companies ought to do about it," says Eve Luppert, author of Rules for the Road: Surviving Your First Job Out of School (Perigee Books, 1998). Luppert, now based in Seattle, logged 15 years in senior level HR for such firms as Chiat/Day Inc. and ConnexT Inc. before becoming a writer and consultant. Luppert says there are several reasons why younger employees aren't committed to their companies. "This is truly a television generation, and not since Lou Grant was Mary's boss have we seen a reasonable, compassionate manager on prime time," Luppert says. She points out that new workers were growing up with parents who often lost their jobs to downsizing and cutbacks. Their parents' worlds were tempered with fear and the loss of the family's livelihood. "Young workers don't believe their companies when they claim to be a family. These kids know better. Younger workers understand management's loyalty lasts only as long as financial statements make it possible," she states. "The new workers have quite rightly placed their first loyalty to themselves and their own careers."

Luppert asserts that if companies are honest with themselves, they know a promise of security and a gold watch is a relic of the past. Commitment is always "purchased" by mutuality; if you commit to me, I'll commit to you. "Now that security is no longer the wage for commitment, organizations need to offer something else," she adds.

She suggests that in the Information Age, the new worker is looking for:

• information and continuous learning opportunities

• companies that devote time and money to socially responsible causes

• merit awards (of money, time or training) for good service.

"I've got a 16-year-old and a 14-year-old, and they see the world very differently from me, a baby-boomer," says Jim Krefft, senior vice president of Six Sigma Qualtec, a consulting firm based in Scottsdale, Arizona. "They're just not going to work in a place that they don't believe in. My son has already announced, 'I'm never going to be in a deadhead job.'" Krefft says these young people are looking for organizational cultures that are amenable to a broad degree of what he calls "vibrant diversity"—a higher level of inclusion than we're experiencing now in the workplace. It's an out-of-the-box orientation that transcends even the most inclusive of today's business cultures—and these younger workers will thrive on it.

—JL

Institute™, an Aon Consulting Worldwide division, based in Ann Arbor, Michigan. "But I'll tell you what they are— they're more aware." Here's the psychology behind it: Workers now are aware that companies are going to do what they have to do to succeed and to survive, and they understand that sometimes companies will have to start doing manufacturing in South America, or eliminate three layers of management or close down plants.

Just as companies have taken stock and taken responsibility for doing what's right for business, employees have also taken a step back and asked: What's in it for me? "That, to me, isn't bitterness, it's a new understanding that the old idea of the paternal company taking care of employees [has died]," explains Stum. Employees have realized they need to take more responsibility for their professional and personal needs, like developing their skills and balancing work with interests outside the office. The whole employee commitment picture is more adult, more honest, more realistic. And employees are coping better than they did in 1995. "There's been a dramatic increase in people's ability to handle the stress and pressures of their jobs," Bookbinder adds.

Reality has hit, and people are dealing with it. They have a lot of energy for their jobs, but they want more in return. They're committed—but they're offering a different kind of commitment: High-impact performance for rewards that are meaningful to them (what they want rather than what their company thinks they need).

Stay longer—but with a different mindset.

There's a popular perception that all this change in the employment contract has made workers more prone to job hopping. In fact, a new 1998 study, "Have Jobs Become Less Stable in the 1990s?: Evidence From Employer Data" by Watson Wyatt Worldwide, a management consulting firm based in Bethesda, Maryland, shows that the average job tenure of American workers at medium and large companies is 13.1 years. In the early 1990s, average tenure was 12.3 years. Watson Wyatt's team examined the employment records of 1.1 million workers at 59 companies and determined that people are staying for longer periods these days, not shorter. And the highest average tenure (14.6 years) was at the nation's largest firms—those with more than 80,000 employees. "The

rush of newspaper stories about downsizing and layoffs gives the impression that there's less job stability than ever," says study author, Sylvester Shieber, vice president and director of research at Watson Wyatt. "This anecdotal evidence simply isn't borne out by our research."

And, interestingly enough, HR pros aren't the only ones who get employee turnover headaches. According to the first-ever "Shell Poll," a quarterly opinion poll of 1,123 Americans sponsored by Shell Oil Co. and conducted by Peter D. Hart Research Associates based in Washington, D.C., most categories of workers share concerns about high turnover rates—72 percent say they prefer the security of long-term employment with one company.

Employees are realizing the grass isn't always greener on the other side. But that doesn't mean they'll stay no matter what. The opportunity for employers and HR managers is that by embracing the concepts of the new deal, you have a good shot at keeping people engaged and employed.

Customization is the new employment deal.

Employees have gotten smarter, tougher, more aware, but they still aren't ready to jump ship at the slightest provocation. They know companies need them more than ever, especially with the U.S. unemployment rate punching in at record lows—4.5 percent at press time. It's a seller's market, putting employees at an advantage, while companies need to have more confidence in their workforce than ever, putting them, ostensibly, at a disadvantage. The tables have been turned. "In this tight job market, loyalty

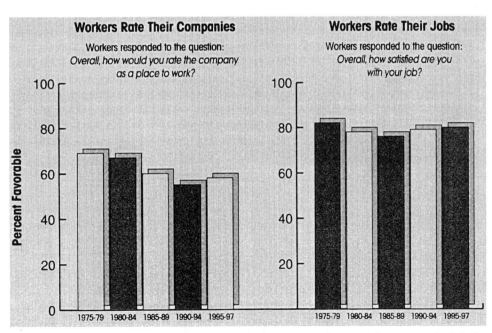

In the past 22 years, workers' satisfaction with their companies as a place to work (left) has gone down, but is on the rise again. The same is true with employees' satisfaction with their jobs (right). While it took a hit in years past, it's now rising.

Source: The 1998–'99 Hay Employee Attitudes Study, Hay Group, Inc., Philadelphia.

The Committed Employee—Then and Now

Every employer needs committed employees to compete and prosper. But employee loyalty isn't what it used to be. American business is at a crossroads in the challenge to develop committed workers. Aon Consulting's 1998 America @ Work℠ survey confirms that even today's most valuable and committed workers often put career development and life/family issues ahead of company goals. The chart below illustrates this shift in workforce commitment.

Characteristic	Then	Now
Attachment to employer	Long-term	Near-term
Readiness to change jobs	Not interested	Not looking (but will listen)
Priorities on the job	The firm and its goals	Personal life and career
Devotion to employer goals	Follow orders	Buys in (usually)
Effort on the job	100 percent	110 percent
Motto	Semper fidelis ("Always faithful")	Carpe diem ("Seize the day")

has taken a back seat as people are more opportunistic," says Gary Beisaw, director of ShopLink Inc., a personal services company (home food delivery) based in Westwood, Massachusetts.

Here's the new deal: Employees won't be checking into Corporate America Inc. for long periods of time anymore, so you'll need to look at employee loyalty in a different way. Define it by performance rather than time, and seek to enhance that performance in ways that are most meaningful to workers for as long as they decide to stay.

Here's the interesting twist for HR professionals: While employee commitment studies generalize what employees want under the new deal, the companies that will be successful are ones that can figure out how to align their business goals with each worker's goals. "The analogy for companies is that mass marketing isn't necessarily working anymore. Everyone's looking for customized solutions these days. Why would employees be any different?" asks Barbara Madden, vice president of North American sales in the San Francisco office of Blessing White, a firm specializing in individual and organizational consulting. If managers are going to get the most out of employees, they need to look at individuals separately, which demands a higher level of communication. "Don't assume that what works for one employee will work for another," adds Madden, whose specialty is employee development. "Although some managers might think it's time-consuming, the small amount of time you can invest with an employee to better understand his or her talents and aspirations will pay back

tenfold. Entering into a sincere conversation will lead to a better understanding of what the individual's self-interest is, and how the organization might begin to satisfy that."

Take the term "one size fits all" out of your vocabulary. You thought you had to customize solutions for customers? Get ready to customize an employment deal with every employee. You no longer can see the workforce as an army in which you treat everyone the same. You'll have to learn how to balance fairness for all with recognizing individual contributions. You thought you were already walking a tightrope? This one's even trickier. Fortunately experts see solid areas in which human resources professionals can have an impact on improving relationships between employees and employers. Employees want improvements in the areas of total rewards, including benefits and compensation; leadership and cultural change issues; employee selection, training and development; and work/life balance. They've already been big issues for HR, but having an employee view of it adds fuel to the fire.

Whether the employee commitment fire burns bright or fizzles out may have a lot to do with what you make of it. Says Art Sharkey, director of HR for Shipley Corp., a chemical manufacturing company in Marlboro, Massachusetts: "The effort starts with human resources. Think: I'm an employee, how do I want the company to treat me?" Perhaps the new employment deal can be summarized by employees as: "Treat me right, and I'll treat you right. Treat me wrong, and I'll leave you faster than you can say 'high turnover.' "

Trust,
An Asset in Any Field

By Roger C. Mayer

Like trust between business partners, trust between employees and their employers matters to the bottom line of the organization.

It's no secret that business is rapidly departing from the stable, traditional business environment that we've known for years. While many TQM programs have brought disappointing results, the popularity of quality management programs has fueled a lingering interest in the importance of building long-term partnerships with suppliers, buyers, and employees. Research has found it's much cheaper to retain a current customer than it is to get a new customer, and it's far cheaper than trying to recover a lost customer. Thus, the importance of nurturing long-term relationships in business is becoming increasingly clear.

The Labor Market

Those responsible for hiring new employees are keenly aware that the labor market in recent years has changed dramatically, and that these trends are projected to continue. A few years ago there was an abundance of labor. When Henry Ford popularized the assembly line, if an employee didn't particularly work out or didn't want to "toe the organization's line" that employee could be replaced easily and cheaply. No longer is this the case. Companies have had to resort to incredibly creative means to recruit new employees.

Once again, research has shown us that if the company makes a good initial hiring decision, it is much more economical to retain and develop present employees than to service the revolving door of continuously replacing and retraining employees. Here again, the relationship—this time between the employer and employees—is critically important.

The Employer-Employee Relationship

The employer-employee relationship has become the focus of a good deal of management research. One of the fundamental aspects of any relationship that determines how well it functions is the extent to which the parties trust one another. While intuitively we've known many things about trust for years, many of the bits of folk wisdom about it disagree with one another. Trust seems to be like something Mark Twain once said of the weather, "Everybody knows about it, but no one is doing much about it." For the past several years my research has focused on understanding trust in business relationships. In many ways it is similar to trust in family relationships.

Most managers are becoming increasingly aware of the importance of empowerment to successful organizations, but now it is becoming clear that management's trust for employees contributes to empowerment. If managers don't trust employees, they won't delegate risky tasks—and the employees won't feel empowered or act empowered.

In studies conducted with research colleagues at Purdue and Notre Dame, we first looked at doctors of veterinary medicine. We asked the "vets" (as they are commonly called) how much they trust a given employee and how they work with that employee. We found that with the employees they trusted—not just the ones they thought were skilled but the ones who could be trusted—the vets delegated risky tasks like administering anesthesia to their animal patients.

> If managers don't trust employees, they won't delegate risky tasks—and the employees won't feel empowered or act empowered.

We conducted a second study over a nine-month period in an entire restaurant chain. We measured the level of trust that employees had for their restaurant's general manager and tracked the performance of each restaurant over the next three quarters. The results were striking. In the restaurants where managers garnered more trust from their employees, three things were markedly different. These restaurants had higher sales volume levels, higher net profits, and lower levels of employee turnover—a factor which is critical to the long-term success of any organization. While this may be intuitively obvious to some managers, it has come as quite a shock to others that something as intangible as "employee trust" has a real impact on the bottom line.

The Role of Trust in Companies

Many managers and academics have a pessimistic view about the future of trust in companies. They believe that given economic uncertainties, downsizing, reengineering, and the like, trust for management will inevitably decline.

We conducted a third study in a manufacturing setting and again assessed the level of trust that employees had for top management. In that particular setting, management was telling employees that their raises and promotions were based on their performance, while employees felt that the company's performance appraisal system was not valid. Employees could not see the link between their performance and their raises and promotions. In a fourteen-month experiment, we found that when the performance appraisal system was changed to one that employees deemed more valid (which clearly linked their pay with their performance), employees' trust in management went up.

The consequences of this research are quite simple. Like trust between business partners, trust between employees and their employers matters to the bottom line of the organization. In order to compete in a complex business environment that is changing with increasing speed, companies need to empower their employees to act. Managers who can't trust their employees are unwilling to empower them. As a result, they surrender the competitive advantage to firms whose managers trust their employees. Employees who trust their managers can focus their attention on adding value to the company, rather than trying to protect their own self-interests.

Building Trust

So what can you do to build others' trust in you? First of all, be honest and fair in your dealings with everyone. Since others, even casual third-party observers, will draw conclusions about how a person treats others, showing that you have good values and that you follow them consistently makes a big difference. Second, sharpening your technical and people skills is also important. People are reluctant to put their fate in the hands of someone they don't think is very competent. Third, show by your actions that you care about others. If someone believes that you would go out of your way to protect their interests, it fosters trust for you.

Building trust between managers and employees is neither quick nor easy. By paying attention to relationships with their employees and seeking to understand what things are limiting trust in their own companies, insightful managers can garner more trust from their employees and unleash their potential to contribute to the company's performance.

Roger C. Mayer is associate professor of management. A member of the Baylor faculty since 1997, Mayer holds a BA degree from Kent State University and a PhD from Purdue University. He also serves on the editorial review board of the Academy of Management Journal.

ORGANIZATIONAL CYNICISM

JAMES W. DEAN, JR.

University of North Carolina at Chapel Hill

PAMELA BRANDES

Southern Connecticut State University

RAVI DHARWADKAR

University of Cincinnati

What is the nature of the extremely negative attitudes expressed by so many employees toward their organizations? To respond to this question, we introduce the concept of organizational cynicism. We review the literature from several disciplines on this concept and suggest that organizational cynicism is an attitude composed of beliefs, affect, and behavioral tendencies toward an organization. Following our review and conceptualization, we derive implications of this concept and propose a research agenda for organizational cynicism.

Cynicism is everywhere—widespread among organization members in the United States (Kanter & Mirvis, 1989), Europe, and Asia (Kouzes & Posner, 1993). Organizational change and quality improvement efforts particularly seem to engender cynicism (Shapiro, 1996). For example, Cunniff notes that employees are increasingly cynical about the "constant parade of initiatives that come with the usual promise of imminent improvement" (1993: 4). Employees in one company circulated clandestine copies of their firm's "adaptation" of the Deming Principles, which included "Humor all employees in phony efforts to include them in process improvement methodologies. . . . Provide slogans, meaningless exhortations [and] numerical goals. . . . Drive in fear by discouraging communication and by instituting a policy of Continuous Layoff."

These observations are echoed in our own experience by the reaction of part-time MBA students to the topic of "teamwork" (cross-functional collaboration) in organizations. These students could see the benefits of teamwork in theory but perceived it, in practice, as merely a slogan used by their organizations to appear progressive, without changing anything about

how work actually gets done (cf., Aktouf, 1992). A young woman in this class was so appalled by her organization that she thought she must be part of "some huge experiment on unmotivating employees." Another young man had been invited to lunch with his coworkers by the management of his organization; he accepted the invitation but worried that management had only made the offer "to keep us off guard." Even the popularity of the comic strip "Dilbert," about an engineer whose organization plumbs the depths of unscrupulousness, suggests that many people perceive their organizations in these terms. In fact, much of the material for the strip actually is sent to the cartoonist via e-mail by frustrated employees (Greilsamer, 1995).

This article is about organization members' cynicism toward their organizations—an attitude that appears to be both widespread and ignored by organizational research. We address one major question: how should organizational cynicism be conceptualized? We organize this article as follows. First, we discuss the origin of the concept of cynicism and briefly review the literature that has begun to appear on this topic. We then propose a conceptualization of cynicism in organizations and discuss a number of issues related to this conceptualization. Next, we compare organizational cynicism to other existing organizational constructs. Finally, we propose a research agenda for organizational cynicism.

We thank Lynne Andersson, Harold Angle, Daniel Brass, Thomas Debbink, Dennis Gioia, Katherine Klein, and Anand Narasimhan for their helpful comments on an earlier draft of this article. This research was supported by a grant from the University of Cincinnati Faculty Summer Research Fellowship.

CONCEPTIONS OF CYNICISM

Origins of the Concept of Cynicism

Cynicism as a school of thought and a way of life originated in ancient Greece. The term itself may have come from the Greek word for dog (kyon) or from Cynosarges, a town near Athens where the Cynics had their school. The first Cynic was Antisthenes, originally a follower of Socrates, but he has been overshadowed in history by his student Diogenes of Sinope, who became famous for carrying a lamp in daylight to help him find one honest man. Believing that the individual, and not the organization, was the natural unit of human life, Cynics felt that even cherished institutions, such as religion and government, were unnatural and unnecessary—worthy only of scorn (Fuller, 1931). Cynics were openly contemptuous of such institutions and were known for using dramatic and obscene displays to draw people into conversations, in which they could proclaim their views (Mack, 1993). Humor was the favorite weapon of the Cynics, the privileged and powerful their favorite target.

Cynicism was, from the beginning, as much a lifestyle as a philosophy (More, 1923). Cynics believed that men's conventions were unnatural and should be avoided, as much as possible, in the name of the independence and self-sufficiency that characterize a good life. Rejecting societal standards, Cynics wore rough clothing and drank out of their hands so as not to need a cup. Diogenes is even said to have lived in a tub instead of a house. In short, the original Cynics held society's institutions in very low regard and expressed contempt for them in both words and actions.

Over the centuries the terms "cynic," "cynical," and "cynicism" have taken their place in our language, with meanings that are loosely derived from the tenets of Cynicism. The *Oxford English Dictionary* (1989) defines a cynic as "one who shows a disposition to disbelieve in the sincerity or goodness of human motives and actions, and is wont to express this by sneers and sarcasms; a sneering fault-finder." In the next section we discuss how various researchers have interpreted the idea of cynicism.

Conceptualizations of Cynicism in Research

Five major conceptualizations of cynicism seem to characterize the literature thus far. A useful review of these should compare and contrast existing conceptualizations in order to demonstrate areas of distinction, as well as areas of overlap between concepts. One method for comparing conceptualizations is facet design (Guttman, 1954; Schwab, 1980; Shapira & Zevulun, 1979). While this technique can be used for hypothesis development and testing on more mature concepts, our purpose in applying this technique will be more "taxonomic," in order to contrast different approaches to cynicism.

Extant conceptualizations of cynicism (see Table 1) can be compared in terms of their related concepts, foci, definitions, epistemic correlations (the relationship between the conceptualization and the measurement of a construct; Northrop, 1959),

overlaps with/preclusion of other cynicism forms, internal reliability, relative importance of determinants (e.g., person versus situational characteristics), and the assumed permanence and means of influencing the construct (Morrow, 1983). In addition to these categories, we include in Table 1 yet another means of comparison: theoretical predecessors. Because of space considerations, we mean the citations included to be illustrative rather than exhaustive.

Personality approaches. Researchers using personality-based approaches to cynicism generally discuss cynicism as an overall outlook on human nature. Studies in this tradition are based on Cook and Medley's (1954) hostility scale—a subset of items from the Minnesota Multiphasic Personality Inventory (MMPI). Graham (1993) suggests that individuals who score high on MMPI cynicism scales see others as selfish and uncaring, question the motives of others, and are guarded and untrusting in relationships. Scholars undertaking current discussions of the hostility concept within psychology and medicine interpret Cook and Medley's work as representing "cynical hostility," which includes distrust in others but not overt expressions of aggression (e.g., Barefoot, Dodge, Peterson, Dahlstrom, & Williams, 1989; Costa, Zonderman, McCrae, & Williams, 1986; Greenglass & Julkunen, 1989). The Cook and Medley hostility scale reflects more individuals' impressions of themselves (e.g., "I have often met people who were supposed to be expert who were no better than I") and less their view of people in general, which has been the focus of Wrightsman's (1974) Philosophies of Human Nature Scale (cynicism subscale). As a result of a trait-based approach, research within this tradition assumes that little can be done to change one's degree of cynicism.

Societal/institutional focus. According to Kanter and Mirvis (1989), Americans' cynical outlook on life has resulted from fluctuating fortunes in the American social and political milieus in the twentieth century. Other contributors to cynicism include exploitation of workers during the early stages of industrialization and the failed promise of modern organizations to improve life at work. Although Kanter and Mirvis discuss cynicism as including disillusionment with society, self, institutions, or others, their operationalization deals with people's impressions of others in general. In other words, because of the nature of their operationalization, there is some overlap between their conception of cynicism and the personality approach to cynicism. Kanter and Mirvis's analysis indicates that cynicism has become an inherent characteristic of many Americans, suggesting that 43 percent of the workforce is cynical. However, their description of the evolution of cynicism as a response to the failed promises of society, as well as their attention to demographic variables (e.g., gender, race, education, and income), suggests a situational component; counter to the personality approach, they propose that cynicism levels can be managed, and they offer several ways that organizations can create work cultures to counter it.

Occupational cynicism focus. In his studies of urban policing, Niederhoffer (1967) noted the development of "police cynicism," which he describes as "a byproduct of anomie in the social structure" (1967: 95) of policing stemming from the interaction of role ambiguities and conflicting pressures re-

TABLE 1

Facet Analysis of Cynicism Studies

Facet of Analysis	Personality Focus	Societal or Institutional Focus	Occupational Cynicism Focus	Employee Cynicism Focus	Organizational Change Efforts Focus
1. Representative concepts	Hostility (Cook & Medley, 1954)	Cynicism (Kanter & Mirvis, 1989)	Work cynicism (Neiderhoffer, 1967; O'Connell, Holzman, & Armandi, 1986)	Employee cynicism (Andersson, 1996; Andersson & Bateman, 1997)	Cynicism about organizational change (Reichers, Wanous, & Austin, 1997; Vance, Brooks, & Tesluk, 1996; Wanous, Reichers, & Austin, 1994)
2. Focus of concept	Negative perceptions of and hostility toward others	Unmet expectations of society, institutions, or other authorities	One's occupation (specifically, police work)	Business organizations, executives, and/or other workplace objects	Organizational change efforts
3. Definition(s)	Individuals with high scores "(have) little confidence in [their] fellowman. . . see people as dishonest, unsocial, immoral, ugly, and mean" (Cook & Medley, 1954: 418)	Cynicism requires: (1) formation of unrealistically high expectations of oneself or others that generalize to expectations of society, institutions, authorities, and the future; (2) experience of disappointment in oneself and others; (3) feelings of disillusion and betrayal by one's self or others	Disparaging mistrust toward the service of the people and enforcement of the law; lost respect/pride for the job (O'Connell, Holzman, & Armandi, 1986)	A general and specific attitude characterized by frustration, hopelessness, and disillusionment, as well as contempt and distrust of business organizations, executives, and/or other workplace objects	Midrange construct encompassing pessimism about the success of future organizational change efforts based on beliefs that change agents are lazy, incompetent, or both (Wanous, Reichers, & Austin, 1994)
4. Theoretical predecessor	MMPI	Expectancy-like	Neiderhoffer (1967)	Attitudes-like; psychological contract violation	Expectancy (Vroom, 1964) and attribution (Jones & Davis, 1965)
5. Epistemic correlations	Moderate	Low	Moderate	Moderate	High
6. Comparative aspect overlaps with other forms of cynicism	Yes	Yes	Yes	Yes	Yes
7. Precludes other cynicisms	No	Yes	No	No	No
8. Reliability	50 items, a = .86 (Cook & Medley, 1954)	7 items, a = .78 (Kanter & Mirvis, 1989)	9 items, a = .87 (O'Connell, Holzman, & Armandi, 1986)	7 items, a = .92 (toward hypothetical organization) 6 items, a = .86 (toward business organizations and executives) (Anderson & Bateman, 1997)	8 items, a = not reported (Reichers, Wanous, & Austin, 1997) 8 items, a = .86 (Wanous, Reichers, & Austin, 1994)
9. Impact of determinants:					
a. person	+++	+	0	0	+
b. situation	0	+++	+++	+++	++
10. Permanence	High	Moderate	Not a major focus	Moderate	Highly
11. Strategies of influence	Very few	Several	Not a major focus	Not a major focus	Many

garding professionalization of police work. O'Connell, Holzman, and Armandi (1986) found that officers had two targets for their cynicism: (1) the organization (organizational cynicism) and (2) the service of the people and of the law (work cynicism). O'Connell et al. (1986) suggest that high and low levels of work and organizational cynicism combine to create four different adaptation styles. Although correlated, the relationship between work and organizational cynicism was not so high as to suggest that they were the same construct. Work cynicism was higher for those officers who (1) had less complex work details, (2) had rotating shifts, (3) had non-preferred details, and (4) worked in the precinct.

Employee cynicism focus. Andersson (1996) and Andersson and Bateman (1997) suggest three potential targets for cynicism: (1) business organizations in general, (2) corporate executives, and (3) "other" workplace objects. Employee cynics within this approach are noteworthy for their negative feelings, such as contempt, frustration, and hopelessness toward these targets. Researchers see employee cynicism as a result of violations of psychological contracts and describe this cynicism within the realm of attitudes. Using a scenario-based methodology, Andersson and Bateman found that employee cynicism toward a hypothetical organization was related to high levels of executive compensation, poor organizational performance, and harsh organizational layoffs. Additionally, cynicism toward three targets was negatively related to self-reported intent to perform organizational citizenship behaviors.

Organizational change focus. Reichers, Wanous, and Austin (1997) suggest that organizational change efforts are the appropriate target of cynicism. Specifically, they describe cynicism as an attitude consisting of the futility of change along with negative attributions of change facilitators. Similarly, Vance, Brooks, and Tesluk suggest that organizational cynicism is a "learned belief that fixable problems at work will not be resolved due to factors beyond the individual's control" (1996: 1), but unlike Reichers et al., they suggest that cynics believe that things could be better. Cynicism about organizational change (CAOC) has a specific target (organizational change efforts) but does not preclude other forms of cynicism. In fact, these authors suggest that negative affect (a personality variable) is positively related to CAOC. While acknowledging the impact of personality variables, Reichers et al. (1997) emphasize the strength of situational variables: being an hourly employee, perceiving less participation in decisions, and perceiving poor information flows and follow-ups all are related to CAOC. Furthermore, Reichers et al. offer several recommendations for managing cynicism, which include efforts at involving people in decisions that affect them, enhancing the credibility of management, and keeping surprising changes to a minimum.

In summary, scholars have observed cynicism through various theoretical lenses and have offered several targets for cynicism, including other people in general, societal institutions, one's occupation, top managers, and organizational change efforts.

A NEW CONCEPTUALIZATION OF ORGANIZATIONAL CYNICISM

Our task now turns to conceptualizing organizational cynicism in a way that captures the generally understood meaning of this term and provides a solid foundation for operationalization and measurement. We will also distinguish organizational cynicism from constructs frequently used in organizational studies. Both of these tasks are essential to the development of constructs within organizational behavior. We hope to add to existing knowledge by creating a unique conceptualization that we believe captures the essence of the construct while defining it in precise terms.

In order to put organizational cynicism on solid conceptual and theoretical footing, we have conceptualized it as an attitude, which is "a disposition to respond favorably or unfavorably to an object, person, institution, or event" (Ajzen, 1994: 114). Psychologists suggest that evaluation is the core of attitudes (Eagly & Chaiken, 1993). We define organizational cynicism as follows:

> *Organizational cynicism is a negative attitude toward one's employing organization, comprising three dimensions: (1) a belief that the organization lacks integrity; (2) negative affect toward the organization; and (3) tendencies to disparaging and critical behaviors toward the organization that are consistent with these beliefs and affect.*

Our conception of cynicism, thus, is multidimensional, corresponding to the three components—beliefs, affect, and behavioral tendencies—that have long characterized attitude theory (Eagly & Chaiken, 1993; Hilgard, 1980; Smith, 1947). All three components vary on an evaluative continuum, from positive to negative (Allport, 1935; Breckler, 1984). Thus, we do not focus on cynicism as a personality trait—a characteristic of people who are cynical about everything—but rather as a state—an aspect of people that may change over time and that is directed at a specific target: their organization (cf., Hart, 1997).

One assumption of our definition is that an organization can be the object of an attitude. Ajzen's (1994) definition of attitudes, which includes "institutions" as potential attitude objects, makes clear that this is consistent with attitude theory. There is also a substantial precedent for this assumption in the literature on organizational commitment (Porter, Steers, Mowday, & Boulian, 1974) and on perceived organizational identity (e.g., Dutton, Dukerich, & Harquail, 1994). Bateman, Sakano, and Fujita (1992) also have demonstrated that people hold attitudes about specific organizations, whereas Levinson (1965) discusses the broader tendencies of individuals to personify organizations.

A further assumption is that people can form an attitude about their employing organization based on the behavior of the people in the organization. Although occasional perceptions that organizational practices lack integrity may be attributed to the specific individuals involved, perceptions that such behavior is widespread and enduring in the organization are more likely to be attributed to organizational characteristics (Dutton et al., 1994). Moreover, some of the perceptions upon which cynical attitudes are based—concerning policies, processes, or other systemic elements of the organization—may be difficult to relate to specific individuals.

Beliefs

The first dimension of organizational cynicism is the belief that the organization lacks integrity. Returning to the *Oxford English Dictionary,* we find integrity defined as "soundness of moral principle; the character of uncorrupted virtue, especially in relation to truth and fair dealing; uprightness, honesty, sincerity." Upon relating this back to the dictionary definition of cynicism ("a disposition to disbelieve in the sincerity or goodness of human motives and actions"), we see that a concise statement of cynical beliefs is that people lack integrity (see Becker, 1998, for an alternative conceptualization of integrity).

Thus, *organizational cynics* believe that the practices of their organizations betray a lack of such principles as fairness, honesty, and sincerity. These cynics may believe that, in their organization, such principles are often sacrificed to expediency and that unscrupulous behavior is the norm. They may also believe that choices of organizational direction are based on self-interest (Goldner, Ritti, & Ference, 1977) and that people are inconsistent and unreliable in their behavior. Cynics often believe there are hidden motives for actions; thus, they expect to see deception rather than candor and are unlikely to accept at face value the official rationale for organizational decisions.

Affect

Attitudes are composed of affect—that is, emotional reactions to the attitude object—as well as beliefs (Eagly & Chaiken, 1993). This implies that cynicism is *felt* as well as *thought*—experienced through emotion as well as cognition. Cynicism is not a dispassionate judgment about the organization; it can include powerful emotional reactions. In conceptualizing this affective component of cynical attitudes, we rely primarily upon the work of Izard (1977), who identifies nine basic emotions, each of which is described in both a mild and strong form: (1) interest-excitement, (2) enjoyment-joy, (3) surprise-startle, (4) distress-anguish, (5) anger-rage, (6) disgust-revulsion, (7) contempt-scorn, (8) fear-terror, and (9) shame-humiliation.

The affective dimension of organizational cynicism comprises several of these emotions. Cynics may, for example, feel contempt for and anger toward their organization. They may also experience distress, disgust, and even shame when they think about their organization. Thus, cynicism is associated with a variety of negative emotions. Ironically, however, cynics may also experience a secret enjoyment of their superiority to the organization, which they have judged by their standards and found wanting. Therefore, we see organizational cynics as not only holding certain beliefs about their organizations but also as experiencing a related set of emotions.

Behavior

The final dimension of organizational cynicism is tendencies toward negative, and often disparaging, behavior. The gen-

eral thrust of the literature indicates that cynical attitudes comprise tendencies toward certain types of behavior, rather than specific behaviors per se (e.g., Ajzen, 1994). Echoing the ancient Cynics, the most obvious behavioral tendency for those with cynical attitudes is the expression of strong criticisms of the organization. This may take a variety of forms, the most direct of which is explicit statements about the lack of honesty, sincerity, and so on, on the part of the organization. Employees also may use humor, especially sarcastic humor, to express cynical attitudes. Expressing interpretations of organizational events that assume a lack of integrity on the part of the organization may be a behavioral tendency that characterizes organizational cynics as well—for example, the employee who says that the only reason the company is interested in environmental issues is to generate good public relations. Organizational cynics may tend to make pessimistic predictions about the future course of action in the organization. For example, they may predict that a quality initiative will be abandoned as soon as it begins to be costly. Finally, tendencies toward certain types of nonverbal behavior may be used to convey cynical attitudes. This includes "knowing" looks and rolling eyes, as well as the smirks and sneers by which cynics (and Cynics) have long been known.

In summary, we have conceptualized organizational cynicism as an attitude composed of beliefs, affect, and behavioral tendencies. Thus, we see organizational cynicism as a multidimensional construct: people are considered cynical about their organization to the extent that they hold certain beliefs about the organization's (lack of) integrity, experience certain types of affect toward the organization, and display certain behavioral tendencies toward the organization. We can conceptualize the strength of the attitude of cynicism as a function of the strength of each of the individual dimensions. However, research generally has shown the three components of attitudes to be highly intercorrelated (e.g., Breckler, 1984). Implicit in this discussion is the assumption that organizational cynicism is a continuum: the world is not divided into cynics and noncynics, and people have widely varying degrees of cynicism.

ADVANTAGES OF OUR CONCEPTUALIZATION OF ORGANIZATIONAL CYNICISM

We believe our conceptualization of organizational cynicism provides a number of advantages over existing conceptualizations. Many of these advantages are based on our use of the tripartite attitude framework. First, our conceptualization makes it clear that organizational cynicism is a state—not a trait—which implies both that it is based on specific organizational experiences and that it is likely to change somewhat over time as individuals' experiences change. By relying on an attitudes framework, we have clearly differentiated organizational cynicism from personality- or trait-based cynicism, which focuses on human nature in general. Second, it is not limited to a particular type of work, such as police work; cynicism certainly is observable in a wide range of occupations.

Third, our conceptualization rounds out the construct by including affect and behavior, as well as beliefs. Although the cognitive element of organizational cynicism is quite important, the construct would be impoverished without a consideration of its emotional and behavioral dimensions. Finally, by focusing on the organization as the target of cynicism, constructs such as cynicism about organizational change are subsumed into a broader whole, from which, perhaps, they can be derived. If employees see organizations as generally insincere and duplicitous, then it makes sense that organizational changes will not be expected to be seriously undertaken and, therefore, will be expected to fail. However, unlike the societal and occupational variants of cynicism, in which targets include governments, education, religion, or occupations, our approach restricts the target of cynicism to one's employing organization.

CONCEPTUAL ISSUES IN DEFINING ORGANIZATIONAL CYNICISM

In attempting to conceptualize a new construct, we must address a number of issues in order to explain and justify our definition. The issues we address here include (1) the validity of cynical beliefs, (2) the value of cynicism, (3) the appropriate level of analysis for organizational cynicism, and (4) the distinction between organizational cynicism and other constructs.

The Validity of Cynical Beliefs

It may well have occurred to some readers that cynics may be right—that is, correct in their evaluations of their organization. Our definition takes no position on the factual basis (or lack thereof) for cynical attitudes. Whatever their real or imagined basis, these attitudes are equally valid to the individuals who hold them. Moreover, it would be virtually impossible to distinguish between "justified" and "unjustified" organizational cynicism because so much of what happens in organizations is open to different interpretations (e.g., Pfeffer, 1981; Weick, 1979). For example, one could argue about whether an organization is being heartless in laying people off or making a principled decision to save as many people as possible. Determining whether cynicism is justified is ultimately a matter of opinion, which would be a very unstable basis for theory. The better approach appears to be to conceive of cynicism simply in terms of attitudes, leaving aside the question of their validity.

The Value of Cynicism

Cynicism is not a particularly valued attribute in our culture; referring to someone as a cynic generally is not intended as a compliment. Cynics may be depressing to be with, their pessimism may undermine their relationships, and their skepticism about the truth of anything they hear may cause them to miss out on attractive opportunities. However, cynicism can be functional (at least up to a point) for both individuals and organizations. At the individual level, people who invariably believe in others' integrity are likely to be taken advantage of by those who lack it. For the organization, cynics may provide a necessary check on the temptation to place expediency over principle or the temptation to assume that self-interested or underhanded behavior will go undetected. In their particular manner cynics may act as the voice of conscience for the organization, much as the Cynics did for their culture. Thus, we should see organizational cynicism as neither an unalloyed good nor an unalloyed evil for organizations.

The Appropriate Level of Analysis

A third issue with which we must deal is the level of analysis for organizational cynicism. The level of organizational cynicism is clearly the individual. By operationalizing organizational cynicism as an attitude, we are targeting an individual's cynicism as the focal construct to be explained. This does not mean that individuals in the same subunit or even organization may not have similarly cynical attitudes. It does mean, however, that we will not assume similarity of attitudes among people at a given level by conceptualizing our construct at any level above that of the individual.

Comparison of Organizational Cynicism with Other Constructs

In proposing a new construct in the general area of employee attitudes, we must differentiate it from those that already exist in order to avoid the appearance of "old wine in new bottles." Several constructs (organizational commitment, trust, job satisfaction, and alienation) appear to have potential overlaps with organizational cynicism (Table 2).

Organizational commitment. This construct has held a prominent position within organizational studies (e.g., Steers, 1977). The question is, does organizational cynicism simply represent a lack of commitment? When we compare each of organizational commitment's elements to those of organizational cynicism, we identify several differences between the constructs. First, within the cognitive realm, an organizationally cynical employee believes that the practices of his or her employing organization lack integrity, whereas commitment deals with whether employees believe their personal values and goals are similar to the organization's. Second, cynical employees may or may not entertain thoughts of quitting their organization, whereas the behavioral component of commitment includes an employee's intent to stay with the employer. Third, within the affective domain, an organizationally cynical employee is likely to experience such feelings as frustration and contempt toward his or her organization, whereas a noncommitted employee is simply likely to lack pride and attachment to the organization. Our discussion suggests that, although the two constructs may be somewhat negatively related, cynicism clearly is different from and more extreme than a lack of commitment.

Trust. Trust is an old concept that scholars recently have shown a resurgence of interest in (e.g., Bromiley & Cummings, 1995; Hosmer, 1995; Mayer, Davis, & Schoorman, 1995). Recent reviews on trust suggest that a truster makes an assessment of the likelihood of another party's willingness to take

TABLE 2

Facet Analyses of Organizational Cynicism with other Constructs[a]

Facet of Analysis	Organizational Commitment	Trust	Job Satisfaction	Alienation	Organizational Cynicism
1. Common citations and representative concepts	Organizational commitment (Steers, 1977)	Trust (Hosmer, 1995; Mayer, Davis, & Schoorman, 1995)	Job satisfaction (Brayfield & Rothe, 1951; Smith, Kendall, & Hulin, 1969)	Work alienation (Blauner, 1964; Leiter, 1985; Podsakoff, Williams, & Todor, 1986)	Organizational cynicism
2. Focus of concept	Devotion and loyalty to one's employing organization	Willingness to be vulnerable to the actions of others	Reactions to global or to specific components of one's job, including pay, autonomy, supervision, coworkers, and working conditions	One's affective reaction to the job and work	Negative attitude toward one's employing organization
3 Definition(s)	Extent to which a person (1) has a strong desire to remain a member of the organization, (2) is willing to exert high levels of effort for the organization, and (3) believes and accepts the values and goals of the organization	The reliance by one party upon a voluntarily accepted duty on the part of another party to recognize and protect the rights and interests of all others engaged in a joint endeavor or economic exchange	Global or facet-specific espressions of a positive affective orientation toward a job	The degree of estrangement that an individual experiences from his/her work, including feelings of powerlessness, meaninglessness, social isolation, and self-estrangement	Beliefs that one's employing organization lacks integrity; negative affect towrd the organization (disappointment, frustration) and behavior toward the organization consistent with beliefs
4. Theoretical predecessors	Attitude-like	Equity, social exchange theory, interpersonal relations, sociology, economics	Attitude-like	Marxian theory	Attitudes
5. Comparative aspects/overlaps with other constructs	Yes	Yes	Yes	Yes	Yes
6. Precludes other constructs	No	No	No	No	No
7. Impact of determinants:					
a. person	+++	+	+	0	?
b. situation	+	+	+	+++	+++
10. Permanence	Moderate over a lifetime	Varies across both transactions and parties	Varies across jobs	Realtively stable	Moderate
11. Strategies of influence	Many	Some	Some	Not a central focus	?

[a]The citations in this table should in no way be construed as exhaustive. We have merely taken some of the more frequently cited works in these areas in order to demonstrate similarities and differences between organizational cynicism and other potentially related constructs.

into account the interests of the parties concerned within a transaction. We should note that trust itself is the willingness to be vulnerable to the actions of others and should not be confused with trusting behavior or actually putting oneself at risk by the actions of others (Mayer et al., 1995). Trust does not include affect, although we may experience negative or positive affect based on the outcomes of a transaction.

Trust and organizational cynicism differ in several dimensions. First, a lack of trust may be based on a lack of experience—that is, when a person has not had enough experience to be confident in trusting the other party. Cynicism, in contrast, almost certainly is based on experience. Although one can easily imagine a lack of trust from one person toward another party based on a lack of experience to justify such trust, it is unlikely that someone in similar circumstances would be cynical about the other party (e.g., proclaim his/her/its lack of values or experience distress, shame, or so on). Second, trust requires a vulnerability to another party to perform a particular action that considers the well-being of the truster. However, cynicism does not require interpersonal vulnerability as a precondition. One certainly can be cynical without being vulnerable, whereas trust has no meaning in the absence of vulnerability. Third, the definition of trust also suggests that it is oriented toward facilitating cooperation between two or more parties. Our definition of cynicism makes no such contention. Fourth, because trust, in contrast to cynicism, is not commonly conceptualized as an attitude, an affective component on the part of the belief holder generally is not included within the definition of trust. Organizational cynicism, unlike trust, involves disappointment and frustration, and perhaps even disgust and shame. There is an intensely emotional aspect to cynicism that is lacking in trust. Finally, Wrightsman's (1974) empirical work demonstrates that cynicism and trust are only weakly related, sharing 10 percent common variance.

Alienation. Extending Blauner's (1964) conceptualization of work alienation, Leiter (1985) suggests that alienation includes four facets: (1) powerlessness, (2) meaninglessness, (3) social isolation, and (4) self-estrangement. Management researchers (Organ & Greene, 1981; Podsakoff, Williams, & Todor, 1986) have tied alienation to other organizational constructs, such as formalization, role conflict and ambiguity, and organizational commitment. Work alienation is people's reactions to perceiving themselves as not a part of the social or work environment because of the nature of their job. Organizational cynicism, however, while possibly including some overlapping feelings, such as frustration, tension, or anxiety, includes completely different types of beliefs and behaviors. Work alienation does comprise some of the behavioral tendencies we suggest are part of organizational cynicism. However, since alienation is more of a reaction to one's job than the organization (Blauner, 1964; Leiter, 1985), its target is distinct from that of organizational cynicism.

Job satisfaction. This is yet another construct having much prominence in organizational studies. Job satisfaction has been treated as a global concept (Brayfield & Rothe, 1951) or as a general orientation to a job (Smith, Kendall, & Hulin, 1969), but also as a more specific construct relating to aspects of jobs, such as pay and supervision (Cook, Hepworth, Wall, & Warr, 1981). Because of this concept's focus on the job per se as opposed to one's employing organization, we recognize organizational cynicism as distinct from job satisfaction.

DISCUSSION AND CONCLUSION

We have attempted, in this article, to address the question of conceptualizing organizational cynicism. We have answered this question by defining organizational cynicism as a negative attitude toward the organization, comprising certain types of belief, affect, and behavioral tendencies. This conceptualization sets the stage for a considerable research agenda on organizational cynicism. One major step will be to operationalize our conception of organizational cynicism using the tripartite structure that we have imported from attitude theory.

A second major step will be to begin—theoretically and empirically—to grapple with the causes of cynicism in organizations. Researchers potentially could employ a variety of models to predict why some people are so much more cynical about their organizations than others. For example, organizational cynicism could be understood as a result of processes involving leadership, power distribution, organizational change, or procedural justice.

A third step will be to determine the effects of organizational cynicism. Outcomes of cynicism could include such constructs as organizational commitment, organizational citizenship, and participation in team-based activities, such as employee involvement and process improvement. Although we have speculated to some degree about cynicism's effects on the organization, empirical work will be needed to answer this question with any confidence.

In conclusion, organizational cynicism presents a new and challenging research opportunity, which builds on but also goes beyond existing constructs and theoretical frameworks. Research on cynicism should help us to better understand a phenomenon that is pervasive in modern organizations, and perhaps to find better ways to manage or prevent it.

REFERENCES

Ajzen, I. 1994. Attitudes. In R. J. Corsini (Ed.), *Encyclopedia of psychology* (2nd ed.): 114–116. New York: Wiley.

Aktouf, O. 1992. Management and theories of the 1990's: Toward an initial radical humanism? *Academy of Management Review,* 17: 407–431.

Allport, G. W. 1935. Attitudes. In C. Murchison (Ed.), *Handbook of Social Psychology:* 798–844. Worcester, MA: Clark University Press.

Andersson, L. 1996. Employee cynicism: An examination using a contract violation framework. *Human Relations,* 49: 1395–1418.

Andersson, L., & Bateman, T. S. 1997. Cynicism in the workplace: Some causes and effects. *Journal of Organizational Behavior,* 18: 449–470.

Barefoot, J. C., Dodge, K. A., Peterson, B. L., Dahlstrom, W. G., & Williams, R. B. 1989. The Cook-Medley hostility scale: Item content and ability to predict survival. *Psychosomatic Medicine,* 51: 46–57.

Bateman, T. S., Sakano, T., & Fujita, M. 1992. Roger, me, and my attitude: Film propaganda and cynicism toward corporate leadership. *Journal of Applied Psychology,* 77: 768–771.

Becker, T. E. 1998. Integrity in organizations: Beyond honesty and conscientiousness, *Academy of Management Review,* 41: 154–161.

Blauner, R. 1964. Alienation and freedom: *The factory worker and his industry.* Chicago: University of Chicago Press.

Brayfield, A. H., & Rothe, H. F. 1951. An index of job satisfaction. *Journal of Applied Psychology,* 33: 307–311.

Breckler, S. J. 1984. Empirical validation of affect, behavior, and cognition as distinct components of attitude. *Journal of Personality and Social Psychology,* 47: 1191–1205.

Bromiley, P. B., & Cummings, L. L. 1995. Transactions costs in organizations with trust. *Research on Negotiation in Organizations,* 5: 219–247.

Cook, J. D., Hepworth, H. J., Wall, T. D., & Warr, P. B. 1981. *The experience of work.* New York: Academic Press.

Cook, W. W., & Medley, D. M. 1954. Proposed hostility and parasaic virtue scales for the MMPI. *Journal of Applied Psychology,* 38: 414–418.

Costa, P. T., Zonderman, A. B., McCrae, R. R., & Williams, R. B. 1986. Cynicism and paranoid alienation in the Cook and Medley HO scale. *Psychosomatic Medicine,* 48: 283–285.

Cunniff, J. 1993. If only the bosses would get out of the way. *Marketing News,* 27(4): 4–5.

Dutton, J. E., Dukerich, J. M., & Harquail, C. V. 1994. Organizational images and member identification. *Administrative Science Quarterly,* 39: 239–263.

Eagly, A. H., & Chaiken, S. 1993. *The psychology of attitudes.* Fort Worth, TX: Harcourt Brace Jovanovich.

Fuller, B. A. G. 1931. *History of Greek philosophy.* New York: Henry Holt.

Goldner, F. H., Ritti, R. R., & Ference, T. P. 1977. The production of cynical knowledge in organizations. *American Sociological Review,* 42: 539–551.

Graham, J. R. 1993. *MMPI-2: Assessing personality and psychopathology* (2nd ed.). New York: Oxford University Press.

Greenglass, E. R., & Julkunen, J. 1989. Construct validity and sex difference in Cook-Medley hostility. *Personality and Individual Differences,* 10: 209–218.

Greilsamer, M. 1995. The Dilbert barometer. *Across the Board,* March: 39–41.

Guttman, L. 1954. An outline of some new methodology in social research. *Public Opinion Quarterly,* 18: 395–404.

Hart, P. M. 1997. *Personality, work-related experiences and organizational cynicism: A longitudinal study.* Paper presented at the Society for Industrial and Organizational Psychology Annual Meeting, St. Louis, MO.

Hilgard, E. R. 1980. The trilogy of mind: Cognition, affection, and conation. *Journal of the History of the Behavioral Sciences,* 16: 107–117.

Hosmer, L. T. 1995. Trust: The connecting link between organizational theory and philosophical ethics. *Academy of Management Review,* 20: 379–403.

Izard, C. E. 1977. *Human emotions.* New York: Plenum.

Jones, E. E., & Davis, K. E. 1965. From acts to dispositions: The attribution process in person perception. In L. Berkowitz (Ed.), *Advances in experimental social psychology,* vol 2. New York: Academic Press.

Kanter, D. L., & Mirvis, P. H. 1989. *The cynical Americans.* San Francisco: Jossey-Bass.

Kouzes, J. M., & Posner, B. Z. 1993. *Credibility.* San Francisco: Jossey-Bass.

Leiter, J. 1985. Work alienation in the textile industry: Reassessing Blauner. *Work and Occupations,* 12: 479–498.

Levinson, H. 1965. Reciprocation: The relationship between man and organization. *Administrative Science Quarterly,* 9: 370–390.

Mack, B. L. 1993. *The lost gospel: The book of Q and Christian origins.* New York: Harper Collins.

Mayer, R. C., Davis, J. H., & Schoorman, F. D. 1995. An integrative model of organizational trust. *Academy of Management Review,* 20: 709–734.

More, P. E. 1923. *Hellenistic philosophies.* Princeton, NJ: Princeton University Press.

Morrow, P. C. 1983. Concept redundancy in organizational research: The case of work commitment. *Academy of Management Review,* 8: 485–500.

Meiderhoffer, A. 1967. *Behind the shield.* Garden City, NJ: Doubleday.

Northrop, F. S. C. 1959. *The logic of modern physics.* New York: Macmillan.

O'Connell, B. J., Holzman, H. H., & Armandi, b. R. 1986. Police cynicism and the modes of adaptation. *Journal of Police Science and Administration,* 14: 307–313.

Organ, D. W., & Greene, C. N. 1981. The effects of formalization on professional involvement: A compensatory process approach. *Administrative Science Quarterly,* 25: 237–252.

Pfeffer, J. 1981. Management as symbolic action: The creation and maintenance of organizational paradigms. *Research in Organizational Behavior,* 3: 1–52.

Podsakoff, P. M., Williams, L. J., & Todor, W. D. 1986. Effects of organizational formalization on alienation among professionals and nonprofessionals. *Academy of Management Journal,* 29: 820–831.

Porter, L. W., Steers, R. M., Mowday, R. T., & Boulian, P. V. 1974. Organizational commitment, job satisfaction, and turnover among psychiatric technicians. *Journal of Applied Psychology,* 59: 465–476.

Reichers, A. E., Wanous, J. P., & Austin, J. T. 1997. Understanding and managing cynicism about organizational change. *Academy of Management Executive,* 11(1): 48–59.

Schwab, D. P. 1980. Construct validity in organizational behavior. In B. M. Staw and L. L. Cummings (Eds.), *Research in organizational behavior,* vol. 2: 3–43. Greenwich, CT: JAI Press.

Shapira, Z., & Zevulun, E. 1979. On the use of facet analysis in organizational behavior research: Some conceptual considerations and an example. *Organizational Behavior and Human Performance,* 23: 411–428.

Shapiro, E. C. 1996. The "glow and tingle" audit. *The Wall Street Journal,* January 26.

Smith, M. B. 1947. The personal setting of public opinions: A study of attitudes toward Russia. *Public Opinion Quarterly,* 11: 507–523.

Smith, P. C., Kendall, L. M., & Hulin, C. L. 1969. *The measurement of satisfaction in work and retirement.* Chicago: Rand McNally.

Steers, R. M. 1977. Antecendents and outcomes of organizational commitment. *Administrative Science Quarterly,* 22: 46–56.

Vance, R. J., Brooks, S. M., & Tesluk, P. E. 1996. *Organizational cynicism and change.* Working paper, Pennsylvania State University, University Park.

Vroom, V. H. 1964. *Work and motivation.* New York: Wiley.

Wanous, J. P., Reichers, A. E., & Austin, J. T. 1994. Organizational cynicism: An initial study. *Academy of Management Best Papers Proceedings:* 269–273.

Weick, K. 1979. *The social psychology of organizing.* Reding, MA: Addison-Wesley.

White, S. E., & Mitchell, T. R. 1976. Organizational development: A review of research content and research design. *Academy of Management Review,* 1: 57–73.

Wrightsman, L. S. 1974. *Assumptions about human nature: A social-psychological analysis.* Monterey, CA: Brooks/Cole.

James W. Dean, Jr., received his Ph.D. from Carnegie-Mellon University. He is an associate professor of management at the Kenan-Flagler Business School, University of North Carolina at Chapel Hill. His current research interests include organizational change, performance improvement, and aesthetic aspects of organizations.

Pamela Brandes is an assistant professor of management at Southern Connecticut State University. Her research interests include employee-organization linkages and strategic human resource management.

Ravi Dharwadkar received his Ph.D. from the University of Cincinnati. He is a visiting assistant professor of management at the University of Cincinnati. His research interests include international management issues in emerging markets and employee attitudes.

WANT PARTICIPATION? HAVE THEM "VOTE WITH THEIR FEET"!

Barbara H. Holmes
Evansville, IN

Almost every management instructor struggles at times with the problem of how to get students to participate more in class. Explaining to students that participation builds involvement and is good "real-world" training does not necessarily guarantee the desired results. Nor do various demands, threats, or incentives (e.g., basing part of the grade on participation) always work. Many students, especially in beginning classes, simply lack confidence in their opinions and are reluctant to say anything that may make them look or feel foolish. Calling on students often makes them uncomfortable; waiting for someone to say *something* may make the instructor uncomfortable. So professors often give in and start the discussion themselves while students settle comfortably into a passive mode.

Many instructors probably believe that it is not possible to force students to participate. This technique, which I call "Voting With Your Feet," does in fact "force" students (gently!) by making them move physically to a place in the room that expresses their viewpoint on a topic. This technique guarantees that everyone participates minimally by at least physically declaring a viewpoint. More importantly, it also seems to open the door in a relatively nonthreatening way to higher levels of participation. The following section will describe the technique and illustrate how I use it in my principles of management class.

Voting With Your Feet—How It Works

Voting With Your Feet may be used to stimulate discussion on many issues, but it is probably most effective when the topic is likely to produce a small number of diverse, firmly held opinions. An example related to social responsibility and management ethics will illustrate how I use this technique in the principles of management class. Our first discussion of these topics comes about the third week of the semester, when participation is still likely to be limited. I use an actual short case from the late 1980s concerning the Eli Lilly Company's refusal to sell their herbicide "Spike" to the U.S. government, which wanted to use it to spray South American cocaine crops. Because issues in the case (e.g., the drug war and the environment) are still timely and because Lilly headquarters are less than 200 miles from our campus, interest is easy to generate. I start with a single question: Was Lilly right or wrong to refuse to sell "Spike" to the government? Before hearing

any discussion, I instruct students to "vote with their feet": sit on one side of the room if they think Lilly was right; sit on the other side if they think Lilly was wrong. Students often look surprised at this request but quickly realize they must make a decision; they must participate at least minimally by choosing a seat that lets everyone see what they think. There is no neutral zone in the room, so even if students stay where they are, they are "saying" something.

At this point, the discussion begins. I instruct the two groups to turn their chairs to face each other for a very informal debate. One student (a volunteer) from the "pro" side (i.e., Lilly was right) begins by standing and explaining to the "con" group (Lilly was wrong) why he or she has chosen that position. This student then chooses (from raised hands) a student from the "con" side who stands and explains his or her position. The procedure continues back and forth until arguments are exhausted. Students may change their minds during the discussion if they wish and move to the other side of the room.

During the debate, I sit off to the side of both groups and try to be as unobtrusive as possible. I may interrupt if I feel a few students are dominating too much; from that point on they must choose as the next speaker someone who has not already spoken. My intervention usually is not necessary; typically a large number of students volunteer during the discussion.

Why It Works

There are various reasons why I think Voting With Your Feet is effective in stimulating student participation.

First, it seems to help students overcome what may be the major hurdle to participation for many: the fear of being wrong. In the usual class discussion, someone must be first to express any given viewpoint; the chances of feeling like you have said something wrong or "stupid" can be high. In Voting With Your Feet, *everyone* must essentially express his or her views at the same time. This aspect takes the pressure off any one individual and also typically shows students that there are many others who feel as they do. Once that fact is known, it seems to become easier for students to articulate orally the reasons behind their physical choices.

Fear of being wrong also seems to be reduced because of the minimal role I play in the discussion. Although students may not forget I am there, they really do get absorbed in ex-

Author's Note: Requests for reprints should be sent to Barbara H. Holmes, 300 Camden Court, Evansville, IN 47715.

plaining their positions to each other, which seems to be less threatening than explaining them to me directly.

Another reason this technique stimulates participation is that students often discover there can be various reasons for choosing a particular side, not all of which are shared by everyone on that side. I have observed students almost "burst" with wanting to explain *their* rationale after hearing a student on their own side give an argument with which they did not agree. Finally, I think the technique is effective because it is unexpected and therefore somewhat of a novelty. I never announce in advance when we will consider a topic using the technique (I often do not decide until I come to class), and I do not use it more than a few times in a semester. It is a change of pace that seems to be "fun." In addition, I suspect that simply introducing a little physical movement into the classroom (remember in grammar school being told to "stand up and stretch"?) is sometimes enough to stimulate the brain and vocal chords as well!

Possible Variations

I use Voting With Your Feet in relatively small classes (around 30 students), which meet in rooms where all chairs can be moved. But the technique could also be adapted to large lecture hall classes, where involvement is often even more difficult to encourage. Students could move to opposite sides of the hall and debate from fixed seats. Not everyone would speak, of course, but everyone would still participate by physically expressing an opinion.

Another possible variation would be to have each group spend a little time sharing member views within the group before the classwide debate begins. This might encourage even more students to speak because they would not have to talk in front of the whole class.

Limitations and Criticisms

As with any idea, this technique has certain limitations. One of these is that it works well with only certain kinds of topics, especially those that elicit a small number of diverse, firmly held opinions. My example has only two opinions/groups, although three or four would probably work too.

There are also some potential negative effects of having students choose sides. First, students may be encouraged to think in oversimplified "black and white" terms (e.g., Lilly was right or wrong) about complex issues that really involve shades of gray. Students may also feel social pressure to conform to a particular position, especially if they have friends in class or if there appears to be a dominant class view. In addition, students may find it difficult to change their minds after publicly picking a position.

An additional criticism some instructors may have is that "forcing" students to participate (however gently) is contrary to a good learning environment. I certainly do not view Voting With Your Feet as the ideal solution to all participation problems. But I do find it one useful technique for getting beginning students involved and willing to take that important first step: saying *something!*

Unit 2

Unit Selections

Diversity and Individual Differences

6. **Building a Rainbow, One Stripe at a Time,** Marc Adams
7. **Why Diversity Matters,** Lee Gardenswartz and Anita Rowe

Values and Ethics

8. **Walking the Tightrope, Balancing Risks and Gains,** Lin Grensing-Pophal

Motivation

9. **Measuring the Effectiveness of Recognition Programs,** Bob Nelson and Patrick Dailey
10. **Motivation: The Value of the Work Ethic,** J. Clifton Williams

Learning and Self-Management

11. **Guide Lines,** Alan Fowler
12. **Will Your Culture Support KM?** Samuel Greengard
13. **Managing Oneself,** Peter F. Drucker

EXERCISE 2: The Twilight Zone of Diversity, Linda Parrack Livingstone and Bradley Thomas Livingstone

Key Points to Consider

❖ What are the ways in which the diversity of the American population can be considered an asset to the society?

❖ How do supervisors have an impact on diversity in the workforce?

❖ What are some of the ways by which an organization and an individual experience dissonance?

❖ Why is motivation of the individual by the organization important?

❖ How can people and organizations best deal with change?

 **Links**   **www.dushkin.com/online/**

9. **American Civil Liberties Organization (ACLU)**
   http://www.aclu.org/issues/worker/campaign.html
10. **Career Magazine: Diversity in the Workplace**
    http://www.careermag.com/newsarts/diversity/fed.html
11. **Diversity in the Workforce**
    http://www.consciouschoice.com/issues/cc083/workdiv.html
12. **Diversity in Workforce Produces Bottom Line Benefits**
    http://www.villagelife.org/news/archives/diversity.html
13. **Knowledge Management and Organizational Learning**
    http://www.brint.com/OrgLrng.htm
14. **Report on Workforce Diversity**
    http://www.fs.fed.us/land/fire/difference.htm
15. **Workforce Diversity Plan for ORNL**
    http://www.ornl.gov/HR_ORNL/WFD/plan_pub.htm

These sites are annotated on pages 4 and 5.

Organizations are made up of individuals, who are all different. In the United States, the history of the country can be traced to these differences. As new groups emigrated to North America, their differences seemed large, but as these various groups settled in, those differences became less important. The United States traces its beginnings to the first English settlers in Massachusetts and Virginia. But soon other groups followed from Scotland and Ireland. While today, we may view these differences between Scots and English as nonexistent, in the 1600s they were very real. There were differences of religion (Catholic vs. Anglican vs. Presbyterian vs. Puritan), and language (English vs. Gaelic), and there were historical animosities that had run deep in the British Isles.

In America different groups, based on religion, ethnic background, national origin, and other criteria, have generally been accepted after what might sometimes seem a rather long period of time. Some groups have taken longer than others and other groups are still waiting to participate fully in American society. But America, while it may not have been the melting pot historians called it 100 years ago, could certainly be compared to a tossed salad. The origins of people may still be identifiable by their surname, religion, or skin tone, but they continue to work with each other to produce the most productive society in the world. Diversity in the United States is a strength that other countries will find difficult to copy.

For an organization to be truly successful in the next century, it is going to have to have to take advantage of the diversity that American society offers. No organization can hope to compete effectively in modern society by deliberately excluding one group over another. An organization must actively engage in "Building a Rainbow, One Stripe at a Time" (see article 6) in its workforce; one that includes all races, religions, and genders. Only by taking advantage of the talents of all of the available personnel in an organization can a company hope to maintain a competitive advantage in the economy. This is "Why Diversity Matters." (See article 7.) It matters, not because it is politically correct, or socially acceptable, or even legally required, but because it makes sense for any organization that is trying to be successful in the marketplace.

Organizations are made up of people, and while the organizations may be credited with certain actions, those actions are actually taken by people. There are many guiding principles that people use when performing certain actions and tasks. Some are external to the individual and involve the policies of the organization, but others are internal and involve the values and ethics of the individual. People may be required to do things in an organization that they may find to be out of balance with their own values and ethics. With the possible exception of the founder, owner, president, and/or chairman of the board, people work for companies, and it is unlikely that their values and ethics will exactly correspond. This is called dissonance.

There are various levels of dissonance caused by situations that are illegal, unethical, and just plain unfair. How much is the individual willing to tolerate within an organization and how close to home does that have to be before it begins to really bother him or her. Managers often find themselves in an ethical or perhaps even legal dilemma. (See "Walking the Tightrope, Balancing Risks and Gains.") The question then becomes, how much can an individual tolerate?

Much has been written about motivation, but relatively little is understood. One thing is certain, however, and that is that there is very little that motivated people cannot accomplish, and there is relatively little that unmotivated people will accomplish. Alexander the Great conquered the known civilized world with 5,000 Greek warriors; Cortez and less than 200 Spanish Conquistadors conquered the Aztecs of Mexico; and Peter Drucker, the well-known management guru has written that "Most things, I have learned, are accomplished by a monomaniac with a mission." While organizations may find it difficult to instill internal motivation in their employees, the advice in the article "Motivation: The Value of the Work Ethic" by J. Clifton Williams should not be underestimated. Organizations can develop reward systems that will encourage external motivation in employees to accomplish organizational goals. But it must be remembered that there will be a trade-off between the benefits of the reward to the individual and the cost of that reward, as well as the benefit of that accomplished goal to the organization. "Measuring the Effectiveness of Recognition Programs" by Bob Nelson and Patrick Daily takes a look at this trade-off for motivating people in an organization.

In this rapidly changing world, the only thing that people and organizations can really do to protect themselves is to continue to learn, adapt, and change to meet the continuing changes in the environment. American society is based on the idea that people can learn and change their behavior, based upon what they have learned. In the United States, millions of people are involved in the education system and hundreds of billions of dollars are spent on education in K–12 schools, colleges, universities, and corporations. American companies spend approximately $100 billion a year on educating and training their employees in a formal setting, to say nothing of the informal training and education that goes on. For the society to grow, change, and develop, the people who make up the society must do the same. Organizations must learn to support this growth and change. This is addressed in the article "Will Your Culture Support KM?" by Samuel Greengard.

Today, people must take responsibility for themselves and their actions as well as for their careers. While organizations may help, Peter Drucker, in his essay "Managing Oneself," contends that it is ultimately the responsibility of the individual. People who do not assume this responsibility are, in fact, leaving their fate to someone else.

Building a Rainbow, One Stripe at a Time

A true commitment to diversity requires a long-term, integrated program for recruitment and retention. With today's competitive labor market, the time to start is now.

By Marc Adams

Every morning from October through April, Judy Wilson unlocks her office at Hampton University in Hampton, Va., scans her calendar and confirms yet another appointment with a recruiter from a major corporation.

As Hampton's recruiting coordinator, Wilson is the referee for hundreds of employers who come to scout the small university's top students in accounting and engineering—or, more precisely, the school's top African-American students in accounting and engineering.

"It's gotten to the point where they're asking for our students by name," Wilson says. "They ask, 'When is this one graduating? When is that one coming out?'"

Such intense recruiting of minority applicants is becoming the norm. Many employers have long believed that a diverse workforce is the key to a well-rounded organization, not to mention bigger profit margins. And now that record business growth and falling unemployment rates have created labor shortages, the hunt for prime talent has shifted into overdrive. Faced with stiffer competition, HR staffs are devising better ways to recruit—and retain—minority employees.

Intel, for example, headquartered in Santa Clara, Calif., hired a top consulting firm to compile a closely guarded list of the 10 colleges and universities with the highest minority enrollments in the field of circuitry design.

At Boeing Co., in Seattle, the HR team launched a slick, nationwide advertising campaign aimed at women and ethnic minorities who feel underutilized in their current jobs.

Some employers are even helping universities fine-tune their curricula so that the most promising students, minority or Caucasian, can more easily step into fields that are becoming more specialized. Others are honing in on historically black colleges and universities such as Hampton, which hosted 300 recruiters last year—roughly one recruiter for every 23 students.

FOCUS ON RETENTION

When it comes to keeping recruits on board, diversity consultants are prodding employers to beef up cultural training programs, recognize employees' hidden skills and transform diversity committees from isolated social clubs into forums that carry clout with upper management. Overall, however, many HR practitioners are convinced that the most effective technique is to develop recruitment and retention strategies at the same time.

"Companies spend all this time aggressively recruiting, their minority hires leave and the employers wonder why," says Lisa

Willis-Johnson, HR director of the Mid-Ohio Regional Planning Commission and vice chair of the Society for Human Resource Management Workplace Diversity Committee. "They think, 'Our recruitment program is failing.' No. It's just that they don't have the proper support mechanisms in place."

RECRUITING FOR THE LONG TERM

"A lot of companies still have the mentality that diversity is compliance," says Enrique Baltiera, an associate with The Pro Group Inc., a diversity consulting firm based in Minneapolis. "Employers figure that as long as they have enough minorities they're OK, and that, in time, the minorities will move up. But those companies aren't thinking of the maximum opportunity for the individual when he's brought in."

Baltiera agrees that long-term opportunities are crucial to whites as well but notes that they "aren't underrepresented." If you lose as many minorities as you do whites, "minorities will continue to be underrepresented in your firm.

"Some people feel that their gender or their cultural background is important," Baltiera says. "They were raised with different ways of doing things, saying things, thinking about things, even selling things, that can benefit the company. But when they're hired, they don't always walk into a situation that's comfortable to them."

At Intel, where the ethnic minority share of management positions jumped from 13 percent to 17 percent between 1993 and 1997, college interns are snapped up as early as the sophomore year and matched with mentors for their entire college careers. Interns who decide to stay onboard are handed over to supervisors who are trained to spot "crossover" skills that can apply to different jobs in the firm.

"We want our interns and new employees to understand the culture at Intel, and we want to understand theirs," says Mike Foster, Intel's manager of college relations. "We make sure that they see the diversity in the company and, for that matter, the diversity in the community. And if a job isn't working out the way an employee thought it would, we'll cross train him from, say, finance to a materials specialty."

Boeing Co. takes its commitment to employee training one step further. The company's lifetime learning program allows employees to

Blacks and Hispanics in the Workforce

According to the U.S. Bureau of Labor Statistics, the number of blacks and Hispanics in professional specialties and management has grown by nearly 40 percent since 1994, compared with an increase of 10 percent for whites. That gives blacks and Hispanics a 12.3 percent share of choice white-collar slots, up from 10.7 percent four years ago.

On the other hand, a closer look at the data shows that the percentage of Hispanics in management declined after 1994, then hit a lull for two years before it rebounded in 1997, when the current economic boom was beginning to hit its stride.

Over the same period, the percentage of blacks in management hardly increased at all.

Clearly, employers are hiring more minorities. But HR experts are starting to question whether counting noses is the best way to ensure that minorities are part of a company's future. It's an even bigger issue for companies that bid for government contracts, which require firms to meet affirmative action guidelines—a tall order in today's tight labor market.

Total Workforce				
	1994	1995	1996	1997
Blacks	10.4%	10.6%	10.6%	10.8%
Hispanics	8.8	8.9	9.2	9.8
Management				
Blacks	6.8	7.2	6.9	7.0
Hispanics	4.9	4.8	4.8	5.5
Professional Specialty				
Blacks	7.4	7.8	7.9	7.8
Hispanics	4.0	4.0	4.3	4.5
Technicians/ sales				
Blacks	7.9	8.2	8.2	8.4
Hispanics	6.5	6.8	6.9	7.3

'Diversity goes beyond your gender and your race. It's whatever it takes to make everybody work together as a team.'

—Lori Jensen, manager of diversity recruiting and advertising, Boeing Co.

develop latent skills they can apply inside—and outside—the firm. "If you decide you want to be, say, a pediatrician, we'll pay for it," says Lori Jensen, Boeing's manager of diversity recruiting and advertising.

Boeing also quickly exposes new hires to programs designed to find employees' comfort zones and makes liberal use of "flex" time and telecommuting. Perhaps as a result, the company-wide ethnic minority ratio is holding firm at 18 percent. What's more, the minority ratio in management is 23 percent. That includes 13.4 percent white female, and a 4 percent rise in ethnic minorities' share of the top 1,500 management slots since 1995.

Still, Boeing appears to focus on what those statistics represent, instead of getting caught up in a numbers game.

"Affirmative action is the process of hiring enough minorities to meet government guidelines or the goals you set for yourself, and that's fine," says Jensen. "And, of course, diversity committees are important, and you want to encourage that. But once you're here and you're an employee, diversity goes beyond your gender and your race. It's whatever it takes to make everybody work together as a team. We see it as all tied together."

DEALING WITH COMPETITION

Sometimes factors that are difficult to control can lower minority representation. For example, the competition is so fierce in high-technology fields that upstart West Coast consulting firms are hiring away some of Intel's top rookies, minority and white alike, for fat starting salaries that Intel can't always match.

Foster, Intel's recruiting manager, laments that new hires who flee for extra cash are giving up the long-term care and feeding that Intel can provide. But piracy is one way that smaller firms are competing in an arena teeming with heavyweights.

Structured Mentoring

Letty Hardy has made a career of nudging minorities up the corporate ladder. Now she has persuaded more than 100 companies to get behind her and push.

Hardy's venture, Inclusion Systems Inc., gives top minority prospects the chance to learn from mentors in other companies. That way, employees can learn the corporate ropes without worrying about making mistakes at their own firms.

About 60 companies will be onboard when the sessions kick off at Inclusion's Southfield, Mich., headquarters in November. Another 45 firms are on the waiting list for the opening of the Chicago office in January 1999.

"You talk to young people who have these big compensation packages and you ask them, 'How happy are you?' And 90 percent of the time, they're miserable," Hardy says. "It's a typical cycle with people of color. They feel isolated when they're brought onboard, and they feel there's no one at the top they can talk to."

Basically, the Inclusion staff teaches mentors the ins and outs of intercultural communication and subtle workplace bias. The mentors then pass along those skills to their protégés, who are selected by their own employers based on their executive potential.

Inclusion Systems is a spinoff of Menttium Corp., a top consulting firm based in Minneapolis that uses the "cross-mentoring" technique for women trying to pierce the glass ceiling. Hardy, a partner in Menttium, launched Inclusion after a series of employer focus groups showed that employers didn't know how to address the frustrations of minority employees.

"We want to catch these young people before they become bitter, cynical and just quit," Hardy says. "We want them to be in a position to make an impact and change the corporate culture."

"Diversity recruiting takes much more effort in today's marketplace," says Lisa Weingarten, employment manager of Mercury Computer Systems Inc., a technology design firm of 360 employees based in Chelmsford, Mass. "Smaller firms that don't have an affirmative action requirement are sort of behind schedule."

In fact, consultants say that small companies are about five years behind larger firms in diversifying their staffs.

Regardless of a company's size, however, "the most important thing is to make sure that practice follows policy," says Mary Jane Sinclair, whose Morristown, N.J., consulting firm, MJS Associates, compiled Intel's "top 10" list of computer engineering schools that have the highest minority enrollments.

"Companies use, say, job sharing as a retention issue, but they don't bother to mention that there's a four-year waiting list," Sinclair says. "If you hire folks based on these great programs that the employees can't access, they don't trust you."

TAPPING THE RIGHT SOURCES

Many employers say they recruit at the college level for the sake of efficiency. Essentially, diversifying a company from the ground up is often cheaper and, retentionwise, more effective than relying on "head hunters" and referrals. But many companies tend to recruit at random instead of targeting schools that fit their HR needs.

For instance, the applied sciences department at a small private college might work better than an engineering school at a large state university with a vaunted reputation. And according to data supplied by the U.S. Department of Education, minority enrollment in four-year private institutions is increasing at twice the rate of minority enrollment in four-year public schools.

Perhaps one of the most fertile pools is the National Association for Equal Opportunity in Higher Education (NAEOHE), composed of 116 historically black colleges and universities with a total enrollment of 375,000. At many of those schools, counselors are recommending courses that steer students toward the hottest industries and away from glutted fields. All the while, the counselors urge recruiters to cast their nets wider. For instance, a counselor might spot a recruiter from a high-technology firm that is launching a mar-keting subsidiary, then match the recruiter to students who have strong backgrounds in liberal arts.

What about recruiting beyond the entry level? At Bank of America in San Francisco, the HR department makes ample use of the usual sources, such as minority job fairs and the Internet. But the company often turns to less conventional techniques.

For example, the bank routinely taps welfare-to-work organizations, "and these aren't necessarily entry-level people," says Henry Bennett, vice president and recruiting manager of the bank's San Francisco office. "These are mid-level people who have been out of the workforce for a while."

Instead of merely posting job openings with key personnel suppliers—such as the National Association of Black Accountants—the bank hosts regular on-site sessions between suppliers and bank managers to nail down mutual needs.

At the executive level, when recruiting became too expensive, the company simply recruited the recruiters. The bank now has its own executive search operation. "We've turned our company into a recruiting center so we can control the costs," says Bennett. "Many of our people were 'head hunters' in a former life."

Executive recruiters confirm that more and more companies are placing orders specifically for females and ethnic minorities. But money isn't always the lure.

"Of all the executives I interview, both minority and Anglo, fewer than half of them mention money in the first five minutes," says Dee Jones, president of Jones & Associates, a Strongsville, Ohio, recruiting firm. "Most of the time, the issue is opportunity."

Opportunity is one benefit that Mercury Computer Systems uses to its advantage. "We really are a niche company," says Weingarten. "So we offer people the opportunity to work in a smaller environment, where their skills will be known and better recognized."

That may be one reason that Mercury has not needed to resort to corporate looting to fill its desks. Instead, the company relies heavily on word of mouth and awards referral bonuses to employees who bring in new blood. The company also trolls minority trade journals and professional groups for minority candidates with highly specialized skills, such as digital processing and systems design.

While long-term strategies, such as providing opportunities to minority applicants, seem to be working, methods designed to create "instant" diversity, such as fast-tracking, are beginning to fade.

"Companies were moving people up too quickly without regard to proper skills," says Madeleine Condit, vice president of Korn/Ferry International, the world's largest executive search firm, based in Chicago. "Where are those people now? Well, they got frustrated and left. Or they moved elsewhere in the company where their goals, and perhaps the company's goals, were not met. Of course, this happens to Anglos, too," Condit says. "But the effect is sometimes more pronounced with minorities who, even today, don't have as many options."

BANKROLLING THE FUTURE

Experts agree that college campuses are the biggest sources of minority talent—and one way to sustain that diversity is to buy it.

Since 1994, minority scholarships from corporate foundations have increased by more than 15 percent a year and colleges are demanding more, raising fears among smaller firms that, eventually, the giants will corner the market.

In 1997, Intel awarded $900,000 in undergraduate minority scholarships, up from $823,000 in 1996. Boeing has awarded $500,000 so far this year, including $250,000 to the United Negro College Fund. Of course, scholarship recipients rarely are required to work for their benefactors after graduation, "but a lot of them do," says Tim Saponas, Intel's manager of corporate contributions.

NAEOHE, the black colleges' organization, will launch its first systemwide fund drive later this year. The schools had to mount aggressive marketing campaigns to attract attention in the first place, so association president Henry Ponder foresees an uphill battle for funds.

On the West Coast, the University of California at Berkeley plans to pass the hat to overcome the effects of Proposition 209, California's 1996 referendum that wiped out racial preferences as an admission standard for state-run schools. Berkeley officials say that 209 might prohibit minority scholarships as well. If so, the school is banking on alumni to fill the gap.

Elsewhere, budget cuts have put a crimp in universities' outreach efforts, so the schools are asking employers to make up the difference. As a result, minority grants and scholarships have become a sort of recruiting fee, and few employers can match the resources of titans like Intel and Boeing. But consultants

---

Words to the Wise

It's tough to recruit talented minorities who will stay aboard your firm, especially in today's competitive market. Here are a few pointers from some top diversity experts.

Spread the task. Don't assume your HR department has to bear the entire load. Assign some key recruiting tasks to marketing or public affairs, then coordinate from the top. That way, your diversity program will keep going—even after key HR personnel leave the organization.

Lower your sights. Minority executives are at a premium, so limit the time and money that you spend recruiting certain positions. For example, instead of recruiting a comptroller, create an assistant comptroller's position. Most likely, this will give you a larger candidate pool. Then you can train the new hire for the top slot. Your recruit will have an instant opportunity for advancement, and you'll add a minority to your executive suite.

Exit interviews. Don't expect an ethnic minority to burn her bridges during an exit interview by telling you that she's disgruntled. Instead, sign a release that guarantees the employee a good reference, then conduct the interview six months later. You're liable to learn plenty that you can use to improve your retention program.

Experts also have some good ideas that are particularly valuable for smaller firms.

Allocate your funds. Don't spend too much on recruiting. Carve out part of the budget for retention items, such as flex time, enrichment programs and seniority pay.

Tutoring. Recruiting at the Ivy Leagues is probably a long shot. Instead, allow your staff to teach part-time at local community colleges, which are full of talented minorities who already have work experience. Establish a permanent network with the schools. The long-term relationships will pay off.

Spread the wealth. Set up a well-defined advancement program that leads to an equity position in the company—much like partnership arrangements in law firms. Match the program to the employee, not the other way around.

Making the Grade
in Minneapolis

At the Metropolitan Airports Commission in Minneapolis, Juan Lopez' job is to wade through the thicket of affirmative action guidelines and hire enough minorities to match the complexion of the community.

Like most small outfits, the commission has to rely on local talent. So far, so good. Ethnic minorities comprise about 9 percent of the commission's 100 professional class, compared with an available pool of only 6 percent in the Hennepin County area. The ratio for the entire 400-member staff is a healthy 10 percent.

"The trick is to maintain it—and increase it if I can," says Lopez, the commission's diversity manager.

Lopez develops contacts in the inner city, posts job openings with 110 organizations and pesters officials at the Employment Commission for Hispanic Opportunities.

He needs only one more female and one more ethnic minority to meet his goal for upper management. But he's fighting high turnover in the police department. The commission pays to train police recruits, but many of them accept more challenging jobs at other law enforcement agencies.

Lopez now is toying with the idea of raiding the other agencies. "I don't know how far I'll get," he says. "We'll see."

say there are plenty of inexpensive ways to tap the college market.

"We see it as an issue of commitment rather than money," says Peter Conte, Boeing's director of corporate relations. Boeing led an unsuccessful drive against Initiative 200, Washington state's version of Proposition 209, slated for the ballot in November. "We weren't able to get an alternative measure on the ballot," says Conte. "But if affirmative action were to go away tomorrow, we would remain committed."

Marc Adams is a Winchester, Va.-based journalist specializing in business, finance and legal affairs. His 32-year career as a writer and editor has included full-time positions as a national correspondent for United Press International and as a senior business writer for The Washington Times. *He can be reached at adam162@ibm.net.*

STRATEGY

Why Diversity Matters

The news about the state of corporate diversity is good, bad and perplexing. On the bright side, as part of the everyday language in most workplaces, diversity is being addressed in some way. Despite the predicted setback from anti-affirmative action legislation and rhetoric, corporations continue to make headway in creating more inclusive, inviting and equitable work environments.

The bad news, however, is that even where there are solid diversity strategies and years of implementation, discrimination complaints are not uncommon, recruitment remains a difficult challenge, and harassment incidents continue to make the news. Breaking through the inertia of entrenched patterns in both individual behavior and organizational systems has shown itself to be much more difficult and long-term than expected.

But most perplexing of all is that in the face of powerful statistical evidence about demographic changes in the workforce and marketplace, staff from the executive suite to the shop floor and front office are still asking, "why?"

Why spend resources, time and energy on diversity, especially when other business needs seem more compelling? A satisfactory answer is a must to get the commitment of those with the power to make the changes necessary to capitalize on diversity.

Here are some of the most important reasons diversity is critical to an organization's bottom line success.

1 GAINING ACCESS TO A CHANGING MARKETPLACE. Today's domestic marketplace is being transformed by powerful demographic forces:

• "Minorities" are the majority in six out of the eight largest metropolitan areas of the U.S. (*Los Angeles Times,* June 9, 1993).

• In Los Angeles County, 16 of the 25 most common surnames of home buyers in 1996 were Hispanic (*Los Angeles Times,* December 4, 1994).

• The combined African-American, Hispanic and Asian buying power is over $500 billion dollars (Gail Baker Woods, *Advertising and Marketing to the New Majority,* Wadsworth Publishing, 1995).

• Women are the primary investors in over half of U.S. households (*USA Today,* May 4, 1998).

Beyond the individual consumer, purchasing agents, proposal review committees and other key decision makers in organizations are an increasingly varied group. Furthermore, potential client companies often ask about an organization's diversity record before they are willing to do business. Reaching these diverse customers/clients demands an understanding of their needs, languages and preferences. What organization can afford to ignore such shifts and expect to gain access to this kaleidoscope of customers without a staff that mirrors the marketplace?

2 GETTING A HEALTHY ROI FROM YOUR HUMAN CAPITAL. The same diversity in the marketplace affects the pool of present and potential employees. While statistics vary by location, it is clear that the workforce will continue to have more women, people of color and immigrants each year. In addition, employees of all groups are expecting more from organizations— from hostile-free, non-discriminatory workplaces to flexible schedules and benefits, childcare and family-friendly policies. Human capital represents one of your organization's biggest investments and your potential competitive edge. That ROI is reduced when commitment and productivity are lost due to the following:

• Employees who feel disregarded or shut out;

• Time wasted with conflicts and misunderstandings;

• Money spent on legal fees and settlements; and

• Morale slumps that result from legal actions and complaints.

3 RECRUITING AND RETAINING THE BEST TALENT. Your organization's future depends on the quality of talent you attract and keep. Today's recruits commonly ask questions about diversity because they want to know what kind of career opportunities await them. When they don't see anyone like them in top positions, they turn their attention to another employer who is more open to developing and promoting a wider array of people.

Not only does dealing effectively with diversity aid recruitment, but it can help you avoid the high cost of losing the retention battle.

When employees feel valued and respected, when there is a fair, open promotional system and when resources are spent on developing staff, they stay. What's more, they often tell others.

4 EXPANDING CREATIVITY. One outcome of the coming together of differences is creativity. Some of the greatest breakthroughs in human history have resulted when people of different backgrounds came in contact. A diverse mix can offer more varied perspectives, come up with a wider array of ideas and solutions, challenge long-accepted views and generate a dynamic synergy that may not emerge on a more homogenous staff.

5 ENSURING SURVIVAL THROUGH RESILIENCE AND FLEXIBILITY. The only certainty ahead is continued change. Responding to varied perspectives and preferences, as well as making the adaptations required by diversity, keeps an organization's flexibility muscle exercised and well-developed. That strengthened ability to respond to changing environments and demands may be the most significant and far-reaching benefit of diversity.

Diversity is not an altruistic venture nor an experiment in social engineering foisted upon organizations. Responding to and capitalizing on a pluralistic workforce is a strategic business imperative to ensure organizational viability.

WHERE DIVERSITY IS GOING

We can track four major trends that signal the evolutionary direction of diversity-related initiatives:

• **Systems changes.** If there is a common complaint about diversity efforts to date, it is that they seem to stop at training without bringing about any significant organizational change. Systemic change is one way of bringing accountability and longevity to diversity initiatives. Expecting training to carry the weight of significant change is ill-conceived and impossible. For example, greater understanding of biases can benefit individual relationships, but it does not necessarily change the work environment or increase productivity and commitment to the organization. New awareness may improve workplace interactions but may not bring about the implementation of flexible hours for working mothers or those responsible for eldercare. Awareness training can open minds but generally does not open the promotional system and create a wider profile of candidates to mentor, coach, hire and promote. Training can serve as a catalyst to systems changes, but it doesn't ensure them.

The desire for systems modification is a reflection of the strategic focus that is designed to bring about long-term culture change. If done right, the organization becomes more humane and productive, clear in its objectives, and flexible enough to respond to multiple employee needs. The key imperative with systems change is not only to think long-term and have patience, but also to hold people accountable for the agreed changes. The result is increased trust and pride, both personally and as a group.

• **Skills set training.** The most common objective to date regarding diversity training has been in the area of awareness, a sort of Diversity Training 101. The future suggests there will be a greater emphasis on managerial and team skills, with a focus on two audiences: internal (employee to employee) and external (employee to customer). Staff at all levels often need conflict resolution, cross-cultural communication and productive problem-solving skills in a pluralistic environment. At a managerial/supervisory level, understanding interviewing biases and assumptions is key to broadening the hiring profile. Giving performance reviews to employees of multiple nationalities or running meetings with employees who may be used to deferential relationships, requires an additional set of skills and competencies.

Externally, the skills focus may be on sales and marketing as a way to understand and appeal to diverse customers, or it may also focus on improving customer service. How you market a hamburger, airplane or a movie to customers in different parts of the world, or how you sell goods and services to various audiences in this country requires understanding a wide array of preferences and norms in order to position products effectively.

Defining what constitutes excellent service in particular contexts, and teaching people how to demonstrate these behaviors, is a central part of skill set training. Take demonstration of respect, for example. What does welcoming behavior look like to various customers? Does it mean direct eye contact or averted eyes? Does it mean shaking hands, bowing or simply nodding one's head in acknowledgment of someone standing in front of you?

• **Integration.** The third trend is one that means diversity is woven into all aspects of the organization. How does diversity become a constant presence in the way your organization does business? If you print a calendar, for example, are holidays, celebrations and acknowledgments made across all cultures and backgrounds? In photographs for promotional material, are all populations reflected? An article in the *Los Angeles Times* editorial section (May 11, 1998) pointed out that Asian and Latino children rarely see themselves reflected in magazines or on television. What toll does this exclusion take on the development of these children's self-esteem. One could also suggest that the exclusion of a group or groups of people from an organization's culture has repercussions on the excluded. Are your policies and procedures inclusive? If not, who is left out? Diversity has to be an ongoing lens through which business decisions are made.

One way to achieve integration is through the addition of a broader array

---

MEASURE YOUR DIVERSITY

Answering these questions may help you make the business case for diversity in your organization:

- In how many countries does your organization operate?
- How many languages are spoken by your customers/clients?
- How much does employee turnover cost your organization?
- How much does your organization spend annually on recruitment?
- How much have discrimination/harassment suits cost your organization in the past year (in both legal fees and settlements?)
- What are the demographics of your customer/client base? (e.g., age, income, gender, education, ethnicity, etc.)
- How frequently does intergroup conflict sap productivity?
- Is there higher level of turnover among certain employee groups?
- Are your policies and benefits attractive to potential recruits?
- Is your organization losing top talent because people do not feel heard, included or valued?
- Do employees feel that their skills and talents are well rewarded?
- Is there some career advancement possibility for employees and a focus on developing people internally?

SEVEN STRATEGIC STEPS

Look at the following questions to see where your organization stands in its diversity strategy:

1 EXECUTIVE LEVEL COMMITMENT. What concrete indicators from executives illustrate their support and commitment?

2 ASSESSMENT AND DIAGNOSIS. What data have you used to identify obstacles and steer your initiative? How current is it? Does it reflect all levels of the organization?

3 DIVERSITY TASK FORCE. What group is acting as shepherd and advocate of the initiative? What kind of team building and education has enabled them to develop common goals and language?

4 SYSTEMS CHANGES. What systems changes are needed? How are people being held accountable for making these changes the norm?

5 TRAINING. What objectives is training designed to accomplish? How has the content been tailored to suit all levels and skills throughout the organization? How is diversity integrated into training?

6 MEASUREMENT AND EVALUATION. What are your stated outcomes and how will you know if you are successful? What data can you collect to use in measurement?

7 INTEGRATION. How will you make your efforts stick?

• **Global focus.** Whether you are a multinational doing business abroad, or a company in the United States dealing with an increasingly immigrant population, the global focus is unavoidable. If you are headquartered in the United States and have a clear sexual harassment or gender equity policy, how does that play in Malaysia or Turkey? How open are people of other cultures to looking at issues around sexual orientation? Does the concept of individualism, or equality and justice have any ring of truth or relevance in other parts of the world or in all parts of your workforce? Any successful business today needs global eyes that pay close attention to all strategic and operational issues.

The diversity arena is rapidly changing and evolving. Areas of focus continue to shift. What doesn't change is the need to address the issues. A culture of inclusion, demographic trends, globalization, competitive marketplaces and the need for top talent all point to the fact that regardless diversity does matter in a highly complex and competitive world.

of skills into all curricula. Whether participants are learning about conflict, time management or stress, culture helps shape realities and should shape content. Its influence needs to be fully a part of all classes, all policies and all procedures because in reality, it effects the work environment daily. (If it doesn't do it consciously, it will do so unconsciously.) Training content as well as policies need to be conceived with a wide range of audiences and potential adaptations in mind.

LEE GARDENSWARTZ, Ph.D., and ANITA ROWE, Ph.D., are diversity consultants/trainers based in Los Angeles, and authors of several books on diversity.

WALKING THE TIGHTROPE, BALANCING RISKS & GAINS

In making judgment calls on ethics issues, HR needs to balance the organization's fundamental values, the needs of employees and the bottom line.

BY LIN GRENSING-POPHAL

A former senior human resource executive for a health care organization in a Southern state tells of some outrageous activities connected with hiring minority workers to fill management positions. "This was a lily-white organization when I joined it," he says. "The only diversity was in the lower end jobs. I brought in two minority managers and, shortly thereafter, started receiving some pressure from the board along some stereotypical lines: 'We don't hire people like that. You're not from here. You don't understand.' They wanted me to fire them. I refused, and it ultimately cost me my job."

Another HR professional lost her job at two companies because, she says, she refused to sit back and do things she considered wrong. What kind of things? Allowing a pay inequity to persist between a male employee whose salary was more than double that of two female colleagues; testing new applicants for HIV and basing hiring decisions on the results; screening out female applicants in their 30s based on the boss's fear that they would miss a lot of work due to child-care issues. "I went through a period of really agonizing over the behavior I was seeing—things I didn't expect to encounter," she says. "It was very discouraging."

HR-related online bulletin boards, such as SHRM's HR Talk, are filled with similar examples of ethical dilemmas and judgments faced by HR professionals every day. Ethical issues spill over into the media and professional literature as well. Consider these two examples:

• A story appearing in newspapers around the country reported that a Catholic nurse in Erie, Pa., was fired for refusing to hand out birth control pills or condoms to single men and women. She wants her job back and feels it was unfair to be terminated because of her deeply held religious beliefs.

• The book *Dante's Dilemma: MBAs from Hell!*, by management consultant Larry Baytos, explores ethical dilemmas involving disparate treatment of minorities, executive compensation rip-offs, sexual harassment and other issues in a fictitious corporation. Baytos, former senior vice president of HR at Quaker Oats Co., says his book is based on real events.

ETHICAL, ILLEGAL OR JUST UNFAIR?

Terminating an employee solely based on race is illegal. So is refusing to consider applicants who are HIV-positive or who are females in their 30s. Many of the issues HR deals with have clear legal ramifications—there is a "right" answer and a "wrong" answer. Where, then, does ethics come in? The distinctions aren't always black and white, and the issues tend to line themselves up along a continuum. Baytos has developed a "scale of transgressions" that may help to clarify the distinctions between illegal, unethical and simply unfair. On one end of the continuum is "unfair." On other end is "illegal." In the middle, and much less well-defined, is "unethical."

An unfair incident might be a CEO receiving a huge pay increase after massive layoffs. "That certainly seems unfair, but it's not illegal, and it's hard to make a case that it's unethical by existing standards," Baytos says. An illegal incident might occur when an employer tells a search firm not to submit names of female applicants. He tells another story of a CEO who confided that he engaged in a large diversity study, using an outside consultant, simply to appease a minority board member. "The CEO had no real commitment to the process or to making any changes," he explains. "This was a real dilemma for the people involved in the study process. To me, that clearly would be an ethical issue—not a fairness one." An unethical situation, according to Baytos, might be a company that puts its employees' retirement security at risk by forcing the investment of the retirement funds in its own securities.

Even when dealing in the center of the spectrum—ethical issues—a distinction should be made between ethical dilemmas and ethical judgments, says Frank Navran. He is senior consultant with the Ethics Resource Center (ERC), a Washington, D.C.-based nonprofit organization which, he says, essentially invented ethics consulting.

"We find that there are fewer ethical dilemmas than there are ethical judgments," Navran explains. "A dilemma occurs when two or more values are in conflict. It's the classic example you get in Philosophy 101 of 'do you steal a loaf of bread to feed a starving child?' "

Here's a recent instance. An article in the *Washington Times* on March 10, 1993, related the story of Lt. David Quint, then a Navy public affairs officer. He was censured for "expressing his opposition to lifting the ban on homosexuals in the military." In this case and that of the Catholic nurse, neither side is "right." The people involved simply have different values, which conflict with those of the organization.

Ethical judgments are different in that the values do not conflict. An example might be an organization in which "fairness" is a shared value between the company and the HR manager. A situation occurs that requires a decision to be made. Both senior management and HR are committed to "fairness," yet they differ in their approach to the issue. "The difficulty occurs when both the employee and management look at the values of the organization and come to different conclusions as to what is the right way to act," Navran says.

THE BOTTOM LINE VS. THE FIRING LINE

As one online bulletin board participant commented, "It has been comforting to know that ethical issues are out there and I'm not alone. But, on the other hand, it's disheartening to know that they're so commonplace." Why are these issues so prevalent in the workplace?

"Maybe there's some ignorance initially, but mostly I think it's disregard," says a woman who is currently working in HR at a nonprofit and actively seeking employment elsewhere. "They're trying to get the HR person to find 'loopholes'— ways to skirt the law," she adds. "I think HR people are willing to find ways to meet the boss's expectations so long as they are ethical and legal. I don't think anybody has any problem with that. When they cross that line, it's difficult."

"High-tech companies and entrepreneurs are used to calculating risk," says the woman who lost two jobs because of value conflicts. "Some of these decisions like 'will we be sued?' are based more on a risk calculation than on principle. If the risk is small enough and the perceived benefit is great enough, I believe they'll take the risk." One of the values shared by every profit-making company is to "maximize the wealth of the shareholders." That's Finance 101. One value shared by virtually every HR manager is to be an advocate for employees. Those two values are, all too frequently, in conflict. It's important, Navran says, "not just for HR, but for every line and support department to understand what the values and culture of the organization demand of them so they're operating in ways that are congruent."

BALACING HR NEEDS AND ORGANIZATION NEEDS

Many HR professionals find themselves caught between a rock (upper management) and a hard place (disgruntled, poorly treated employees). When making decisions they want to do "what's right." But sometimes it's hard to know what that

SURVEY REINFORCES NEED TO DEVELOP WORKPLACE ETHICS GUIDELINES

Despite growth in the field of business ethics since 1980, ethical dilemmas in the workplace continue to challenge HR professionals, according to the *1997 SHRM/Ethics Research Center Business Ethics Survey*. The findings were based on responses from 747 HR professionals.

Overall survey results show that although an increasing number of organizations have developed written standards of ethical conduct, many still need to do more to integrate the standards into daily operations. Of the 73 percent in organizations with written ethical standards, 61 percent reported that their organizations do not provide training on the standards.

Here are a few telling findings on ethics challenges for HR:
• Almost half of the respondents (47 percent) said they had felt at least some pressure from other employees or managers to compromise their organization's standards of ethical business conduct in order to achieve business objectives.
• Those who felt some pressure to compromise their organization's ethical business standards cited three principal causes: overly aggressive financial or business objectives (50 percent), schedule demands (38 percent) and the need to help the organization survive (30 percent).
• Respondents tend to think their own ethical standards are more in line with those of subordinates' than with those of peers and senior management.

• 53 percent of survey respondents reported that, either occasionally or often, they observed conduct in the organization that they believed violated the law or the organization's ethical standards, and 79 percent of that group said they reported their observations to management or another appropriate person.

REACTIONS TO SPECIFIC ETHICAL DILEMMAS

When presented with hypothetical ethical situations at work, the HR professionals gave the following responses:
• 88 percent would report to their supervisor the accidental discovery of information related to a major downsizing initiative in the HR department.
• 83 percent would encourage a key employee, whose position would be difficult to fill, to notify the company of their plans to leave.
• 81 percent would further investigate a third-party report of an employee abusing legal substances on the job, such as prescription medicine, and 31 percent would further investigate a third-party report of an employee abusing illegal substances off the job.
• 34 percent would further investigate a third-party report that an employee is HIV-positive; an equal number would do nothing.

means. In fact, as Navran points out, often it's not even an issue of "what's right," but of balancing divergent perspectives and holding decisions up against the organization's stated values.

In one of the corporations he has consulted with, the benefits administration and medical departments were engaged in an ongoing struggle. "Members of the medical department saw themselves as the employees' advocates, and their concern was to protect the health of employees," Navran explains. "Those in the benefits department saw themselves as managing the company's health care benefits budget. There was a tension between the two departments in terms of how long to allow an employee to be away from work, for example, after a surgical procedure.

"The way these issues get resolved," he says, "is not by arguing the medical facts, but really by understanding the organization's core beliefs. If one of the organization's fundamental principles is to be compassionate and caring about employees, then the decision needs to be tested against the compassion and caring standard. The organization's values become a benchmark." In this instance, he says, "we have an obligation to be good to shareholders, so we have to manage our costs. We also have an obligation to employees. The struggle is, how do we balance those issues? If you remember to talk about the issues in terms of the fundamental principles you're working to-

ward, it helps you reach a balance that is palatable and appropriate."

Consultant Lynn Brailsford believes "it really does boil down to the issue of 'money vs. people' or 'bottom line vs. people.' It's short-term vs. long-term thinking. The tendency of most business managers is to really look at things in a quantifiable, bottom-line perspective." Brailsford is former vice president of training and development for Chase Manhattan, and now works with financial services companies, helping them to review their employment practices and come up with suggestions and recommendations for how to create more respectful environments.

HR managers, she says, often have a credibility problem. It stems from not taking a broader, more strategic, view of the issues they're dealing with and framing those issues in terms that upper management understands. Brailsford learned that lesson firsthand from her experience as president of a small company in New Jersey. "Senior management will look at these issues if you can quantify them—if you can say 'here are the costs,' or 'here's what will happen—let me quantify it for you.' It's taking the same language they're using and framing your positions in the same way, instead of constantly trying to harp on them from an HR point of view."

Baytos agrees. "There are other priorities that CEOs are wont to look at such as earnings per quarter, how analysts are looking at the company, and how the stock is going to do next year. You'd better be familiar with these priorities. If you're not at a high level in the organization, at least find a way to have access to that high level, or your voice will be lost."

WHEN YOU MUST AGREE TO DISAGREE

What if you are truly are taking a broad view of the issues you deal with? What if your recommendations are clearly aligned with the corporation's stated values and you still feel that you're beating your head against the wall?

Navran says that when he conducts focus groups of employees, one of the most frequent criticisms he hears is that management "doesn't walk the talk." What makes the HR manager's job especially difficult, he says, is when management sends mixed messages—"when the rhetoric says 'we really believe in caring for employees' and everyone knows what they really care about is the bottom line." What to do? Know yourself. Know your own values. And live by them.

David Quint is in the private sector today, working as an HR professional in the construction industry. He admits that his experience was a difficult one, but what helped, he says, was having a solid understanding of his own guiding principles and values. "If you have a foundation of character, when difficult issues come up you can address them as easily as possible. Decide ahead of time what hills you're going to die on," Quint advises. Clarifying your values, he says, "doesn't make it easy, but it does make it less difficult."

Quint's advice is echoed by the HR manager who refused to terminate minority employees without cause. His advice: "Don't back down."

Baytos agrees. "If it's something that you really feel strongly about, you have to be willing to put your career at risk. Unless the HR person is willing to take these risks they're really not part of the solution, they're just going along with the tide and riding it out."

"The real myth that needs busting is the myth of powerlessness," Navran says. "Too many HR managers tell me what they can't do as opposed to doing what they can. I would suggest to people that powerlessness is a convenient place to hide but, very often, it's a lie. We often have more power than we're willing to accept, because we

don't want to put ourselves at risk. We use the excuse of powerlessness so that we don't have to make the decision, whether or not we have the moral fortitude to do what's difficult."

WHEN IT'S TIME TO MOVE ON

Several HR professionals who expressed frustrations about ethical issues they face in their current positions are changing jobs. "Life's too short," says one HR professional who wants to make a job change. "It's just not worth it. You have to know when it's time to move on." Here they share some suggestions on how to screen prospective employers to determine if they're the right "ethical fit."

One job seeker comments, "I would ask questions of the person interviewing me to get a feel for how they have handled certain dilemmas. Listen to your intuition. If you get a feeling that something's not quite right, it probably isn't."

"It's tough to assess from the outside, but I think there may be some clues," says Baytos. "One clue to me is 'what has been the tenure of HR people at key levels?' Constant turnover at the top may indicate that anybody who tries to come forward with a strong HR agenda quickly meets a sudden death."

David Quint offers some suggestions on the types of questions to pose to prospective employers:
- Is this a new position? If not, why did the last person leave?
- What characteristics does a successful person have in your organization?
- And, perhaps most telling: Is there anything unusually demanding about this job that I should know about?

Quint encourages HR professionals to ask the tough questions. "They're either going to respect you for that—or they won't and they won't hire you. If that happens, you're really better off."

Lin Grensing-Pophal, SPHR, is a business journalist with HR consulting experience in employee communication, training and management issues. Her articles have previously appeared in HR News *and other business and trade journals. She is the author of* A Small Business Guide to Employee Selection *and* Motivating Today's Workforce: When the Carrot Can't Always Be Cash *(Self-Counsel Press).*

Measuring the Effectiveness Of Recognition Programs

Companies spend money on recognition programs, but often give little attention to evaluating these investments. There is a way to measure their effectiveness by borrowing from Donald Kirkpatrick's training evaluation model and then applying it to your recognition program.

- Reaction—Did participants like the training?
- Learning—Did participants learn something?
- Behavior—Did participants apply what they learned back on the job?
- Results—Did participants' application on the job affect the organization?

1 REACTION. Evaluating reaction to recognition programs is the easiest, and probably most common, measure of recognition. A systematic approach to gauging participants' reactions to the program could include questions such as the following:

- Did the program describe how and why you should recognize others?
- Are the program guidelines clear and communicated well?
- Is the nomination and award process simple to use?

If no other form of measurement is taken, it is important to find out how employees feel about the program. Their reaction—especially if it is positive—can provide you with information for continued support and enable you to build on the success of the programs.

2 LEARNING. It takes additional effort to evaluate whether participants understand how and why they should use the recognition program. You can measure if certain skills or awareness levels have changed since implementation of the program. Participants can be asked how important it is to recognize employees, how often they should do so, in what types of situations, and in what ways. Other measurable skills include knowing how to use formal, informal and day-to-day recognition; how to praise publicly; and how to write a persuasive nomination for an employee award. Tools used at this level of evaluation include tests or surveys administered before and after the training event or program launch.

3 BEHAVIOR. Showing that learning has occurred does not guarantee the learning translates to new behavior on the job. Determining if employees apply what they learned can involve direct observation, but more often consists of feedback from management and peers. The most effective approach is to build tracking systems—targeted at specific behaviors—directly into the program. Simple, trackable forms of behavior change include: How frequently managers recognize their employees; how many employees receive written praise from managers, peers or customers; and how many employees are nominated for awards.

Tracking such information can be useful in examining variations over time and identifying behavior change throughout the organization.

4 RESULTS. Measuring the results of your program is the most critical part of evaluating recognition, but the least pursued. Many recognition programs focus on direct results such as productivity award programs based directly upon increased performance, sales incentive programs linked to sales revenue, and employee suggestion programs tied to percentage of dollars earned or saved. Indirect measures should focus specifically on the behavior the recognition is designed to reinforce.

Recognition programs are then evaluated for the intent of their design: attendance programs that reduce absenteeism; customer service awards that improve care given to the customer; team awards that enhance cooperation; safety programs that reduce on-the-job injuries; and quality award systems that enhance product quality.

Even when the program's focus is simply to increase overall morale, measures exist or can be built to examine the results. Employee surveys or exit interviews can include questions that evaluate the level of recognition or indicate the program's effectiveness. For example, when morale is low, employees typically rank one or more of the following survey items very low: My manager makes time for me when I need to talk; my manager has discussed my career aspirations with me; I feel appreciated for the work I do; I feel I am a valuable member of the team.

Surveying attitudes can help determine whether employee perceptions of the company are improving and can help quantify morale at the individual, group and organizational level. The more recognition programs are geared toward driving significant organizational performance and strategic results, the easier it is to justify their use.

A challenge for sustaining and improving recognition initiatives is how to evaluate the program's organizational impact. One way to do this is to begin with the end—that is, define the results first to be sure the program can achieve them. Starting with a clear idea of your goals and desired performance will strengthen the link of recognition to results and ensure that you can answer with confidence, "Yes, the program works."

BOB NELSON is author of the best-selling books, "1001 Ways to Reward Employees" and "1001 Ways to Energize Employees," both published by Workman Publishing. PATRICK DAILEY is manager of Global Employee Recognition and Organization Development for Mary Kay Inc. in Dallas.

Motivation:
The Value of a Work Ethic

by J. Clifton Williams

The motivation challenge of an organization's leaders is extremely complex. Employees enter an organization with very different needs, personality traits, levels of formal education, skills, aptitudes, interests, and other attributes. They most certainly have different expectations of their employer and different views of what their employer has a right to expect of them. These differences provide leaders their greatest opportunity to become effective motivators and their greatest risk of failing the motivational challenge.

Employee Selection

Given the legal constraints surrounding personnel hires today, managers often give up trying to make professional selection decisions and decide primarily on the basis of intuition. That is not to say that intuition should play no part in the selection process. It is regrettable however when 75 years of research on personnel selection is ignored because managers are so afraid of discriminating illegally that they become totally non-discriminating.

In every position certain personal qualities correlate more highly with

> **Hire people who are self-motivated because of _their_ self-expectations, and do everything possible to help them live up to both your expectations and theirs.**

on-the-job effectiveness than do others, and the law allows for selecting on the basis of those characteristics. Some organizations select employees who have a high probability of being productive. Others play a guessing game and hire applicants who are likely to be mediocre performers at best.

Many employees who otherwise have the qualities needed to serve their employer well, lack the motiva-

tion to do so. Many are highly motivated but not highly motivated to do what their employer needs done. Some, for example, are past masters at keeping their jobs and getting raises without ever making an effort to solve problems, develop new skills, or seriously identify with the mission and goals of their employer.

The actions of leaders and the policies and practices of organizations can greatly influence employee motivation, but what employees bring to the employment situation may influence their motivation even more. Some more than fulfill their employer's highest expectations because it is their nature to do their best; others barely meet acceptable standards despite their employer's most cleverly contrived motivational efforts.

The Protestant Work Ethic

The so-called Protestant or Puritan work ethic was important in the theology of John Calvin. It is thought to have supported the industrial revolution by creating a large pool of highly motivated workers—workers who believed it was their duty to put their God-given talents to work. They responded to the usual work incentives, but aside from those sources of motivation, they were productive because of their belief that it was the right thing to do.

Furthermore, the financial prosperity resulting from productive work, simple living, and saving part of their earnings was viewed as a sign of God's favor and evidence of their *elect* position. Similar beliefs about one's moral obligation to be productive are also present in other cultures. A Confucian work ethic, for instance, plays an important motivational role in Eastern cultures.

Modern studies of work motivation indicate that the Protestant work ethic is far from dead in the United States. Many Christians and others whose values have been influenced by Christianity still believe they have a moral obligation to be productive.

The point to remember is that employees who hold some version of the Protestant work ethic have a special faith-related motivation to work. If you are such a person, you know from experience that you don't need close supervision to keep you working and you are probably as effective when your pay is low as when it is high.

High Self-Expectations

Internal motivation need not be linked psychologically to religious values. Many people whose behavior is virtually identical to that of those with a strong Protestant work ethic have learned from their families or other subcultures a sense of "oughtness" about work. They feel good about themselves when they are productive and bad about themselves when they are not. When they perceive that the quantity and or quality of their work falls below their high self-imposed standards, they become anxious. They have a *need* to excel in their work as surely as they have a need for food and drink. A leader is indeed fortunate when a significant number of his or her direct reports possess this characteristic. One caveat is in order: these subordinates will have no respect for supervisors who lack such motivation.

High Organizational Expectations

Employees who are committed to a Protestant work ethic, or whose culture has conditioned them to make productivity a high priority, are motivated by deeply embedded *acquired* personality characteristics. Fortunately, employees who lack such motivation can often learn it.

Some leaders build high productivity expectations into the value systems of their organizational cultures. They expect a high sense of responsibility, high productivity, and high quality of output from all of their employees. These expectations are impressed upon new employees. The ac-

tions of pace setters demonstrate that the organization is serious about them and social pressures also reinforce them. Employees who don't fulfill those expectations soon find occasion to seek work elsewhere.

Conversely, in organizations with few pressures for high productivity, individual differences in productivity can be enormous. Some secretaries and clerks may produce two or three times as much as others. Employers' expectations can have quite an impact. Early in my career as a professor I had a typing and library assistant whose atrocious typing I tolerated only because she seemed to be a conscientious and good person. Was I surprised when she returned from a summer of working in the executive suite of a large corporation. Apparently at the end of her first day there, her supervisor carefully explained that she had the rest of the week to quit making typing mistakes and to increase her speed to that of the top secretaries in the office. She did exactly that! By the time she came back to work for me she had tripled her typing speed and rarely had to correct a mistake. It was a good learning experience for both of us.

Clif Williams is Distinguished Professor Emeritus of Management at Baylor University and also serves as an organizational consultant to the university.

How to mentoring

Many organisations now use mentoring as part of management development, but the relationship between mentor and mentee can be fraught with difficulties. **Alan Fowler** explains how to overcome them and introduce an effective mentoring programme

Guide lines

Although it is only since the early 1970s that mentoring became a formal component of many development programmes, the concept of experienced individuals handing down their wisdom to their young protégés is centuries old. The term comes from Greek mythology—Mentor being the friend to whom Ulysses entrusted the education of his son before he went off on his odyssey. Historically, the relationship between master and apprentice has strong mentoring characteristics.

In modern times, mentoring has been used outside the business environment. There are mentoring programmes in the social services to help disturbed young people, for instance, and other schemes that assist academic high-flyers in higher education. But its most common use is in management development.

Organisations wishing to introduce a mentoring scheme first need to consider its main objectives. They then have to decide whether mentors should be internal or external, how to select them, the level of support they need and the type of relationship required between the mentor, mentee and the mentee's manager.

It might seem that the objectives are obvious—to aid the development of inexperienced managers—but in reality priorities can differ considerably between organisations. The goal could be to contribute to a culture-change programme by helping to change mentees' behaviour. But it might also be to improve people's performance, develop their skills or improve their long-term career development. Or it could be to assist mentees in disadvantaged or un-der-represented groups to break into management roles.

These objectives affect the selection of the participants and the type of guidance offered. They will also influence the decision on whether to use mentors from inside or outside the organisation. If the emphasis is on helping mentees to attain the skills of existing high-performers or technical specialists, internal mentors may more readily provide the necessary expertise.

Alternatively, an emphasis on more general personal and career development may indicate the selection of a mentor from another organisation who can help to broaden the mentee's horizons. External mentors can be valuable when an organisation is trying to achieve a culture change. One example is the use of private-sector mentors for senior managers in public-sector organisations that are having to become more commercial. They can also be of particular help to mentees who are having difficulties that they are reluctant to discuss with anyone in their own organisation.

It is generally accepted that if mentors are to be internal, they should not be the mentees' line managers. The mentoring relationship differs from that between individuals and their line managers, and they should not be confused. It is not uncommon for mentees to need to discuss issues involving their line management relationships. This can't be done if the mentor is the manager. A common approach is for an internal mentor to be in a different function and to be one or two hierarchical levels above the mentee.

There are several criteria for selecting mentors. In addition to having specific, job-related skills, they need to be fully committed to the role—they should always be volunteers. Excellent communication skills are vital, but mentors must also be patient and avoid offering solutions too readily. The role is most effective when people are encouraged to form their own solutions. Mentors should recognise that they too can learn from the process and treat it as part of their own continuous development.

The selection of mentees will also be influenced by the scheme's aims. If it is designed to develop high-flyers, the results of appraisals or assessments may be needed for the initial selection. If it is aimed at under-represented groups such as women or ethnic minorities, this will largely dictate the preliminary selection. (Positive action of this kind is not in breach of equal opportunities legislation if it is specifically to correct a significant imbalance in the workforce. It is also necessary for the scheme to be categorised clearly as a training initiative.)

Another approach, sometimes used for graduate trainees or for skilled technical jobs, is for mentoring to be arranged for all staff involved in a particular activity. In this case, mentors may be selected from the same function.

Reciprocal recipe

For a mentoring relationship to be successful, both individuals need to possess certain personal qualities. Mentees must be honest, open-minded and willing to learn. They should also be prepared to consider their weaknesses and be able to develop a high level of self-aware-

From *People Management*, October 1998, pp. 48-50. © 1998 by Alan Fowler. Reprinted by permission.

ness. But they should not be reluctant to challenge their mentor's views.

While potential mentees may be strongly encouraged to embark on a mentoring relationship, there is little point in forcing this on someone who feels uncomfortable with it. As with mentors, they should be able to opt into—or out of—the scheme.

Matching mentor to mentee is critical, as the relationship is a personal one. It might be thought that the best match is one in which both parties have similar personalities, but experience has shown that this is not the case. Indeed, if the individuals are too similar, they may avoid discussing issues they both feel uncomfortable about, and the mentor may not be able to bring new insights to bear.

There must, of course, be mutual respect and confidence. Mentors have to be able to identify with their mentees, while mentees should feel that their mentors really have valuable know-how and experience that they can tap. But some of the most effective relationships can be between two people with very different personalities who can gain insights from each other's different perspectives.

In the matching process it may be necessary to consider the issues involved in mixed-sex mentoring. Mentoring by an older man of a younger woman needs particular care. There have been examples of outstandingly successful mentoring of this kind, in which women at a junior level are helped to break through the glass ceiling by highly respected senior male managers. In addition to the conventional mentoring role, his support can give her greater visibility and legitimacy within the organisation, which may be needed before her managerial potential is fully recognised.

But there can be problems beyond that of the possibility of unpleasant office gossip about the relationship. Male mentors need to have a constructive at-titude towards the different attributes that women may bring to the management role. A male mentor who tries to turn his female mentee into "one of the boys" instead of helping her to develop her own qualities is doing neither her nor the organisation any favours.

The mentoring of a young male manager by a more senior woman may not only carry much less risk, it can also make a positive contribution towards breaking down the sexual stereotyping that in some organisations still influences male managers' attitudes. But in all mixed-sex mentoring there is a need for care about personal behaviour and the problems that can be generated by the relationship going beyond the purely professional—actual or perceived.

The eternal triangle

There is a tendency to think of mentoring as involving only two people, but successful arrangements also recognise the involvement of line managers. Problems are likely to arise if managers think that mentors are undermining their authority, perhaps if mentees are given advice that they see as conflicting with the needs of their department. They may also be suspicious that mentees are telling mentors about their shortcomings, and that these tales out of school will adversely affect their relationships with senior management. This is a particular risk when the mentor is more senior in the hierarchy than the manager, but the dangers are reduced by the organisation clearly defining the objectives of the mentoring programme and distinguishing the role of the mentor from that of the line manager.

Mentors should also never arrange for the mentee to be away from the workplace—for example, to accompany them to a meeting—without first seek-ing the consent of the line manager. It is essential for mentors to make it clear that a key aspect of the whole process is to assist, not undermine, the mentees' relationships with their line managers.

From a broader organisational viewpoint, too, the whole scheme needs to be monitored to ensure that it is not developing into an alternative power base.

The launch of any mentoring scheme should include training sessions for both mentors and mentees. Mentors need to understand the primary aim of the programme and the implications this has for the type of guidance they should offer. Some training in the principles of effective counselling is also appropriate.

Mentees require briefings on the objectives of the scheme and the nature of the mentoring relationship. It is important, for example, to avoid misunderstandings about the purpose of a relationship, and to explain that decisions about job changes and promotions will be made through the normal channels and do not lie with the mentor.

The fourth person in the mentoring relationship, of course, is the personnel and development professional. All he or she has to do is design the scheme, secure top management backing, administer the selection and matching process, provide the necessary training, deal with any individual problems that may arise and monitor the impact of the scheme.

Further reading

A selection of Alan Fowler's "how to" articles was published in two books launched at the IPD's national conference in Harrogate.

Get More—And More Results—From Your People and **Get More—And More Value—From Your People** are available, price £9.95 each, from Plymbridge Distributors (01752 202301).

Will Your Culture Support KM?

By Samuel Greengard

When consulting firm Arthur Andersen embraced knowledge management (KM) in the early 1990s, executives knew it would take more than sophisticated technology and leading-edge software to make the initiative fly. They also knew that cultural barriers would need to be broken down, and that this would take effort from everyone in the company. "It requires a total commitment from management and a total buy-in from workers," explains Mark T. Stone, director of internal knowledge management for the firm's business consulting division based in Atlanta.

That's because organizations usually run into three major cultural problems when adopting a knowledge management initiative. First, people don't like to share their best ideas. They believe doing so dilutes their standing in the organization, and can impede their ability to get ahead. "Most of us were raised in an environment that's highly competitive, and we've never learned to share," states Thomas Koulopoulos, president of the Delphi Group, a Boston consulting firm specializing in knowledge management. Adds Eric Austvold, director of product marketing at Infinium Software: "In today's highly political corporate environment, knowledge equals power. Getting people to understand that knowledge sharing is for the

greater good of all requires significant culture change." Second, people don't like to use other people's ideas for fear it makes them look less knowledgeable, and that they're suddenly dependent on others to do their job. Third, people like to consider themselves experts, and prefer not to collaborate with others.

Communicate the concept.

Changing this mindset isn't easy. Because most workers have operated within a knowledge-hoarding environment for so long, it can take weeks or months to spot the first hint of significant change, but it *can* be done. To create the desired culture, Arthur Andersen established an array of programs which includes occasional seminars and workshops, and a cross-functional team comprised of both technologists and non-technologists to make decisions about knowledge management processes. Says Stone: "It's a tremendous and ongoing challenge, but once people begin to see the true value of sharing knowledge, you break through the barriers and see a transformation in thinking and action."

At Buckman Laboratories, a Memphis-based producer of specialty chemicals for the paper, leather and plastics industries, the change has been slow and steady. CEO Bob Buckman conjured up the idea of sharing knowledge in 1991 while laying in bed with a ruptured disk. He thought,

---

Samuel Greengard is a contributing editor to WORKFORCE. *E-mail sam@greengard.com to comment.*

"Why should people be forced to constantly re-invent the wheel when a steady stream of information and knowledge is available within the organization?" A year later, after establishing a knowledge-sharing network known as K'Netix, Buckman had built a foundation for the future.

But getting employees to understand, let alone use the system, required enormous effort. "We had to assist them in understanding what the system is, what it does and how it can benefit them personally," says Mark Koskiniemi, vice president, human resources. "Managers had to learn they no longer can oversee the flow of information within the company; they have to help employees get the information they need."

Early on, the firm began offering workshops to communicate the power of KM. The organization's top executives, including Buckman and Koskiniemi, immediately began contributing to forums and discussion groups to show management's unwavering commitment and monitor the proceedings. Those with something intelligent to say finally had a public forum, Buckman pointed out. But as the culture became more collaborative, those who couldn't or wouldn't participate might find their opportunities for advancement more limited than in the past.

Provide incentives.

Incentives were also a key component. Although Buckman Laboratories doesn't offer financial rewards for posting knowledge, it has dangled a few carrots along the way. At one point, Buckman organized a one-time event at a fashionable Scottsdale, Arizona, resort for 150 employees who had contributed the most widely used information. At the event, these individuals helped map out the future of the program, and shared ideas on how to make it better. The selected employees also received computer gear, listened to a presentation by Tom Peters, and participated in discussions which further defined K'Netix. Some of those who didn't make the cut let management know they were a bit irked at being left behind, but participation in the online forums spiked immediately following the event, and it has never dropped off.

Experts say creating appropriate rewards, recognition and compensation to drive KM is essential. Therefore, besides encouraging consultants to contribute information out of "social responsibility," Arthur Andersen also provides monetary incentives and other rewards that can amount to several thousand dollars a year for those who regularly contribute knowledge.

The challenge is to ensure that people are contributing valuable information, not just reams of information. "Knowledge management can collapse under information overload. It's essential to manage the process," says Joel Summers, vice president of HR systems development for Oracle Corp. of Redwood City, California, a database and HRMS provider. That's not so much a problem with HRMS and ERP (Enterprise Resource Planning) tools that take existing data and information and manipulate it to fit a user's needs. But for companies that rely on personal Web sites to spot competencies and those that use classic knowledge sharing techniques, it's a make-or-break proposition.

At Arthur Andersen, the problem has attracted a good deal of attention. "The trick is to create incentives for quality, rather than quantity," says Stone. The company has appointed a group of knowledge managers who review every contribution and certify that it's of significant value to the organization before posting it. Consultants who contribute receive cash bonuses based on both the amount of knowledge they contribute and how often it's used. "While that's not a direct assessment of quality, it's an indirect indication of the value to the organization," Stone explains. Arthur Andersen also uses recognition programs, and includes a knowledge management skills assessment as part of all employee performance evaluations.

Make people accountable.

Employee evaluations are another way Buckman Laboratories encourages involvement. After establishing K'Netix, Koskiniemi revamped the evaluation process to include an evaluation of online participation and contributions. "We've created mechanisms to encourage teamwork. The ultimate incentive is to use the system to become more productive and successful in satisfying customers." And more often than not, that's exactly how things have played out. Over the years, Buckman Laboratories has grabbed lucrative contracts away from larger competitors on the basis of its knowledge network. "When potential clients see what we're able to deliver with K'Netix, they understand they have the support of the entire company behind them," boasts Koskiniemi.

Getting to this point takes time, but is worth the effort. "Once people begin to see the true value of sharing knowledge, they embrace the concept," says Arthur Andersen's Stone. "Ultimately, they recognize that it arms them with better solutions. It allows them to get work done in a fashion that's superior to our competitors. In any organization, the value of knowledge management must be clearly demonstrated. You don't succeed by simply introducing an intranet and telling people to share information. You find ways to provide value for both the individual and the organization."

Success in the knowledge economy comes to those who know themselves—their strengths, their values, and how they best perform.

MANAGING ONESELF

By Peter F. Drucker

Hᴉsᴛᴏʀʏ's ɢʀᴇᴀᴛ ᴀᴄʜɪᴇᴠᴇʀs—A Napoleon, a daVinci, a Mozart—have always managed themselves. That, in large measure, is what makes them great achievers. But they are rare exceptions, so unusual both in their talents and their accomplishments as to be considered outside the boundaries of ordinary human existence. Now, most of us, even those of us with modest endowments, will have to learn to manage ourselves. We will have to learn to develop ourselves. We will have to place ourselves where we can make the greatest contribution. And we will have to stay mentally alert and engaged during a 50-year working life, which means knowing how and when to change the work we do.

What Are My Strengths?

Most people think they know what they are good at. They are usually wrong. More often, people know what they are not good at—and even then more people are wrong than right. And yet, a person can perform only from strength. One cannot build performance on weaknesses, let alone on something one cannot do at all.

Throughout history, people had little need to know their strengths. A person was born into a position and a line of work: the peasant's son would also be a peasant; the artisan's daughter, an artisan's wife, and so on. But now people have choices. We need to know our strengths in order to know where we belong.

Peter F. Drucker is the Marie Rankin Clarke Professor of Social Science and Management at Claremont Graduate University in Claremont, California.

From *Harvard Business Review,* March/April 1999, pp. 65-74. Excerpted from *Management Challenges for the 21st Century,* by Peter F. Drucker. © 1999 by HarperCollins Publishers. Reprinted by permission.

The only way to discover your strengths is through feedback analysis. Whenever you make a key decision or take a key action, write down what you expect will happen. Nine or 12 months later, compare the actual results with your expectations. I have been practicing this method for 15 to 20 years now, and every time I do it, I am surprised. The feedback analysis showed me, for instance—and to my great surprise—that I have an intuitive understanding of technical people, whether they are engineers or accountants or market researchers. It also showed me that I don't really resonate with generalists.

Feedback analysis is by no means new. It was invented sometime in the fourteenth century by an otherwise totally obscure German theologian and picked up quite independently, some 150 years later, by John Calvin and Ignatius Loyola, each of whom incorporated it into the practice of his followers. In fact, the steadfast focus on performance and results that this habit produces explains why the institutions these two men founded, the Calvinist church and the Jesuit order, came to dominate Europe within 30 years.

Practiced consistently, this simple method will show you within a fairly short period of time, maybe two or three years, where your strengths lie—and this is the most important thing to know. The method will show you what you are doing or failing to do that deprives you of the full benefits of your strengths. It will show you where you are not particularly competent. And finally, it will show you where you have no strengths and cannot perform.

Several implications for action follow from feedback analysis. First and foremost, concentrate on your strengths. Put yourself where your strengths can produce results.

Second, work on improving your strengths. Analysis will rapidly show where you need to improve skills or acquire new ones. It will also show the gaps in your knowledge—and those can usually be filled. Mathematicians are born, but everyone can learn trigonometry.

Third, discover where your intellectual arrogance is causing disabling ignorance and overcome it. Far too many people—especially people with great expertise in one area—are contemptuous of knowledge in other areas or believe that being bright is a substitute for knowledge. First-rate engineers, for instance, tend to take pride in not knowing anything about people. Human beings, they believe, are much too disorderly for the good engineering mind. Human resource professionals, by contrast, often pride themselves on their ignorance of elementary accounting or of quantitative methods altogether. But taking pride in such ignorance is self-defeating. Go to work

on acquiring the skills and knowledge you need to fully realize your strengths.

It is equally essential to remedy your bad habits—the things you do or fail to do that inhibit your effectiveness and performance. Such habits will quickly show up in the feedback. For example, a planner may find that his beautiful plans fail because he does not follow through on them. Like so many brilliant people, he believes that ideas move mountains. But bulldozers move mountains; ideas show where the bulldozers should go to work. This planner will have to learn that the work does not stop when the plan is completed. He must find people to carry out the plan and explain it to them. He must adapt and change it as he puts it into action. And finally, he must decide when to stop pushing the plan.

At the same time, feedback will also reveal when the problem is a lack of manners. Manners are the lubricating oil of an organization. It is a law of nature that two moving bodies in contact with each other create friction. This is as true for human beings as it is for inanimate objects. Manners—simple things like saying "please" and "thank you" and knowing a person's name or asking after her family—enable two people to work together whether they like each other or not. Bright people, especially bright young people, often do not understand this. If analysis shows that someone's brilliant work fails again and again as soon as cooperation from others is required, it probably indicates a lack of courtesy—that is, a lack of manners.

Comparing your expectations with your results also indicates what not to do. We all have a vast number of areas in which we have no talent or skill and little chance of becoming even mediocre. In those areas a person—and especially a knowledge worker—should not take on work, jobs, and assignments. One should waste as little effort as possible on improving areas of low competence. It takes far more energy and work to improve from incompetence to mediocrity than it takes to improve from first-rate performance to excellence. And yet most people—especially most teachers and most organizations—concentrate on making incompetent performers into mediocre ones. Energy, resources, and time should go instead to making a competent person into a star performer.

How Do I Perform?

Amazingly few people know *how* they get things done. Indeed, most of us do not even know that different people work and perform differently. Too many people work in ways that are not their ways, and that almost guarantees nonperformance. For knowledge workers, How do I perform?

may be an even more important question than What are my strengths?

Like one's strengths, how one performs is unique. It is a matter of personality. Whether personality be a matter of nature or nurture, it surely is formed long before a person goes to work. And *how* a person performs is a given, just as *what* a person is good at or not good at is a given. A person's way of performing can be slightly modified, but it is unlikely to be completely changed—and certainly not easily. Just as people achieve results by doing what they are good at, they also achieve results by working in ways that they best perform. A few common personality traits usually determine how a person performs.

Am I a reader or a listener? The first thing to know is whether you are a reader or a listener. Far too few people even know that there are readers and listeners and that people are rarely both. Even fewer know which of the two they themselves are. But some examples will show how damaging such ignorance can be.

When Dwight Eisenhower was commander in chief of the Allied forces in Europe, he was the darling of the press. His press conferences were famous for their style—General Eisenhower showed total command of whatever question he was asked, and he was able to describe a situation and explain a policy in two or three beautifully polished and elegant sentences. Ten years later, the same journalists who had been his admirers held President Eisenhower in open contempt. He never addressed the questions, they complained, but rambled on endlessly about something else. And they constantly ridiculed him for butchering the King's English in incoherent and ungrammatical answers.

Eisenhower apparently did not know that he was a reader, not a listener. When he was commander in chief in Europe, his aides made sure that every question from the press was presented in writing at least half an hour before a conference was to begin. And then Eisenhower was in total command. When he became president, he succeeded two listeners, Franklin D. Roosevelt and Harry Truman. Both men knew themselves to be listeners and both enjoyed free-for-all press conferences. Eisenhower may have felt that he had to do what his two predecessors had done. As a result, he never even heard the questions journalists asked. And Eisenhower is not even an extreme case of a nonlistener.

A few years later, Lyndon Johnson destroyed his presidency, in large measure, by not knowing that he was a listener. His predecessor, John Kennedy, was a reader who had assembled a brilliant group of writers as his assistants, making sure that they wrote to him before discussing their memos in person. Johnson kept these people on his staff—and they kept on writing. He never, apparently, understood one word of what they wrote. Yet as a senator, Johnson had been superb; for parliamentarians have to be, above all, listeners.

Few listeners can be made, or can make themselves, into competent readers—and vice versa. The listener who tries to be a reader will, therefore, suffer the fate of Lyndon Johnson, whereas the reader who tries to be a listener will suffer the fate of Dwight Eisenhower. They will not perform or achieve.

How do I learn? The second thing to know about how one performs is to know how one learns. Many first-class writers—Winston Churchill is but one example—do poorly in school. They tend to remember their schooling as pure torture. Yet few of their classmates remember it the same way. They may not have enjoyed the school very much, but the worst they suffered was boredom. The explanation is that writers do not, as a rule, learn by listening and reading. They learn by writing. Because schools do not allow them to learn this way, they get poor grades.

Schools everywhere are organized on the assumption that there is only one right way to learn and that it is the same way for everybody. But to be forced to learn the way a school teaches is sheer hell for students who learn differently. Indeed, there are probably half a dozen different ways to learn.

There are people, like Churchill, who learn by writing. Some people learn by taking copious notes. Beethoven, for example, left behind an enormous number of sketchbooks, yet he said he never actually looked at them when he composed. Asked why he kept them, he is reported to have replied, "If I don't write it down immediately, I forget it right away. If I put it into a sketchbook, I never forget it and I never have to look it up again." Some people learn by doing. Others learn by hearing themselves talk.

A chief executive I know who converted a small and mediocre family business into the leading company in its industry was one of those people who learn by talking. He was in the habit of calling his entire senior staff into his office once a week and then talking at them for two or three hours. He would raise policy issues and argue three different positions on each one. He rarely asked his associates for comments or questions; he simply needed an audience to hear himself talk. That's how he learned. And although he is a fairly extreme case, learning through talking is by no means an unusual method. Successful trial lawyers learn the same way, as do many medical diagnosticians (and so do I).

Of all the important pieces of self-knowledge, understanding how you learn is the easiest to acquire. When I ask people, "How do you learn?"

most of them know the answer. But when I ask, "Do you act on this knowledge?" few answer yes. And yet, acting on this knowledge is the key to performance; or rather, not acting on this knowledge condemns one to nonperformance.

How do I perform? and How do I learn? are the first questions to ask. But they are by no means the only ones. To manage yourself effectively, you also have to ask, Do I work well with people or am I a loner? And if you do work well with people, you then must ask, In what relationship?

Some people work best as subordinates. General George Patton, the great American military hero of World War II, is a prime example. Patton was America's top troop commander. Yet when he was proposed for an independent command, General George Marshall, the U.S. chief of staff—and probably the most successful picker of men in U.S. history—said, "Patton is the best subordinate the American army has ever produced, but he would be the worst commander."

Some people work best as team members. Others work best alone. Some are exceptionally talented as coaches and mentors; others are simply incompetent as mentors.

Another crucial question is, Do I produce results as a decision maker or as an adviser? A great many people perform best as advisers but cannot take the burden and pressure of making the decision. A good many other people, by contrast, need an adviser to force themselves to think; then they can make decisions and act on them with speed, self-confidence, and courage.

This is a reason, by the way, that the number two person in an organization often fails when promoted to the number one position. The top spot requires a decision maker. Strong decision makers often put somebody they trust into the number two spot as their adviser—and in that position the person is outstanding. But in the number one spot, the same person fails. He or she knows what the decision should be but cannot accept the responsibility of actually making it.

Other important questions to ask include, Do I perform well under stress or do I need a highly structured and predictable environment? Do I work best in a big organization or a small one? Few people work well in all kinds of environments. Again and again, I have seen people who were very successful in large organizations flounder miserably when they moved into smaller ones. And the reverse is equally true.

The conclusion bears repeating: do not try to change yourself—you are unlikely to succeed. But work hard to improve the way you perform. And try not to take on work you cannot perform or will only perform poorly.

What Are My Values?

To be able to manage yourself, you finally have to ask, What are my values? This is not a question of ethics. With respect to ethics, the rules are the same for everybody, and the test is a simple one. I call it the "mirror test."

In the early years of this century, the most highly respected diplomat of all the great powers was the German ambassador in London. He was clearly destined for great things—to become his country's foreign minister, at least, if not its federal chancellor. Yet in 1906 he abruptly resigned rather than preside over a dinner given by the diplomatic corps for Edward VII. The king was a notorious womanizer and made it clear what kind of dinner he wanted. The ambassador is reported to have said, "I refuse to see a pimp in the mirror in the morning when I shave."

That is the mirror test. Ethics requires that you ask yourself, What kind of person do I want to see in the mirror in the morning? What is ethical behavior in one kind of organization or situation is ethical behavior in another. But ethics are only part of a value system—especially of an organization's value system.

To work in an organization whose value system is unacceptable or incompatible with one's own condemns a person both to frustration and to nonperformance.

Consider the experience of a highly successful human resources executive whose company was acquired by a bigger organization. After the acquisition, she was promoted to do the kind of work she did best, which included selecting people for important positions. The executive deeply believed that a company should hire people for such positions from the outside only after exhausting all the inside possibilities. But her new company believed in first looking outside "to bring in fresh blood." There is something to be said for both approaches—in my experience, the proper one is to do some of both. They are, however, fundamentally incompatible—not as policies but as values. They bespeak different views of the relationship between organizations and people; different views of the responsibility of an organization to its people and their development; and different views of a person's most important contribution to an enterprise. After several years of frustration, the executive quit—at considerable financial loss. Her values and the values of the organization simply were not compatible.

Similarly, whether a pharmaceutical company tries to obtain results by making constant, small improvements or by achieving occasional, highly expensive, and risky "breakthroughs" is not primarily an economic question. The results of either strategy may be pretty much the same. At bottom, there is a conflict between a value system that sees the company's contribution in terms of helping physicians do better what they already do and a value system that is oriented toward making scientific discoveries. Whether a business should be run for short-term results or with a focus on the long term is likewise a question of values. Financial analysts believe that businesses can be run for both simultaneously. Successful businesspeople know better. To be sure, every company has to produce short-term results. But in any conflict between short-term results and long-term growth, each company will determine its own priority. This is not primarily a disagreement about economics. It is fundamentally a value conflict regarding the function of a business and the responsibility of management.

Value conflicts are not limited to business organizations. One of the fastest-growing pastoral churches in the United States measures success by the number of new parishioners. Its leadership believes that what matters is how many newcomers join the congregation. The Good Lord will then minister to their spiritual needs or at least to the needs of a sufficient percentage. Another pastoral, evangelical church believes that what matters is people's spiritual growth. The church eases out newcomers who join but do not enter into its spiritual life.

Again, this is not a matter of numbers. At first glance, it appears that the second church grows more slowly. But it retains a far larger proportion of newcomers than the first one does. Its growth, in other words, is more solid. This is also not a theological problem, or only secondarily so. It is a problem about values. In a public debate, one pastor argued, "Unless you first come to church, you will never find the gate to the Kingdom of Heaven."

"No," answered the other. "Until you first look for the gate to the Kingdom of Heaven, you don't belong in church."

Organizations, like people, have values. To be effective in an organization, a person's values must be compatible with the organization's values. They do not need to be the same, but they must be close enough to coexist. Otherwise, the person will not only be frustrated but also will not produce results.

A person's strengths and the way that person performs rarely conflict; the two are complementary. But there is sometimes a conflict between a person's values and his or her strengths. What one does well—even very well and successfully—may not fit with one's value system. In that case, the work may not appear to be worth devoting one's life to (or even a substantial portion thereof).

If I may, allow me to interject a personal note. Many years ago, I too had to decide between my values and what I was doing successfully. I was doing very well as a young investment banker in London in the mid-1930s, and the work clearly fit my strengths. Yet I did not see myself making a contribution as an asset manager. People, I realized, were what I valued, and I saw no point in being the richest man in the cemetery. I had no money and no other job prospects. Despite the continuing Depression, I quit—and it was the right thing to do. Values, in other words, are and should be the ultimate test.

Where Do I Belong?

A small number of people know very early where they belong. Mathematicians, musicians, and cooks, for instance, are usually mathematicians, musicians, and cooks by the time they are four or five years old. Physicians usually decide on their careers in their teens, if not earlier. But most people, especially highly gifted people, do not really know where they belong until they are well past their mid-twenties. By that time, however, they should know the answers to the three questions: What are my strengths? How do I perform? and, What are my values? And then they can and should decide where they belong.

Or rather, they should be able to decide where they do *not* belong. The person who has learned that he or she does not perform well in a big organization should have learned to say no to a position in one. The person who has learned that he or she is not a decision maker should have learned to say no to a decision-making assignment. A General Patton (who probably never learned this himself) should have learned to say no to an independent command.

Equally important, knowing the answer to these questions enables a person to say to an opportunity, an offer, or an assignment, "Yes, I will do that. But this is the way I should be doing it. This is the way it should be structured. This is the way the relationships should be. These are the kind of results you should expect from me, and in this time frame, because this is who I am."

Successful careers are not planned. They develop when people are prepared for opportunities because they know their strengths, their method of work, and their values. Knowing where one belongs can transform an ordinary person—hardworking and competent but otherwise mediocre—into an outstanding performer.

What Should I Contribute?

Throughout history, the great majority of people never had to ask the question, What should I contribute? They were told what to contribute, and their tasks were dictated either by the work itself—as it was for the peasant or artisan—or by a master or a mistress, as it was for domestic servants. And until very recently, it was taken for granted that most people were subordinates who did as they were told. Even in the 1950s and 1960s, the new knowledge workers (the so-called organization men) looked to their company's personnel department to plan their careers.

Then in the late 1960s, no one wanted to be told what to do any longer. Young men and women began to ask, What do *I* want to do? And what they heard was that the way to contribute was to "do your own thing." But this solution was as wrong as the organization men's had been. Very few of the people who believed that doing one's own thing would lead to contribution, self-fulfillment, and success achieved any of the three.

But still, there is no return to the old answer of doing what you are told or assigned to do. Knowledge workers in particular have to learn to ask a question that has not been asked before: What *should* my contribution be? To answer it, they must address three distinct elements: What does the situation require? Given my strengths, my way of performing, and my values, how can I make the greatest contribution to what needs to be done? And finally, What results have to be achieved to make a difference?

Consider the experience of a newly appointed hospital administrator. The hospital was big and prestigious, but it had been coasting on its reputation for 30 years. The new administrator decided that his contribution should be to establish a standard of excellence in one important area within two years. He chose to focus on the emergency room, which was big, visible, and sloppy. He decided that every patient who came into the ER had to be seen by a qualified nurse within 60 seconds. Within 12 months, the hospital's emergency room had become a model for all hospitals in the United States, and within another two years, the whole hospital had been transformed.

As this example suggests, it is rarely possible—or even particularly fruitful—to look too far ahead. A plan can usually cover no more than 18 months and still be reasonably clear and specific. So the question in most cases should be, Where and how can I achieve results that will make a difference within the next year and a half? The answer must balance several things. First, the results should be hard to achieve—they should require "stretching," to use the current buzzword. But also, they should be within reach. To aim at results that cannot be achieved—or that can be only under the most unlikely circumstances—is not being ambitious; it is being foolish. Second, the results should be meaningful. They should make a difference. Finally, results should be visible and, if at all possible, measurable. From this will come a course of action: what to do, where and how to start, and what goals and deadlines to set.

Responsibility for Relationships

Very few people work by themselves and achieve results by themselves—a few great artists, a few great scientists, a few great athletes. Most people work with others and are effective with other people. That is true whether they are members of an organization or independently employed. Managing yourself requires taking responsibility for relationships. This has two parts.

The first is to accept the fact that other people are as much individuals as you yourself are. They perversely insist on behaving like human beings. This means that they too have their strengths; they too have their ways of getting things done; they too have their values. To be effective, therefore, you have to know the strengths, the performance modes, and the values of your coworkers.

That sounds obvious, but few people pay attention to it. Typical is the person who was trained to write reports in his or her first assignment because that boss was a reader. Even if the next boss is a listener, the person goes on writing reports that, invariably, produce no results. Invariably the boss will think the employee is stupid, incompetent, and lazy, and he or she will fail. But that could have been avoided if the employee had only looked at the new boss and analyzed how this boss performs.

Bosses are neither a title on the organization chart nor a "function." They are individuals and are entitled to do their work in the way they do it best. It is incumbent on the people who work with them to observe them, to find out how they work, and to adapt themselves to what makes their bosses most effective. This, in fact, is the secret of "managing" the boss.

The same holds true for all your coworkers. Each works his or her way, not your way. And each is entitled to work in his or her way. What matters is whether they perform and what their values are. As for how they perform—each is likely to do it differently. The first secret of effectiveness is to understand the people you work with and depend on so that you can make use of their strengths, their ways of working, and their values. Working relationships are as much based on the people as they are on the work.

The second part of relationship responsibility is taking responsibility for communication.

Whenever I, or any other consultant, start to work with an organization, the first thing I hear about are all the personality conflicts. Most of these arise from the fact that people do not know what other people are doing and how they do their work, or what contribution the other people are concentrating on and what results they expect. And the reason they do not know is that they have not asked and therefore have not been told.

This failure to ask reflects human stupidity less than it reflects human history. Until recently, it was unnecessary to tell any of these things to anybody. In the medieval city, everyone in a district plied the same trade. In the countryside, everyone in a valley planted the same crop as soon as the frost was out of the ground. Even those few people who did things that were not "common" worked alone, so they did not have to tell anyone what they were doing.

Today the great majority of people work with others who have different tasks and responsibilities. The marketing vice president may have come out of sales and know everything about sales, but she knows nothing about the things she has never done—pricing, advertising, packaging, and the like. So the people who do these things must make sure that the marketing vice president understands what they are trying to do, why they are trying to do it, how they are going to do it, and what results to expect.

If the marketing vice president does not understand what these high-grade knowledge specialists are doing, it is primarily their fault, not hers. They have not educated her. Conversely, it is the marketing vice president's responsibility to make sure that all of her coworkers understand how she looks at marketing: what her goals are, how she works, and what she expects of herself and of each one of them.

Even people who understand the importance of taking responsibility for relationships often do not communicate sufficiently with their associates. They are afraid of being thought presumptuous or inquisitive or stupid. They are wrong. Whenever someone goes to his or her associates and says, "This is what I am good at. This is how I work. These are my values. This is the contribution I plan to concentrate on and the results I should be expected to deliver," the response is always, "This is most helpful. But why didn't you tell me earlier?"

And one gets the same reaction—without exception, in my experience—if one continues by asking, "And what do I need to know about your strengths, how you perform, your values, and your proposed contribution?" In fact, knowledge workers should request this of everyone with whom they work, whether as subordinate, superior, colleague, or team member. And again, whenever this is done, the reaction is always, "Thanks for asking me. But why didn't you ask me earlier?"

Organizations are no longer built on force but on trust. The existence of trust between people does not necessarily mean that they like one another. It means that they understand one another. Taking responsibility for relationships is therefore an absolute necessity. It is a duty. Whether one is a member of the organization, a consultant to it, a supplier, or a distributor, one owes that responsibility to all one's coworkers: those whose work one depends on as well as those who depend on one's own work.

The Second Half of Your Life

When work for most people meant manual labor, there was no need to worry about the second half of your life. You simply kept on doing what you had always done. And if you were lucky enough to survive 40 years of hard work in the mill or on the railroad, you were quite happy to spend the rest of your life doing nothing. Today, however, most work is knowledge work, and knowledge workers are not "finished" after 40 years on the job, they are merely bored.

We hear a great deal of talk about the midlife crisis of the executive. It is mostly boredom. At 45, most executives have reached the peak of their business careers, and they know it. After 20 years of doing very much the same kind of work, they are very good at their jobs. But they are not learning or contributing or deriving challenge and satisfaction from the job. And yet they are still likely to face another 20 if not 25 years of work. That is why managing oneself increasingly leads one to begin a second career.

There are three ways to develop a second career. The first is actually to start one. Often this takes nothing more than moving from one kind of organization to another: the divisional controller in a large corporation, for instance, becomes the controller of a medium-sized hospital. But there are also growing numbers of people who move into different lines of work altogether: the business executive or government official who enters the ministry at 45, for instance; or the midlevel manager who leaves corporate life after 20 years to attend law school and become a small-town attorney.

We will see many more second careers undertaken by people who have achieved modest success in their first jobs. Such people have substantial skills, and they know how to work. They need a community—the house is empty with the children gone—and they need income as well. But above all, they need challenge.

The second way to prepare for the second half of your life is to develop a parallel career. Many people who are very successful in their first careers stay in the work they have been doing, either on a full-time or a part-time or consulting basis. But in addition, they create a parallel job, usually in a nonprofit organization, that takes another ten hours of work a week. They might take over the administration of their church, for instance, or the presidency of the local Girl Scouts Council. They might run the battered women's shelter, work as a children's librarian for the local public library, sit on the school board, and so on.

Finally, there are the social entrepreneurs. These are usually people who have been very successful in their first careers. They love their work, but it no longer challenges them. In many cases they keep on doing what they have been doing all along but spend less and less of their time on it. They also start another activity, usually a nonprofit. My friend Bob Buford, for example, built a very successful television company that he still runs. But he has also founded and built a successful nonprofit organization that works with Protestant churches, and he is building another to teach social entrepreneurs how to manage their own nonprofit ventures while still running their original businesses.

People who manage the second half of their lives may always be a minority. The majority may "retire on the job" and count the years until their actual retirement. But it is this minority, the men and women who see a long working-life expectancy as an opportunity both for themselves and for society, who will become leaders and models.

There is one prerequisite for managing the second half of your life: you must begin long before you enter it. When it first became clear 30 years ago that working-life expectancies were lengthening very fast, many observers (including myself) believed that retired people would increasingly become volunteers for nonprofit institutions. That has not happened. If one does not begin to volunteer before one is 40 or so, one will not volunteer once past 60.

Similarly, all the social entrepreneurs I know began to work in their chosen second enterprise long before they reached their peak in their original business. Consider the example of a successful lawyer, the legal counsel to a large corporation, who has started a venture to establish model schools in his state. He began to do volunteer legal work for the schools when he was around 35. He was elected to the school board at age 40. At age 50, when he had amassed a fortune, he started his own enterprise to build and to run model schools. He is, however, still working nearly full-time as the lead counsel in the company he helped found as a young lawyer.

There is another reason to develop a second major interest, and to develop it early. No one can expect to live very long without experiencing a serious setback in his or her life or work. There is the competent engineer who is passed over for promotion at age 45. There is the competent college professor who realizes at age 42 that she will never get a professorship at a big university, even though she may be fully qualified for it. There are tragedies in one's family life: the breakup of one's marriage or the loss of a child. At such times, a second major interest—not just a hobby—may make all the difference. The engineer, for example, now knows that he has not been very successful in his job. But in his outside activity—as church treasurer, for example—he is a success. One's family may break up, but in that outside activity there is still a community.

In a society in which success has become so terribly important, having options will become increasingly vital. Historically, there was no such thing as "success." The overwhelming majority of people did not expect anything but to stay in their "proper station," as an old English prayer has it. The only mobility was downward mobility.

In a knowledge society, however, we expect everyone to be a success. This is clearly an impossibility. For a great many people, there is at best an absence of failure. Wherever there is success, there has to be failure. And then it is vitally important for the individual, and equally for the individual's family, to have an area in which he or she can contribute, make a difference, and be *somebody*. That means finding a second area—whether in a second career, a parallel career, or a social venture—that offers an opportunity for being a leader, for being respected, for being a success.

The challenges of managing oneself may seem obvious, if not elementary. And the answers may seem self-evident to the point of appearing naïve. But managing oneself requires new and unprecedented things from the individual, and especially from the knowledge worker. In effect, managing oneself demands that each knowledge worker think and behave like a chief executive officer. Further, the shift from manual workers who do as they are told to knowledge workers who have to manage themselves profoundly challenges social structure. Every existing society, even the most individualistic one, takes two things for granted, if only subconsciously: that organizations outlive workers, and that most people stay put.

But today the opposite is true. Knowledge workers outlive organizations, and they are mobile. The need to manage oneself is therefore creating a revolution in human affairs.

THE TWILIGHT ZONE OF DIVERSITY——

Linda Parrack Livingstone
Baylor University
Bradley Thomas Livingstone
Vanguard College Preparatory School

What does it mean to manage diversity? According to a study of human resource managers conducted by the Society for Human Resource Management and the Commerce Clearing House, managing diversity is "the management of an organization's culture and systems to ensure that all people are given the opportunity to contribute to the business goals of the company" (Nelton, 1995, p. 25). Thus, a diverse workforce takes into consideration not only race, gender, and age but also family status, sexual orientation, and disabilities (Nelton, 1995). Issues related to the management of workforce diversity have become increasingly important to organizations because the makeup of the workforce has changed dramatically in recent years and is expected to continue to change in the future. White males, once the majority in the workplace, are expected to comprise only 40% of the workforce by the year 2000, whereas minorities will comprise 25% of the workplace (Powell, 1993). The role of women in the labor force will also continue to grow. Between 1970 and 1989, the number of women in the work force increased from 31.5 million to 56 million (U.S. Bureau of the Census, 1991). By the year 2000, women will comprise 47% of the workforce (Powell, 1993). With the passage of the Americans with Disabilities Act, organizations are also beginning to realize the importance of employing individuals with disabilities. The unemployment rate among the estimated 43 million disabled people in the United States is more than 60% (Laabs, 1991). In spite of these statistics, many people do not have an appreciation for the value of diversity in society and the workplace, and they continue to hold stereotypical and discriminatory views of others.

This activity uses a clip from *Twilight Zone: The Movie* (Spielberg & Landis, 1983) as a catalyst for increasing awareness about diversity and about some of the false assumptions (e.g., about character, work ethic, intelligence, and economic status) associated with diversity that lead to stereotypical and

Authors' Note: An earlier version of this article was presented at the 1994 Organizational Behavior Teaching Conference. Requests for reprints and correspondence should be sent to Linda Parrack Livingstone, Department of Management, Hankamer School of Business, Baylor University, Waco, TX 76798-8006; (phone) 254-710-6243, (fax) 254-710-1093, (e-mail) linda_livingstone@baylor.edu.

discriminatory views. In addition, the activity explores the implications of discrimination for organizations and the means by which discrimination can be alleviated. Effective in any setting in which diversity and discrimination are concerns, this activity can stand alone as a good discussion of those issues or it can be used to introduce discussions of attitudes, stereotyping, perceptions, or legal issues related to discrimination. Although most effective in a 50-minute class period, the activity can be modified for shorter sessions.

The Activity

To conduct this activity, you will need a VCR and monitor; a chalkboard, flip chart; or overhead projector; and a copy of the video *Twilight Zone: The Movie*. The movie should be available at most video rental stores.

To initiate discussion, ask students to define discrimination, racism, and bigotry. After the students define these terms, it is helpful to have an overhead with formal definitions of each term to compare with the student definitions. (We use the following definitions of each term from the *American Heritage Dictionary* (1985): *discrimination*—the act of recognizing or drawing fine distinctions; *racism*—the notion that one's own ethnic stock is superior; and *bigotry*—the attitude, state of mind, or behavior characteristic of a person who is intolerant of those who differ.) Explain that many people who discriminate do so based on race, gender, physical abilities, and so forth, ignorant to the fact that these are characteristics beyond the individual's control.

Next, show the first segment of *Twilight Zone: The Movie*. This segment is approximately 18 minutes long. The movie is made up of three mini-movies, so it will be easy to identify the correct place to start and stop the movie. This segment is about a bigot who, while in the twilight zone, takes on the characteristics of three people against whom he has historically discriminated: a Jewish person, a person of color, and an Asian person. He has to live their lives and experience being the target of the discrimination that they historically have experienced. The movie always has a strong impact on students.

After watching the movie clip, begin a discussion by focusing on the students' reactions to the movie and then move into a more general discussion of the causes of discrimination, its implications for organizations, and how it can be alleviated. The following is a list of a number of questions that can be used to stimulate discussion after showing the video. Questions should, however, be designed to meet the specific goals of each instructor.

- What is your reaction to the man portrayed in the movie clip?
- What types of discrimination are revealed in the film?
- How might the types of discrimination revealed in the film be related to when the film was made?
- What other stereotypes could be included in a film such as this if it were made today?
- Why do people discriminate?
- What implications does discrimination have for organizations (in terms of performance and legal implications)?
- Why is diversity important to organizations?
- What can be done to increase awareness about diversity and to alleviate discrimination? (This can be discussed from the perspective of the individual, the organization, and society.)

Students can also be asked to share about a time when they have experienced discrimination. In the discussion, focus on how this made them feel and what their reaction was to the discrimination. The discussion of discrimination becomes more personal to the students and also helps them realize that we are all discriminated against for various reasons, thus enhancing their sensitivity to the concept of discrimination.

Student Learning and Reactions

After completion of this activity, students always comment on what an impact it had on them and how it helped them view diversity in a different light. When asked what they like most about the activity in a postactivity survey, students' typical responses include the following:

- The activity was informative and interesting.
- It should have an impact on racism in our school.
- It caught my attention about the seriousness of racism.
- I liked the self-involvement in the activity.

- That was one of the most interesting activities I've done all year.

When asked what insights they gained from the activity or how it changed their mind, typical student responses include the following:

- I've never thought of discrimination in that light.
- I never realized how destructive bigotry was.
- I saw what it was like to be in a group that is discriminated against.
- It forced me to accept my own prejudice.
- I learned that we all have a part in preventing racism.
- It emphasized the reality of racism.

It is our experience that this activity is very effective at heightening students' awareness of diversity and the problems associated with discrimination. Student reactions following the activity, as illustrated above, seem to bear this out. For further reading on the topic of diversity, see Cox (1991), Gentile (1994), Morrison and Crabtree (1992), Powell (1994), and Rice (1994).

References

American Heritage Dictionary (2nd ed.). (1985). Boston: Houghton Muffin.

Cox, T., Jr. (1991). The multicultural organization. *Academy of Management Executive, 5*(2), 34–47.

Gentile, M. C. (Ed.). (1994). *Differences that work: Organizational excellence through diversity.* Cambridge, MA: Harvard Business School Press.

Laabs, J. J. (1991, July). The golden arches provide golden opportunities. *Personnel Journal,* pp. 52–57.

Morrison, A. M., & Crabtree, K. M. (1992). *Developing diversity in organizations: A digest of selected literature.* Greensboro, NC: Center for Creative Leadership.

Nelton, S. (1995, June). Nurturing diversity. *Nation's Business,* pp. 25–27.

Powell, G. N. (1993). *Women and men in management* (2nd ed.). Newbury Park. CA: Sage.

Powell, G. N. (1994). *Gender and diversity in the workplace: Learning activities and exercises.* Thousand Oaks, CA: Sage.

Rice, F. (1994, August 8). How to make diversity pay. *Fortune,* pp. 78–86.

Spielberg, S., & Landis, J. (Producers). (1983). *Twilight zone: The movie* [Film]. (Available from Warner Brothers, Inc., 4000 Warner Blvd., Burbank, CA 91522)

U.S. Bureau of the Census. (1991). Statistical abstract of the United States. Washington, DC: U.S. Government Printing Office.

Unit 3

Unit Selections

Key Points to Consider

❖ What is the importance of status in organizations? Give some examples.

❖ Why is it important for people to cooperate with others to achieve their goals?

❖ Why is inter- and intragroup communication important?

❖ How can socialization in the group be accomplished?

❖ In what ways is leadership developed and implemented in an organization?

❖ What is the importance of teams in an organization?

 **Links** **www.dushkin.com/online/**

16. **IIR Library Site Map**
 http://socrates.berkeley.edu/~iir/sitemap.html
17. **Journal of Organizational Behavior: Aims and Scope**
 http://www.interscience.wiley.com/jpages/0894-3796 /aims.html
18. **Organizational Behavior and Human Decision Processes**
 http://www.apnet.com/www/journal/ob.htm
19. **Teams, Teambuilding, and Teamwork**
 http://www.organizedchange.com/teamhome.htm

These sites are annotated on pages 4 and 5.

Human beings are social animals. Since before the dawn of recorded history they have lived in groups, whether in small bands of hunter-gathers, in a nuclear family, or in urban centers. Psychologists, sociologists, and anthropologists have recognized this for years. Indeed, two of the five steps in Abraham Maslow's hierarchy of needs involves the group: belongingess and status. Maslow recognized this when he devoted 40 percent of his hierarchy of human needs to these concerns. They occur in importance right after the physiological needs of food, clothing, shelter, and safety. In other words, after people are reasonably certain that they will have enough food to eat, will not die from exposure to the elements, and will not be killed by a saber-toothed tiger or their fellow man, they want to have someone to talk to. Once that has been achieved, issues of status within the group become important. Nobody wants to be the proverbial "low man on the totem pole." Status is important within the group because it helps to define who and what people are and how they relate to others. The higher an individual's status, the more power, the more prestige, and the more control that person has over his or her own fate. People live in groups because it is necessary for self-protection, nurturing, propagation of the human race, and achievement. There are only a few things that individuals can accomplish strictly on their own. The help and assistance of others become necessary even in the accomplishment of simple tasks such as lifting a heavy object, and great accomplishments have become almost impossible without help. Leo Tolstoy wrote *War and Peace* on his own, but someone taught him how to read and write; Ludwig van Beethoven created some of the greatest music in the history of civilization, but he needed an orchestra to play it; and Albert Einstein developed the theory of relativity, but he had to stand on the shoulders of the giants who preceded him. Human beings need each other if they are going to fully achieve their potential.

Group dynamics, or the way groups work, has always been one of the major focuses of organizational behavior. People make up groups and, over time, will develop groups within larger groups or cliques. How people interact within the cliques and how those cliques interact within particular networks or groups is the subject of the report "Networks within Networks: Service Link Overlap, Organizational Cliques, and Network Effectiveness."

Communication is one of the chief activities that occurs in any group. A function of any group is educating its members on the expectations of the group. This is called the socialization process. Members become socialized when they become conversant with the group's rules, both written and unwritten. For groups to succeed and to continue, those norms must be adopted by new members. Often, the unwritten rules are more important to the individual's success in the group than the written

ones, and violating those rules can result in the termination of the individual's membership.

Leadership may be the least understood aspect of human behavior. Leaders are not limited to any particular group or social status. Winston Churchill was a member of the English aristocracy, and his distant cousin, Franklin Roosevelt, was a member of the American upper class. Both were successful leaders and great orators who became symbols of their country's struggle against Adolf Hitler, who was also a great orator, who symbolized his country's struggle in World War II, and who was a member of the Austrian middle class. Hitler wrote about his warped vision in *Mien Kampf,* and he was able to communicate it to the German people, who then adopted it as their own. Hitler possessed the qualities of great leadership in leading his evil crusade against mankind. Leadership requires more than just a high IQ, ability to communicate, and a vision. To be successful, it requires other skills, sometimes called emotional intelligence, as discussed by Daniel Goleman in "What Makes a Leader?"

Power is often the goal of individuals within an organization. The amount of power that a person has in an organization is often a direct indicator of the status of the individual in that organization. Power is essential for the individual to survive and prosper in the organization. One of the primary reasons for unionization in the United States has been an attempt on the part of the workers to equalize the power relationship between themselves and the corporation. A single worker, negotiating with General Motors or Ford, has very little power. But, if the entire workforce is negotiating for pay, benefits, and working conditions, then the balance of power has changed and the workers have more power at the bargaining table. A large organization, such as GM or Ford, will find it difficult to ignore the entire workforce if it wants to continue to produce cars.

In most organizations, individuals are placed in teams to work together to accomplish the goals of the organization. They must make decisions that are affected by a variety of factors, including the feedback that the team receives. Sometimes conflicts occur within well-intended groups. As Shari Caudron contends in her article, "Keeping Team Conflict Alive," conflict can be a good thing when it is managed effectively.

Intergroup behavior is yet another aspect of the social and group process. How groups interact with each other is as important as how individuals act with each other inside the group. There are many factors that can play a role in this, including status, culture, and experience, as shown in "Inter- and Intracultural Negotiations: U.S. and Japanese Negotiators."

The group process is highly important to the success of any organization. Successful social and group behaviors are the hallmarks of successful organizations that have been, are, and will be able to meet the coming challenges of the next millennium.

Social and Group Process

NETWORKS WITHIN NETWORKS: SERVICE LINK OVERLAP, ORGANIZATIONAL CLIQUES, AND NETWORK EFFECTIVENESS

KEITH G. PROVAN
University of Arizona

JULIANN G. SEBASTIN
University of Kentucky

This study explored the use of clique analysis for explaining network effectiveness. In data from networks of mental health agencies in three cities, effectiveness, measured as client outcomes, was negatively related to the integration of full networks. In contrast, effectiveness was positively related to integration among small cliques of agencies when these cliques had overlapping links through both reciprocated referrals and case coordination. The findings have implications for both theory and research, demonstrating the value of studying network clique structure and developing clique-based explanations of network behavior and outcomes.

Despite strong recent interest in the study of interorganizational networks (see, for example the special issue of the *Academy of Management Journal* published in April 1997), very little attention has been devoted by researchers to assessing the effectiveness of multifirm networks (as opposed to that of dyadic alliances and partnerships) or to explaining the network structural properties associated with effectiveness. Most of the research on networks in both profit and not-for-profit contexts has not addressed effectiveness explicitly, focusing instead on such issues as network formation, structure, and governance (Larson, 1992), or examining firm-level outcomes like power and influence (Marsden, 1990). Recent work has touted the presumed advantages of networks (Powell, 1990), but the lack of empirical evidence on why some networks might be more effective than others has limited the contribution of network scholars to both practice and the development of a network theory (Salancik, 1995).

For those studying networks of business firms, the lack of interest in network effectiveness is to some extent justified, since firms typically become network members to enhance their own individual performance. Nonetheless, there may be substantial network-level outcomes in the form of new product development, customers who are able to receive more comprehensive services, or the

This research was funded by a grant from the National Institute of Mental Health (R01-MH43783). We would like to thank Brint Milward and Michael Berren for their earlier contribution to the project. We would also like to express our appreciation to the three anonymous reviewers for their many helpful and insightful comments on previous versions.

generation of jobs in a region. In health and human services, agencies can and do join networks to lower operating costs and gain competitive advantage. However, network-level outcomes are especially salient because clients often have multiple needs, and many of the services typically provided in community-based settings are highly fragmented. This fragmentation is due in part to categorical funding streams that pay for one type of service but not another and in part to traditions of service organized around a single, narrowly defined problem or illness.

The prevailing assumption among researchers, planners, and practitioners in health care and human services about the dilemma of multiple client problems and service fragmentation across many providers has been that treatment outcomes will be enhanced when provider organizations form an integrated network of service delivery (Alter & Hage, 1993; Dill & Rochefort, 1989). Integration occurs when organizations that provide services to a particular client group work together to coordinate the services these clients need. Integration may be formal or informal and may involve a simple exchange of information about a client or a full-scale sharing of resources and programs. The presumed tie between the integration of services and client outcomes has been especially prevalent for noninstitutionalized clients with severe and chronic conditions, like mental illness, HIV, and drug abuse, and for the homeless, in part because of the breadth of likely services needed and in part because these clients are very likely to have difficulty navigating the intricacies of an unintegrated system on their own. Yet there has been scant empirical evidence that integrated networks are effective (Department of Health and Human Services, 1991).

The few studies that have examined the relationship between network structure and effectiveness have focused on networks as wholes (Lehman, Postrado, Roth, McNary, & Goldman, 1994; Provan & Milward, 1995). Although this approach seems intuitively obvious, concerns about network bounding (Doreian & Woodard, 1994; Laumann, Marsden, & Prensky, 1983)—about which organizations to include and which not to include in a study—can lead researchers to oversample, making findings and conclusions about the relationship between organizational integration and network outcomes somewhat misleading. Specifically, many organizations that might be included as network members may have little real impact on network outcomes. Network effectiveness may owe far less to integration across a network as a whole than to ties among a few organizations that provide the bulk of relationships and services to clients. Even in networks of for-profit business firms, network success is likely to be the result of effective interaction among small, overlapping subsets of firms, often linked through a lead firm (Lorenzoni & Ornati, 1988) or an administrative entity (Human & Provan, 1997), rather than the result of integration across the network as a whole.

Especially in health and human services, many organizations in a community may well be considered part of a broadly defined delivery system and connected to one another in a variety of ways. The reality of integrated services, however, is that outcomes for a particular clientele are likely to be more affected by the activities of a small group, or clique, of tightly connected providers than by the activities of the complete network. For instance, although homeless individuals may need many different services, their primary needs are for temporary shelter, food, physical health care, and perhaps mental health and substance abuse treatment. Even though the entire system of agencies that serves this population may not be highly integrated, client and network effectiveness may be quite high owing to close coordination among the small clique of agencies that provide these core services. The basic point applies to business firms as well: stronger cooperative ties can develop among small clusters of firms (Barley, Freeman, & Hybels, 1992), mutually dependent constellations of a few key firms (Lorenzoni & Ornati, 1988), and small-scale buyer-supplier networks (Larson, 1992) than can develop among the multiple firms that may compose a broadly defined network.

This study explored the relationship between network effectiveness and the structure of service integration within each of three health and human services networks. Since we measured effectiveness using client outcomes, we also assessed service integration at the client level, using referrals and case coordination rather than administrative-level links. The study is unique in that we attempted to explain network effectiveness, not by examining integration across full networks, but by examining the links, or interorganizational ties, among small subsets, or cliques, of provider agencies. We focused in particular on overlapping cliques whose members shared multiple ties with the members of one or more other cliques. A clique is a group of mutually connected actors within a larger network (Alba, 1982; Scott, 1991). Each member of a clique must be directly linked to every other member.

Because the approach was new, because the findings were from only three networks, and because much of the analysis was descriptive, this research was exploratory. The goal of the study was to examine and compare clique structure and overlap across the three networks, relate these findings to measures of network effectiveness, and discuss the implications for both network methods and the development of network theory.

METHODS

The study examined the mental health systems in Providence, Tucson, and Albuquerque, three U.S. cities that were selected in part because of their comparable size. Data were collected in 1991 and early 1992 from the individual health and human service agencies that composed the system at each site and from a sample of adult clients having severe and persistent mental illness and their families. The research was part of a larger study of the general relationship between system structure and client outcomes (Provan & Milward, 1995). The three cities displayed a range of effectiveness, measured in terms of client outcomes, from low, through medium, to high.[1]

At each site, we first identified the organizations that composed the full system of service delivery to adults with severe mental illness by meeting with key professionals and administrators involved with mental health services. These agencies were mostly small to midsized (under 100 employees), private, and not-for-profit, although some were large public agencies or their subunits in such areas as housing, vocational rehabilitation, and criminal justice. Once a full list of agencies had been developed for each site, questionnaires were sent out to the highest-level administrator at each agency who would be knowledgeable about services for adults with severe mental illness. The primary purpose of the questionnaire was to determine the interorganizational service links maintained by each agency with every other organization in the system.

The lead author and another researcher flew to each site and conducted personal interviews with administrators at each agency. The purpose of the interviews was to go over the questionnaire to ensure its full and accurate completion and to seek additional information about the agency and the system. Extensive follow-up procedures enabled us to collect nearly complete network data at each site. The number of organizations from which data were obtained and specific response rates were as follows: Providence ($N = 35$, 92%), Albuquerque ($N = 35$, 92%), and Tucson ($N = 32$, 97%).

The key survey data obtained from agencies concerned their ties to other organizations in the community through reciprocated referrals and case coordination for adults with severe mental illness. Clients who are able to move from one provider agency to another through intensive, service-level links like reciprocated referrals and case coordination enhance the prospect that their multiple problems will be addressed in a truly integrated fashion. Many of the agencies in the networks were also linked through board ties, information sharing, planning, and the like, but these administrative links need not involve clients. It was our intent to examine only those links that would involve the direct provision of client services and then to relate these to client-level outcomes.

Data were collected for both referrals sent and received, and those data were then combined into a single measure of reciprocated referrals. We used both reciprocated referrals and case coordination because both require considerable interorganizational involvement and

commitment to client outcomes. When referrals are reciprocated, it means that agencies develop an ongoing pattern of interaction with one another through the exchange of clients. Reciprocated referral flows are likely to generate considerable knowledge among the staffs of participating agencies concerning client needs and approaches to treatment. Simple nonreciprocated referrals reflect what Alter and Hage (1993: 97) discussed as sequential task integration and do not necessarily provide the level of coordination required to achieve favorable outcomes. With case coordination, case workers actively manage the treatment of clients across agencies to ensure that all needed services are obtained and client progress is monitored. In Alter and Hage's (1993) model, task integration through reciprocated referrals and case coordination is reciprocal and often collective, so the two highest levels of integration are achieved.

Since no interaction data were available from agency records, we confirmed links in two ways to ensure validity and reliability. First, whenever possible, at least two respondents per agency were asked to participate in completing the survey. Discrepancies were discussed and resolved at the time of the interviews. Second, only data on confirmed links were used in the actual data analysis (Marsden, 1990). Thus, for instance, we only considered agency A to have case coordination with agency B if each agency separately indicated that it had such a link with the other. For reciprocated referrals, not only did each type of referral link have to be confirmed, but agencies A and B had to exchange clients with each other through *both* referrals sent and referrals received. Confirmed data on each of the two types of referrals and the single measure of case coordination were dichotomously coded (0 = no link, 1 = a link) and organized into three separate matrixes, one for each type of link. A reciprocated referral matrix was then constructed from the two separate confirmed referral matrixes (referrals sent and referrals received). We then analyzed the two final matrixes, reflecting organizational link data on reciprocated referrals and case coordination, using UCINET IV (Borgatti, Everett, & Freeman, 1992) network analysis software and a plotting subroutine called Krackplot (Krackhardt, Lundberg, & O'Rourke, 1993).

Data on client outcomes were obtained from 5 percent samples of severely mentally ill clients and their families drawn in each city. This procedure resulted in samples of 64 clients in Tucson, 59 in Albuquerque, and 62 in Providence. Clients were selected randomly from a coded list provided by the core mental health agency at each site.[2] Each of these agencies was responsible for de-

---

[1] A fourth site, Akron, was part of the larger study but was not included in the present research because it had recently undergone a major system overhaul that appeared to have had a negative impact on outcomes.

[2] The process of random selection minimized the risk that a larger proportion of more (or less) severely ill clients would be sampled at any one site. Although it is possible that the overall level of illness at one site might have been higher than it was at the others, data we were able to collect at two sites on client functioning (based on the Global Assessment of Functioning Scale) gave no indication that this was the case.

TABLE 1

Factors Scores of Client Outcome Data for Each Site[a]

Perspective[b]	Tucson	Albuquerque	Providence
Client: Quality of life/ satisfaction	-.18	-.17	.43
Client: Psychiatric/ medical status	-.29	.05	.56
Family	-.10	.06	.26
Mean factor score	-.19	-.02	.42

[a]The numbers of clients sampled at each site were as follows: Tucson, 64; Albuquerque, 59; Providence, 62.

[b]Outcome scores in Providence were significantly higher ($p < .05$) for all three perspectives than they were in either Tucson or Albuquerque. Outcomes in Albuquerque were significantly higher ($p < .05$) for client psychiatric/medical status than in Tucson.

livering and coordinating care and services to all or most of the publicly funded adult clients with severe mental illness in their respective communities. Clients who were institutionalized or unstable at the time of data collection were not interviewed.

Clients and their families (when available) were interviewed by people trained by a clinical psychologist who was a member of the research team. The interviews were structured and involved recording five-point Likert-scale responses to questions concerning the clients' quality of life, adjustment, satisfaction with services, and psychopathology. We selected the interview items from several standard assessment instruments, most notably, the Colorado Client Assessment Record and the New York Functioning Scale, and modified them to fit the study. Other assessment instruments were considered, and many of the items we used were very similar to items from those instruments. However, other aspects of these alternative instruments were not appropriate for our work (too many questions, predominant focus on a less severely ill population, and so forth). In pretests conducted by Bootzin, Berren, Figueredo, and Sechrest (1989) as part of an earlier project, both methods and measures were found to be reliable and valid.

Once data were collected, results from all sites were pooled and factor analyses (with "varimax" rotation) were conducted on the items, first for the client data, then for families. The purpose of the factor analysis was to reduce the data, if possible, so that a single broad measure of effectiveness might be obtained. For the client data, this analysis produced two relatively distinct factors, one related to quality of life and one to psychiatric/medical status, collectively explaining 48 percent of the total variance in client scores. A single factor emerged from the family perspective data, reflecting both client

quality of life and psychiatric/medical status and accounting for 42 percent of total variance.

Factor scores were then calculated for each of the three factors, and these scores were then broken down by site (see Table 1). Despite some differences, the overall patterns of results within each system were similar. That is, the three factor scores for Tucson were the lowest of the four sites initially studied, the scores for Providence were consistently highest, and the scores for Albuquerque were generally in the middle. We then averaged the three factor scores generated for each site to produce a single mean factor score for that site, reflecting the overall effectiveness of each system regarding client outcomes. In terms of this final outcome figure, Providence was a particularly effective system (achieving a positive mean factor score), Tucson was an ineffective system (a negative score), and Albuquerque was in the middle (a neutral score). Outcome scores were found to be statistically unrelated to differences in client age, gender, race, and ethnicity.

ANALYSIS AND RESULTS

As a first step in the analysis, the overall level of integration at each site through each of the two types of links was computed and expressed as a percentage of the maximum possible number of links of each type at each site ($n[n - 1]$). These network density scores (Scott, 1991) based on dyadic links indicated that the most effective site, Providence, had the lowest network-wide integration measured as both reciprocated referrals (10.1%) and case coordination (6.1%), and that Tucson, the least effective site, had the highest scores (13.3% and 9.3%, respectively). Albuquerque, with moderate effectiveness, fell in the middle on integration, with density scores of 12.9 percent for referrals and 6.7 percent for case coordination. The differences across sites were statistically significant at the .05 level according to Pearson chi-square tests for both referrals ($\chi^2 = 6.57$) and case coordination ($\chi^2 = 9.04$). These results appear to shed considerable doubt on the generally held belief that integrated networks of service delivery are more effective than less integrated systems (Department of Health and Human Services, 1991; Dill & Rochefort, 1989). However, it was our belief that the underlying argument for service integration was not incorrect—only its implicit focus on dyadic, nonoverlapping links across an entire network.

Before we could begin the analysis of clique overlap, a key issue to resolve concerned the size of cliques. Since no research existed to guide a decision, we simply examined the data and based our decision on findings from the three networks. A major assumption of the research was that greater and more intensive integration within and across cliques would be more effective than less integration. Thus, the first phase of the clique analysis was simply to determine the largest clique size that could be compared across the three systems. Determining this involved generating a list of the cliques in each network, based first on reciprocated referral links and then on case coordination links.

Using UCINET software (Borgatti et al., 1992), we analyzed the agency data for each site to determine which agencies were directly connected to which others, first in groups/cliques of three agencies, then four, and so on until the data yielded no cliques of a given size at each site. Using this approach, we found that all three sites could be compared using a minimum set size of four or more agencies per clique. We found four-member cliques at all three sites for both types of links, although Albuquerque (for referrals only) and Tucson (for case coordination only) had some cliques of five agencies.

The results of the clique analysis are reported in Table 2. The analysis consisted of first calculating both the number of cliques with four or more agencies each network had and the total number of agencies in the network involved in one or more of these cliques. We then calculated the overlap across cliques and across types of service links. Each approach is explained below.

The top half of Table 2 is simply a count of the number of cliques and the agencies involved in cliques in each network, with no consideration of overlap. One obvious finding is that the most effective site, Providence had fewer cliques (especially reciprocated referral cliques) and fewer agencies involved in cliques than either Tucson or Albuquerque, despite roughly similar city sizes and similar numbers of agencies in the cities' networks. This finding suggests that the coordination of clients and their needs may be most effective when only a small number of closely connected subgroups of agencies are involved. The results are mixed and not especially strong, however, and do not consider integration across cliques, or what we refer to as clique overlap.

Clique overlap was calculated in several ways. We first examined, for each network, the extent to which those agencies in a particular type of clique (either reciprocated referrals or case coordination) appeared in at least half the cliques of that type. It might be that a network would have eight case coordination cliques of four agencies each, for example, but each of these cliques might contain agencies that were members of few or none of the other seven case coordination cliques. Such low overlap would mean that the members of one clique would interact among themselves but not across cliques, thus depriving clients who might need the services of agencies in other cliques of the benefits of a strongly integrated service system. In contrast, in a system with high clique overlap, many clique members would also be members of other cliques, thus providing a highly integrated core of provider agencies spanning multiple cliques.

Findings for this part of the clique overlap analysis were not consistent across the sites, making interpretation difficult. Providence, the most effective system for client outcomes, had the highest clique overlap for reciprocated referrals (four, or 57.1 percent, of the seven agencies involved in the community's four referral cliques were members of at least half of those referral cliques). However, clique overlap in Tucson (27.3%), the least effective site, was more than twice as high as in Albuquerque (13.3%). Results for case coordination were even more puzzling, with Tucson having the highest level of clique overlap: 71.4 percent of clique members were involved in at least half the cliques, whereas the score was 50 percent for both the other two sites.

TABLE 2

Clique Characteristics and Client Outcomes: Minimum Set Size of Four[a]

Clique Characteristics	Tucson	Albuquerque	Providence
Number of cliques			
Reciprocated referrals	14 cliques	13 cliques	4 cliques
Case coordination	3 cliques	5 cliques	3 cliques
Number of agencies in cliques,			
Reciprocated referrals	11 agencies	15 agencies	7 agencies
Case coordination	7 agencies	8 agencies	6 agencies
Clique overlap[b]			
Reciprocated referrals	3/11 = 27.3%	2/15 = 13.3%	4/7 = 57.1%
Case coordination	5/7 = 71.4%	4/8 = 50%	3/6 = 50%
Service link overlap			
Multiplexity[c]	2/7 = 28.6%	6/8 = 75%	5/6 = 83.3%
Identical overlap[d]	0/3 = 0%	1/5 = 20%	2/3 = 66.7%

[a]Client outcomes were the lowest in Tucson and the highest in Providence, with Albuquerque in the middle.

[b]Clique overlap was the number of agencies in at least half the cliques of a particular type expressed as a percentage of the total number of agencies in that clique type.

[c]Service link overlap/multiplexity was the percentage of agencies in case coordination cliques that were also members of reciprocated referral cliques.

[d]Identical overlap was the percentage of case coordination cliques exactly matching reciprocated referral cliques.

FIGURE 1
Reciprocated Referral and Case Coordination Links in Providence

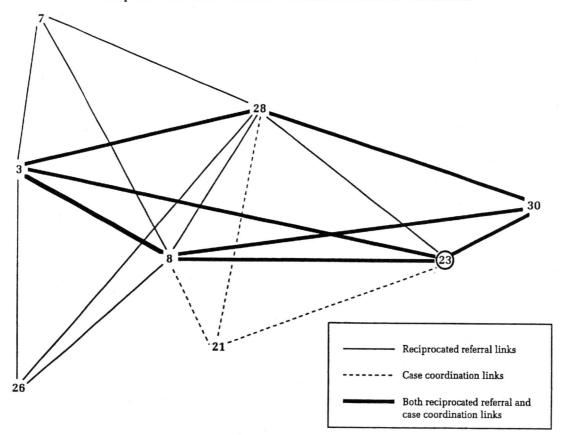

Legend:
——————— Reciprocated referral links

- - - - - - - Case coordination links

━━━━━━━ Both reciprocated referral and
case coordination links

Results become clearer, however, when we examined service link overlap, or multiplicity. Rather than focusing on the extent to which agencies in one clique were also members of other cliques of the same type (overlap across case coordination cliques, for instance), this second measure reflected overlap in service link type. That is, the focus was on examining the extent to which agencies in a case coordination clique were also members of a reciprocated referral clique. Systems with substantial service link overlap would have a core group of agencies that were heavily integrated and involved with one another in multiple ways that were critical for the overall well-being and satisfaction of their clients.

Table 2 indicates that the site with the best client outcomes, Providence, also had the highest level of service link overlap. Specifically, in Providence five of the six agencies (83.3%) involved in the city's three case coordination cliques were also members of reciprocated referral cliques. Tucson, the low-outcome site, had little overlap, with only two of seven (28.6%) members of case coordination cliques also belonging to reciprocated referral cliques. Albuquerque, with moderate client outcomes, was in-between, although its figures were quite close to those of Providence (six of eight, or 75 percent service link overlap).

An alternative way of computing service link overlap resulted in further evidence of the relationship between network clique structure and client outcomes. For this measure, overlap in clique membership for the two types of service links had to be identical. Results indicated that in Providence, two of the three case coordination cliques consisted of exactly the same agencies as the reciprocated referral cliques. This pattern of identical overlap in cliques based on different types of links occurred only once in Albuquerque (20%), the site with moderate outcomes, and not at all in Tucson, the least effective site.[3]

The clique data for each site were displayed graphically as a final way of examining the findings regarding clique structure and overlap. Using the network-plotting subroutine Krackplot (Krackhardt et al., 1993) as a starting point, we developed plots of all clique members at each site. Figures 1, 2, and 3 present these plots. Included are all members of each reciprocated referral clique (thin solid lines) and each case coordination clique (dotted lines). Clique overlap, in which both types of links occur among clique members, is indicated by a thick solid line connecting each pair of agencies within a clique for which overlap exists.

The plots make it very clear that the overlap structures of cliques at each site are quite different. Link overlap among clique members in Providence (Figure 1) was sub-

---

[3]The analysis of service link overlap was also conducted for cliques having a minimum set size of three agencies. Results were consistent with those reported for cliques of four or more agencies, although the differences across sites were not as strong.

FIGURE 2
Reciprocated Referral and Case Coordination Links in Albuquerque

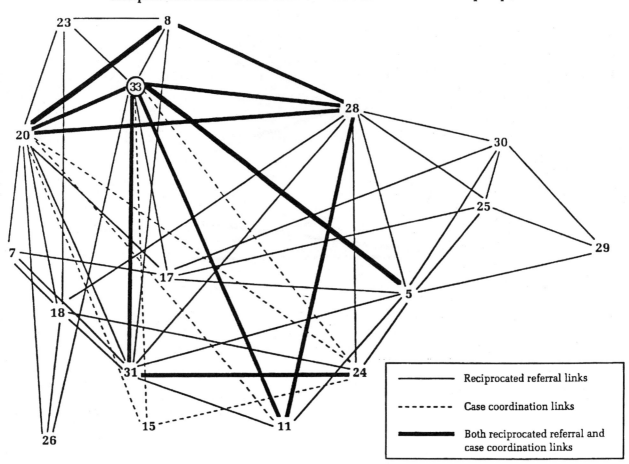

Reciprocated referral links

Case coordination links

Both reciprocated referral and case coordination links

stantial, with five of the eight clique-member agencies included in both types of cliques (referrals and case coordination). Albuquerque (Figure 2) had many (seven) overlapping agencies, but most (ten) of the members of one type of clique did not overlap with the other type. Finally, although Tucson (Figure 3), the least effective site, had many agencies involved in cliques of each type, only two agencies (a single dyad, not a four-member clique) in one of the cliques shared both reciprocated referral and case coordination links. It is also interesting to note that the core mental health agency in Tucson (Figure 3, agency number 1, circled) had no reciprocated referral ties to any other agencies involved in the city's clique structure. This situation is in contrast to the situations in Providence and Albuquerque, where the core mental health agencies (Figure 1, agency 23, and Figure 2, agency 33, respectively) maintained both types of links to many of the other agencies involved in the cliques. Thus, overlap in service links across cliques appears to be important in a general way for explaining system effectiveness, but the specific composition of these overlapping cliques also seems to matter, particularly when the cliques involve agencies, like the core mental health agencies, that may be critical to overall network success.[4]

DISCUSSION AND CONCLUSIONS

The findings of this study offer preliminary evidence that network effectiveness can be explained by intensive integration through network cliques but that integration across a full network is likely to be a poor predictor of network effectiveness. Our data on systems of service delivery for severely mentally ill clients generally supported the idea that differences in client outcomes across

[4]Chi-square analyses revealed few or no statistically significant differences when we compared clique overlap across sites. Specifically, the Pearson chi-square statistic for overlap through referrals was 4.68 (p. 10), and it was 0.87 (n.s.) for overlap through case coordination. For the two measures of service link overlap, chi-squares were 5.04 (p. 10) for multiplexity and 3.61 (n.s.) for identical overlap. The weakness of these statistical results is not surprising, since there were relatively few cliques and only three networks. These small numbers represent a general problem for research on cliques, which will typically be few in number in all but the largest networks. In addition, since collecting reliable link and outcome data on multiple networks and getting high response rates is extremely time consuming and costly, most network studies will inevitably suffer from problems of small sample size. Since this research was exploratory, we based our interpretations on the magnitude of the differences in overlaps across sites, particularly for the two measures of service link overlap, and on the linear relationship between these clique overlap measures and effectiveness scores. The findings were supported by our clique plots shown in Figures 1–3.

FIGURE 3
Reciprocated Referral and Case Coordination Links in Tucson

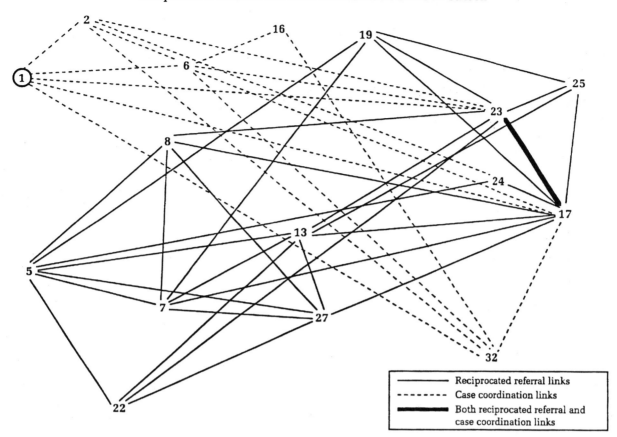

	Reciprocated referral links
	Case coordination links
	Both reciprocated referral and case coordination links

systems could be explained reasonably well by focusing on the overlap among cliques of provider agencies through both reciprocated referrals and case coordination.

Although it is risky to generalize about findings from a sample of only three networks in a single area of health and human services, the results of this exploratory study are suggestive for the study of networks in a number of ways. Most notably, the study points to the need to consider networks and network structure in a more microanalytic way than has been done previously. Integration across an entire network of organizations, whether in the health care, manufacturing, or service sectors, is difficult to achieve and is probably not a very efficient way of organizing. Nonetheless, one should not draw the conclusion that integration is undesirable. Rather, if networks are to perform well, especially regarding client outcomes, integration must occur, but at the clique, or subnetwork, level. To be most effective, clique integration must be intensive, involving multiple and overlapping links both within and across the organizations that compose the core of a network. When this sort of intensive, multiplex integration occurs, clique members learn a great deal about each other, minimizing their transaction costs and establishing working relationships built on norms of cooperation and trust (Larson, 1992; Uzzi, 1997). Other organiza-

tions that are more loosely linked to these cliques can also benefit, contributing to the effectiveness of the entire network.

The logic of clique integration is also likely to hold in networks outside of health and human services. For instance, R&D links in biotechnology networks (Barley et al., 1992; Powell, Koput, & Smith-Doerr, 1996) appear to be most prevalent among clusters or cliques of firms working on a common problem. When cliques overlap, the ideas developed in one cluster of firms can be built on by others, and learning can be disseminated effectively throughout a network, enhancing product development. Full-scale integration among the scores of firms that compose the complete network is neither needed nor desirable. Exactly what sizes and kinds of cliques and what types of clique overlap are needed to maximize effectiveness will depend on the unique characteristics of each type of network studied, including which activities are critical to achieving network-level outcomes.

The study also points to the need to examine and assess network effectiveness at the level of the client or customer. Both case coordination and reciprocated referrals are important mechanisms by which health and human service agencies can integrate their activities to have a direct impact on client outcomes. Unlike administrative links through governing boards or top managers involving financial, managerial, or planning issues, service links involve the professional staff members who actually serve clients daily (Bolland & Wilson, 1994). Thus, if integration among providers is to affect client outcomes, the impact is likely to be greatest when integrative efforts are through links that are meaningful to clients.

The findings also have implications for interorganizational and network theory. Salancik (1995) recently expressed the concern of many organization theorists that the study of networks has primarily been an exercise in analysis and methods. He suggested that "a network theory of organization should propose how structures of interactions enable coordinated interaction to achieve collective and individual interests" (Salancik, 1995: 348). This study introduces an alternative method for network analysis and, rather than simply demonstrating that this method can be utilized, it makes a contribution to building network theory by examining and explaining how one unique aspect of network structure, overlapping cliques, might promote the interests of network members and the clients they serve. The findings clearly build on Granovetter's (1973) theory of weak ties by demonstrating that, at least in certain contexts, strong, multiplex, reciprocal ties among small network subgroups can be particularly effective. This conclusion has significant implications for network governance, implying that network administrative organizations or lead firms might focus on building and maintaining intensive integration among cliques of key member firms, who will then have weaker ties to other members, rather than on attempting to loosely integrate entire networks.

There are clearly some shortcomings of the research. Most obvious is the small sample size, which is, unfortunately, a common problem when the unit of analysis is an organizational network. Other problems are perhaps less obvious. For instance, the clients we evaluated were served by the systems being studied, but we cannot be certain that the particular clients sampled were actually served by the specific agencies involved in the cliques, except for the core mental health agency in each system. It also may be that client outcomes, although related to clique overlap, could be better explained by other variables not considered here, like the mix of services within the cliques, commitment of key staff, or the use of certain treatment methods. Finally, despite our efforts to the contrary, it is certainly possible that the client outcome measures used, which were tied to individuals, did not accurately reflect network effectiveness at each site, especially in view of the difficulty in accurately assessing mental health care.

To summarize, the results of this study point to several suggestions for future research and theory development. First, network researchers should consider the role of strongly connected and overlapping cliques of organizations, rather than focusing solely on full network integration, particularly when attempting to explain network-level outcomes, or effectiveness. Second, it is

critical in such analyses to be certain that the types of interorganizational links used to construct cliques have relevance for the level at which network outcomes are being measured. Thus, for instance, it would probably be inappropriate to examine board interlocks and CEO friendship ties among cliques of manufacturing firms to explain network outcomes regarding the level of new product development achieved by the R&D staffs of these firms. For health and human service agencies like those studied here, client outcomes will be most affected by multiplex, overlapping links at the client level, rather than by broader, organization-level integration. Finally, it seems important to measure and analyze clique overlap using complementary linkage mechanisms, like the referral and case coordination links studied here. If clique overlap is to have an impact on effectiveness, it is likely to be through multiple links that build and reinforce competencies rather than through links that only contribute superficially to organizational outcomes. In general, research on networks should shift from a concern with firm-level outcomes to a concern with network effectiveness. At the same time, the analysis of networks needs to become more narrowly focused, especially when broad, poorly specified structural issues like integration are considered.

REFERENCES

Alba, R. D. 1982. Taking stock of network analysis: A decade's results. In S. B. Bacharach (Ed.), *Research in the sociology of organizations,* vol. 1: 39-74. Greenwich, CT: JAI Press.

Alter, C., & Hage, J. 1993. *Organizations working together*. Newbury Park, CA: Sage.

Barley, S., Freeman, J., & Hybels, R. 1992. Strategic alliances in commercial biotechnology. In N. Nohria & R. Eccles (Eds.), *Networks and organizations: Structure, form, and action:* 311-347. Boston: Harvard Business School Press.

Bolland, J. M., & Wilson, J. V. 1994. Three faces of integrative coordination: A model of interorganizational relations in community-based health and human services. *Health Services Research,* 29: 341-366.

Bootzin, R. R., Berren, M., Figueredo, A. J., & Sechrest, L. 1989. *Evaluation of the Arizona Pilot Project on capitation financing for the severely mentally ill*. Phoenix: Arizona Psychological Association.

Borgatti, S. P., Everett, M. G., & Freeman, L. C. 1992. *UCINET IV*. Columbia, SC: Analytic Technologies.

Department of Health and Human Services. 1991. *Services integration: A twenty year retrospective*. Washington, DC: Office of the Inspector General.

Dill, A., & Rochefort, D. A. 1989. Coordination, continuity, and centralized control: A policy perspective on service strategies for the chronic mentally ill. *Journal of Social Issues,* 45(3): 145-159.

Doreian, P., & Woodard, K. L. 1994. Defining and locating cores and boundaries of social networks. *Social Networks,* 16: 267-293.

Granovetter, M. S. 1973. The strength of weak ties. *American Journal of Sociology,* 78: 1360-1380.

Human, S. E., & Provan, K. G. 1997. An emergent theory of structure and outcomes in small-firm strategic manufacturing networks. *Academy of Management Journal,* 40: 368-403.

Krackhardt, D., Lundberg, M., & O'Rourke, L. 1993. Krackplot: A picture's worth a thousand words. *Connections,* 16(1 & 2): 37-47.

Larson, A. 1992. Network dyads in entrepreneurial settings: A study of the governance of exchange processes. *Administrative Science Quarterly,* 37: 76-104.

Laumann, E. O., Marsden, P. V., & Prensky, D. 1983. The boundary specification problem in network analysis. In R. S. Burt & M. J.

Minor (Eds.), *Applied network analysis: Structural methodology for empirical social research:* 18-34. Beverly Hills, CA: Sage.

Lehman, A. F., Postrado, L. T., Roth, D., McNary, S. W., & Goldman, H. H. 1994. Continuity of care and client outcomes in the Robert Wood Johnson Foundation program on chronic mental illness. *Milbank Memorial Quarterly,* 72: 105-122.

Lorenzoni, G., & Ornati, O. A. 1988. Constellations of firms and new ventures. *Journal of Business Venturing,* 3: 41-57.

Marsden, P. V. 1990. Network data and measurement. In W. R. Scott (Ed.), *Annual review of sociology,* vol. 16: 435-463. Palo Alto, CA: Annual Reviews.

Powell, W. W. 1990. Neither market nor hierarchy: Network forms of organization. In B. M. Staw & L. L. Cummings (Eds.), *Research in organizational behavior,* vol. 12: 295-236. Greenwich, CT: JAI Press.

Powell, W. W., Koput, K. W., & Smith-Doerr, L. 1996. Interorganizational collaboration and the locus of innovation: Networks of learning in biotechnology. *Administrative Science Quarterly,* 41: 116-145.

Provan, K. G., & Milward, H. B. 1995. A preliminary theory of interorganizational network effectiveness: A comparative study of four community mental health systems. *Administrative Science Quarterly,* 40: 1-33.

Salancik, G. R. 1995. Wanted: A good network theory of organization. *Administrative Science Quarterly,* 40: 345-349.

Scott, J. 1991. *Social network analysis: A handbook.* London: Sage.

Uzzi, B. 1997. Social structure and competition in interfirm networks: The paradox of embeddedness. *Administrative Science Quarterly,* 42: 35-67.

Keith G. Provan is a professor in the School of Public Administration and Policy, which is part of the College of Business and Public Administration at the University of Arizona. He also holds a joint appointment with the Department of Management and Policy. Professor Provan received his Ph.D. from the State University of New York at Buffalo. His primary research interests are in the areas of interorganizational and network relationships. Recent empirical work in these areas has focused on health care systems and small-firm manufacturing networks.

Juliann G. Sebastian is an associate professor and the assistant dean for advanced practice at the University of Kentucky College of Nursing. She received her Ph.D. in management from the University of Kentucky College of Business and Economics. Her research interests include understanding the structure and behavior of organizational systems such as health care under imperfect market conditions and, in particular, interorganizational dynamics within a network context.

STRATEGY

Managing Staff Relationships

Traditionally, the chief role of human resources has been to perform internally focused administrative functions that seemingly connect little to an organization's larger purpose—to serve its external customers. Even today, HR managers and their staffs often function in a tactical capacity, left out of senior management's decision-making loop. Many times, new company directions and HR "initiatives" develop in management meetings without the presence of a single HR manager.

How times have changed. In the era of reengineering, more companies than ever before are looking to human resources for help with change management, acquisitions, competency models and development of new ideas for relating to customer service and company strategy. While these new roles have placed new expectations and pressures on the HR department, they have also opened new doors of opportunity. With senior management inviting HR to become a major player in the overall management process, HR's potential influence in business has significantly grown, but has so far been largely unrealized.

What's been missing has been the willingness of HR to connect with customer results. How can HR executives become strategic coaches for organizational effectiveness without such connections, especially measurable ones? Today, everyone in a company manages points of customer contact. To take its rightful place in this emerging paradigm, HR must cease identifying itself as an "internal" function.

How can HR managers and their departments convert not only their thinking and self-image but their day-to-day operations and responsibilities? How can they link a traditionally "inside" focus with external forces and demands? One approach that managers in other arenas have begun practicing suggests an answer. Designed to facilitate more effective interaction within the workplace and beyond, relationship management (RM) provides a guide for systematically orchestrating business relationships in order to produce win-win outcomes for all involved. While many sales and marketing departments utilize it to develop new business, RM also offers HR departments a blueprint for acclimating themselves to the future.

A commonly held view is that relationships develop on their own, for good or ill. We either luck out with the right "chemistry" or we don't. More and more companies are hoping, however, that such assumptions are simply not true. With so many excellent companies competing against each other these days, they recognize that the defining difference is frequently "customer intimacy." Thus, millions of training dollars are spent each year on customer service seminars, teamwork programs and job selection criteria, all in an effort to discover the gateway to such a difference.

MEASUREMENT

These limited approaches, however, will never be enough. What's needed are systematic, periodic measurements of business relationships to identify which provide the highest return on time and resource investments. Companies may then literally "rate" their customers on a best-to-least profitable scale, thereafter targeting their best efforts toward those customers on the upper end of the scale.

SHARED VALUES

Likewise, companies are deciding they must reach beyond conventional marketing techniques (such as advertising, price wars and public relations stunts) and concentrate instead on values shared with their customers. In this way, they solidify a trust and customer dialogue that extends beyond price alone. Think Home Depot, Jeep, Disney, Federal Express: Such enormously successful products and services demonstrate the potency of relationship marketing and management, instilling a sustainable competitive advantage in their customer base.

COMMITMENT

To succeed in such an effort, however, managers, workers, customers and vendors must all be deeply committed to the company's mission and work together on the same page. Fortunately for HR, this might be the area of their greatest advantage. As possibly the most visible and pivotal internal function in the organization, HR managers have the power to see to it that a relationship management process succeeds or fails. With everyone in the company watching, HR's actions can provide the model, vision, impetus and inspiration for sound relationship management practices. It also can arrange direct actions, such as sponsoring intensive training sessions, to ensure that the company has a fighting chance to achieve its goals. If, however it acts as if RM doesn't matter, everyone else may act that way too.

Relationship management succeeds best when concrete RM skills are put into action. Moreover, such skills can be periodically measured, improved, polished—all but perfected. Are you already an effective business relationship manager? Perhaps, but most likely, even if you're among the best, there may be ways you could improve your own skills further and utilize them in even more effective ways for the good of the company as a whole, as well as the HR department and your own career. Take a look here at five key relationship management skills and decide for yourself where you fit in:

1 POSITIONING. Communicate your credible role as a major force in the organization. You want everyone within earshot to understand how they can help. At meetings, for example, grab attention with a powerful "impact message," conveying clearly and concisely the high value you and your team bring to the company table.

Try this, for example: "My name is Sue Withers, and I'm director of human resources. We are responsible for organizational effectiveness by educating company associates to best practices in relationship management and by conducting training and mentoring." Wow! A tad more impressive than "I'm in personnel, call anytime," wouldn't you say?

Positioning is about articulating your credibility and value and making certain your listeners understand exactly what you can contribute.

2 HUNTING. Hunters seek out relationships with opinion leaders and role models capable of advancing their company's goals. How good a hunter are YOU? To find out, try this quiz:

• Do you typically work side by side with your company's highest performing managers?
• Do you routinely search out new opportunities?
• Do you take time to contemplate how you might create new opportunities, both for yourself and for your department?

3 FARMING. You need to grow, cultivate and harvest that value you've been creating and demonstrating while you position yourself and hunt for good allies. Expert RM farmers wisely tap into their ever-expanding garden of trusted relationships on a regular basis, tilling their rich soil for such nourishing "cash crops" as feedback, information, ideas and introductions. They always

ask their allies about resources that can help them achieve their objectives.

For example, rather than spending inordinate amounts of time and money on "help wanted" ads, recruitment firms and job fairs, "farm" the company's workforce. By establishing referral fees, organizing internal recruitment drives or simply asking individual employees for help, HR managers cultivate their rich employee soil, extracting from it "nutrients" immediately available and costing nothing.

4 COACHING. In contrast to RM skills #1, #2 and #3, in which high value is extracted from others primarily for your personal benefit, coaching allows your allies to extract value from you. HR professionals, of course, tend to be naturally inclined toward coaching, so this skill will probably already be well-developed. However, a new attitude on the part of the HR manager may need formulating.

When we help others, we produce a value deposit that our "coachees" are willing to reciprocate. Yet HR managers frequently don't bother to act on that willingness. Remember that coaching is, or can be, a two-way street.

Take the case of HR manager Brian Farrell, who decided one day to work on upgrading his company's family leave policies. Due to Brian's tireless lending of an ear to all department managers over the years, and his continual wise and generous counsel, these managers wanted very much to help him transform the company for the better and achieve his goals. They were determined to work cooperatively with him and to support him. As a result, Brian won approval on many of the toughest issues, such as paternity leave, employee sabbaticals and flextime.

5 LEADING. As we can see in the case of Brian Farrell, your own generosity to others will frequently enable you to establish atmospheres that inspire your business allies to support you in achieving your goals. By carefully applying the other essential RM skills (positioning, hunting, farming, coaching), you might then find leading to be a snap. That's because leading simply means enlisting others to help you attain your objectives and when you've laid the groundwork they will often jump quickly in line behind you.

Imagine, for example, that one of your HR objectives is to link your company's

salary structures to their impact on customer contact. Rather than taking an internal employee survey on the issue, a traditional HR way of doing things, you propose to the company president that customers be included in a survey too. Can you find a correlation between customer satisfaction and salary levels?

If you've adequately demonstrated your value (positioning), nurtured individuals you can trust (hunting), listened and acknowledged others for their competence and good ideas (farming), and counseled your allies to help them achieve their goals (coaching), you couldn't be in any better condition to ask your allies for support as you make your radical proposal to the president. Deftly wielding your RM skills, you turn your attention in more customer-focused directions as your proposal sails through.

When applied to human resources, then, effective relationship management frequently creates a "circular effect." Relationships throughout the company deepen, employees generate more positive attitudes, there's an upswing in the number of rewarding company-customer relations, and customer intimacy and the bottom line grows vital and strong. As job security grows, "internal" relationships elevate another notch and the HR/RM dynamic swings full circle.

The biggest winner in this success chain will likely be HR. As morale rises and "negative" issues fall (absenteeism, turnover, low productivity), HR can concentrate on more positive, affirming matters, building the company's spirits ever higher. Though everyone involved gains in such a scenario, HR wins recognition as an integral and primary factor in making it happen. Thus, once HR masters relationship management skills, its ability to influence the whole organization is possible.

***

JAMES P. MASCIARELLI is founder of Archer Consulting in Gloucester, Ma., a leadership, organization and business development firm offering seminars, consulting and CEO coaching. He is also a principal of Walnut Venture Associates, an investment group for early stage high technology companies, and a board member of the National Association of Corporate Directors/New England. To quantify your own relationship management skills, visit his website at www.archerconsulting.com.

This research explored how employees perceived and articulated organizational "rules" in describing specific communication problem incidents. The research elicited and analyzed 560 short narratives from MBA students describing an actual on-the-job communication problem caused by another organization member's weak understanding of "how we communicate here." Respondents cited many more unwritten than written sources of guidance, naming 22 different means by which organizations conveyed guidance on "how we communicate here." Categorizing types of communication problems showed that about 20 percent could have been prevented or solved by communication policy guidelines; other kinds of managerial intervention are recommended for those owing more to bad individual judgment, poor managerial oversight, or dearth or inappropriateness of cues from corporate culture. Organizations with some written policy on communicating may have thought more about "how we communicate here" and how to convey that information to employees. Respondents' cost estimates suggest that communication problems are a drain on profitability and effectiveness. Most organizations should examine how employees learn the communication rules at present and should introduce measures that reduce uncertainty. If employees can make sense of their work environments sooner and more accurately, errors are likely to diminish.

Organizational Rules on Communicating: How Employees Are—and Are Not—Learning the Ropes

Jeanette W. Gilsdorf

California State University—Long Beach

How do employees of an organization know how the organization wants them to communicate on the job? How do organizations tell them? *Do* they tell them? Do organizations rely on corporate culture to inform employees? Do organizations rely on their ability to recruit observant people and to train them thoroughly? Do some rely on employees' peers and co-workers? Do some decline to think about the matter at all? A study based on 560 critical incidents narrated by MBA-level respondents permits some inferences.

Organizations, relying on human beings to create and deliver products and services, lose serious money and see productivity eroded when errors are made. Many, many errors trace back to a problem in communication. Human beings make decisions about what to do and say based on interpretation of a changing, moving mass of cues from others in their environment. Some organizations give employees excellent guidance on how they expect them to communicate; some organizations give little or none. As this study suggests, most organizations could do more to help employees reduce uncertainty and make better and more profitable communication decisions.

The study analyzed 560 questionnaires completed by students in MBA-level human resource management classes at 18 universities from across the United States. The questionnaire was administered at a point in the term when students had already been introduced to the concept of corporate culture. Respondents were asked to narrate the problem incident, discuss what went wrong, and state what the originator of the problem should have known to avoid the problem. What someone "should have known" amounted to a rule for communicating in that situation in that organization.

Research Questions

This study sought *to draw inferences about how employees enrolled in MBA programs perceived and articulated organizational "rules" as they described specific communication problem incidents and commented on what their organizations expected.* Earlier research has offered little firm information on where and how employees learn the organization's rules. Therefore, another important goal of the study was *to try to infer the origin of the rules whose violation led to financial costs: Were the rules written or unwritten? If unwritten, by what means should the individual have obtained knowledge of them?*

The literature (e.g., Schein, 1985) suggests that corporate culture is an important conduit of organizational expectations. Accordingly, this study also sought *to learn whether the*

From *The Journal of Business Communication*, April 1998, pp. 173-201. © 1998 by Jeannette W. Gilsdorf. Reprinted by permission.

strength of corporate culture is related to the degree to which employees understand communication expectations. Also, following previous research (Gilsdorf, 1987, 1992), the study *examined whether organizations with strong corporate cultures are likely to put more of their communication expectations in writing.*

Another goal of the study was *to try to infer how many of the problems cited by respondents could have been mitigated or solved if the organization had developed clearer rules.* To be sure, rules cannot cover all eventualities, nor can they compensate for an individual employee's bad judgment or imperceptiveness, or an individual manager's inattention or incompetence. But *would having clear rules be important in enough cases that organizations should attend to them more?*

Rules, Policies, and Culture

The term *rules* as used here denotes the assumptions organizational members make about the right way to communicate in given situations in their particular organization. Rules might be formal or informal; written or oral; implicit or explicit; general (an organization-wide policy, for instance) or particular (specific to a department or even to a task); positively stated or implied ("do this") or negatively stated or implied ("avoid this"; Gilsdorf, 1987).

A *policy* usually sets forth, at a high level, an organization's firm belief and/or course of action on a given important matter. Strategic planners create policy, but so also do lower-level staff or line people responsible for departments. For instance, the corporate communication department might generate crisis communication policy, and human resources might formulate policy forbidding sexual harassment. One also sees the word *policy* attached to statements with narrower focus than the organization as a whole: Guidelines and procedures are often referred to as policies.

Some rules are expressed in policies, but many rules exist outside policies. A priori, these rule categories were of interest:

1. Written and acknowledged (e.g., cited, posted, provided to organization members). For example, a policy encountered fairly frequently in writing is "Your manager's door is open. Ask questions or raise concerns as needed." Or "Our customer is always first."
2. Written but unacknowledged (e.g., outdated or not widely available).
3. Unwritten and explicitly stated/acknowledged. For example, a rule fairly common as an oral but explicit policy is "We work as a team here. Ask for help in solving problems."
4. Unwritten, definitely present, but unacknowledged and unlikely to be viewed as policy. For example,

- A rule such as "When you use someone else's good idea, give the person credit and don't try to hog the rewards" might be implicit and helpful to the organization's goals.
- A rule like "People can come in up to 20 minutes late in the morning without calling" might be implicit rather than explicit and might be very harmful to the organization's goals.
- An unwritten rule such as "CYA" (cover your ass) may or may not be congruent with many organizational goals. "CYOA" (cover your organization's ass) is generally consistent with at least some organization goals.

Written rules are conveyed by familiar means such as policy statements, memos, or posters. In contrast, unwritten rules are not always easy to trace. Some are clear; some are "fuzzy." The more they are understood rather than explicit, the more they blur into the area that is considered *culture*—that is, an organization's shared vision, values, beliefs, goals, and practices. Rules are sometimes formulated deliberately but sometimes coalesce from practice. Whatever their origin, rules exist, and they guide the decisions of organizational actors.

To succeed in organizations, employees have to find out that the rules exist and what they are and decide whether it is in their interests to follow them. Though one might initially think it would always be in employees' interests to follow the rules, this is not always so. For instance, in cases where employees hear conflicting rules from different sources or where rewards do not follow compliance, people might well decide to ignore rules. Furthermore, skilled communicators may make communication decisions that promote organizational objectives better than those suggested by the "rules." In fact, rules often evolve for the better in exactly this way.

Managers in organizations think about "how we communicate here" only some of the time, and some managers do so infrequently or not at all. Since people assign meaning to experience, correctly or incorrectly, rules are formed in abundance. If an organization's management does not consider which communication behaviors it wishes to foster for its success, the signals it sends to employees may be inconsistent or counterproductive. Desirable behaviors may not be reinforced. Resulting patterns may be dysfunctional to the organization.

This article will argue that greater emphasis on deliberate, workable, and consistent messages about "how we communicate here" will increase an organization's chances of obtaining useful communication behavior more of the time and avoiding costly errors.

It is a given that "how we communicate here" can be an elusive set of concepts. Rules can exist in combinations, admit of many exceptions by their very nature, and depend on one's level in the organization. In clusters of rules, different organizational actors will sometimes perceive different ones as salient. Some rules have metarules. For example, in a department of one technical organization, employees understood that they were to listen politely to how the manager told them to do a task but then go and ask a long-term staffer how they should actually do it. The work group's rule about the manager was, in essence, "He's a manager, not a technical expert. He doesn't understand this function, doing it his way would create problems, and he doesn't know how to check on you anyway." This arrangement was functional, because the manager was out of his depth in this case. Clearly, however, this kind of "rule" setup is laden with peril. On the part of both the manager and the work group, there are too many unexamined assumptions.

Research on Communication Rules

Learning the ropes in organizations is a challenge to newcomers but also a continuing process for longer-term organizational members. Employees move up or transfer; new managers make changes in "how we do things here"; organizational culture itself evolves overtime. Many scholars (e.g., Daft & Weick, 1984) agree that organizations are complex systems that interpret events for their members and create meanings that guide actions. Numerous sources, including Van Maanen (1976), Jablin (1987), Miller and Jablin (1991), Mills and Murgatroyd (1991), and Teboul (1994) describe how newcomers to organizations become socialized. Louis (1980, pp. 231, 246) emphasizes that most newcomers have prior cultural assumptions and behaviors to unlearn as well as new ones to perceive, interpret, and take on. Weick (1995) emphasizes the continuousness and complexity of sensemaking. Thomas, Clark, and Gioia (1993) explore the processes linking cognition (scanning, interpretation, etc.) to action and the effects on what the actors do in the organization.

Deal and Kennedy (1982) link strong corporate culture, effective communication, and cost savings: "By knowing what exactly is expected of them, employees will waste little time in deciding how to act in a given situation. In a weak culture, on the other hand, employees waste a good deal of time just trying to figure out what they should do and how they should do it. The impact of a strong culture on productivity is amazing. In the extreme, we estimate that a company can gain as much as one or two hours of productive work per employee per day" (p. 15).

Where employees understand management's expectations, they apparently contribute better to management's goals. Clampitt and Downs (1993), building on previous studies by Downs and Hain (1982) and Downs, Clampitt, and Pfeiffer (1988), demonstrated a close link between effective communication and productivity. Trombetta and Rogers (1988, p. 510) showed that information adequacy directly predicts commitment and job satisfaction. Guzley (1992) showed that employees' commitment to the organization correlates positively with organizational clarity and is maintained even when changes are occurring in the organization "if they sense some form of clarity or orderliness exists for work activities, goals, objectives, and the like" (p. 398). Ibarra and Andrews (1993) found that the more closely connected employees were to the firm's informal communication network, the more positively those employees viewed the organization's climate and the more likely they were to believe that that climate allowed employees to take risks, gain access to information, and hope for their decisions to be accepted.

Informal, nonhierarchical means of communication appear to fill in gaps between what employees want to know and what management has time, attention, or inclination to tell them. Katz and Kahn (1966) discuss the asymmetrical communication needs of superiors and subordinates. An individual in a direct-report relationship does not always want to send or receive the information desired or offered by the other. "The greater the conflict between the communication needs of these two hierarchically situated senders and recipients of information, the more likely is an increase in lateral communication. . . . Horizontal exchange can be an escape valve for frustration in communicating upward and downward; and sometimes it can operate to accomplish some of the essential business of the organization" (p. 247). Comer (1991) suggests that managers not merely allow but actively encourage newcomers to rely on peers as sources of information. Louis (1980, p. 245) recommends that managers make knowledgeable insiders the primary associates of newcomers. Wilson (1992) explores nonpeer information-seeking outside the chain of command. Individuals' cognitive styles, the uncertainty level, and the nature of the organization (organic or mechanistic) regulate what kinds of organizational linkages (vertical, horizontal, or diagonal) are relied on for information (Wilson & Malik, 1995).

Employees generally enter the organization intending to learn and fulfill the firm's expectations and prosper by doing so. They form schemata (see Harris, 1994) based on formal and informal information from supervisors, formal and informal guidance from co-workers, observation of results of their own and others' behavior, and the organization's own statements about itself and its expectations. To convey cultural values, which drive much communication behavior, informal channels are used even more than formal ones (Johnson, Donohue, Atkin, & Johnson, 1994, p. 119) and the channels are interrelated in complex ways (p. 120). Newcomers infer what alliances to build, and with whom, whose opinions are and are not influential, when and when not to communicate, whom to trust and under what circumstances, and many other subtleties of communication behavior. Southard (1990) lists numerous cues organizational newcomers use in learning official and unofficial corporate protocol. They process the information as it is salient—that is, as they perceive it to apply to problems they face.

Learning rules is a continuing process. Events occur and people interpret them. As Gray, Bougon, and Donnellon observe (1985), action-taking causes observers to amend meanings; leaders are powerful insofar as they can cause others to accept their interpretations of events; and some (not all) organizational meanings will be widely agreed upon and "crystallized as informal and formal structures" (p. 91). Schall (1983) examined an organization's communication "rules" using multiple methods, defining these rules as "tacit understandings (generally unwritten and unspoken) about appropriate ways to interact (communicate) with others in given roles and situations; they are choices, not laws (though they constrain choice through normative, practical, or logical force), and they allow interactors to interpret behavior in similar ways (to share meanings)" (p. 560). Goldhaber (1990) adds, "If these rules are followed extensively throughout an organization, we state that 'communication policies' are in effect, especially if they are put in writing" (p. 129).

A firm's rules on communicating are sometimes summed up as a firm's "communication climate," here defined by Poole: "A communication climate is a molar description of communication practices and procedures in an organization or subunit. It consists of collective beliefs, expectations, and values regarding communication, and is generated in interaction around organizational practices via a continuous process of structuration" (1985, p. 107). Czarniawska-Joerges and Joerges (1988) say that managers can and should construct linguistic artifacts that convey shared meaning about the organization's values and cultural assumptions. Such statements, they believe, reduce uncertainty and facilitate control. Stohl (1986) analyzed messages that employees found memorable and found that, first, organizational members do remember value statements from higher-status persons that seem to embody what an organization desires; and second, managers can formulate these statements deliberately and helpfully. But where individual managers' or whole organizations' communication signals are mixed and undeliberate, employees might never be sure what they are expected to do. Indeed, in a study by Harcourt, Richerson, and Wattier (1991) a national sample of middle managers rated as poor the quality of the information they received on their job responsibilities, company policies and objectives, and other elements regarding expected behaviors. They also said that formal communication was less reliable than informal.

Some linguistic artifacts, such as value statements or organizational guidelines, are put in writing. Gilsdorf (1987, 1992) examined the nature and incidence of written organizational policy on selected aspects of communicating and found that it is not abundant. Her studies also suggest that formulating written policy on communicating could clarify organizational expectations to employees by revealing where expectations are uncertain or unshaped and by making explicit those expectations that are implicit and/or misunderstood. Francis and Woodcock (1990) recommend that organizations examine, write down, and exemplify their values. "It is what managers do—symbolic communication—that is vital. The actions of managers must reinforce their value statements. . . . Until a set of values is clear enough to be committed to paper, it will not have the authority to be a leadership statement" (p. 35). In Schein's (1985) opinion, however, formal written policy "will highlight only a small portion of the assumption set that operates in the group and, most likely, will highlight those aspects of the leader's philosophy or ideology that lend themselves to public articulation" (p. 242). Schein listed many other mechanisms for embedding and reinforcing values, including what leaders consistently view as important enough to measure; how leaders react to critical incidents and crises; leaders' deliberate role modeling and coaching; what things they reward; and what bases they use for recruiting, selecting, promoting, and terminating or isolating (pp. 224–225).

Employees look at an organization's reward system, as well as its messages, for signals about what the organization really values. Vroom (1964) and Porter and Lawler (1968) say employees are more likely to perform desired behaviors if they are told what is expected, offered incentives toward those behaviors, shown they are feasible, and rewarded fairly for desired behaviors. Though it should be clear that an organization's reward system should reinforce the behaviors it

desires, Kerr's famous article "On the Folly of Rewarding A, While Hoping for B" (1975, updated 1995) is, according to a survey taken by the editors of *Academy of Management Executive* (Dechant & Veiga, 1995), still descriptive of actuality. "Ninety percent of our respondents told us that Kerr's folly is still prevalent in corporate America today. Over half concluded that the folly is widespread in their companies" (p. 15).

If organizations reward the behaviors they say they reward, their messages are congruent and credible. If these messages are inconsistent, employees' responses will be at worst antagonistic (because contradictory and equivocal signals generate resentment) and at best unpredictable (because no clear signal is available to guide the well-intentioned). While it is true that an equivocal message can sometimes serve useful purposes (Eisenberg, 1984), the present study's findings suggest strongly that many mixed or nonexistent messages result from inadvertence—that is, from managerial inattention to the need for clear, consistent communication with employees—rather than from purpose.

Employees do not always feel free to ask what managers really want. In their article on individual feedback seeking, Ashford and Cummings (1985) refer to the risk employees take in exposing their ignorance and asserting their needs. They believe managers should reduce that risk by "communicating their positive interpretation of such an act" (p. 78) and should also "become more self-conscious about their own actions and how employees are interpreting them as feedback . . . . Managers need to be aware that through their behaviour they signal to employees those behaviours they most value, those employees they most esteem, and what strategies *really* lead to goal attainment in that setting" (p. 78).

To be sure, only some of the communication problems gathered in the present study trace to unclearly understood expectations. Many stem from the bad judgment of individual employees or some other unforeseeable element. Organizational "rules" on communicating cannot cover all eventualities. Where managers and organizations can avert waste or loss by providing helpful direction, however, it would seem that they err if they overlook the opportunity.

Research Methods

Twenty-five instructors at 18 graduate business programs agreed to distribute a two-page instrument in their human resource management classes at the MBA level and allocate 20 minutes to its completion. Classes of this kind were chosen because these students could be assumed to be familiar with the concept of corporate culture and organizational norms, because many MBA-level students have professional work experience, and because MBA-program entrance requirements make it probable that respondents will in general be intelligent and perceptive observers.

Using a questionnaire, respondents were asked to think of an organization where they had worked and which they knew well—an organization where they knew the ropes—and then to think of a person who didn't know the ropes, a person who did not have a good feel for the culture of the organization. Respondents were then asked to recall and narrate an incident where this person made a mistake that had adverse consequences for the organization. (Respondents were asked about a third party's actions for two reasons: to get around individuals' tendency to self-justify when reporting problem situations, and to induce respondents to reflect on rules they perceive to be in effect.)

The purpose was to position the respondent as an observer in an organization where s/he felt s/he fit in; and next, to get the respondent to examine what there was to know about the organization's operating rules, how s/he learned what to do there, and how clearly the organization communicated its expectations to employees in general.

Respondents were asked to rate the strength of the organization's culture on a scale of 1 (very weak) to 10 (very strong). (An even number was used because previous pilot-testing of the instrument revealed no tendency for respondents to seek an exact middle point on the scale.)

After narrating the incident, respondents were asked

- To estimate the cost of the mistake in actual dollars, in soft terms, or both.
- To state what the erring individual should have known about the organization's communication expectations in order to avoid creating the problem.
- To attempt to explain why that person did not know.

The latter two questions aimed at getting the respondent to voice the "rule" in force on "how we communicate here."

Respondents were asked to indicate whether most employees of the organization know clearly how management wants them to communicate. If respondents believed employees received guidance from management in how to communicate, they were asked to state the ways in which management guided them. The last content question asked whether written policy on communicating exists in the organization and, if yes, where an employee finds it. The formal written policy did not have to address the specific "rule" violated. The question was intended to discover whether the respondent was aware of any written organizational guidelines on communicating.

Last of all, to make sure the respondent was qualified to observe and comment on the incident, the instrument asked the observer's position in the organization, the core business of the organization, and the size of the organization. Since MBA programs tend to enroll students who are within the 25–40 age range and about 55 percent male and 45 percent female, the usual demographic items (e.g., age, salary) were not requested.

Returned questionnaires were entered into a database for tallying and analysis. The rules (what the individual "should have known") were recorded and studied in the context of their narratives. One of the study's research questions was to infer how often an explicit policy would have mitigated or prevented the communication error and, where policy would not have been applicable, what other sources of influence guided organizational actors. I anticipated that a clear policy would help in some cases, that individuals' communication skill and common

sense would be more important in others, and that still other cases would be amenable to other kinds of cues, either from organizational culture or from managers. I also anticipated that some cases would be mixed or difficult to classify. I categorized the means by which respondents said their management typically conveyed communication expectations to employees in order to gain respondents' perceptions of which media their managers generally used and how frequently each medium was cited overall.

Four factors limit this study: The information gathered depended on respondents' reports of remembered incidents. The questions about managers' use of communication media and about the existence of written policy were not connected with the critical incident narrated. Some of the data (e.g., strength of corporate culture) depended on how respondents interpreted terms used and motives for others' behavior. Finally, the sample was not random and therefore cannot represent U.S. organizations as a whole.

Returned questionnaires with usable narratives numbered 560. N varied slightly for some items; though some respondents declined to answer one or more items, nonresponse to one item did not necessarily invalidate responses to others. Where nonresponse or unclear response was problematical, that questionnaire was disqualified.

Culture Strength, Employee Understanding, and the Rules

The more than 500 organizations that respondents represented ranged in size from small proprietorships to some of the nation's largest firms, and cut across business, governmental, nonprofit, and even military organizations. All but three of the respondents had at least some work experience; these three, however, also usefully narrated an incident they had observed. Categorizing responses by position of respondent, core business, and size of firm was not a goal of the study and did not permit useful inferences.

The "core business" question did not produce neat categories. In answering the "how big is the organization" question, some people clearly meant a whole organization of 1200 people while others meant their department of 30. The information was useful in that it indicated the size of the unit an individual was thinking about. Job title was useful because it showed what the person could observe but was not used in categorizing because organizations are wildly inconsistent in what it means to be a vice president or an executive assistant.

Culture and Employee Understanding of Communication Rules

Most respondents viewed their organization's corporate culture as fairly strong and believed employees knew pretty clearly how the organization wanted them to communicate. Thus it seems clear that strong corporate culture is associated with effective transmission of communication rules in many organizations.

Early in the questionnaire, respondents were asked whether the organization they had in mind had a strong or weak culture and to mark a scale in answer to this question:

Along this continuum, please indicate how strong you believe this organization's culture is.

very strong									very weak
10	9	8	7	6	5	4	3	2	1

The overall response on this item was 6.83 Mean, 7 Median, and 8 Mode.

Toward the end of the questionnaire, respondents were asked,

Do most employees of this organization know how management wants its people to communicate? or not? Please mark this continuum:

most employees know clearly									most employees don't know clearly
10	9	8	7	6	5	4	3	2	1

Overall response on this item was 6.55 Mean, 7 Median, 8 Mode. A Pearson product moment correlation coefficient was calculated ($r = .495$; $p = .0001$). In the social sciences an r of .4 to .5 is considered good to strong. The p of .0001 suggests that this correlation coefficient of .495 is significant; strong corporate culture is associated with effective transmission of the rules in many organizations. The literature links strong culture with understanding of "the way we do things around here" (Deal & Kennedy, 1982); this correlation indicates that *in organizations with strong cultures, employees are more likely to understand the organization's communication expectations.*

Respondents were not at all at a loss for problem incidents to narrate. (Some said, "What? Only one?!") Based on the median responses, considerable numbers of employees are likely *not* to clearly understand their organization's communication expectations. It is important to examine the responses of those who did not assign high marks to strength of culture and employees' understanding. With 7 as a median response for both items, let us assume for the purposes of discussion that respondents who marked 5 or below on the culture statement felt that the culture was relatively weak and that those marking 5 or below on the "do most employees" item were not very willing to say that most employees understood the organization's communication expectations. A cross-tabulation using a 5 response as a cutoff yields these numbers:

Relationship Between Culture Strength and Understanding of Communication Expectations

	5 or under Most employees don't know	>5 Most employees know
5 or under Culture relatively weak	91	46
>5 Culture relatively strong	76	328

Of the 541 who answered both questions, the right-hand column shows that 374 felt positive (>5) about employees' understanding of communication expectations. Of those, however, 46 responses (8.5 percent of 541) appear to indicate that employees' understanding came from something other than a strong culture. Adding the left-hand column shows 167 respondents who were *not* very willing (5 or under) to say that most employees understood communication expectations. Of those, 76 marked the strength of culture item higher than 5. These responses would seem to suggest that in these cases (14 percent of 541) strong culture did not work well in guiding employees' communication decisions. The following incident shows an example (this example and some others are abridged slightly, and respondents' minor haste errors have been silently corrected):

> The company is a small but growing information service firm. We sell data that has had "value added." The company has been acquiring several products from other companies in the last four months and marketing kits need to be revised so clients understand everything we now offer.
>
> One person from sales (call him Bob) is assigned to create new marketing pieces for new products. Bob carefully reviews the previous owners marketing pieces and uses information from those to create new ones. These new pieces are sent to press and eventually to customers. The company gets lots of calls about new products and Bob is pretty happy. The problem, however, is that Bob did not have anyone on the operations side review the marketing pieces. First, major computer programming was required to get new products up and running, and several products would not be available for a couple of months. Meanwhile, sales had already sold them. Second, one of the marketing pieces that a previous owner had written contained some erroneous information and essentially promised a service that was impossible to deliver. (Again, several clients had already "bought" products for this specific service.) All of the operations managers were aware of the problems, but sales had not consulted any of them before marketing information went out to hundreds of clients. Products therefore could not be delivered although we had promised them. Several clients were very upset.

What should the employee have known? "All internal and external communications should be reviewed by the department head. . . . Even the president has someone review ALL his external communication to make sure it is the best that it can be." The policy (one-over-one review) was known to the respondent, yet no one had told Bob. The respondent said that "people get told when they screw up" and that, although there is some written policy on communicating, it is not distributed reliably. This incident cost the firm $15,000, as well as client goodwill, when products bought could not be delivered.

This respondent rated strength of corporate culture at 7 but employees' understanding of communication expectations at 5. Seventy-five other respondents also marked corporate culture at 7 or higher and employees' understanding of communication expectations at 5 or lower. Thus it is tenable to infer that *strong corporate culture often helps guide employees' communication decisions but cannot always be relied on to do so.*

Identifying the Rules and Their Sources

Analysis of the incidents and responses to the "What should the person have known?" question divided the incidents roughly into these categories:

• Cases where a clear, well supported policy would have helped.

- Cases where the culture should have shaped the behavior of the individual.
- Cases involving individual bad judgment or imperceptiveness.
- Cases due to management shortcomings.

From respondents' answers to the "what should the employee have known" question and from study of the incidents, the "rules" were recorded. The rules were numerous and various; thus Table 1 shows *examples* of the kinds of rules that, in the context of their incident, fell into the four main categories.

To be sure, many of the incidents gathered in this study show mixed causes. Note that no category is absolute. The distinction of most interest to this study was the one between cases where an explicit rule would help and cases where an explicit rule would be largely irrelevant.

About 20 percent of the answers to "What should the person have known to avoid creating the problem" were matters where *a clear, well-supported policy would have helped greatly.* These communication problems sometimes happened because policy, whether oral or written, didn't exist, as in the following example, where a work-flow diagram was sorely needed:

> This individual did not communicate the changes made to a specific engineering drawing. She made the changes and continued with her work. She did not know the flow of information and who should be told about these changes. As a result, when

Table 1
What to Know and Where to Learn It

Respondents evaluated what the erring person should have known and where s/he should have learned it. Examples follow:

Solution needed: *Refer to an existing oral or written policy*
- Obtain review/approval of external communications before sending.
- Preserve the organization's image.
- Make your best effort to keep customers satisfied.
- Guard confidential information.
- Observe regular communication channels.
- Don't obligate the organization.
- Obtain appropriate clearances.
- Convey information to need-to-know people.

Solution needed: *Better understanding of cues from culture*
- Peers don't direct new employees; supervisors do.
- Don't withhold problems from the boss.
- Pitch in! It's all everybody's job.
- Join off-duty activities to help team effectiveness on the job.
- Ask questions and learn reasons.
- Don't ask a lot of questions; "just do it."
- Consult and collaborate, or don't expect any support.
- Individuals here are independent but no throat-cutting is tolerated.

Solution needed: *Better individual judgment*
- Don't embarrass your manager.
- Adapt to the people around you.
- Keep your expectations reasonable.
- Seek job information proactively.
- Support a decision once it's made.
- Don't be too frank in public when you're new.
- Don't grab and make a decision you don't understand.
- Understand and respect "turf."

Solution needed: *Management needs to send better cues*
- Don't set low performance examples.
- When you delegate, follow up.
- Manage, but don't micromanage.
- Inform people about work priorities and expectations.
- Never spread the blame undeservedly.
- Give constructive feedback.
- Don't blow up in front of people.
- When a department works well as a team, don't disrupt it.

the customer came in for a review, the changed drawings did not match the rest of the information. As a result many changes had to be made to other documents, technical manuals, teaching materials and requirements of the equipment.

In other cases a written policy existed but was not sufficiently reinforced, as in this instance:

> I worked as a senior customer service specialist for [XYZ] Savings & Loan for approx. 1 and ½ years. The firm has a customer service credo. On Saturdays [XYZ] closes at 1 p.m. One Saturday right at 1 o'clock X had just closed the doors and was returning to her terminal. One of our long-time customers, a loyal customer for years, began to knock on the door showing a check she needed to cash. X screamed at the customer that we closed at 1 p.m. and she would have to come back on Monday. The customer again knocked on the door desperately as X began to shake her head.
>
> Just then our district manager, who frequently visits the branch, walked up to the door and told X to open the door. The district manager politely apologized to the customer, while I assisted her with her transaction. After the customer left, our D.M. pulled out our operations manual and showed us that we are required to help any demanding customer up to 15 minutes after we close. X soon after was placed on P.I.P. (Performance Improvement Program).

The bulk of the incidents—the 80 percent—were less easy to classify, as the next examples will illustrate. Many of the communication problems would *not* have been amenable to a stated policy but were instead matters where the *culture should have shaped the behavior of the individual,* as in this case:

> A product that our group in quality control was testing gave results outside specifications, which was very unusual. It turned out that the person responsible for submitting it to our group failed to inform us about a problem with a different test—one that is repeated and that provides data that we base our testing on. This person did not inform us of this problem because it did not directly impact his immediate responsibilities. It caused our group to waste significant time and energy. The norm in our workplace is for everyone to be aware of as much as possible and to approach problems as a team, giving assistance whenever possible, even if it is something not "defined" in a person's immediate duties.

As the last sentence implies, culture at this firm calls for attentiveness, proactive communication, and mutual assistance. The other employees evidently understood the norms well. A policy would probably not have helped; to have guided this individual in this instance, a statement would have needed to be so concrete and specific that, if offered as a policy, it would sound absurd and possibly insulting to the intelligence of other employees. Instead, cultural cues would convey that where B depends on A, we always make sure the people who work on B find out about A.

Some others had little to do with culture or policy but instead occurred owing mainly to *individual bad judgment or imperceptiveness,* as here:

> "M" would at times yell at subordinates or fellow members of the executive team. He was bright, with an educational background well suited for the position he was in. However, his means of communication were totally

unacceptable to the workings and inner culture of the organization. In one instance, this executive yelled at another executive with less seniority who simply wanted to pin down and identify particular problems that existed in his department. . . . This and other inconsistent behavior finally led to the elimination of his entire department and the subsequent layoff of approximately 30 employees and staff.

The "should have known" rule was to exercise self-control and treat others courteously, especially other executives. This basic, common-sense rule would hardly need to be set forth as policy. At lower organizational levels, disciplinary options are available for controlling outbursts. Here, the firm got rid of the executive-level offender, but only after many complications and at a high cost.

Still other problem incidents stemmed from *management shortcomings* that would probably not have been influenced either by explicit policy or strong organizational culture:

> We were at the client's office having a meeting. The manager presented a proposal which [had not been] taken up in the office. All of us in the meeting were lost. The manager [had] not consulted us about the new proposals. There were a lot of things wrong about the proposal. After the meeting, one of the client's personnel approached me. He said they weren't too happy about the proposal. I could not tell him that we were not informed.

Some cases had multiple causes: An individual was insufficiently acculturated, and both individual judgment and managerial oversight were at fault as well.

> Another manager from a different functional group casually asked the employee in question to "look into" an issue. The request was very informal and vague, and was not documented. The employee failed to raise the issue with his manager. A week or two later, the issue took several sharp, negative turns, and the employee in question was accused of dropping the ball—although the request and the actual event that followed were not really one and the same.
>
> The culture here dictates that employees take initiative to inform their managers of EVERYTHING and take every suggestion or comment from a superior as an order (request for action), [though] the communication channels and the nature of the information passed through them did not obviously match in formality, speed of response, and so on.

Metarules apply. The visible rule is "We are low-key and casual here," but the rule about the rule is that the casual term "look into" means "solve the problem," and a suggestion means an order. Policy statements rarely enter territory such as this. *Stating clear policy would have headed off about 20 percent of the problems narrated by this study's respondents.* For communication to be most effective, however, all the factors need to work well: The organization's expectations need to be clear, the culture needs to support them, individuals need good judgment, and managers need to be good at their jobs.

Ways Organizations Guide Employees in Communicating

An organization has many means of shaping behavior: culture, training, cultivation of the grapevine, and many other media. As Table 2 shows, the most common ways that my respondents' organizations shared expectations were meetings; training, orientation, role-play; one-on-one conversations with supervisors; and memos, postings, and newsletters. (Note: The question "In what ways does management let employees know how it wants its people to communicate?" regarded usual practice at the respondent's organization, not merely the practices affecting the incident narrated.) Not all respondents answered; indeed, respondents who felt management at their firms did not give good guidance on communicating (based on their earlier response to "Do most employees know?") were less likely to respond to this item.

Table 2 further subclassifies numbers of responses with regard to whether the organization had any written guidelines on communicating that were known to the respondent.

Naturally enough, respondents in organizations with written communication guidelines answered "memos, postings, news-

Table 2
How Management Lets Employees Know Communication Expectations

Communication Medium $N = 433$, arranged in order of total frequency of mention. Some respondents named more than one means.	Does Organization Have Written Policy?				Total Mentions
	Yes $n = 240$	No $n = 125$	Don't know $n = 66$	No response $n = 2$	
Meetings	35 (14.5%)	40 (32%)	14 (21%)	0	89
Training, orientation, role-play	30 (12.5%)	38 (30.4%)	7 (10.5%)	0	75
One-on-one with boss, "tells them directly," mbwa	37 (15.5%)	16 (12.8%)	14 (21%)	0	67
Memos, postings, newsletter	16 (6.6%)	34 (27.2%)	10 (15%)	2	62
Co. manual, handbook, written policies	4 (1.5%)	36 (28.8%)	2 (3%)	0	42
Management sets the example	26 (11%)	7 (5.6%)	7 (10.5%)	0	40
Not well; doesn't tell, "laissez-faire"; dysfunctionally, unhelpfully, "ha!"	28 (11.5%)	4 (3.2%)	5 (7.5%)	0	37
After-the-fact criticism	19 (8%)	7 (5.6%)	2 (3%)	0	28
You just watch; experience	18 (7.5%)	3 (2.4%)	6 (9%)	0	27
Frequent interaction	14 (5.8%)	7 (5.6%)	4 (6%)	0	25
Informal network, grapevine, word of mouth	15 (6.2%)	5 (4%)	5 (7.5%)	0	25
Open door	17 (7%)	6 (4.8%)	0 (0%)	1	24
Evaluations, counseling sessions	15 (6.2%)	7 (5.6%)	2 (3%)	0	24
Immediate praise/censure	14 (5.8%)	6 (4.8%)	3 (4.5%)	0	23
Senior peers tell or help; mentoring	13 (4%)	5 (4%)	3 (4.5%)	0	21
Teams	14 (5.8%)	3 (2.4%)	2 (3%)	0	19
Hierarchy/chain of command	6 (2.5%)	2 (1.6%)	1 (1.5%)	0	9
Culture	6 (2.5%)	1 (0.8%)	1 (1.5%)	0	8
Voice mail, e-mail	1 (0.4%)	3 (2.4%)	3 (4.5%)	0	7
Setting goals and objectives	2 (0.8%)	3 (2.4%)	1 (1.5%)	0	6
Figure it out or GET out	3 (1.2%)	0 (0%)	0 (0%)	0	3
Peer pressure	2 (0.8%)	0 (0%)	0 (0%)	0	2

letter" and "manual, handbook, policies" in considerable numbers. Interestingly, however, respondents representing firms with written policy also referred to "meetings" and "training . . . role-play" at more than twice the rate of respondents in no-written-policy organizations. *This seems to suggest a deliberateness about some organizations with written policies: Many such appear not only to have considered "how we communicate here," but also to use multiple channels in conveying their guidance to employees.*

The first six categories would strike most managers as beneficial, reliable channels. "After-the-fact criticism" is at least reliable feedback that helps the next time a similar problem arises. "Frequent interaction," "open door," "evaluations and counseling sessions" and most other categories can be considered helpful. The seventh category, however, suggests that the 37 respondents who marked it felt disappointed or angered over the organization's failure.

Several other categories, such as "just watch," "peer pressure," and "informal network, grapevine," are reliable only if the behavior models or informal informants themselves know and follow behavior of which management approves. These can and often do convey salutary guidance. However, since they are less easily monitored, individuals with defensive agendas or grievances would select means like these to promote rules that the organization would not countenance if it were aware of them. The "figure it out or GET out" category suggests a rather bitter view of the organization in the minds of those who answered that way.

As organizations become flatter, as more mid-level jobs are lost, and as more is expected of those who remain, it would seem that fewer individuals and organizations are likely to be ideally matched, and more proactive behavior will be needed. Managers desiring to shape employees' behavior and employees wishing to meet the organization's expectations could increase their success by using a greater variety of channels for information flow. Employees' relying on peers or on persons outside the chain of command works only if the organization has ensured that clear information is available and persons possessing it are motivated to share it. Part of a manager's job should be to place reliable guidance information in channels employees use. Another part is to ensure that public statements on "how we do things here" are borne out when individuals "reality-test" those statements.

Costs of Communication Problem Incidents

As mentioned earlier, the questionnaire asked these MBA-level students, most of whom had professional work experience, to estimate hard costs if possible and, if not, to specify types of soft costs incurred owing to the incident narrated. This was done partly to make sure the incident they chose was not trivial. (Respondents were permitted to specify both hard and soft costs if appropriate.) Though respondents were only estimating and these data cannot be considered solid, their estimates are sobering. Of 560 respondents, 247 cited dollar estimates.

Estimated Costs of Not Knowing the Ropes

n respondents	Cost in U.S. $
11	< $100
34	$100-$499
14	$500-$999
82	$1,000-$9,999
25	$10,000-$19,999
35	$20,000-$49,999
11	$50,000-$99,999
21	$100,000-$499,999
3	$500,000-$999,999
11	$1,000,000-$10,000,000

Even if approximate, the "costs" these respondents estimated suggest that ineffective communication is a serious drain on organizations' finances. Few of the estimates fell below $100. Less than a quarter of the 247 respondents citing hard costs placed those costs under $1,000. The largest share of the estimates fell between $1,000 and $9,999—82 respondents set the price of the mistake in this range. Eleven estimates exceeded $1 million.

Most of the respondents (514 of 560) in this study referred to one or more soft costs, as follows.

Soft Costs of Not Knowing the Ropes

n respondents	Cost
124	Lost time
111	Lost employee(s)
101	Lowered productivity, efficiency, or quality
82	Bad image, word of mouth, publicity
80	Ill will
79	Grave erosion of individual's effectiveness
72	Damaged working environment or relationship
57	Lowered morale
56	Stupid risk or liability
51	Lowered team spirit
46	Lowered trust
46	Lost revenue
34	Waste of money
25	Lost customer(s)
18	Lost opportunity

"Soft costs" have heavy consequences. Managers are well aware of the expenses surrounding, for instance, voluntary or involuntary employee turnover. (Problems leading to the separation, waste of training costs for the lost employee, disarray during the time the position is vacant, and costs of recruiting, hiring, and training the replacement do not exhaust the reasons why an employee's quitting or being fired is so expensive.) Negative image or word of mouth is gravely injurious to an organization. Exposure of the firm to risk or liability is more dangerous every year, as the United States becomes increasingly litigious.

It would seem reasonable that where organizations can give well-considered and explicit guidance, more employees would do the right thing more of the time. Organizational life moves quickly, however, and the many competing demands on managers' time tend to distract their attention from the act of communicating guidance and expectations. Still, as suggested here, the costs of ignoring this task can be heavy.

A Taxonomy of Rules: Written? Acknowledged? Reinforced? Functional?

A great variety of rules was invoked, some general, some particular, some commonsensical, some rather idiosyncratic. Many cases entailed combinations of causes and influences. Indeed, the categories of policy, individual judgment, culture, and management are interrelated in complex ways.

As we have seen, a given rule can be written or unwritten, acknowledged or unacknowledged, reinforced or not reinforced, functional or dysfunctional, and complied with or not complied with. The branching tree diagram in Figure 1 shows these categories. It would seem that the more visible a rule is, the more confident the employees feel in following it and the clearer it is that management intends and supports what the rule says. *The uppermost branch on both trees is the configuration for a rule, whether written or unwritten, that is likely to be working well for both employee and organization.*

Of the critical incidents that related to unwritten rules, most fell into Figure 1's categories F (acknowledged [explicit] and functional) and J (not acknowledged [implicit] and functional). This makes intuitive sense; observers who knew the rules were asked to comment on organizational actors who either did not understand the rules or understood them but violated them anyway.

This incident illustrates the former; clearly the individual would have been told that his job was to clarify the customer's needs before implementing a solution:

> In a data processing department for an insurance company, a programmer on my team was expected to deal with customers on a one-to-one basis. The instance I am thinking of was an error that could have been prevented in the implementation of a program enhancement. Due to his shyness and fear of appearing unintelligent, key questions were not asked. As a result, program errors existed that resulted in important financial information being lost. Resulting reruns of information, late fees, etc. amounted to $25,000. This was the first step in a chain of events that resulted in his termination.

An implicit, functional rule was violated in this next incident: That people in this organization need to build relationships before trying to impose major changes.

> A very bright woman broke the glass ceiling and moved into the lower executive level. Rather than doing some one-on-one groundwork before introducing a new performance appraisal system, she tried to demand acceptance of her new program by asserting her new authority. Resistance developed quickly and the program failed miserably.

An interesting example follows of an implicit, reinforced policy ("Mind your own business") that resulted in harm when people complied with it.

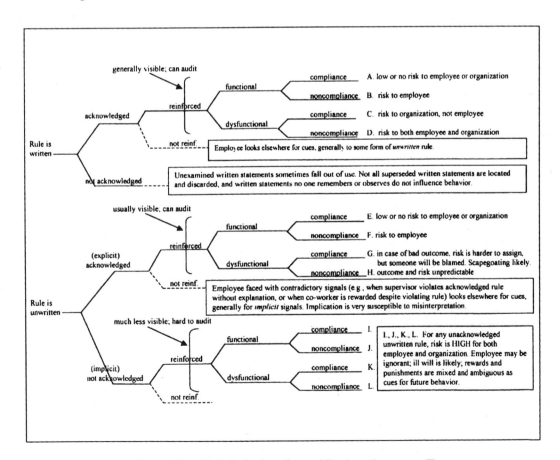

Figure 1. Possible Rule Configurations and Employee Response to Them

The accounting supervisor held communication to a minimum. The subordinates had no dialogue with him except the most minimal work instructions. After he was promoted, problems came to light in his former department and as a result, one person (not the supervisor) lost his job. It was discovered that many accounts were "fudged" and most employees were doing their jobs without realizing what was happening around them. The supervisor took advantage of the corporate culture, which was one of tacit trust, to discourage checking and controlling of this department. The wrong person took the fall and was fired. In this organization there is also little or no "backstabbing," so the whole incident was kept silent.

Many other incidents were so mixed that to attempt to assign them to categories with any kind of accuracy would have been unproductive. Especially where rules are implicit, unexplained, or dysfunctional, they might be at war with other rules linked to other schemata (from sources as varied as rumor mongers, union organizers, external pressure groups, or an individual's ego or conscience). Where rules compete, individuals have decisions to make, and they may have to defend their decisions. "This doesn't fit what I know." "What will really work here?" "What does the company really want? "What makes sense?" "How can I protect myself?" And, of course, where the rules themselves are not clear, the need for intelligent exceptions to the rules cannot even have a context.

This study elicited relatively few cases involving written guidelines, either functional or dysfunctional. (Recall that respondents were asked if they were aware of any written organizational policies on communicating, not if their organizations had written policy addressing the kind of incident they narrated.) Where written guidelines figured in the stories respondents narrated, they tended to be rules that would have been functional but were not well reinforced—in which case the erring person would turn to an unwritten rule for guidance. Written but unreinforced policies tend to enter the picture after the mistake is made, when someone unearths the policy either to instruct or to justify punishment.

The inference to be drawn is that *unwritten rules, whether explicit (acknowledged) or implicit (not acknowledged), tend to apply to more eventualities.* By their very nature, unwritten rules on communicating will be more numerous than written rules, because many aspects of communicating are particular. A spoken instruction exists in a situational context and thus can often be brief. A warning facial expression or some other type of symbolic guidance might not even be subject to articulation. Written guidelines are appropriate for more encompassing matters, where an immediate situation is less important (see Table 1), or for highly specific tasks—proposal preparation, for instance. Unwritten rules are also more adaptable to change as an organization's culture evolves.

Figure 1 shows a branch for a written, unacknowledged rule, although intuitively this may at first seem unlikely. Respondents in this study were asked (at the very end of the questionnaire) "Is there written policy on communicating?" Some who answered "yes" or "don't know" made comments such as, "We wrote one once—I think"; "If there is one, the secretary in administration has the only copy"; or "We might have one, but it would be way out of date." Although it would

seem that a guideline important enough to put in writing would also be perceived as a living document and updated as needed, clearly not all organizations do so.

Where a written guideline is buried and unused, I would argue that a guidance-seeking employee will "default" to the informal and unwritten communication channels for information. Similar behavior will occur if a written guideline exists but is not reinforced: "We have a written policy, but that's not what we really *do* here." A written guideline could also be dysfunctional; for instance, it might be inflexible, bureaucratic, or formulated so as to privilege some and disadvantage others. A well-intentioned but noncompliant employee might think, "We'd be crazy to follow that policy. What do people say to do?"

The point of the discussion of employees' choices among rules is that *organizations whose managers clarify what they really want employees to do lower the likelihood that employees will do something they do not desire.*

Discussion

As we have seen, most respondents felt that their organization's culture was moderately strong (median of 7) and that "most employees know pretty well how management wants people to communicate" (median of 7). These facts suggest that corporate culture transmits communication rules in many organizations. But respondents who marked their organizations considerably lower on both questions suggest that culture does not operate universally in this way. Cues come from many sources.

Stating clear policy would have helped head off 20 percent of the problems narrated by this study's respondents. Analyzing their communication expectations and making them more explicit, then, is a good start for organizations with communication problems. If some of a firm's "rules" are misunderstood, or underground, or dysfunctional, or local, or contradictory, policy analysis—a communication audit, for instance—can make the rules more visible. In addition, if, in examining policy, management focuses more attention on "how we communicate here," that emphasis is likely to improve the other problem categories: Managers are likely to see improvements in individual employees' judgment and managers' oversight and are likely to increase salutary effects of the organizational culture.

Respondents mentioned many more unwritten than written means by which communication expectations were conveyed in their organizations. Meetings, training activities, and one-on-one interaction with supervisors were the most frequently named. Of written media, the category containing more ephemeral but more immediate means such as memos, postings, and newsletters was cited more often than the category containing company manuals and policy handbooks.

Organizations with some written policy on communicating may have thought more, on the average, about "how we communicate here" and how to convey that information to employees, as the data in Table 2 suggest. These data support findings by Rogers (1988) that, compared to companies without formal policies, companies having or considering written communication policies were more likely to believe in the importance of 15 of the 20 communication values on which he queried them. (On four other values, no difference appeared.)

Recommendations for Further Research

Future research might address the extent to which the strength of organizational culture might be related to the kinds of rules people mentioned—or violated. It would be useful to study a limited number of specific organizations to see whether respondents within each organization had similar or different perceptions about the strength of the culture and the communication rules in effect, and whether differences of perception existed among top management, middle management, and professional support staff. Another direction might explore similarities and differences between perceptions of female and male respondents; or similarities and differences in perceptions of respondents based on age, ethnicity, type of organization, functional area of the respondent, or position of the respondent within the organization.

Implications for Managerial Practice

Employees joining and succeeding in an organization have to figure out how to communicate effectively there. Learning the ropes takes time. While it is true that, because the questionnaire asked for examples, the narratives tended to exemplify people who had not learned the ropes, numerous incidents exemplified people who tried to act in the organization's best interests but could not be sure how to do so.

Costs of the communication problem incidents were high— high enough in a number of cases to make a serious difference in profit-and-loss statements. At the high end of the cost scale, the incident narrated led to one medium-sized company's having to cease doing business. One very large company saw an entire department collapse. *Especially where many policies are implicit, organizations should examine what norms are shaping employees' communication behaviors,* since organizations comprise many employees who are capable workers but not very intuitive or attentive to implicit messages.

The finding that explicit rules would probably have helped in about 20 percent of the problem incidents suggests a worthwhile opportunity: Managers can reduce problems substantially if they analyze their communication expectations and state them explicitly. In the other categories (poor individual judgment, poor management practice, unhelpful culture), *attention to what "rules" the offenders were using would often have shed light on how similar errors could be avoided in the future.* Based on this study and the literature that supports it, *organizations should study the messages they send employees about "how we communicate here," the means by which they send them, and the consistency or inconsistency of those messages.* Indeed, communication executives (Gilsdorf, 1992, pp. 336–341) indicated that the benefits of analysis would greatly

outweigh the costs. Whether an organization writes policy guidelines or not, the act of examining communication practices and expectations is likely to be instructive and beneficial.

Where weaknesses are revealed, organizations should clarify their expectations. Written guidelines may be appropriate for some situations, training for others, example for others, grapevine for still others, and so on through the many other options. Respondents named 18 positive means and several negative means of shaping communication behaviors; the literature and everyday experience show still others.

Based on the wide variety of incidents narrated by subjects, expensive communication problems are sometimes local, personal, or departmental, but sometimes pervasive in organizations. *Managers should consider the conveying of clear communication-behavior expectations as a fundamental element of strategy.*

Achieving this clarity may take, for different organizations, one or several of the following: *analysis of organizational culture,* especially where culture is weak or is idiosyncratic among departments; *analysis of existing strong corporate cultures for communication values;* and *communication audits.* Firms might also perform *ethnographic analyses, including observation and interviewing, to learn exactly what organizational communication policies are operating* (see Whitney, 1989). Firms should consider *communication training for managers, especially in giving performance feedback.* Organizations should examine how their *reward system* affects communication behaviors. Most employees are concerned for the organization's success but are also moved strongly by the "WIIFM factor": What's in it for me? It would be useful for organizations to *analyze managers' behaviors and words that send messages about communicating.*

One set of rules will not fit all organizations: For instance, service organizations generally will need to emphasize customer communications more, whereas product organizations' more crucial communications are likely to regard quality, schedule, and quantity goals. To be sure, organizations cannot foresee all information needs and should not attempt to formulate guidelines for all situations. Henderson's (1987) model of interpersonal managerial communication shows the range and complexity of influences on what managers say and do. This study suggests, however, that many organizations could be far more deliberate than they are at present about sending consistent, workable messages about communication expectations and could conserve time and money by doing so.

NOTES

This research was supported by a sabbatical semester from California State University—Long Beach. Appreciation is extended to Jone Rymer of Wayne State University and to N. Lamar Reinsch, Jr., of Georgetown University, who read and critiqued an earlier draft of this article.

Jeanette W. Gilsdorf, PhD (University of Nebraska–Lincoln), has published about 40 articles in journals including *The Journal of Business Communication, Management Communication Quarterly,* and *Public Relations Review.* She was president of ABC in 1994. Her research interests include organizational policy on communicating, business lexicon, and persuasion. Her textbooks are with Irwin and Wiley.

Send correspondence to Jeanette W. Gilsdorf, Information Systems, College of Business Administration, California State University–Long Beach, 1250 Bellflower Blvd., Long Beach, CA 90840-8506 <gilsdorf@csulb.edu or gilsdorf@earthlink.net.>

References

Ashford, S. J., & Cummings, L. L. (1985). Proactive feedback seeking: The instrumental use of the information environment. *Journal of Occupational Psychology, 58,* 67–79.

Clampitt, P. G., & Downs, C. W. (1993, January). Employee perceptions of the relationship between communication and productivity: A field study. *The Journal of Business Communication, 30*(1), 5–28.

Comer, D. R. (1991, August). Organizational newcomers' acquisition of information from peers. *Management Communication Quarterly, 5*(1), 64–89.

Czarniawska-Joerges, B., & Joerges, B. (1988, November). How to control things with words: Organizational talk and control. *Management Communication Quarterly, 2*(2), 170–193.

Daft, R. L., & Weick, K. E. (1984). Towards a model of organizations as interpretation systems. *Academy of Management Review, 9*(2), 284–295.

Deal, T. E., & Kennedy, A. A. (1982). *Corporate cultures: The rites and rituals of corporate life.* Reading, MA: Addison-Wesley.

Dechant, K., & Veiga, J. F. (1995). More on the folly. *Academy of Management Executive, 9*(1), 15–16.

Downs, C. W., & Ham, T. (1982). Communication and productivity. In M. Burgoon (Ed.), *Communication yearbook, 5* (pp. 435–471). New Brunswick, NJ: Transaction Books.

Downs, C. W., Clampitt, P. G., & Pfeiifer, A. (1988). Communication and organizational outcomes. In G. Goldhaber & G. Barnett (Eds.), *Handbook of organizational communication* (pp. 171–211). Norwood, NJ: Ablex.

Eisenberg, E. M. (1984). Ambiguity as strategy in organizational communication. *Communication Monographs, 51,* 227–242.

Francis, D., & Woodcock, M. (1990). *Unblocking organizational values.* Glenview, IL: Scott, Foresman.

Gilsdorf, J. W. (1987, Fall). Written corporate communication policy: Extent, coverage, costs, benefits. *The Journal of Business Communication, 24*(4), 35–52.

Gilsdorf, J. W. (1992, February). Written corporate policy on communicating: A Delphi survey. *Management Communication Quarterly, 5*(3), 316–347.

Goldhaber, G. M. (1990). *Organizational communication.* (5th ed.) Dubuque, IA: Wm. C. Brown.

Gray, B., Bougon, M. G., & Donnellon, A. (1985). Organizations as constructions and deconstructions of meaning. *Journal of Management, 11*(2), 83–98.

Guzley, R. M. (1992, May). Organizational climate and communication climate: Predictors of commitment to the organization. *Management Communication Quarterly, 5*(4), 379–402.

Harcourt, J., Richerson, V., & Wattier, M. J. (1991, Fall). A national study of middle managers' assessment of organization communication quality. *The Journal of Business Communication, 28*(4), 348–365.

Harris, S. G. (1994). Organizational culture and individual sensemaking: A schema-based perspective. *Organization Science, 5*(3), 309–321.

Henderson, L. S. (1987, August). The contextual nature of interpersonal communication in management theory and research. *Management Communication Quarterly, 1*(1), 7–31.

Ibarra, H., & Andrews, S. B. (1993). Power, social influence, and sense making: Effects of network centrality and proximity on employee perceptions. *Administrative Science Quarterly, 38,* 277–303.

Jablin, F. M. (1987). Organizational entry, assimilation, and exit. In F. M. Jablin, L. L. Putnam, K. H. Roberts, & L. W. Porter (Eds.), *Handbook of organizational communication: An interdisciplinary perspective* (pp. 679–740). Newbury Park, CA: Sage.

Johnson, J. D., Donohue, W. A., Atkin, C. K., & Johnson, S. (1994, April). Differences between formal and informal communication channels. *The Journal of Business Communication, 31*(2), 111–122.

Katz, D., & Kahn, R. L. (1966). *The social psychology of organizations.* New York: John Wiley & Sons.

Kerr, S. (1975). On the folly of rewarding A, while hoping for B. *Academy of Management Journal, 18,* 769–783. Updated for *Academy of Management Executive, 9*(1), 7–14.

Louis, M. R. (1980, June). Surprise and sense making: What newcomers experience in entering unfamiliar organizational settings. *Administrative Science Quarterly, 25,* 226–251.

Miller, V. D., & Jablin, F. M. (1991). Information seeking during organizational entry: Influences, tactics, and a model of the process. *Academy of Management Review, 16*(1), 92–120.

Mills, A. J., & Murgatroyd, S. J. (1991). *Organizational rules: A framework for understanding organizational action.* Philadelphia: Open University Press.

Nadler, D. A., & Lawler, E. E., III. (1983). Motivation: A diagnostic approach. In J. R. Hackman, E. E. Lawler III, & L. W. Porter (Eds.), *Perspectives on behavior in organizations* (2nd ed., pp. 67–87). New York: McGraw-Hill.

Poole, M. S. (1985). Communication and organizational climates: Review, critique, and a new perspective. In R. McPhee & P. K. Tompkins (Eds.), *Organizational communication: Traditional themes and new directions* (pp. 79–108). Beverly Hills, CA: Sage.

Porter, L. W., & Lawler, E. E., III. (1968). *Managerial attitudes and performance.* Homewood, IL: Irwin.

Rogers, D. P. (1988). The relationship between written communication policies and internal communication philosophies. *Proceedings of the International Meeting of the Association for Business Communication,* Indianapolis, IN, 15–22.

Schall, M. S. (1983). A communication-rules approach to organizational culture. *Administrative Science Quarterly, 28,* 557–581.

Schein, E. H. (1985). *Organizational culture and leadership: A dynamic view.* San Francisco: Jossey-Bass.

Southard, S. G. (1990, September). Interacting successfully in corporate culture. *Journal of Business and Technical Communication, 4*(2), 79–90.

Stohl, C. (1986). The role of memorable messages in the process of organizational socialization. *Communication Quarterly, 34*(3), 231–249.

Teboul, J. C. B. (1994, November). Facing and coping with uncertainty during organizational encounter. *Management Communication Quarterly, 8*(2), 190–224.

Thomas, J. B., Clark, S. M., & Gioia, D. A. (1993). Strategic sensemaking and organizational performance: Linkages among scanning, interpretation, action, and outcomes. *Academy of Management Journal, 36*(2), 239–269.

Thombetta, J. J., & Rogers, D. P. (1988, May). Communication climate, job satisfaction, and organizational commitment: The effects of information adequacy, communication openness, and decision participation. *Management Communication Quarterly, 1*(4), 494–514.

Van Maanen, J. (1976). Breaking in: Socialization to work. In R. Dubin (Ed.), *Handbook of work, organization, and society* (pp. 67–130). Chicago: Rand McNally College.

Vroom, V. H. (1964). *Work and motivation.* New York: John Wiley & Sons.

Weick, K. E. (1995). *Sensemaking in organizations.* Thousand Oaks, CA: Sage.

Wellmon, T. A. (1988, May). Conceptualizing organizational communication competence: A rules-based perspective. *Management Communication Quarterly, 1*(4), 515–534.

Whitney, M. A. (1989). Analyzing corporate communications policy using ethnographic methods. *IEEE Transactions on Professional Communication, 32*(2), 76–80.

Wilson, D. O. (1992, Spring). Diagonal communication links within organizations. *The Journal of Business Communication, 29*(2), 129–143.

Wilson, D. O., & Malik, S. D. (1995, January). Looking for a few good sources: Exploring the intraorganizational communication linkages of first line managers. *The Journal of Business Communication, 32*(1), 31–47.

IQ and technical skills are important, but emotional intelligence is the sine qua non of leadership.

What Makes a Leader?

BY DANIEL GOLEMAN

Every businessperson knows a story about a highly intelligent, highly skilled executive who was promoted into a leadership position only to fail at the job. And they also know a story about someone with solid—but not extraordinary—intellectual abilities and technical skills who was promoted into a similar position and then soared.

Such anecdotes support the widespread belief that identifying individuals with the "right stuff" to be leaders is more art than science. After all, the personal styles of superb leaders vary: some leaders are subdued and analytical; others shout their manifestos from the mountaintops. And just as important, different situations call for different types of leadership. Most mergers need a sensitive negotiator at the helm, whereas many turnarounds require a more forceful authority.

I have found, however, that the most effective leaders are alike in one crucial way: they all have a high degree of what has come to be known as *emotional intelligence.* It's not that IQ and technical skills are irrelevant. They do matter, but mainly as "threshold capabilities"; that is, they are the entry-level requirements for executive positions. But my research, along with other recent studies, clearly shows that

Daniel Goleman is the author of Emotional Intelligence *(Bantam, 1995) and* Working with Emotional Intelligence *(Bantam, 1998). He is cochairman of the Consortium for Research on Emotional Intelligence in Organizations, which is based at Rutgers University's Graduate School of Applied and Professional Psychology in Piscataway, New Jersey. He can be reached at Goleman@javanet.com.*

emotional intelligence is the sine qua non of leadership. Without it, a person can have the best training in the world, an incisive, analytical mind, and an endless supply of smart ideas, but he still won't make a great leader.

Effective leaders are alike in one crucial way: they all have a high degree of emotional intelligence.

In the course of the past year, my colleagues and I have focused on how emotional intelligence operates at work. We have examined the relationship between emotional intelligence and effective performance, especially in leaders. And we have observed how emotional intelligence shows itself on the job. How can you tell if someone has high emotional intelligence, for example, and how can you recognize it in yourself? In the following pages, we'll explore these questions, taking each of the components of emotional intelligence—self-awareness, self-regulation, motivation, empathy, and social skill—in turn.

Evaluating Emotional Intelligence

Most large companies today have employed trained psychologists to develop what are known as "competency models" to aid them in identifying, training, and promoting likely stars in the leadership firmament. The psychologists have also developed such models for lower-level positions. And in recent years, I have analyzed competency models from 188 companies, most of which were large and global and included the likes of Lucent Technologies, British Airways, and Credit Suisse.

In carrying out this work, my objective was to determine which personal capabilities drove outstanding performance within these organizations, and to what degree they did so. I grouped capabilities into three categories: purely technical skills like accounting and business planning; cognitive abilities like analytical reasoning; and competencies demonstrating emotional intelligence such as the ability to work with others and effectiveness in leading change.

To create some of the competency models, psychologists asked senior managers at the companies to identify the capabilities that typified the organization's most outstanding leaders. To create other models, the psychologists used objective criteria such as a division's profitability to differentiate the star performers at senior levels within their organizations from the average ones. Those

individuals were then extensively interviewed and tested, and their capabilities were compared. This process resulted in the creation of lists of ingredients for highly effective leaders. The lists ranged in length from 7 to 15 items and included such ingredients as initiative and strategic vision.

When I analyzed all this data, I found dramatic results. To be sure, intellect was a driver of outstanding performance. Cognitive skills such as big-picture thinking and long-term vision were particularly important. But when I calculated the ratio of technical skills, IQ, and emotional intelligence as ingredients of excellent performance, emotional intelligence proved to be twice as important as the others for jobs at all levels.

Moreover, my analysis showed that emotional intelligence played an increasingly important role at the highest levels of the company, where differences in technical skills are of negligible importance. In other words, the higher the rank of a person considered to be a star performer, the more emotional intelligence capabilities showed up as the reason for his or her effectiveness. When I compared star performers with average ones in senior leadership positions, nearly 90% of the difference in their profiles was attributable to emotional intelligence factors rather than cognitive abilities.

Other researchers have confirmed that emotional intelligence not only distinguishes outstanding leaders but can also be linked to strong performance. The findings of the late David McClelland, the renowned researcher in human and organizational behavior, are a good example. In a 1996 study of a global food and beverage company, McClelland found that when senior managers had a critical mass of emotional intelligence capabilities, their divisions outperformed yearly earnings goals by 20%. Meanwhile, division leaders without that critical mass underperformed by almost the same amount. McClelland's findings, interestingly, held as true in the company's U.S. divisions as in its divisions in Asia and Europe.

In short, the numbers are beginning to tell us a persuasive story about the link between a company's success and the emotional intelligence of its leaders. And just as important, research is also demonstrating that people can, if they take the right approach, develop their emotional intelligence. (See "Can Emotional Intelligence Be Learned?")

Self-Awareness

Self-awareness is the first component of emotional intelligence—which makes sense when one con-

The Five Components of Emotional Intelligence at Work

	Definition	Hallmarks
Self-Awareness	the ability to recognize and understand your moods, emotions, and drives, as well as their effect on others	self-confidence realistic self-assessment self-deprecating sense of humor
Self-Regulation	the ability to control or redirect disruptive impulses and moods the propensity to suspend judgment—to think before acting	trustworthiness and integrity comfort with ambiguity openness to change
Motivation	a passion to work for reasons that go beyong money or status a propensity to pursur goals with energy and persistence	strong drive to achieve optimism, even in the face of failure organizational commitment
Empathy	the ability to understand the emotional makeup of other people skill in treating people according to their emotional reactions	expertise in building and retaining talent cross-cultural sensitivity service to clients and customers
Social Skill	proficiency in managing relationships and building networks an ability to find common ground and build rapport	effectiveness in leading change persuasiveness expertise in building and leading teams

siders that the Delphic oracle gave the advice to "know thyself" thousands of years ago. Self-awareness means having a deep understanding of one's emotions, strengths, weaknesses, needs, and drives. People with strong self-awareness are neither overly critical nor unrealistically hopeful. Rather, they are honest—with themselves and with others.

People who have a high degree of self-awareness recognize how their feelings affect them, other people, and their job performance. Thus a self-aware person who knows that tight deadlines bring out the worst in him plans his time carefully and gets his work done well in advance. Another person with high self-awareness will be able to work with a demanding client. She will understand the client's impact on her moods and the deeper reasons for her frustration. "Their trivial demands take us away from the real work that needs to be done," she might explain. And she will go one step further and turn her anger into something constructive.

Self-awareness extends to a person's understanding of his or her values and goals. Someone who is highly self-aware knows where he is headed and why; so, for example, he will be able to be firm in turning down a job offer that is tempting financially but does not fit with his principles or long-term goals. A person who lacks self-awareness is apt to make decisions that bring on inner turmoil by treading on buried values. "The money looked good so I signed on," someone might say two years into a job, "but the work means so little to me that I'm constantly bored." The decisions of self-aware people mesh with their values; consequently,they often find work to be energizing.

How can one recognize self-awareness? First and foremost, it shows itself as candor and an ability to assess oneself realistically. People with high self-awareness are able to speak accurately and openly—although not necessarily effusively or confessionally—about their emotions and the impact they have on their work. For instance, one manager I know of was skeptical about a new personal-shopper service that her company, a major department-store chain, was about to introduce. Without prompting from her team or her boss, she offered them an explanation: "It's hard for me to get behind the rollout of this service," she admitted, "because I really wanted to run the project, but I wasn't selected. Bear with me while I deal with that." The manager did indeed examine her feelings; a week later, she was supporting the project fully.

Self-aware job candidates will be frank in admitting to failure—and will often tell their tales with a smile.

Such self-knowledge often shows itself in the hiring process. Ask a candidate to describe a time he got carried away by his feelings and did something he later regretted. Self-aware candidates will be frank in admitting to failure—and will often tell their tales with a smile. One of the hallmarks of self-awareness is a self-deprecating sense of humor.

Self-awareness can also be identified during performance reviews. Self-aware people know—and are comfortable talking about—their limitations and strengths, and they often demonstrate a thirst for constructive criticism. By contrast, people with low self-awareness interpret the message that they need to improve as a threat or a sign of failure.

People who have mastered their emotions are able to roll with the changes. They don't panic.

Self-aware people can also be recognized by their self-confidence. They have a firm grasp of their capabilities and are less likely to set themselves up to fail by, for example, overstretching on assignments. They know, too, when to ask for help. And the risks they take on the job are

calculated. They won't ask for a challenge that they know they can't handle alone. They'll play to their strengths.

Consider the actions of a mid-level employee who was invited to sit in on a strategy meeting with her company's top executives. Although she was the most junior person in the room, she did not sit there quietly, listening in awestruck or fearful silence. She knew she had a head for clear logic and the skill to present ideas persuasively, and she offered cogent suggestions about the company's strategy. At the same time, her self-awareness stopped her from wandering into territory where she knew she was weak.

Despite the value of having self-aware people in the workplace, my research indicates that senior executives don't often give self-awareness the credit it deserves when they look for potential leaders. Many executives mistake candor about feelings for "wimpiness" and fail to give due respect to employees who openly acknowledge their shortcomings. Such people are too readily dismissed as "not tough enough" to lead others.

In fact, the opposite is true. In the first place, people generally admire and respect candor. Further, leaders are constantly required to make judgment calls that require a candid assessment of capabilities—their own and those of others. Do we have the management expertise to acquire a competitor? Can we launch a new product within six months? People who assess themselves honestly—that is, self-aware people—are well suited to do the same for the organizations they run.

Self-Regulation

Biological impulses drive our emotions. We cannot do away with them—but we can do much to manage them. Self-regulation, which is like an ongoing inner conversation, is the component of emotional intelligence that frees us from being prisoners of our feelings. People engaged in such a conversation feel bad moods and emotional impulses just as everyone else does, but they find ways to control them and even to channel them in useful ways.

Imagine an executive who has just watched a team of his employees present a botched analysis to the company's board of directors. In the gloom that follows, the executive might find himself tempted to pound on the table in anger or kick over a chair. He could leap up

Can Emotional Intelligence Be Learned?

For ages, people have debated if leaders are born or made. So too goes the debate about emotional intelligence. Are people born with certain levels of empathy, for example, or do they acquire empathy as a result of life's experiences? The answer is both. Scientific inquiry strongly suggests that there is a genetic component to emotional intelligence. Psychological and developmental research indicates that nurture plays a role as well. How much of each perhaps will never be known, but research and practice clearly demonstrate that emotional intelligence can be learned.

One thing is certain: emotional intelligence increases with age. There is an old-fashioned word for the phenomenon: maturity. Yet even with maturity, some people still need training to enhance their emotional intelligence. Unfortunately, far too many training programs that intend to build leadership skills—including emotional intelligence—are a waste of time and money. The problem is simple: they focus on the wrong part of the brain.

Emotional intelligence is born largely in the neurotransmitters of the brain's limbic system, which governs feelings, impulses, and drives. Research indicates that the limbic system learns best through motivation, extended practice, and feedback. Compare this with the kind of learning that goes on in the neocortex, which governs analytical and technical ability. The neocortex grasps concepts and logic. It is the part of the brain that figures out how to use a computer or make a sales call by reading a book. Not surprisingly—but mistakenly—it is also the part of the brain targeted by most training programs aimed at enhancing emotional intelligence. When such programs take, in effect, a neocortical approach, my research with the Consortium for Research on Emotional Intelligence in Organizations has shown they can even have a *negative* impact on people's job performance.

To enhance emotional intelligence, organizations must refocus their training to include the limbic system. They must help people break old behavioral habits and establish new ones. That not only takes much more time than conventional training programs, it also requires an individualized approach.

Imagine an executive who is thought to be low on empathy by her colleagues. Part of that deficit shows itself as an inability to listen; she interrupts people and doesn't pay close attention to what they're saying. To fix the problem, the executive needs to be motivated to change, and then she needs practice and feedback from others in the company. A colleague or coach could be tapped to let the executive know when she has been observed failing to listen. She would then have to replay the incident and give a better response; that is, demonstrate her ability to absorb what others are saying. And the executive could be directed to observe certain executives who listen well and to mimic their behavior.

With persistence and practice, such a process can lead to lasting results. I know one Wall Street executive who sought to improve his empathy—specifically his ability to read people's reactions and see their perspectives. Before beginning his quest, the executive's subordinates were terrified of working with him. People even went so far as to hide bad news from him. Naturally, he was shocked when finally confronted with these facts. He went home and told his family—but they only confirmed what he had heard at work. When their opinions on any given subject did not mesh with his, they, too, were frightened of him.

Enlisting the help of a coach, the executive went to work to heighten his empathy through practice and feedback. His first step was to take a vacation to a foreign country where he did not speak the language. While there, he monitored his reactions to the unfamiliar and his openness to people who were different from him. When he returned home, humbled by his week abroad, the executive asked his coach to shadow him for parts of the day, several times a week, in order to critique how he treated people with new or different perspectives. At the same time, he consciously used on-the-job interactions as opportunities to practice "hearing" ideas that differed from his. Finally, the executive had himself videotaped in meetings and asked those who worked for and with him to critique his ability to acknowledge and understand the feelings of others. It took several months, but the executive's emotional intelligence did ultimately rise, and the improvement was reflected in his overall performance on the job.

It's important to emphasize that building one's emotional intelligence cannot—will not—happen without sincere desire and concerted effort. A brief seminar won't help; nor can one buy a how-to manual. It is much harder to learn to empathize—to internalize empathy as a natural response to people—than it is to become adept at regression analysis. But it can be done. "Nothing great was ever achieved without enthusiasm," wrote Ralph Waldo Emerson. If your goal is to become a real leader, these words can serve as a guidepost in your efforts to develop high emotional intelligence.

---

and scream at the group. Or he might maintain a grim silence, glaring at everyone before stalking off.

But if he had a gift for self-regulation, he would choose a different approach. He would pick his words carefully, acknowledging the team's poor performance without rushing to any hasty judgment. He would then step back to consider the reasons for the failure. Are they personal—a lack of effort? Are there any mitigating factors? What was his role in the debacle? After considering these questions, he would call the team together, lay out the incident's consequences, and offer his feelings about it. He would then present his analysis of the problem and a well-considered solution.

Why does self-regulation matter so much for leaders? First of all, people who are in control of their feelings and impulses—that is, people who are reasonable—are able to create an environment of trust and fairness. In such an environment, politics and infighting are sharply reduced and productivity is high. Talented people flock to the organization and aren't tempted to leave. And self-regulation has a trickle-down effect. No one wants to be known as a hothead when the boss is known for her calm approach. Fewer bad moods at the top mean fewer throughout the organization.

Second, self-regulation is important for competitive reasons. Everyone knows that business today is rife with ambiguity and change. Companies merge and break apart regularly. Technology transforms work at a dizzying pace. People who have mastered their emotions are able to roll with the changes. When a new change program is announced, they don't panic; instead, they are able to suspend judgment, seek out information, and listen to executives explain the new program. As the initiative moves forward, they are able to move with it.

Sometimes they even lead the way. Consider the case of a manager at a large manufacturing company. Like her colleagues, she had used a certain software program for five years. The program drove how she collected and reported data and how she thought about the company's strategy. One day, senior executives announced that a new program was to be installed that would radically change how information was gathered and assessed within the organization. While many people in the company complained bitterly about how disruptive the change would be, the manager mulled over the reasons for the new program and was convinced of its potential to improve performance. She eagerly attended training sessions—some of her colleagues refused to do so—and was eventually promoted to run several divisions, in part because she used the new technology so effectively.

I want to push the importance of self-regulation to leadership even further and make the case that it enhances integrity, which is not only a personal virtue but also an organizational strength. Many of the bad things that happen in companies are a function of impulsive behavior. People rarely plan to exaggerate profits, pad expense accounts, dip into the till, or abuse power for selfish ends. Instead, an opportunity presents itself, and people with low impulse control just say yes.

By contrast, consider the behavior of the senior executive at a large food company. The executive was scrupulously honest in his negotiations with local distributors. He would routinely lay out his cost structure in detail, thereby giving the distributors a realistic understanding of the company's pricing. This approach meant the executive couldn't always drive a hard bargain. Now, on occasion, he felt the urge to increase profits by withholding information about the company's costs. But he challenged that impulse—he saw that it made more sense in the long run to counteract it. His emotional self-regulation paid off in strong, lasting relationships with distributors that benefited the company more than any short-term financial gains would have.

The signs of emotional self-regulation, therefore, are not hard to miss: a propensity for reflection and thoughtfulness; comfort with ambiguity and change; and integrity—an ability to say no to impulsive urges.

Like self-awareness, self-regulation often does not get its due. People who can master their emotions are sometimes seen as cold fish—their considered responses are taken as a lack of passion. People with fiery temperaments are frequently thought of as "classic" leaders—their outbursts are considered hallmarks of charisma and power. But when such people make it to the top, their impulsiveness often works against them. In my research, extreme displays of negative emotion have never emerged as a driver of good leadership.

Motivation

If there is one trait that virtually all effective leaders have, it is motivation. They are driven to achieve beyond expectations—their own and everyone else's. The key word here is *achieve*. Plenty of people are motivated by external factors such as a big salary or the status that comes from having an impressive title or being part of a prestigious company. By contrast, those with leadership potential are motivated by a deeply embedded desire to achieve for the sake of achievement.

If you are looking for leaders, how can you identify people who are motivated by the drive to achieve rather than by external rewards? The first sign is a passion for the work itself—such people seek out creative challenges, love to learn, and take great pride in a job well done. They also display an unflagging energy to do things better. People with such energy often seem restless with the status quo. They are persistent with their questions about why things are done one way rather than another; they are eager to explore new approaches to their work.

A cosmetics company manager, for example, was frustrated that he had to wait two weeks to get sales results from people in the field. He finally tracked down an automated phone system that would beep each of his salespeople at 5 p.m. every day. An automated message then prompted them to punch in their numbers—how many calls and sales they had made that day. The system shortened the feedback time on sales results from weeks to hours.

That story illustrates two other common traits of people who are driven to achieve. They are forever raising the performance bar, and they like to keep score. Take the performance bar first.

During performance reviews, people with high levels of motivation might ask to be "stretched" by their superiors. Of course, an employee who combines self-awareness with internal motivation will recognize her limits—but she won't settle for objectives that seem too easy to fulfill.

And it follows naturally that people who are driven to do better also want a way of tracking progress—their own, their team's, and their company's. Whereas people with low achievement motivation are often fuzzy about results, those with high achievement motivation often keep score by tracking such hard measures as profitability or market share. I know of a money manager who starts and ends his day on the Internet, gauging the performance of his stock fund against four industry-set benchmarks.

Interestingly, people with high motivation remain optimistic even when the score is against them. In such cases, self-regulation combines with achievement motivation to overcome the frustration and depression that come after a setback or failure. Take the case of another portfolio manager at a large investment company. After several successful years, her fund tumbled for three consecutive quarters, leading three large institutional clients to shift their business elsewhere.

Some executives would have blamed the nosedive on circumstances outside their control; others might have seen the setback as evidence of personal failure. This portfolio manager, however, saw an opportunity to prove she could lead a turnaround. Two years later, when she was promoted to a very senior level in the company, she described the experience as "the best thing that ever happened to me; I learned so much from it."

Executives trying to recognize high levels of achievement motivation in their people can look for one last piece of evidence: commitment to the organization. When people love their job for the work itself, they often feel committed to the organizations that make that work possible. Committed employees are likely to stay with an organization even when they are pursued by headhunters waving money.

It's not difficult to understand how and why a motivation to achieve translates into strong leadership. If you set the performance bar high for yourself, you will do the same for the organization when you are in a position to do so. Likewise, a drive to surpass goals and an interest in keeping score can be contagious. Leaders with these traits can often build a team of managers around them with the same traits. And of course, optimism and organizational commitment are

The very word *empathy* seems unbusinesslike, out of place amid the tough realities of the marketplace.

fundamental to leadership—just try to imagine running a company without them.

Empathy

Of all the dimensions of emotional intelligence, empathy is the most easily recognized. We have all felt the empathy of a sensitive teacher or friend; we have all been struck by its absence in an unfeeling coach or boss. But when it comes to business, we rarely hear people praised, let alone rewarded, for their empathy. The very word seems unbusinesslike, out of place amid the tough realities of the marketplace.

But empathy doesn't mean a kind of "I'm okay, you're okay" mushiness. For a leader, that is, it doesn't mean adopting other people's emotions as one's own and trying to please everybody. That would be a nightmare—it would make action impossible. Rather, empathy means thoughtfully considering employees' feelings—along with other factors—in the process of making intelligent decisions.

For an example of empathy in action, consider what happened when two giant brokerage companies merged, creating redundant jobs in all their divisions. One division manager called his people together and gave a gloomy speech that emphasized the number of people who would soon be fired. The manager of another division gave his people a different kind of speech. He was upfront about his own worry and confusion, and he promised to keep people informed and to treat everyone fairly.

The difference between these two managers was empathy. The first manager was too worried about his own fate to consider the feelings of his anxiety-stricken colleagues. The second knew intuitively what his people were feeling, and he acknowledged their fears with his words. Is it any surprise that the first manager saw his division sink as many demoralized people, especially the most talented, departed? By contrast, the second manager continued to be a strong leader, his best people stayed, and his division remained as productive as ever.

Empathy is particularly important today as a component of leadership for at least three reasons:

the increasing use of teams; the rapid pace of globalization; and the growing need to retain talent.

Consider the challenge of leading a team. As anyone who has ever been a part of one can attest, teams are cauldrons of bubbling emotions. They are often charged with reaching a consensus—hard enough with two people and much more difficult as the numbers increase. Even in groups with as few as four or five members, alliances form and clashing agendas get set. A team's leader must be able to sense and understand the viewpoints of everyone around the table.

Social skill is friendliness with a purpose: moving people in the direction you desire.

That's exactly what a marketing manager at a large information technology company was able to do when she was appointed to lead a troubled team. The group was in turmoil, overloaded by work and missing deadlines. Tensions were high among the members. Tinkering with procedures was not enough to bring the group together and make it an effective part of the company.

So the manager took several steps. In a series of one-on-one sessions, she took the time to listen to everyone in the group—what was frustrating them, how they rated their colleagues, whether they felt they had been ignored. And then she directed the team in a way that brought it together: she encouraged people to speak more openly about their frustrations, and she helped people raise constructive complaints during meetings. In short, her empathy allowed her to understand her team's emotional makeup. The result was not just heightened collaboration among members but also added business, as the team was called on for help by a wider range of internal clients.

Globalization is another reason for the rising importance of empathy for business leaders. Cross-cultural dialogue can easily lead to miscues and misunderstandings. Empathy is an antidote. People who have it are attuned to subtleties in body language; they can hear the message beneath the words being spoken. Beyond that, they have a deep understanding of the existence and importance of cultural and ethnic differences.

Consider the case of an American consultant whose team had just pitched a project to a potential Japanese client. In its dealings with Americans, the team was accustomed to being bombarded with questions after such a proposal,

but this time it was greeted with a long silence. Other members of the team, taking the silence as disapproval, were ready to pack and leave. The lead consultant gestured them to stop. Although he was not particularly familiar with Japanese culture, he read the client's face and posture and sensed not rejection but interest—even deep consideration. He was right: when the client finally spoke, it was to give the consulting firm the job.

Finally, empathy plays a key role in the retention of talent, particularly in today's information economy. Leaders have always needed empathy to develop and keep good people, but today the stakes are higher. When good people leave, they take the company's knowledge with them.

That's where coaching and mentoring come in. It has repeatedly been shown that coaching and mentoring pay off not just in better performance but also in increased job satisfaction and decreased turnover. But what makes coaching and mentoring work best is the nature of the relationship. Outstanding coaches and mentors get inside the heads of the people they are helping. They sense how to give effective feedback. They know when to push for better performance and when to hold back. In the way they motivate their protégés, they demonstrate empathy in action.

In what is probably sounding like a refrain, let me repeat that empathy doesn't get much respect in business. People wonder how leaders can make hard decisions if they are "feeling" for all the people who will be affected. But leaders with empathy do more than sympathize with people around them: they use their knowledge to improve their companies in subtle but important ways.

Social Skill

The first three components of emotional intelligence are all self-management skills. The last two, empathy and social skill, concern a person's ability to manage relationships with others. As a component of emotional intelligence, social skill is not as simple as it sounds. It's not just a matter of friendliness, although people with high levels of social skill are rarely mean-spirited. Social skill, rather, is friendliness with a purpose: moving people in the direction you desire, whether that's agreement on a new marketing strategy or enthusiasm about a new product.

Socially skilled people tend to have a wide circle of acquaintances, and they have a knack for finding common ground with people of all kinds—a knack for building rapport. That doesn't mean they socialize continually; it means they work according to the assumption that nothing important gets done alone. Such people have a network in place when the time for action comes.

Social skill is the culmination of the other dimensions of emotional intelligence. People tend to be very effective at managing relationships when they can understand and control their own emotions and can empathize with the feelings of others. Even motivation contributes to social skill. Remember that people who are driven to achieve tend to be optimistic, even in the face of setbacks or failure. When people are upbeat, their "glow" is cast upon conversations and other social encounters. They are popular, and for good reason.

Because it is the outcome of the other dimensions of emotional intelligence, social skill is recognizable on the job in many ways that will by now sound familiar. Socially skilled people, for instance, are adept at managing teams—that's their empathy at work. Likewise,they are expert persuaders—a manifestation of self-awareness, self-regulation, and empathy combined. Given those skills, good persuaders know when to make an emotional plea, for instance, and when an appeal to reason will work better. And motivation, when publicly visible,makes such people excellent collaborators; their passion for the work spreads to others, and they are driven to find solutions.

But sometimes social skill shows itself in ways the other emotional intelligence components do not. For instance, socially skilled people may at times appear not to be working while at work. They seem to be idly schmoozing—chatting in the hallways with colleagues or joking around with people who are not even connected to their "real" jobs. Socially skilled people, however, don't think it makes sense to arbitrarily limit the scope of their relationships. They build bonds widely because they know that in these fluid times, they may need help someday from people they are just gettin to know today.

For example, consider the case of an executive in the strategy department of a global computer manufacturer. By 1993, he was convinced that the company's future lay with the Internet. Over the course of the next year, he found kindred spirits and used his social skill to stitch together a virtual community that cut across levels, divisions, and nations. He then used this de facto team to put up a corporate Web site, among the first by a major company. And, on his own initiative, with no budget or formal status, he signed up the company to participate in an annual Internet industry convention. Calling on his allies and persuading various divisions to donate funds, he recruited more than 50 people from a dozen different units to represent the company at the convention.

Emotional intelligence can be learned. The process is not easy. It takes time and commitment.

Management took notice: within a year of the conference, the executive's team formed the basis for the company's first Internet division, and he was formally put in charge of it. To get there, the executive had ignored conventional boundaries, forging and maintaining connections with people in every corner of the organization.

Is social skill considered a key leadership capability in most companies? The answer is yes, especially when compared with the other components of emotional intelligence. People seem to know intuitively that leaders need to manage relationships effectively; no leader is an island. After all, the leader's task is to get work done through other people, and social skill makes that possible. A leader who cannot express her empathy may as well not have it at all. And a leader's motivation will be useless if he cannot communicate his passion to the organization. Social skill allows leaders to put their emotional intelligence to work.

It would be foolish to assert that good-old-fashioned IQ and technical ability are not important ingredients in strong leadership. But the recipe would not be complete without emotional intelligence. It was once thought that the components of emotional intelligence were "nice to have" in business leaders. But now we know that, for the sake of performance, these are ingredients that leaders "need to have."

It is fortunate, then, that emotional intelligence can be learned. The process is not easy. It takes time and, most of all, commitment. But the benefits that come from having a well-developed emotional intelligence, both for the individual and for the organization, make it worth the effort.

INTEREST ALIGNMENT AND COALITIONS IN MULTIPARTY NEGOTIATION

JEFFREY T. POLZER
University of Texas at Austin

ELIZABETH A. MANNIX
Columbia University

MARGARET A. NEALE
Stanford University

This study tested hypotheses developed from the distinct literatures on negotiations and coalitions and hypotheses integrating the two. In a complex, three-person negotiation simulation, subjects had to decide jointly how to allocate two resource pools. They were given multiple pieces of information regarding their negotiation preferences, coalition alternatives, and entitlements. Coalition alternatives and entitlement cues affected only the resource pool to which they were directly linked, but compatible interests, through the coalitions they generated, affected both resource pools, including the one to which these interests were not directly linked. We discuss the importance of integrating negotiation and coalition research in a way that incorporates the social dynamics of the negotiation interaction.

Resource allocation decisions in small groups can be usefully analyzed from a negotiations perspective (Brett, 1991). Conflicting interests are resolved through multiparty negotiation in both formal and everyday social interaction, within groups ranging from governments and organizational task forces to research teams (Ancona, Friedman, & Kolb, 1991; Bazerman, Mannix, & Thompson, 1988; Brett & Rognes, 1986). In multiparty negotiations, bargainers are faced with cooperating enough to reach mutually acceptable agreements while simultaneously competing enough to satisfy individual interests—interests that may align with others' interests in ways that are distributive, integrative, or compatible (Fisher & Ury, 1981; Froman & Cohen, 1970; Kelley, 1966; Neale & Bazerman, 1991; Pruitt, 1981; Thompson, 1990). Multiparty negotiations are complex social interactions because of both the multiple sets of

preferences that must be considered in fashioning agreements and the interpersonal dynamics that grow increasingly complicated as more people interact (Bazerman et al., 1988). An especially important source of complexity in multiparty negotiations, and one that is the focus of this article, is the inherent potential for coalition membership to influence the negotiated outcomes (Caplow, 1956; Chertkoff, 1967; Gamson, 1961; Luce & Raiffa, 1957; Miller & Komorita, 1986; Murnighan, 1986).

A coalition is defined as two or more parties who cooperate to obtain a mutually desired outcome that satisfies the interests of the coalition rather than those of the entire group within which it is embedded (Komorita & Kravitz, 1983; Murnighan, 1986).[1] Coalition researchers have explored how features of a bargaining context affect coalition activity and subsequent resource allocation decisions (Miller & Komorita, 1986; Murnighan, 1978). Compared to negotiation research, however, coalition research tends to

We thank Max Bazerman, Sally Blount, Gerald Davis, Karen Jehn, and Gregory Northcraft for their assistance in data collection and Jackie Paytas for her assistance in data analysis. We also thank the three anonymous reviewers for their contributions. We collected these data while the first and third authors were at the Kellogg Graduate School of Management, Northwestern University, and the second author was at the Graduate School of Business at the University of Chicago. This research was partially supported by an award from the IBM Faculty Research Fund at the University of Chicago to the second author.

[1] This definition of a coalition is consistent with the definition found in the influence tactics literature. The coalition tactic of one party's seeking the aid of another to persuade a third or of using the support of another as an argument for the third's agreement (Yukl & Falbe, 1990) would result in a coalition as we define it: two or more parties who cooperate to obtain a mutually desired outcome. The use of this coalition tactic, if successful, results in a set of parties who form a coalition.

From *Academy of Management Journal*, February 1998, pp. 42-54. © 1998 by the Academy of Management, P.O. Box 3020, Briar Cliff Manor, NY 10510-8020. Reproduced by permission of the publisher via Copyright Clearance Center, Inc.

examine relatively constrained and information-limited problems, focusing on allocation processes that are purely distributive. One result of this focus is a prevailing view that coalitions are inherently unstable. From this perspective, coalitions are temporary alliances designed to increase individual coalition members' outcomes on a particular issue; when the issue is resolved, the coalition dissolves.

The purpose of this study was to extend this view of coalitions to incorporate the effects of both preference alignments that are not purely distributive and social psychological forces that occur within multiparty negotiations. We propose that the alignment of negotiators' preferences in multiparty negotiations has direct implications for whether and how coalition activity affects negotiated outcomes. In addition, coalitions may be more stable than coalition researchers have suggested, primarily because of the social psychological forces that accompany coalition activity. Coalition researchers have called for research that examines bargaining tasks in "a larger, more . . . social context" (Komorita & Parks, 1995: 189). Such advice led us to consider the bond between the parties who form a coalition, the boundary around the coalition, and the consequences of coalition formation that reach beyond the issue that motivated it.

We drew from the literatures on both coalitions and negotiations, two areas of research that have continued relatively independently (see Murnighan & Brass (1991) for an exception). In the next sections of this article, we first address the coalition and negotiation literatures separately. We then integrate ideas from the two literatures, along with ideas from the literature on social categorization processes, to explore an issue relevant to, but missing from, each: How are resource allocation decisions made through a multiparty negotiation process likely to be affected by relatively stable coalitions formed around compatible preferences? This integration allows us to analyze an unexplored but important connection between these research domains.

THEORY AND HYPOTHESES

Power and Entitlement in Multiparty Negotiation

Coalition researchers typically study multiparty contexts in which alternative coalitions have different values based on the inputs of the parties who form the coalition (Kahan & Rapoport, 1984; Komorita & Hamilton, 1984). In these situations, known as variable-sum or characteristic function games, power is determined by the number and value of the alternative coalitions an individual might form (cf. Aumann & Maschler, 1964; Davis & Maschler, 1965; Horowitz, 1973). High-power players are defined as those who add more value (or greater inputs, in the lexicon of coalition researchers) to the coalitions that include them (Aumann & Maschler, 1964). Adding more value to coalitions increases an individual's power

because other players are dependent on that party if they wish to acquire a portion of that value.

To clarify this type of power, consider a simple example of a two-party negotiation. Although the two parties are interdependent, the extent to which each is dependent on the other can differ. Party A may be more dependent on party B to reach an agreement than party B is on A. The more net dependence party A has on party B, the more power party B has to influence party A regarding the terms of the outcome. In this view, power is the inverse of dependence (Emerson, 1964; Pfeffer & Salancik, 1977; Thibaut & Kelley, 1959). Because parties low in power have more net dependence on parties high in power for attaining outcomes of high value, parties with high power should be able to demand a greater share of the resources (Emerson, 1964; Greenberg & Cohen, 1982; Leventhal, 1976; Thibaut & Kelley, 1959). This research implies that parties with higher power should attain higher individual outcomes than parties with lower power from the resource pool created by their combined inputs.

Social psychological models of coalitions also highlight the importance of entitlement cues in determining outcomes (Komorita, 1974, 1979; Komorita & Chertkoff, 1973; Komorita & Tumonis, 1980). Entitlement cues, which are distinct from the value a party adds to a coalition, are pieces of information that influence what an individual believes to be a reasonable or fair distribution of a resource (Homans, 1961; Komorita & Hamilton, 1984). Entitlement cues can be linked to distribution rules, such as equality (Ashenfelter & Bloom, 1984), formalized egalitarianism (Rawls, 1971), equity (Adams, 1963; Homans, 1961), need (Deutsch, 1975), precedent (Bazerman, 1985), or promised future productivity (Mannix, Neale, & Northcraft, 1995). Group members tend to diverge systematically in their perceptions of what constitutes a fair outcome because each player tends to invoke a different distribution rule, with the choice depending on which would make him or her better off (Bettenhausen & Murnighan, 1985; Kelley & Thibaut, 1978; Leventhal, 1980). For example, in many studies of coalition formation, the only cue to the appropriate distribution of resources that is given is the inputs of each party. In such cases, although low-power players may argue for an equal resource distribution, high-power players are more likely to demand a higher outcome based on their inputs, invoking the fairness of an equity distribution rule to support their claim (Kelley & Thibaut, 1978; Komorita & Chertkoff, 1973; Shaw, 1981). In this way, resources are used as a frame of reference, or a cue, to which a particular distribution rule may be applied (Komorita & Kravitz, 1983). To the extent that other parties can be persuaded to agree with the fairness of a particular distribution rule, entitlement cues are a potential source of influence in multiparty negotiation (Greenberg & Cohen, 1982; Komorita & Hamilton, 1984; Leventhal, 1976).

Cues to entitlement other than inputs often exist in multiparty negotiation. Additional entitlement cues can be consistent or inconsistent with inputs in supporting a particular allocation of resources that is based on the application of a single distribution rule. For example, the party with the highest inputs to the group may also have the highest potential for productivity, in which case both entitlement cues are consistent in indicating that this player should get the highest outcome. In another instance, the party with the highest inputs may have the lowest potential for productivity, in which case the cues are inconsistent; one cue indicates this player should get the highest outcome, but the other indicates this player should get the lowest outcome. Leventhal argued that one component determining the strength of a fairness response in a particular situation was the extent to which the "social system . . . imposes consistent, stable rules of fair procedure and fair distribution" (1980: 50). Compared to consistent cues, multiple inconsistent cues may cause greater disagreement among group members about which distribution rule (e.g., equity versus equality) is most appropriate, or about which cue (e.g., inputs versus potential productivity) they should use when applying a particular distribution rule (Bettenhausen & Murnighan, 1985; Kelley & Thibaut, 1978; Komorita & Chertkoff, 1973; Mannix & White, 1992; Shaw, 1981). This research suggests that additional entitlement cues should interact with power position (which is based on inputs) to affect individual outcomes. Specifically, parties in high-power positions should attain higher outcomes when additional entitlement cues are consistent with power, and parties with low power should attain higher outcomes when additional entitlement cues are inconsistent with their power positions.

Reviewing the coalition literature reveals that coalition researchers have focused on issues, such as the distribution of a pool of inputs, that are zero-sum, or distributive, in nature. Each player has interests that are diametrically opposed to the interests of the other parties; any gain made by one player necessarily means the other players will get less. In the current study, we built on some of the findings from this body of research. With these replications as cornerstones, we then extended these ideas by considering how social forces affected the stability of coalitions. We now turn to the negotiation literature to broaden our perspective on various alignments of interests and their effect on negotiated outcomes.

Interest Alignment in Multiparty Negotiations

Like coalition researchers, negotiation researchers examine contexts in which the interests of negotiating parties may be diametrically opposed. However, because they typically study negotiations involving multiple issues, negotiation researchers can simultaneously examine interests that are compatible and sets of interests that have integrative potential (Thompson, 1990). In studying the effects of varying degrees of interest alignment, re-searchers have found that negotiators tend to assume that their own interests are diametrically opposed to the other parties' interests, an assumption labeled the "fixed-pie bias" (Bazerman & Neale, 1983). This assumption gets tested as negotiators exchange information about their interests. New information may indicate to negotiators that their fixed pie assumptions are wrong and that other parties' interests are not completely at odds with their own. In contrast, coalition researchers typically study bargaining situations in which all parties not only have preferences that are diametrically opposed but also have full information prior to the negotiation about the inputs and preferences of the other parties (Komorita & Parks, 1995). In this study, we were especially interested in the consequences of parties' discovering, during the course of a negotiation, that their interests on some issues were compatible.

In multiparty negotiations, subsets of parties often have compatible interests on one or more issues. Indeed, the more issues that are being negotiated, the higher the probability that at least some interests among some parties will be compatible (Raiffa, 1982). The discovery of compatible interests can have a variety of effects. If the parties in a negotiation discover that they all have compatible interests on an issue, they should agree on the option they all prefer. A more complex set of consequences may unfold when only a subset of parties, rather than all parties, has compatible preferences on an issue.

When some parties share compatible interests, they can band together to influence the incompatible party. Although a single negotiator's interests are not by themselves a source of power, when two or more negotiators have compatible interests, they may coordinate their efforts, or coalesce, to influence another party to consent to an agreement more favorable to the subset. To the extent that multiple parties can be more persuasive than a single party, compatibility should help parties achieve their desired outcomes. Further, depending on the decision rule used by the group, the coalescing parties may wield enough influence based on the structure of the decision rule to dominate the final allocation of resources. For example, if the commonly used majority rule is in effect, enough parties (i.e., a majority) may have compatible preferences to forge an agreement without the consent of an incompatible party.

In this majority rule situation, the incompatible party is at a serious disadvantage, because his or her inclusion in the final agreement is dependent on the decisions of the coalesced parties. This situation is likely to result in the incompatible party's being either excluded from the final agreement or included in an agreement in which the terms are dictated by the compatible parties. The preceding discussion suggests these hypotheses:

Hypothesis 1. Parties who have compatible interests will attain higher outcomes on the issues on which their interests are compatible than will those who have incompatible interests.

Hypothesis 2. Parties whose interests are compatible will be more likely to form coalitions that completely exclude other parties from the final agreement than will parties whose interests are not compatible.

In the next section, we consider how compatible interests on one issue may influence the outcomes for other, unrelated, issues. We propose that this effect may occur through the influence of relatively stable coalitions.

The Social Process of Coalition Formation

The prevailing view in the coalition literature is that coalitions are issue-based and, as such, inherently unstable (cf. Murnighan & Brass, 1991). When parties resolve one issue and proceed to the next, the current coalition is likely to disband and a different coalition, based on new sets of preferences for the new issue, is likely to form. According to this view, preferences on one issue, even if they lead parties to form a coalition, should not affect group decisions on other issues. In contrast with this view, we present an alternative proposition that integrates to ideas: (1) that coalitions are likely to influence outcomes in multiparty contexts and (2) that compatible interests are likely to exist in multiparty negotiations. By incorporating social psychological forces, we extend this integration to predict that coalitions that form because of compatible preferences on one issue may remain intact to influence outcomes on other issues, even those for which the coalition members *do not* have compatible preferences. In other words, coalitions may be more stable than coalition researchers have suggested.

We propose that once a coalition is formed, the parties in the coalition will continue to cooperate with each other as further issues are resolved, favorably influencing their own outcomes at the expense of noncoalition members. Several mechanisms contribute to the stability of coalitions. When preferences are revealed during the process of a negotiation, coalitions based on compatibility are likely to form explicitly. As coalition members cooperate to influence others, it is likely that both members and nonmembers will perceive the coalition as a relevant social group. The boundary around the coalition, demarcating who is in it and who is not, is real, as coalition members actually are working together as a subgroup.

In addition, once a coalition begins to form, cognitive processes of social categorization may combine with motivationally based processes of (sub)group identification to amplify the salience of the boundary around the coalition (Kramer & Brewer, 1984; Tajfel & Turner, 1986; Turner, 1987). An "us versus them" categorization can emerge, whereby coalition members are viewed as distinct from nonmembers (Gaertner, Mann, Murrell, & Dovidio, 1989; Tajfel, Billig, Bundy, & Flament, 1971). Resistance from a noncoalition party that is directed at the coalition as an entity may strengthen the bond between

the coalition members, making it more likely they will continue to cooperate with each other and compete with the noncoalition party (Homans, 1950; Tajfel, 1982). Because the distinction between subgroups is based on social psychological processes as well as objective interests, we argue that identification with a coalition may not recede immediately after the issue that motivated it is resolved. The more that coalition members come to identify with the coalition rather than with the larger group, the greater the likelihood that they will continue to act in the coalition's interests (Kramer, 1993).

When compatible interests are the basis for coalition formation, coalition members are able to see their preferences satisfied without having to compete with each other (Thompson, 1990). This cooperation is likely to result in increased stability, because of the social psychological processes described above. In contrast, when coalition members have opposing preferences on the issue around which the coalition formed (that is, the issue is distributive), they must still decide how to distribute those resources among themselves after securing resources for the coalition. This distribution is an inherently competitive activity; a gain for one coalition member comes at the expense of another. Such competition between coalition members may weaken the bond between them or even drive them apart. The lack of competition in the former case may, however, lead to greater coalition stability.

For these reasons, coalitions that form because of compatible preferences on a particular issue are likely to be more stable and to have farther-reaching effects than would be predicted by a strict analysis of preference compatibility. Drawing on this reasoning, we predict:

Hypothesis 3. Interest compatibility on one issue will result in better individual outcomes for compatible parties on other, unrelated, issues.

Support for Hypothesis 3 would indicate that a coalition has effects that extend beyond the particular issue for which it was formed. In addition, the presence of such extended effects would suggest that coalition activity, to the extent that it fulfills its purpose of benefiting coalition members rather than the larger group (Mannix, 1993; Murnighan & Brass, 1991), may be more detrimental to the larger group than previously thought.

METHODS

Subjects and Procedures

Subjects were 495 graduate business students who participated in the study as a classroom exercise. The sample was 26 percent women; the average age was 27.3 years, and the average work experience was 4.6 years. Exercises were conducted in eight separate sessions, with each session including approximately 62 subjects. Each subject participated as a member of 1 of 165 three-person groups, as described below.

The experimental design was a three-by-two-by-three (power position, entitlement cues, and interest compatibility) factorial design. Power position was manipulated within-group, and entitlement cues and interest compatibility were manipulated between-groups.

The task, designed to test our hypotheses, was meant to reflect an integration of negotiation and coalition research. Subjects were randomly assigned to three-person groups, and then, within each group, randomly assigned to represent one of three departments in the research and development division of a large company. Subjects were told that the three departments currently operated separately and had little interaction. The company's CEO had expressed a desire to change that. As a result, he was willing to supply funding to start a new R&D consortium. The CEO specified that any set of two departments, or all three departments, could comprise the new consortium.

Players were told that their objective was to gain as many dollars as they could for their departments. The task of the three players, therefore, was to decide both who would be in the consortium and how the available resources would be allocated. The sequence in which subjects made decisions about these two topics was left up to them; no instructions were given to discuss the two topics in any particular order. They were also free to move back and forth between the two topics or to discuss them simultaneously. Subjects were given 45 minutes to reach an agreement. Either a majority rule agreement (Two out of three) or a unanimous agreement (three out of three) was acceptable. Agreements signed by only two players indicated that a two-way coalition had formed and the third player had received no resources. Players who did not sign the agreement could not be included or assigned resources. The experimenter who ran each session instructed subjects not to talk to people in other groups and monitored the subjects to ensure that this did not occur while they were negotiating or completing the questionnaires.

At the end of the negotiation, subjects completed a contract form and a postquestionnaire that included a manipulation check. On the contract form, subjects specified their final agreement, noting which parties were in the consortium and how the resources were allocated. After completing the questionnaire, subjects returned it immediately to the experimenter.

Experimental Manipulations

Power position. Power (high, medium, or low) was manipulated within-group. Each group contained a high-power player (the manager of department A), a medium-power player (the manager of department B), and a low-power player (the manager of department C).

Power was operationally defined through the use of a variable-sum resource pool, commonly used in coalition research (cf. Kahan & Rapoport, 1984). For simplicity, we will call this the coalition pool, although it was not referred to as such in the experimental materials. Subjects were told that they had a pool of money to divide, the size of which would vary with the composition of the consortium. The amount of money in this resource pool was based on the size of each department (the number of researchers in it). The amount of money the CEO would contribute to this fund could be calculated by summing the number of researchers in each department included in the consortium and multiplying by 10,000. Thus, the value of consortia varied with their composition.

Department A had 40 researchers, department B had 25 researchers, and department C had 10 researchers, so that the values of the coalition pools were as follows: A + B = $650,000, A + C = $500,000, B + C = $350,000, and A + B + C = $750,000. Earlier, we noted that high-power players are defined as those who add more value, or inputs, to the coalitions that include them. Thus, player A had greater power than player B, and player B had greater power than player C. The term "combined inputs," as it was used earlier in the article, refers to the total value of the coalition pool (e.g., $750,000 if A, B, and C were included).

Entitlement cues. Entitlement cues were manipulated between-groups as either consistent or inconsistent with power. The entitlement cue was operationally defined as information regarding each department's projected profitability for the coming year. Subjects were told that this information was sometimes used to allocate resources. When the entitlement cues were consistent with power, the future profitability was projected as follows: A = $400,000, B = $250,000, and C = $100,000. When entitlement cues were inconsistent, the projection was: A = $100,000, B = $250,000, and C = $400,000. Note that these figures map onto the departmental size (multiplied by 10,000), or power position, of each player.

Interest compatibility. Interest compatibility was manipulated as a between-groups variable with three conditions: (1) compatibility between the high- and medium-power players (2) compatibility between the high- and low-power players, and (3) compatibility between the medium- and low-power players. The two compatible parties had identical preferences on two issues (computer equipment and staff support) that made up a second resource pool, which we will call the negotiation pool.

Regarding the negotiation pool, players were told that they had to allocate money to be used specifically for computer equipment and staff support. Five options (A–E) were given for both computer equipment (issue 1) and staff support (issue 2) in a traditional negotiation payoff schedule with integrative potential (Bazerman, Magliozzi, & Neale, 1985). Players were told that members of the consortium had to agree on one of these options for computer equipment and on one option for staff support.

The dollar values within the payoff schedules manipulated which of the two players had compatible interests on the two issues. When two players had compatible interests, they both preferred option A for the two issues, and the third player preferred option E for the two issues. In all cases, option A for the players with compatible interests would result in a $400,000 payoff to each, and the third player would receive $0. However, a solution of higher joint gain was also available, consisting of option E for computer support and option A for staff support, resulting in a payoff of $300,000 for each of the three players.[2]

Analyses

Because we were testing hypothesized differences among the outcomes of individuals in different power positions within groups, our unit of analysis was the individual. Although power position was a within-group manipulation, our other manipulations were between-groups in the sense that they affected players in the same power positions differently across groups. We were interested, however, in the effects of these manipulations on the individual outcomes attained by the players in different power positions in each experimental condition. For example, although interest compatibility was manipulated between-groups (for instance, the high- and medium-power players had compatible interests in some groups, but the high- and low-power players or medium- and low-power players had compatible interests in other groups), we were interested in how individual outcomes were affected by a player's having interests that were compatible (versus incompatible) with another player's. Because we randomly assigned subjects to groups and groups to conditions, and because all groups had the same instructions except for our experimental manipulations, we did not expect the particular group to which subjects belonged to account for a significant amount of variance in individual outcomes. To be sure, we tested this assumption by submitting group as a factor in a multivariate analysis of variance with individual outcomes on the coalition and negotiation pools as dependent variables. The group factor did not significantly affect outcomes on either the coalition pool ($F_{157, 291} = 0.21$, n.s.) or the negotiation pool ($F_{157, 291} = 0.04$, n.s.; multivariate test, $F_{314, 578} = 0.13$, n.s.). Because it did not account for significant variance or substantively affect any of the other results when included in the equation, we excluded the group factor from all subsequent analyses.

In our analysis of the outcome data, the two-way agreements were fundamentally different from the three-

way agreements, which made comparisons that combined the two types of agreements difficult. The occurrence of two-way coalitions had a disproportional impact on outcome means and variances because the parties that were excluded from the coalitions always received $0 (excluded parties could not be assigned resources without their consent). The interpretation difficulty stemmed from the differential distortion of outcome means and variances across conditions caused by including the outcomes of $0. To circumvent this problem while including all of the groups in the analyses, we excluded the outcomes of individual group members who received $0 when two-way coalitions were formed but included all individuals who were part of those agreements. The tests reported in the results section include all groups (i.e., those that reached both two-way and three-way agreements) but exclude those individuals who were left out of the two-way agreements. In addition, for completeness, we conducted separate analyses for groups that reached three-way agreements and for groups that reached two-way agreements. There were no substantive differences between the two sets of results.

We used a multivariate analysis of variance (MANOVA) to test Hypotheses 1 and 3. This MANOVA examined the effects of all three independent variables (power position, interest compatibility, and entitlement cues) on the two outcome dependent variables (individual gain from the coalition pool and individual gain from the negotiation pool). If the multivariate test was significant, the univariate test for individual gain from the negotiation pool was used to test Hypothesis 1, and the univariate test for individual gain from the negotiation pool was used to test Hypothesis 3. Finally, we conducted a chi-square test for Hypothesis 2 to determine whether significantly more two-way agreements occurred between compatible than incompatible parties.

RESULTS

All of the 165 groups reached agreement. Agreements including all three players were reached by 142 groups, and 23 groups reached agreements including only two players.[2]

Manipulation Check

After they had reached an agreement, subjects completed a questionnaire in which they were asked "How powerful were you and the other two department heads?" They rated themselves and each of the other two subjects on a seven-point scale (1 = not at all, 7 = extremely). A MANOVA was conducted that examined the effects of power position (as an independent variable) on ratings of the perceived overall power of the high-, medium-, and low-power players (the dependent variables). Although the power position of the party *being*

---

[2]The specific payoff schedules for each condition are available from the first author upon request.

rated did affect perceived power (reported below), the power position of the *rater* did not affect perceptions of power (that is, there was no significant main effect for power position as an independent variable).

We analyzed the mean power of each party as rated by the other two parties in each group. Comparisons across the three dependent variables revealed that the high-power player ($\bar{X}$ = 4.94, s.d. = 1.63) had higher perceived power than the medium-power player ($\bar{X}$ = 4.42, s.d. = 1.66; t_{594} = 4.94, p < .001), and the medium-power than the low-power player ($\bar{X}$ = 4.07, s.d. = 1.67; t_{589} = 3.30, p < .001). These patterns indicate that our power manipulation worked as intended.

Negotiation Outcomes

Replications of power and entitlement effects. For our results to be consistent with those of other coalition studies, parties with higher power should have attained higher individual outcomes than parties with lower power from the resource pool created by their combined inputs. The MANOVA revealed a significant effect for power position ($F_{4, 858}$ = 57.19, p < .001). In the univariate tests, the effect of power position was significant for the coalition pool only ($F_{2, 431}$ = 114.57, p < .001, η^2 = .35). Power position did not affect distribution of the negotiation pool ($F_{2, 413}$ < 1, n.s.). We conducted Tukey post hoc comparisons at the .05 level among mean outcomes for the coalition pool. These comparisons showed the high-power player's outcome to be significantly higher than the outcome of the medium-power player and the medium-power player's outcome to be significantly higher than the outcome of the low-power player (high $\bar{X}$ = 320,390.73, s.d. = 90,916.66; medium $\bar{X}$ = 250,729.73, s.d. = 70,035.33; low $\bar{X}$ = 180,960.00, s.d. = 86,067.78).

We also expected additional entitlement cues to interact with power to affect individual outcomes. Specifically, parties with high power should have attained higher outcomes when additional entitlement cues were consistent with power, and parties with low power should have attained higher outcomes when additional entitlement cues were inconsistent with power. Consistent with our expectation, the overall MANOVA ($F_{4, 858}$ = 3.77, p < .01) indicated a significant interaction between power position and entitlement cues for the coalition pool only ($F_{2, 431}$ = 6.55, p < .01, η^2 = .03). As can be seen in the pattern of means in Table 1, the size of the differences among the outcomes of the high-, medium-, and low-power players depended on the entitlement cue condition. The significance of the interaction effect between these variables indicates that, as expected, the differences among these means are attenuated, or less extreme, under inconsistent entitlement cues. These findings for power position and entitlement suggest that our manipulations of these factors worked as intended to replicate past research in the coalition domain.

The effect of interest compatibility on the negotiation pool. Hypothesis 1 predicts that parties who have compatible interests on some issues will have higher outcomes on those issues than will parties who have incompatible interests. A significant interaction between power position and interest compatibility occurred in both the multivariate test ($F_{8, 858}$ = 59.08, p < .001) and the univariate ANOVA for individual gain from the negotiation pool ($F_{4, 431}$ = 113.97, p < .001, η^2 = .51). The pattern of means for this effect, reported in the top half of Table 2, indicates that for each power position, players obtained less from this pool when their interests were incompatible with the other parties than they did when their interests were compatible. This result supports Hypothesis 1.

Hypothesis 2 predicts that parties whose interests are compatible will be more likely to form coalitions that completely exclude one party from the final agreement than will parties whose interests are not compatible. To test this hypothesis, we looked at the agreements that included only two of the three parties. Formal two-way

---

TABLE 1

Mean Individual Outcomes by Power Position and Entitlement Cues for the Coalition Pool[a]

Entitlement Cue Condition	Power Position		
	High	Medium	Low
Consistent	332,486.84 (104,923.15)	257,500.00 (76,146.26)	163,094.59 (81,901.57)
Inconsistent	308,133.33 (72,766.07)	243,583.33 (62,686.06)	198,355.26 (86,982.86)

[a] Values in parentheses are standard deviations. A univariate test of interaction had the following results: $F_{2, 431}$ = 6.55, p < .01, η^2 = .03.

---

coalitions were formed in only 23 instances—less than 14 percent of the time (χ^2 [1, N = 165] = 85.82, p < .001). The data indicate that group members with compatible interests were more likely to form two-way coalitions than group members whose interests were incompatible—15 two-way coalitions occurred between compatible parties, and only 8 occurred between incompatible parties (χ^2 [4, N = 23] = 13.04, p < .02). Although this result supports Hypothesis 2, the analysis must be tempered by the fact that some of the cells had low expected frequencies (see Table 3).

The effect of interest compatibility on the coalition pool. Hypothesis 3 predicts that interest compatibility for one issue will increase the individual outcomes of compatible members on other, unrelated, issues. To test this predic-

TABLE 2
Mean Individual Outcomes by Interest Compatibility and Power Position[a]

Power Position	Interest Compatibility Condition		
	High-Medium	High-Low	Medium-Low
Negotiation pool[b]			
High	347,395.83	334,183.67	165,000.00
	(48,989.68)	(71,205.01)	(120,533.85)
Medium	348,863.64	153,888.89	334,000.00
	(44,445.73)	(112,178.27)	(80,774.31)
Low	147,340.43	336,000.00	345,212.77
	(124,480.88)	(62,507.14)	(49,077.99)
Coalition pool[c]			
High	330,812.50	349,244.90	264,177.78
	(139,312.70)	(98,222.86)	(117,896.00)
Medium	256,772.73	214,111.11	259,380.00
	(99,634.88)	(98,467.17)	(93,468.29)
Low	150,531.91	198,700.00	194,212.77
	(117,001.64)	(122,656.85)	(81,653.55)

[a] Values in parentheses are standard deviations.
[b] The results of a univariate test of interaction were $F_{4, 431} = 113.97$, $p < .001$, $\eta^2 = .51$.
[c] The results of a univariate test of interaction were $F_{4,431} = 6.91$, $p < .001$, $\eta^2 = .06$.

TABLE 3
Number of Two-Way Coalitions by Interest Compatibility and Coalition Composition[a]

Interest Compatibility	Parties in Two-Way Coalitions		
	High-Medium	High-Low	Medium-Low
High-medium	4	2	1
High-low	2	7	1
Medium-low	2	0	4

[a] χ^2 (4 df) = 13.04, $p < .02$.

tion, we looked at the effect of interest compatibility on individual outcomes from the coalition pool. The multivariate test revealed a significant interaction effect between power position and interest compatibility ($F_{8, 858} = 59.08$, $p < .001$), as did the univariate ANOVA on individual gain from the coalition pool ($F_{4, 431} = 6.91$, $p < .001$, $\eta^2 = .06$), supporting Hypothesis 3. The means for this interaction are reported in the bottom half of Table 2. Inspection of the means within each row reveals that, for each power position, parties obtained the lowest mean outcome from the coalition pool when their interests on the negotiation pool issues were incompatible with those of the other parties (compared to the conditions in which they had compatible interests). Therefore, our interpretation of this significant interaction is that the outcomes for power position depended on the level of interest compatibility or, more specifically, on whether a particular power position was compatible with another position. These results support Hypothesis 3; compatible interests for one resource pool (the negotiation pool) affected outcomes on another resource pool (the coalition pool) for which the parties' interests were not compatible.

To facilitate our understanding of the negotiation pool agreements, we categorized the agreements as either internal coalition, integrative, or compromise. Agreements for computer support and staff support of AA, AB, BA, or BB indicated the formation of an internal coalition whereby the two compatible players received the vast majority of the resources. Agreements of EA, EB, DA, and DB indicated a relatively integrative outcome of high joint benefit in which each player conceded on the issue that was less important to him or her than it was to another party. All other agreements indicated a compromise, somewhere between an agreement characterized as an internal coalition or as integrative. Almost half (47%) of the groups agreed in AA, AB, BA, or BB solutions, indicating the presence of internal coalitions. About one-third (35%) of the groups reached integrative agreements, and the remaining 18 percent of the groups reached compromise agreements. The high incidence of internal coalition agreements on the negotiation pool issues is consistent with the interpretation that compatibility on the negotiation pool issues affected outcomes on the coalition pool through the operation of relatively stable coalitions.

DISCUSSION

The purpose of this study was to integrate negotiation and coalition research in examining resource allocations in a multiparty context. In a complex task that permitted both the formation of coalitions and the creation of integrative agreements, the value of an agreement was predicated on two potential sources of value: the coalition pool and the negotiation pool. Players who had compatible interests on the two negotiation issues were able to achieve higher individual outcomes from *both* the negotiation and coalition portions of the task. This was true even when compatible players did not form exclusive two-way coalitions. These findings indicate that compatible players formed internal coalitions, acting as allies against the incompatible third party—not necessarily to lock the third party out of the final agreement, but to force him or her to accept a reduced share of both resources pools. Power position and entitlement cues also affected the allocation of resources. However, these factors only increased or decreased players' outcomes on the coalition pool, the portion of the task to which these forms of power were directly linked.

Evidence that compatible players formed two-way internal alliances can also be seen in the pattern of the agreements that were observed. First, we noted that agreements were more likely to include all three members in a coalition rather than to leave anyone out. This result might be attributed to the dominance of group rationality in that a three-way coalition was worth more at the group level than any two-way coalition, increasing the coalition pool from a possible low of $350,000 up to $750,000. However, this concern with high joint gain did not necessarily extend to the negotiation pool, where compatible players would have had to sacrifice some gain to reach fully integrative three-way agreements, jointly worth $900,000. The pattern of agreements indicates that only one-third of the groups selected this option, compared with almost half of the groups in which the two compatible parties prevented the incompatible third party from acquiring resources from the negotiation pool. This is one piece of supporting evidence that compatible players formed internal alliances. The second, and perhaps more compelling, piece of evidence is that compatible players used their power to obtain mutually acceptable outcomes, while leaving the third player with significantly fewer resources from *both* pools.

Implications

The results of this study suggest some interesting implications for the effects of interest compatibility. Our findings indicate that interest compatibility, unlike power position or entitlement cues, can go beyond the narrow range of outcomes that are delimited by the congruence of interests. If interest compatibility on one issue has effects on multiple resource pools, its presence could lead to inefficient and possibly irrational outcomes in some contexts. Further, to the extent that interest compatibility, and the resulting correspondence of outcomes, is a necessary condition in the development of relationships among negotiators (Davis & Todd, 1985; Heidere, 1958), such compatibility signals to the players two potential outcomes: (1) the ability to extract additional resources from other parties because of the strength of the alliance *in this interaction* and (2) the likely future interdependence of the compatible parties as they find themselves again on the same side of an issue *in other interactions* (Ben-Yoav & Pruitt, 1984; Berscheid, Snyder, & Omoto, 1989; Kelley & Thibaut, 1978). These results suggest that relationships among coalition partners—which are more likely to occur when interests are compatible—not only will make coalitions more stable, but also will unify the demands of coalition members.

Another finding from this study that has implications for future research is the influence of entitlement cues. Consider the experimental condition in which additional entitlement cues were inconsistent with power based on inputs. In this condition, the low-power party is likely to invoke entitlement based on future profitability as a justification for more resources, raising the level of ambient conflict. The high-power party should reject such a justification and, instead, press a claim to resources based on ability to add to the size of the resource pool. However, low-power parties were, in fact, able to increase their outcomes based on their entitlements, demonstrating that multiple and even ambiguous sources of power were able to affect the ability of group members to obtain resources.

These results begin to elucidate how it is that parties with different levels of power can press claims for resources based on different distribution norms (Kelley & Thibaut, 1978; Komorita & Chertkoff, 1973; Shaw, 1981). It seems necessary that for entitlement-based arguments to be effective, the medium-power party must at least partially influence the expectations of the other parties about what is reasonable. Since the medium-power position was unchanged by the entitlement conditions, its incumbents would have been most easily able to assess the quality of the arguments from a neutral vantage point (Leventhal, 1976) and thus become more influential. A medium-power party's relative neutrality combined with the ability to form a two-way coalition, if one party were viewed as making demands that were out-of-line, would have made the medium-power party's evaluation of the arguments and subsequent outcome preferences powerful predictors of the final outcomes. In effect, the medium-power player had the swing vote, influencing the outcome to a much greater extent than might initially appear possible (Mannix, 1994).

This ability for one party to draw power from the constellation of the power and interests of the other parties is a relatively unexplored aspect of personal power. There are hints of the sway that perceived neutrality can have in self-interested decision processes in both the managerial dispute intervention literature (Pinkley, Brittain, Neale, & Northcraft, 1995) and the procedural justice literature (Leventhal, 1976). Empirical research has repeatedly illustrated that the appearance of neutrality is central to the perception of a procedurally just decision process and can enhance the acceptability of managerial decisions, even when the outcome is unfavorable (Bies, Tripp, & Neale, 1993; Lind & Lissak, 1985). Thus, to the extent that an individual can argue a position that is not obviously self-interested, the power of that persuasive attempt is considerably greater (Fisher & Ury, 1981).

Another important aspect of coalitions that remains unaddressed by the current research endeavor is the process by which internal coalitions are formed. In this study, we were only able to surmise this process by the constellation of coalitions created and the outcomes associated with different interest compatibility conditions. Theoretically, interest compatibility may reflect relationship potential among the participants. More than simple expectations for future interaction (a common laboratory manipulation of relationship), interest compatibility signals that a basis for relationship formation—similarity (Heider, 1958)—already exists. Relationships have been shown to influence not only the process of negotiation but also the ways in which outcomes are evaluated (Valley, Neale, & Mannix, 1995). Thus, it is important for researchers to consider more carefully the process through which interests are discovered and internal coalitions are formed.

A key practical implication of our results is that managers in multiparty negotiations should anticipate how coalition activity is likely to be affected by factors other than preferences on current issues. These factors include preference alignment on seemingly unrelated issues (including issues in temporally separate negotiations), the existing relationships between parties, shared group memberships (defined demographically or organizationally), successful past alliances, and even shared dislike of another party. Such factors, especially when working in combination, may draw certain parties together while driving other parties apart. Managers should explicitly seek information about connections between other parties that go beyond current issues. This information can be used to anticipate likely coalitions and then to analyze whether the best course of action is to attempt to join, block, dissolve, or ignore them. Considering such coalitional dynamics may help managers protect and further their own (or their organizations') interests in multiparty negotiations.

Limitations

In laboratory studies such as this, one must always consider the extent to which the findings generalize to real-world settings. Neale and Northcraft (1990), in their review of work on negotiator expertise, reported that studies that directly compared the behavior of professional negotiators with that of students found no difference in the patterns of responses, with the exception that the professional negotiators were more likely to implement integrative strategies earlier than the student subjects (Neale & Northcraft, 1986; Northcraft & Neale, 1987). Thus, although professional negotiators might be expected to reach integrative agreements more quickly, there is little reason to expect either that real-world managers or employees would differ significantly in their negotiation behavior from the graduate students in this study or that the social dynamics of these two groups would differ significantly.

A second limitation is that this study used a negotiation simulation. Thus, motivations, relationships, and reputational issues do not come into play at nearly the level they would in a real-world situation. However, the differences among experimental conditions we found with subjects in this relatively constrained laboratory environment suggest that the relationships we have identified may be quite powerful. In addition, in this study, we used a task that more closely mirrored the complexity of negotiation tasks faced

in everyday organizational life. Unlike most negotiation experiments, this one required subjects to choose with whom to negotiate, allowed development of internal coalitions, and required distribution of the value that arose from the various pools of resources.

A further limitation concerns our manipulation check. We measured perceived power with only a one-item scale, although we did obtain a rating of each subject's power from two other players. Further, we did not provide a direct check for our manipulations of additional entitlement cues or interest compatibility. Nevertheless, we hold that the most plausible explanation for these independent variables' having significant effects on our dependent variables in the predicted directions is that our manipulations worked as intended.

Conclusions

This research brings together two seemingly disparate aspects of negotiation: the search for a coalition partner and the development of a negotiated agreement. These findings suggest that negotiators can focus on these two aspects of negotiations simultaneously. In many respects, these processes are analogous to, but more complex than, negotiating distributive and integrative issues simultaneously. In typical negotiation tasks, the issues that are being negotiated have been clearly explicated. In this study, value was increased not only by the way a party negotiated the issues within the negotiation pool, but also by the way he or she attempted to claim value from the coalition pool while determining the particular constellation of the consortium. Clearly, adding the "with-whom-to-negotiate" component to this mixture dramatically increased the cognitive and social complexity of the interaction.

Our primary goal in this article has been to present an initial study with a large sample that combined several factors identified by previous empirical research as integral to multiparty negotiation. We found that negotiators were able to understand, integrate, and use various and conflicting pieces of information regarding claims to resources in reaching resource allocation agreements. Some of these pieces of information—specifically, the compatibility of interests—have farther-reaching effects than one would predict on the basis of past research. Considering the social dynamics that are likely to come into play, particularly the waxing and waning of social categorization processes, reveals a more complex, but more complete, picture of multiparty negotiations.

REFERENCES

Adams, J. S. 1963. Toward an understanding of inequity. *Journal of Abnormal and Social Psychology,* 67: 422–436.

Ancona, D., Friedman, R., & Kolb, D. 1991. The group and what happens on the way to "yes." *Negotiation Journal,* 7: 155–174.

Ashenfelter, O., & Bloom, D. E. 1984. Models of arbitrator behavior: Theory and evidence. *American Economic Review,* 74: 111–124.

Aumann, R. J., & Maschier, M. 1964. The bargaining set for cooperative games. In M. Dresher, L. S. Shapley, & A. W. Tucker (Eds.), *Advances in game theory:* 443–476. Princeton, NJ: Princeton University Press.

Bazerman, M. H. 1985. Norms of distributive justice in interest arbitration. *Industrial and Labor Relations Review,* 38: 558–570.

Bazerman, M. H., Magliozzi, T., & Neale, M. A. 1985. Integrative bargaining in a competitive market. *Organizational Behavior and Human Performance,* 34: 294–313.

Bazerman, M. H., Mannix, E., & Thompson, L. 1988. Groups as mixed-motive negotiations. In E. J. Lawler & B. Markovsky (Eds.), *Advances in group processes: Theory and research:* 195–216. Greenwich, CT: JAI Press.

Bazerman, M. H., & Neale, M. A. 1983. Heuristics in negotiation: Limitations to dispute resolution effectiveness. In M. H. Bazerman & R. J. Lewicki (Eds.), *Negotiation in organizations:* 51–67. Beverly Hills: Sage.

Ben-Yoav, O., & Pruitt, D. 1984. Resistance to yielding and the expectation of cooperative future interaction in negotiation. *Journal of Experimental Social Psychology,* 20: 323–353.

Berscheid, E., Snyder, M., & Omoto, A. M. 1989. Issues in studying close relationships: Conceptualizing and measuring closeness. In C. Hendrick (Ed.), *Close relationships:* 63–91. Newbury Park, CA: Sage.

Bettenhausen, K., & Murnighan, J. K. 1985. The emergence of norms in competitive decision-making groups. *Administrative Science Quarterly,* 30: 350–372.

Bies, B., Tripp, T., & Neale, M. 1993. Procedural fairness, framing and profit seeking: Perceived legitimacy of market exploitation. *Journal of Behavioral Decision Making,* 6: 243–256.

Brett, J. 1991. Negotiating group decisions. *Negotiation Journal,* July: 291–310.

Brett, J., & Rognes, J. 1986. Intergroup relations in organizations: A negotiation perspective. In P. S. Goodman (Ed.), *Designing effective work groups:* 202–236. San Francisco: Jossey-Bass.

Caplow, T. A. 1956. A theory of coalitions in the triad. *American Sociological Review,* 21: 489–493.

Chertkoff, J. M. 1967. A revision of Caplow's coalition theory. *Journal of Experimental Social Psychology,* 3: 172–177.

Davis, K. E., & Todd, M. J. 1985. Assessing friendship: Prototypes, paradigm cases and relationship description. In S. Duck & D. Perlman (Eds.), *Understanding personal relationships: An interdisciplinary approach:* 17–38. London: Sage.

Davis, M., & Maschler, R. J. 1965. The kernel of a cooperative game. *Naval Research Logistics Quarterly,* 12(3): 223–259.

Deutsch, M. 1975. Equity, equality, and need: What determines which value will be used as the basis of distributive justice? *Journal of Social Issues,* 31(3): 137–149.

Emerson, R. M. 1964. Power-dependence relations: Two experiments. *Sociometry,* 27: 282–298.

Fisher, R., & Ury, W. 1981. *Getting to yes.* Boston: Houghton-Mifflin.

Froman, L., & Cohen, M. 1970. Compromise and logroll: Comparing the efficiency of two bargaining processes. *Behavioral Science,* 30: 180–183.

Gaertner, S., Mann, J., Murrell, A., & Dovidio, J. 1989. Reducing intergroup bias: The benefits of recategorization. *Journal of Personality and Social Psychology,* 57: 239–249.

Gamson, W. A. 1961. A theory of coalition formation. *American Sociological Review,* 26: 373–382.

Greenberg, J., & Cohen, R. L. 1982. *Equity and justice in social behavior.* New York: Academic Press.

Heider, F. 1958. *The psychology of interpersonal relationships.* New York: Wiley.

Homans, G. 1950. *The social group.* New York: Harcourt Brace Jovanovich.

Homans, G. 1961. *Social behavior: Its elementary forms.* New York: Harcourt Brace.

Horowitz, A. D. 1973. The competitive bargaining set for cooperative n-person games. *Journal of Mathematical Psychology,* 10(3): 265–289.

Kahan, J. P., & Rapoport, A. 1984. *Theories of coalition formation.* Hillsdale, NJ: Erlbaum.

Kelley, H. H. 1966. A classroom study of the dilemmas in interpersonal negotiation. In K. Archibald (Ed.), *Strategic interaction and conflict:* 49–73. Berkeley: Institute of International Studies, University of California.

Kelley, H. H., & Thibaut, J. W. 1978. *Interpersonal relations: A theory of interdependence.* New York: Wiley.

Komorita, S. S. 1974. A weighted probability model of coalition formation. *Psychological Review,* 81: 242–256.

Komorita, S. S. 1979. An equal-excess model of coalition formation. *Behavioral Science,* 24: 369–381.

Komorita, S. S., & Chertkoff, J. M. 1973. A bargaining theory of coalition formation. *Psychological Review,* 80: 149–162.

Komorita, S. S., & Hamilton, T. P. 1984. Power and equity in coalition bargaining. In S. B. Bacharach & E. J. Lawler (Eds.), *Research in the sociology of organizations:* 189–212. Greenwich, CT: JAI Press.

Komorita, S. S., & Kravitz, D. 1983. Coalition formation: A social psychological approach. In P. B. Paulus (Ed.), *Basic group processes:* 179–203. New York: Springer-Verlag.

Komorita, S. S., & Parks, C. D. 1995. Interpersonal relations: Mixed-motive interaction. In J. T. Spence, J. M. Darley, & D. J. Foss (Eds.), *Annual review of psychology,* vol. 46: 183–207. Palo Alto, CA: Annual Reviews.

Komorita, S. S., & Tumonis, T. M. 1980. Extensions and tests of some descriptive theories of coalition formation. *Journal of Personality and Social Psychology,* 39: 256–268.

Kramer, R. M. 1993. Cooperation and organizational identification. In J. K. Murnighan (Ed.), *Social psychology in organizations:* 244–268. Englewood Cliffs, NJ: Prentice-Hall.

Kramer, R. M., & Brewer, M. B. 1984. The effects of group identity on resource use in a simulated commons dilemma. *Journal of Personality and Social Psychology,* 46: 1044–1057.

Leventhal, G. S. 1976. The distribution of rewards and resources in groups and organizations. In L. Berkowitz & E. Walster (Eds.), *Advances in experimental social psychology:* 91–131. New York: Academic Press.

Leventhal, G. S. 1980. What should be done with equity theory? In K. J. Gergen, M. S. Greenberg, & R. H. Willis (Eds.), *Social exchange: Advances in theory and research:* 27–55. New York: Plenum.

Lind, E. A., & Lissak, R. I. 1985. Apparent impropriety and procedural fairness judgments. *Journal of Experimental Social Psychology,* 21: 19–29.

Luce, D., & Raiffa, H. 1957. *Games and decision: Introduction and critical survey.* New York: Wiley.

Mannix, E. A. 1993. Organizations as resource dilemmas: The effects of power balance on group decision making. *Organizational behavior and Human Decision Processes,* 55: 1–22.

Mannix, E. A. 1994. Will we meet again? The effects of power, distribution rules, and the scope of future interaction in small group negotiation. *International Journal of Conflict Management,* 5: 343–368.

Mannix, E. A., Neale, M., & Northcraft, G. 1995. Equity, equality or need? The effects of organizational culture and resource valence on allocation decisions. *Organizational Behavior and Human Decision Processes,* 63: 276–286.

Mannix, E. A., & White, S. 1992. The effect of distributive uncertainty on coalition formation in organizations. *Organizational Behavior and Human Decision Processes,* 51: 198–219.

Miller, C., & Komorita, S. 1986. Coalition formation in organizations: What laboratory studies do and do not tell us. In R. Lewicki, B. Sheppard, & M. Bazerman (Eds.), *Research on negotiation in organizations:* 117–138. Greenwich, CT: JAI Press.

Murnighan, K. 1978. Models of coalition behavior: Games theoretic, social psychological and political perspectives. *Psychological Bulletin,* 85: 1130–1153.

Murnighan, K. 1986. Organizational coalitions: Structural contingencies and the formation process. In R. Lewicki, B. Sheppard, & M. Bazerman (Eds.), *Research on negotiation in organizations:* 155–173. Greenwich, CT: JAI Press.

Murnighan, K., & Brass, D. 1991. Intraorganizational coalitions. In R. Lewicki, B. Sheppard, & M. Bazerman (Eds.), *Research on negotiation in organizations:* 283–306. Greenwich, CT: JAI Press.

Neale, M. A., & Bazerman, M. H. 1991. *Cognition and rationality in negotiation.* New York: Free Press.

Neale, M. A., & Northcraft, G. B. 1986. Experts, amateurs, and refrigerators: Comparing expert and amateur decision making in a novel task. *Organizational Behavior and Human Decision Processes,* 38: 228–241.

Neale, M. A., & Northcraft, G. B. 1990. Experience, expertise, and decision bias in negotiation: The role of strategic conceptualization. In

B. Sheppard, M. Bazerman, & R. Lewicki (Eds.), *Research in negotiation in organizations:* 55–76. Greenwich, CT: JAI Press.

Northcraft, G. B., & Neale, M. A. 1987. Experts, amateurs, and real estate: An anchoring-and-adjustment perspective on property pricing decisions. *Organizational Behavior and Human Decision Processes*, 39: 228–241.

Pfeffer, J., & Salancik, G. 1977. Organizational design: The case for a coalitional model of organizations. *Organizational Dynamics*, 6(2): 15–29.

Pinkley, R. L., Brittain, J. W., Neale, M. A., & Northcraft, G. B. 1995. Managerial third-party dispute intervention: An inductive analysis of intervenor strategy selection. *Journal of Applied Psychology*, 80: 386–402.

Pruitt, D. G. 1981. *Negotiation behavior.* New York: Academic Press.

Raiffa, H. 1982. *The art and science of negotiation.* Cambridge. MA: Belknap.

Rawls, J. 1971. *A theory of justice.* Cambridge, MA: Harvard University Press.

Shaw, M. E. 1981. *Group dynamics: The psychology of small group behavior.* New York: McGraw-Hill.

Tajfel, H. 1982. Social psychology of intergroup relations. In M. R. Rosenzweig & L. W. Porter (Eds.), *Annual review of psychology*, vol. 33: 1–39. Palo Alto, CA: Annual Reviews.

Tajfel, H., Billig, R., Bundy, C., & Flament, C. 1971. Social categorization and intergroup behavior. *European Journal of Social Psychology*, 1(2): 149–178.

Tajfel, H., & Turner, J. 1986. The social identity theory of intergroup behavior. In S. Worchel & W. G. Austin (Eds.), *Psychology of intergroup relations:* 7–24. Chicago: Nelson-Hall.

Thibaut, J. W., & Kelley, H. H. 1959. *The social psychology of groups.* New York: Wiley.

Thompson, L. 1990. Negotiation behavior and outcomes: Empirical evidence and theoritical issues. *Psychological Bulletin*, 108: 515–532.

Turner, J. C. 1987. *Rediscovering the social group: A self-categorization theory.* Oxford, England: Blackwell.

Valley, K., Neale, M. A., & Mannix, E. A. 1995. Relationships in negotiations: The role of reputation, the shadow of the future, and interpersonal knowledge on the process and outcome of negotiations. In R. J. Bies, R. Lewicki, & B. Sheppard (Eds.), *Research in bargaining and negotiation in organizations:* 65–93. Greenwich, CT: JAI Press.

Yukl, G., & Falbe, C. M. 1990. Influence tactics and objectives in upward, downward, and lateral influence attempts. *Journal of Applied Psychology*, 75: 132–140.

Jeffrey T. Polzer is an assistant professor of management in the Graduate School of Business at the University of Texas at Austin. He received his Ph.D. in organizational behavior at Northwestern University. His current research interests include intergroup relations, conflict resolution and negotiation, social dynamics in work teams, and social dilemmas.

Elizabeth A. Mannix is an associate professor in the Graduate School of Business at Columbia University. She received her Ph.D. in social and organization psychology at the University of Chicago. Her current research interests include negotiation, power, and relationships and alliances, with a focus on managerial teams.

Margaret A. Neale is the academic associate dean and a professor of organizational behavior in the Graduate School of Business at Stanford University. She received her Ph.D. from the University of Texas. Her research interests currently include negotiation, group decision making, and learning in groups.

KEEPING TEAM CONFLICT ALIVE

**Conflict can be a good thing.
Here's what you can do to make
the most of this creative force.**

By Shari Caudron

Not long ago, Michael Leonetti, director of organization effectiveness at Boehringer Ingelheim, was part of a corporate team created to turn the company's North American operations into a learning organization. The team was made up of organizational development specialists from the company's offices in Canada, the United States, and Mexico. You would think because the team members were all skilled trainers that they'd have similar ideas about how to create a learning-oriented culture, right? Wrong.

As soon as the team was formed, conflicts arose. Within six months, the tension among team members was so great that they were close to giving up. Fortunately, they didn't. As experienced employee-development professionals, they knew that disagreement is a healthy part of the collaborative process. Instead of shying away from the conflict, they wrestled with it head-on until they eventually reached consensus on the best corporate-wide learning strategy. The process didn't always feel good, says Leonetti, but it did work.

His is a lesson that many training professionals can learn from: Instead of trying to stamp out the weeds of conflict, they should do everything they can to nurture them. From the roots of conflict come the fruits of innovation. Ironically, what a lot of trainers do to "manage" conflict may actually push it underground, making it worse. To engender constructive conflict in

organizations, trainers themselves must become comfortable with the general idea of conflict and then work to create a culture in which conflict is allowed and acknowledged as a necessary part of the business process.

That's not as far-fetched as it may sound. Conflict is a natural part of the human experience, especially in organizations and especially these days.

According to Alice Pescuric, vice president and practice leader at Development Dimensions International located near Pittsburgh, research shows that line managers now list "managing conflict" as number 7 on their top-10 list of priorities. "It used to be much further down the list," says Pescuric. There are many reasons for that.

In the current highly competitive global marketplace, most employees feel pressured to "do more with less," and they're cracking under the strain. Better-faster-cheaper may be a good goal for companies, but it creates stress for the people who run them. Stress can make people intolerant, which, left unchecked, inevitably leads to conflict. But stress is only part of the reason organizational conflict is escalating. The decentralization of management means that more employees are being asked to make the kind of decisions they never had to make before. Instead of only executives dealing with the tough stuff, most employees now have the responsibility to deal with vexing issues. And that causes conflict.

"The structure of the hierarchy [once protected us] from conflict because employees could stay in their silos and take sides," explains Annette Simmons, author of *Territorial Games* (Amacom Books, 1998). "It wasn't so damaging for engineers to promote their way [or for] marketing to promote its way. But now, employees are having to resolve differences among themselves and that means they get to experience more conflict."

In fact, nothing has contributed more to the escalation of conflict than the advent of collaborative, team-based work. The premise is that a lot of people working together can't help but achieve better results than any one person working alone. Though that's often true, the convergence of many different kinds of personalities can create friction unlike any we've seen before. Add to that the inherent conflict in the business environment—quality versus quantity, short-term results versus long-range planning, and so forth—and you begin to see how many employees are living in a pressure cooker in which conflict is constantly simmering. But instead of putting a lid on it, training professionals should find a way for employees to let off steam. Says Pescuric, "Conflict is healthy, even though it does raise angst and anxiety."

It's a good thing

By now, you may be thinking about all of the conflicts you've been involved in, and you're perhaps wondering how on Earth they could be perceived as "healthy." And, how could something that feels so terrible and makes you so angry be good for the organization? Because when you allow conflict, you let employees be themselves.

Says David Stiebel, author of *When Talking Makes Things Worse!* (Whitehall & Nolton, 1997), "Employees are smart enough to know what managers want and, in most cases, what they want is conformity and obedience." Stiebel believes that when employees think conflict is a no-no, they won't

> If everything is going smoothly, there's no need to innovate. "Trainers should forget about being nice. . . ."

voice their objections, concerns, or dissenting opinions—or suggest new ways of doing things.

"In that kind of environment," says Fred Cunningham, senior EOD specialist at Keane, an information technology firm based in Boston, "we can agree our way into horrendous decisions." But when people are allowed to express their opinions, no matter how disagreeable, magic can occur. More ideas are put on the table, which can lead to more discovery, which can lead to quantum leaps in improvement and innovation. Put simply, conflict is a potent source of creativity—especially in troubled times. After all, if everything is going smoothly, there's no need to innovate or move to a higher level. Says Simmons, "When marketing and engineering disagree violently about something, you've got a wonderful opportunity to figure out how to make improvements by meeting both [of their] objectives."

Jerry Hirshberg, president of Nissan Design International in San Diego, has great respect for the creative value of conflict. In fact, he encourages it on projects by purposefully putting together people from different professional and cultural backgrounds. What he's after is something he calls "creative abrasion," which he describes as "the ability to transform pregnant moments of friction and collision into opportunities for breakthroughs."

So, why with all this creative potential is conflict still viewed as something to be avoided or squelched? Two reasons: Because it feels bad and

because employees usually are not prepared to deal with it. Typically, they haven't been taught the difference between constructive conflict that leads to innovation and destructive conflict that damages relationships. Without that framework, it's easy to believe all conflict is bad. This is where training professionals come in. Working with upper management, they have a significant role in reframing an organization's concept of conflict. But before addressing what trainers can do to nurture constructive conflict, here are some of the things they do that can increase destructive conflict.

It's a bad thing

Ironically, one of the ways that training professionals may (unwittingly) escalate organizational conflict is through the use of traditional conflict management programs. Says Stiebel, "Many trainers have a fundamental belief that conflict is merely the result of poor communication and that, deep down, we are all compatible and share the same interests. I call this 'the myth of hidden harmony.'" Because of that myth, many trainers use conflict management as a way to improve people's communication skills. But by acting as if every conflict is a communication problem, they ignore very real disagreements. "Better communication about true disagreements can actually increase the conflict around those disagreements," says Stiebel. "That's because, typically, the more we understand someone's position, the more we dislike that person."

Another way that trainers contribute to conflict is through the use of traditional group process. Says Simmons, "Often, many of the facilitation techniques that trainers use push conflict under the surface, making it worse." For example, if a team discussion gets tense, many trainers will divide the team into smaller groups. "That's a way to avoid conflict, not confront it."

Another potentially harmful technique is to try to break an impasse by taking a vote. Simmons points out that "majority rules" is not consensus.

Sure, you might get 10 people to agree to go in a certain direction, but you risk having eight people still pissed off. She says, "If people were cows, traditional group process would work because we could corral them through a chute labeled Agreement. But people aren't cows. Whenever we try to herd them in a direction that they don't want to go, they go back to the gate and let themselves out."

The way that many trainers are evaluated may also serve to fuel organizational conflict. "Trainers are trained to be nice because their evaluation sheets typically measure how happy and satisfied employees are with a program," says Simmons. But learning doesn't always feel good, especially when participants are learning about something as inherently uncomfortable as conflict. To help people understand conflict, trainers have to be willing to get them to stare this uncomfortable subject in the face. Says Simmons, "Trainers should forget about being nice and start thinking about being effective."

Granted, it's tricky trying to create the kind of culture in which conflict is nurtured but not allowed get out of hand. There might be a temptation to think: If a little conflict is good, wouldn't a lot be better? The key is to encourage constructive conflict, which leads to better decisions, and discourage destructive conflict, which erupts into turf wars. But how do you distinguish between the two?

"Look at how employees relate to each other in public settings," suggests Jim Lucas, president of Luman Consulting, Shawnee Mission, Kansas. "It's usually the opposite of what is going on under the surface." Lucas says, for example, that if 10 people in a meeting appear unwilling to disagree, the seeds of destructive conflict are probably at work.

Think about it: How many times have you been in a meeting in which people nodded politely at new ideas but went right back to doing things the same old way? Such behavior indicates the kind of culture in which any conflict or disagreement is considered taboo—the kind of culture

---

How To Encourage Good Disputes

Here are some approaches for encouraging productive conflict, from *Workplace Wars and How to End Them* by Kenneth Kaye of Kaye & McCarthy, a Chicago-based management consulting firm. Writes Kaye: "It must not be our goal to prevent conflict or discourage disputes. Our goal is to encourage good disputes. We want people to disagree with one another freely, constructively—not always pleasantly or kindly, but always respecting the legitimacy of other points of view and the value of the other person."

▫ Look for shared goals and win-win situations.

▫ Clarify, sort, and value differences.

▫ Gain people's commitment to change their own attitudes and modes of communication when necessary.

▫ Analyze why conflicts keep occurring. Usually, people aren't really fighting about what they say they're fighting about.

▫ Encourage individuals to take the initiative to change personally.

Kaye says, " A single individual can do much to stimulate positive change within an organization."

---

that's ripe for destructive, covert conflict. But when people are willing to disagree publicly and challenge each other, you have the makings of constructive conflict. That's because when people are allowed to speak their minds, resentment doesn't have a chance to fester. Disagreements can lead to well-rounded decisions. Says Lucas, "There is no one best way to do anything." Companies that realize that let employees make suggestions no matter how contrary to popular opinion they may be.

Part of the scenery

So how can you, as a training professional, help create the kind of culture

in which constructive conflict is encouraged? Recommends Simmons, "Start by getting comfortable with conflict." You can experiment with it and stretch your own comfort zone. Look for apparently unsolvable conflicts. Instead of relegating them to the "unsolvable basket," examine those conflicts more closely for opportunities for creativity.

Simmons recalls a time when she was designing a performance-review system for a client and wanted to involve all managers. The client, however, was used to making all of the decisions and couldn't see how everyone could possibly be involved, especially given the time constraints. She says, "By hashing it out, we were able to create a process that not only heightened organizational performance, but also allowed the managers to feel heard."

Once you're comfortable with conflict, you can begin to influence the kind of organizational change necessary for constructive conflict to become part of the scenery. Conflict isn't something that can be "solved" by teaching employees how to communicate more effectively or work together better in teams–important as those activities are. The best way to deal with conflict is to create the kind of culture in which it's acknowledged and supported as a natural part of the business process.

Here are some of the elements that need to be in place for companies to foster the kind of work environment that allows healthy conflict.

Respect individuals and individual differences. Before you can do anything to help employees develop conflict management skills, the organization must create the kind of culture that supports diversity of all kinds, including diversity of thought and opinion. A corporate values statement is a great place to start. At Keane, one of its corporate values is respect for the individual, which implies respect for individual differences. That value goes a long way toward helping employees understand the need to see other points of view. Says Cunningham, "If I'm involved in a conflict and I see our values statement hanging on the wall, it forces me to step back and see how I can adjust my message to respect the other person or people involved."

Managers must model healthy conflict if it has any hope of becoming a reality. According to Stiebel, managers can model the value of conflict by demonstrating their willingness to learn from others and experiment with those counter-intuitive approaches:

□ publicly praising employees who are willing to suggest new and different approaches

□ celebrating the success of counter-intuitive decisions by telling stories about such successes

□ modeling the kind of behavior that shows a comfort level with conflict.

Glenn Gienko, executive vice president of human resources for Motorola in Schaumburg, Illinois, agrees that leadership, public praise, and storytelling are the keys to making constructive conflict a reality. He says, "Fifteen years ago during an officers' meeting, in which everyone was celebrating the success of the company, one employee stood up in front of his peers and their spouses and proclaimed that Motorola's quality stunk. The willingness of [that lone] employee to speak against the grain ultimately turned into Motorola's highly praised Six Sigma quality effort. Today, we tell this story over and over as a way to show employees what constructive dissent can do for a company."

Reward the behavior you want to encourage. As any good trainer knows, what gets rewarded gets reinforced. If you expect employees to work through difficult problems and take the initiative to find new and better ways to do things, then you had better spell out those expectations in the performance-review system. But don't stop with lower-level employees; managers must also be held accountable. At Flint Ink, an ink manufacturer based in Detroit, managers are held accountable for communicating job expectations to employees, for providing ongoing employee development, and for creating a trusting work environment.

Says Tom Emerson, director of employee relations, "Destructive conflict occurs when employees feel insecure and don't trust management. We hold managers accountable for developing and exhibiting the kind of behaviors that allow employees to trust them."

Make sure employees are equipped to do their jobs. One of the primary sources of conflict in many organizations is that employees often work outside of their comfort zones. Says Emerson, "We ask employees to do things that are outside their previous area of experience. That makes them feel uncomfortable, which can lead to frustration and conflict." Because of that, Emerson believes that one of the best services a trainer can provide is to make sure employees are prepared to do the jobs they've been assigned.

Provide individualized training when and where needed. Trainers who assume that conflict management, better communication, or management training is the key to nurturing constructive conflict are on the right track, but they're likely to waste an enormous amount of money along the way. Yes, a lot of employees do need to improve their skills in reflective listening, problem solving, collaboration, negotiation, and communication. But not everyone does. Instead of wasting training dollars trying to create a one-size-fits-all conflict management program, the time would be better spent two ways. One, teach managers how constructive conflict adds value and how they can model the kind of behaviors that encourage positive dissent or creative abrasion. Two, provide training in communication and conflict management only to employees who need it. You determine which ones by holding managers accountable for employee development. In the end, it's a tricky proposition to encourage the kind of ripe and juicy conflict that leads to innovation. Motorola's Gienko says, "It's definitely more of an art form than a formula." But when conflict is harnessed, amazing things can happen.

As Hirshberg of Nissan put it in his book, *The Creative Priority* (HarperBusiness, 1998): "Friction between individuals and groups is typically thought of as something harmful. And it usually is. It generates heat and discomfort, disrupts interactions, and can destroy relationships. Between a couple, it can lead to divorce. Between countries, it can lead to war. Within corporations, it can distort and disrupt communication and ruin cohesiveness. Businesses of all types spend considerable time and money trying to reduce or eliminate conflict. But in human terms, it's surely one of the most plentiful and volatile sources of energy on the planet."

So, go for it. Just be careful.

Shari Caudron *is a Denver-based freelance writer.*

INTER- AND INTRACULTURAL NEGOTIATION:
U.S. AND JAPANESE NEGOTIATORS

JEANNE M. BRETT
Northwestern University

TETSUSHI OKUMURA
Shiga University

In this study, we propose that culture provides scripts and schemas for negotiation. The implications for negotiation of two cultural values, individualism/collectivism and hierarchy/egalitarianism, are discussed. The primary hypothesis, that joint gains will be lower in intercultural negotiations between U.S. and Japanese negotiators than in intracultural negotiations between either U.S. or Japanese negotiators, was confirmed with data from 30 intercultural, 47 U.S.-U.S. Intracultural, and 18 Japanese-Japanese intracultural simulated negotiations. Tests of secondary hypotheses indicated that there was less understanding of the priorities of the other party and the utility of a compatible issue in inter- than in intracultural negotiations. When information about priorities was available, intercultural negotiators were less able than intracultural negotiators to use it to generate joint gains.

In order to remain competitive, organizations are increasingly engaging in international business ventures (Lewis, 1990). Intercultural buyer-seller transactions and joint ventures between companies have grown exponentially during the 1990s, bringing midrange and smaller companies into international ventures, some for the first time (Lewis, 1990). Managing these intercultural transactions requires knowing not just how to negotiate successfully with buyers and sellers from your own culture, but also how to negotiate with buyers and sellers from other cultures.

Western scholars have produced substantial research on negotiation over the past decade. (See Neale and Bazerman [1991], Pruitt and Carnevale [1993], and Thompson [1997] for reviews.) There has been some cross-cultural research comparing negotiations in different cultural contexts (Graham, 1993). However, research on negotiations between members of different cultures, or intercultural negotiation, has lagged (Leung, 1997). In this study, we developed hypotheses contrasting inter-

The authors would like to acknowledge the helpful comments on a draft of this article provided by Wendi Adair, Max Bazerman, Don Moore, Anne Lytle, Margaret Neale, Debra Shapiro, and Catherine Tinsley and the financial support of the Dispute Resolution Research Center, Northwestern University.

and intracultural negotiations and tested these hypotheses on simulation data gathered from Japanese and U.S. managers negotiating interculturally and intraculturally.

Japan and the United States are major business partners (Graham & Sano, 1989). Successful negotiations between Japanese and U.S. companies have implications for the economies of both countries. Yet descriptions of Japanese and U.S. negotiating styles suggest substantial differences in approach (Graham, 1993; Kato & Kato, 1992; March, 1990) that may affect intercultural negotiations. For example, a vice president in the Japan merchant banking operation at Bankers Trust noted in the *New York Times Magazine* that information is viewed as an important source of power in negotiations in both the United States and Japan (Yoshimura, 1997). U.S. negotiators, he suggested, exercise the power of information by disclosing it, and in return, they get information from other people. In contrast, the Japanese exercise the power of information by hiding it, he noted, going on to point out another fundamental difference between Japanese and U.S. negotiating styles: "For Japanese, negotiation is usually a process of reaching a point that is acceptable to both parties. For Americans, it's a competition dividing winners and losers" (Yoshimura, 1997). Americans, he continued, often open negotiations at a level that is

From *Academy of Management Journal*, October 1998, pp. 495-510. © 1998 by the Academy of Management, P.O. Box 3020, Briar Cliff Manor, NY 10510-8020. Reproduced by permission of the publisher via Copyright Clearance Center, Inc.

totally unacceptable to the Japanese, seeing the opening offer as a starting point, but the Japanese cannot see trust in such behavior.

The purpose of this research was to determine just how great the cultural differences between Japanese and U.S. negotiators are and whether these cultural differences interfere with the negotiation of joint gains in intercultural as opposed to intracultural negotiations. We chose joint gains as the dependent variable in our study because joint gains are relatively difficult to negotiate in any culture (Neale & Bazerman, 1991), and we thought that strategies for negotiating joint gains might be different across cultures. Joint gains are only one of the outcomes of negotiation. However, they are an important outcome, since the creation of joint gains can bridge a nonoverlapping bargaining zone, thus making an agreement possible when no agreement seemed likely; and, when an overlapping bargaining zone exists, the creation of joint gains means taking maximum advantage of available resources (Raiffa, 1982).

We begin with a review of the research identifying the knowledge structures (or schemas and scripts, in the parlance of social cognition) that are associated with the negotiation of joint gains. We propose that such knowledge structures are fanned by culture (among other influences) and develop hypotheses about differences between U.S. and Japanese schemas for negotiation. These hypotheses lead to the study's major research question, whether intercultural negotiations between U.S. and Japanese negotiators are less effective in generating joint gains than intracultural negotiations between U.S. or Japanese negotiators.

THEORY AND HYPOTHESES

Culture and Negotiation

Culture, or a society's characteristic profile with respect to values, norms, and institutions (Lytle, Brett, Barsness, Tinsley, & Janssens, 1995) provides insight into the different solutions that societies evolve to manage social exchanges such as negotiation. Culture is a socially shared knowledge structure, or schema, giving meaning to incoming stimuli and channeling outgoing reactions (Triandis, 1972). Cultural values (what is important) and norms (what is appropriate) provide the members of a cultural group with schemas, or templates, for interpreting both the situation and the behavior of others (Fiske & Taylor, 1991), and scripts, or sequences of appropriate social action (Shank & Abelson, 1977). Cultural institutions provide contexts for negotiations. Negotiation schemas are cognitive warehouses of information and expectations about negotiation (Thompson, 1997). Negotiation scripts are subsets of negotiation schemas. They store action plans in the form of behavioral sequences. These plans can be drawn upon for enacting schemas.

Prior research, carried out within the U.S. culture, has identified several scripts and schemas that contribute to the negotiation of joint gains. For example, there appear to be two different information-sharing scripts—seeking and sharing information about preferences and priorities (Olekalns, Smith, & Walsh, 1996; Pruitt, 1981; Weingart, Thompson, Bazerman, & Carroll, 1990) and heuristic trial-and-error search (Pruitt & Lewis, 1975; Tutzauer & Roloff, 1988)—that facilitate the negotiation of joint gains. Negotiation schemas (preconceptions about negotiation) related to the negotiation of joint gains include avoidance of premature closure (Olekalns & Smith, 1996) and eschewal of power (Pruitt, 1981; Pruitt & Lewis, 1975). A cooperative motivational orientation, defined as a negotiator's having goals for self and for the dyad or group (Weingart, Bennett, & Brett, 1993), and a mixed motive orientation, defined as expectations that preferences may not be completely opposed (Pinkley, Griffith, & Northcraft, 1995), in contrast to a fixed-pie schema, defined as the assumption that negotiations are necessarily distributive (Thompson & Hastie, 1990), also appear to be schemas associated with the negotiation of joint gains.

Comparative cross-cultural research documenting differences between U.S. and Japanese cultural values (Hofstede, 1980; Schwartz, 1994) provides a basis for developing hypotheses about how negotiation scripts and schemas differ in the U.S. and Japanese cultures. The Japanese culture is collectivist and hierarchical; the U.S. culture is individualistic and egalitarian (Hofstede, 1980; Schwartz, 1994). Both of these cultural values appear to have implications for the scripts and schemas that a culture's members bring with them to a negotiation.

Individualism versus collectivism and the self-interest schema. In individualist cultures, the definition of self is independent from in-group membership; in collectivist cultures, it is interdependent with in-group membership (Marcus & Kityama, 1991; Triandis, 1989). In individualist cultures, goals are independent of those of the in-group; in collectivist cultures, goals are aligned with those of the in-group (Triandis, 1989). In individualist cultures, there is an emphasis on personal needs; in collectivist cultures, the emphasis is on social obligations (Triandis, 1989). The linkage of goals to self as opposed to the collective and the emphasis on personal needs as opposed to social obligations suggest that individualists should be more self-interested in negotiations than collectivists.

Hypothesis 1. The cultural value of individualism versus collectivism will be related to a high self-interest negotiation schema.

Prior research has shown that when all negotiators in a dyad or group subscribe to a self-interest schema, or an individualistic social or motivational orientation, they may risk impasse; however, when they do reach agreements, their goals appear to motivate them to realize high joint gains (Weingart et al., 1993). Huber and Neale

(1986) also found that joint gains were facilitated when both negotiators in a dyad had moderate to difficult goals.

Hierarchy versus egalitarianism and the power schema. The cultural value hierarchy versus egalitarianism has implications for how power is perceived in a culture. In hierarchical cultures, there is a preference for differentiated social status. Social status implies social power in a variety of contexts, including negotiations. Low-status members of a society are expected to concede to high-status members, who in turn have a social responsibility to look out for the needs of the lower-status members (Leung, 1997).

Social status differences exist in egalitarian cultures, but people are less receptive to power differences in egalitarian societies than in hierarchical ones (Leung, 1997). Social status may not automatically convey negotiating power in egalitarian societies, because status differences may be downplayed, in keeping with the cultural value of egalitarianism. Egalitarians expect equal engagement in social intercourse, but those from hierarchical cultures have unidirectional expectations (Leung, 1997). In an egalitarian culture, a party's negotiating power may be tied to the best alternative to a negotiated agreement (BATNA) and may therefore vary from one negotiation to another. In a hierarchical culture, power is associated with the party's status in the social structure. Since this status is unlikely to change drastically from one negotiation to another, power in hierarchical cultures may be viewed as fixed.

The relative emphasis on power in hierarchical cultures, compared to egalitarian cultures, suggests that power will be a more important schema for negotiators in hierarchical cultures than in egalitarian cultures.

Hypothesis 2. The cultural value of hierarchy versus egalitarianism will be related to a power schema for negotiation.

Scripts for information exchange in negotiation. Descriptive accounts (March, 1990; Yoshimura, 1997), theory (Ting-Toomey, 1988), and some empirical research (Ohbuchi & Takahashi, 1994) suggest that the scripts U.S. and Japanese negotiators use to gather information are quite different. Yoshimura (1997) observed that U.S. negotiators share information in order to get information but that Japanese negotiators hide information. In her face-negotiation theory, Ting-Toomey (1988) proposed that individualists communicate directly and collectivists, indirectly. When Ohbuchi and Takahashi (1994) asked Japanese and American people to describe their conflict management behavior, the Japanese said they used more indirect methods, such as suggestions, ingratiation, impression management, and appeasement; the Americans said they used more direct methods, such as persuasion, bargaining, and compromise. Thus, although it may seem to a U.S. negotiator that a Japanese negotiator does not engage in information sharing, it may only be that the two cultures' scripts for information sharing are incompatible. Furthermore, the individualist

negotiator whose own style is direct may not know how to glean information from the collectivist's indirect communication script.

In intercultural negotiations between U.S. and Japanese negotiators, if scripts for information sharing are different, there should be less understanding than there is in intracultural negotiations, where scripts are similar. If Japanese negotiators follow their culturally appropriate script and search for and provide information indirectly, U.S. negotiators may not be able to interpret the information conveyed indirectly. U.S. negotiators in intercultural negotiations therefore may end up understanding less about the preferences and priorities of their Japanese opponents than U.S. negotiators in intracultural negotiations, whose opponents are likely to share a similar information script.

Hypothesis 3. U.S. negotiators in intercultural negotiations with Japanese negotiators will have less understanding of their opponents' priorities and preferences than U.S. negotiators in intracultural negotiations.

Japanese negotiators in intercultural negotiations should understand the direct communications of U.S. negotiators regarding their own preferences and priorities. However, if the Japanese negotiators do not reciprocate with direct information sharing, the U.S. negotiators may provide less information when negotiating cross-culturally than when negotiating with same-culture partners.

Hypothesis 4. Japanese negotiators in intercultural negotiations with U.S. negotiators will have less understanding of their opponents' priorities and preferences than Japanese negotiators in intracultural negotiations.

Intercultural Negotiations and Joint Gains

U.S. negotiators do not always reach optimal agreements (Neale & Bazerman, 1991; Pruitt & Carnevale, 1993). A comparative, cross-cultural negotiation study that used a three-issue exercise with integrative potential (Pruitt, 1981) showed that Japanese pairs received the highest joint profits of any national group; U.S. negotiators' joint profits were in the middle of the range (Graham, 1993). We expected that relatively compatible cultural values and negotiation schemas and scripts regarding self-interest, power, and information sharing would facilitate intracultural negotiators' reaching better agreements than intercultural negotiators.

When negotiators' schemas and scripts are incompatible owing to culture or other reasons, their negotiation process may be ineffective and their negotiated outcomes suboptimal. It may be as though two actors in the same play have two different scripts and two different sets of stage directions, each contributed by a different playwright. Although intercultural negotiators may still reach agreements, their agreements, compared to those of intracultural negotiators, may be suboptimal in that opportunities for joint gains are missed.

The research on norm development (Bettenhausen & Murnighan, 1985) and conflict frames (Pinkley, 1990; Putnam & Holmer, 1992) suggests that negotiators whose norms or frames do not match may have difficulty reaching agreement. Bettenhausen and Murnighan (1985) proposed that when parties define a situation (such as a negotiation) similarly but have different scripts, their initial interaction may go smoothly, but resolving differences later may be problematic, unless they negotiate their scripts and take a common approach to the task. The research and theorizing about conflict frames suggest that disputants with similar frames or frames that converge are likely to reach agreement but that disputants whose frames are very different may fail to reach agreement (Drake & Donohue, 1994; Pinkley & Northcraft, 1994).[1] The implication of the norm development and conflict frames literatures for our research on intercultural negotiation is that when cultural differences result in different or conflicting negotiation scripts and schemas, a negotiated agreement may be less than optimal, unless schemas and scripts can themselves be negotiated. However, it seems unlikely that incompatible negotiation schemas and scripts embedded in cultural values can be easily changed or even adjusted during the course of a single negotiation. Thus, we expected that joint gains would be lower in intercultural than in intracultural negotiations.

Hypothesis 5. Intercultural negotiators will realize lower joint gains than intracultural negotiators.

We expected cultural differences in schemas and scripts to impact information sharing in intercultural negotiations in such a way that intercultural negotiators would be less likely than intracultural negotiators to identify optimal integrative tradeoffs. We also thought that cultural differences would limit heuristic trial-and-error search for better alternatives and contribute to premature closure. This reasoning suggested intercultural negotiators would be less likely than intracultural negotiators to include a compatible but optional issue in their agreements.

Low joint gains may result from negotiators' having incompatible schemas and scripts that lead to a lack of information sharing or a lack of motivation to continue searching for better alternatives. For example, if a negotiator from a collectivist culture uses indirect communication and a negotiator from an individualist culture uses direct information sharing, the "disconnect" in information-sharing scripts may result in low information sharing and low joint gains.

Hypothesis 6. When intercultural negotiators' scripts and schemas are incompatible, joint gains will be lower than they

will be when intercultural negotiators' scripts and schemas are compatible.

Intercultural negotiators may anticipate that their approaches to negotiation will be incompatible, or they may sense the incompatibility once a negotiation begins and try to make adjustments. If their adjustments are successful, intercultural negotiators should be as capable of generating high joint gains as intracultural negotiators, nullifying Hypothesis 6.

METHODS

Simulation

The data were collected in conjunction with the simulated negotiation of a buyer-seller transaction. The simulation, "Cartoon," is based on the exercise "Working Women" (Tenbrunsel & Bazerman, 1995). In "Cartoon," the seller is a major film production company and the buyer is an independent television station in a large metropolitan area. The seller wishes to syndicate (sell the rerun rights for) a 100-episode cartoon, *Ultra Rangers*. The issues include the price per episode, the number of times each episode will be allowed to run, the financing arrangement, and whether another cartoon, *Strums*, is to be added to the deal. The alternatives are quantified, as is the BATNA. There is the potential for an integrative trade-off between the number of runs, which is more important to the buyer than to the seller, and financing, which is more important to the seller than to the buyer. *Strums* is a compatible issue; inclusion generates value for both parties, although that value must still be distributed. Table 1 shows the positions of each party on the issues. Table 1 also shows the explicit information negotiators were given about the value to them of their alternative deal (BATNA).

The program in the original exercise, "Working Women," is a sitcom. We decided to change the program to a cartoon, because cartoons are popular television shows in both the United States and Japan. Furthermore, film companies in both countries produce cartoons and syndicate them worldwide. (For further information about the worldwide syndication of cartoons, see Mifflin [1995].)

Two versions of each role were produced: (1) a U.S. buyer (a U.S. television station) and a Japanese buyer (a Japanese television station) and (2) a U.S. seller (a U.S. film company) and a Japanese seller (a Japanese film company). The U.S. and Japanese buyers received the same substantive information, as did the U.S. and Japanese sellers. Participants, who were American and Japanese managers, always played the role of a party from their own culture. In the intercultural simulation, half the teams had a U.S. buyer (played by a U.S. participant) and a Japanese seller (played by a Japanese participant); the other half of the teams had a Japanese buyer (played by a Japanese participant) and a U.S. seller (played by a U.S. participant). In the intracultural simulations, U.S.

---

[1] A conflict frame is a perceptual set or orientation that leads disputants to focus on some characteristics of a conflict while ignoring others (Deutsch, 1975) and that invokes particular schemas and scripts (Pinkley & Northcraft, 1994).

TABLE 1
"Cartoon": Positions of the Parties

Issue	T.V. Station	Film Company
Revenue	$ 8,400,000	n.a.
Price per episode		
Limit	$ 60,000	$ 35,000
Aspiration	$ 30,000	$ 70,000
Runs-per-episode adjustment		
4	$(1,680,000)	$ 500,000
5	(840,000)	250,000
6	0	0
7	840,000	(250,000)
8	1,680,000	(500,000)
Financing savings/cost		
Year 1	10%	−20%
Year 2	20	−35
Year 3	30	−50
Year 4	40	−60
Year 5	50	−70
Strums[a]		
Reservation price	$ 20,000	$ 10,000
Ratings[b]		
6–7	20%	10%
7–8	50	10
8–9	10	10
9–10	10	50
10–11	10	20
Alternative deal		
Value[c]	$3.0	$2.5

[a] This was the additional cartoon that was available.
[b] The percentages given are estimated likelihoods of a range.
[c] Values are millions of dollars.

buyers negotiated with U.S. sellers, and Japanese buyers negotiated with Japanese sellers.

Participants

To obtain the intercultural data set, we invited U.S. and Japanese managers to participate in a one-day executive program on intercultural negotiation. U.S. participants were selected from the alumni of a major Midwest business school who lived in the greater metropolitan area close to the school and worked in finance, banking, manufacturing, or trading. Japanese participants were identified as follows: First, 210 Japanese companies with offices in the metropolitan area were identified. The top local manager was sent a letter describing the intercultural negotiation program and asking him (all were men) to select a Japanese manager whose day-to-day business for the company was conducted in English. The invitation made it clear that the program would be conducted in English. Once a manager was nominated for the program, he (all were men) was sent information about the program (the time and location, etc.), as well as notification that the program would be conducted in English. We emphasized that the program would be conducted in English in order to discourage Japanese managers who might be uncomfortable negotiating in English from attending.

Participants providing the intracultural U.S.-U.S. data participated in the study as the first negotiation exercise in their master's-level course on negotiations. Data from pairs of foreign nationals who were in the course were not included in the analysis. Men were paired with men and women with women. Since there were no outcome differences between the male and female pairs, the latter were included in the data set.

Participants providing the intracultural Japanese-Japanese data set were full-time managers who were taking part in a management training program paid for by their companies. All were men.

There were 60 participants in the intercultural negotiation sample, 30 American managers and 30 Japanese foreign assignees; 94 in the U.S. sample; and 36 in the Japanese-Japanese sample. Both intercultural data and intracultural U.S.-U.S. data were collected at two different times approximately one year apart. Intracultural Japanese-Japanese data were collected at two different times in the intervening year. There were no significant differences on any measure for any group between the first and second data collections.

Participants in the U.S.-Japanese sample were older (mean, 38 years) than those in the Japanese-Japanese sample (mean, 27 years) and in one of the two classes in the U.S. sample (mean, 28 years). The average age of the participants in the other U.S. class was 37 years. U.S. participants in the intercultural negotiation were likely to have had previous negotiation training (64%), because there was a negotiation training program at the school. Japanese participants in the intercultural negotiation were less likely to have had prior negotiation training (50%). Participants in the U.S.-U.S. and Japanese-Japanese samples took part in the simulation prior to negotiation training.

Procedures

We wrote a standard introduction to the negotiation exercise and used it each time data were collected. This introduction provided an outline of activities and timing and described "Cartoon," the exercise. Participants were given a short questionnaire asking about negotiation norms. They were assigned to play the role of buyer or seller and given confidential information for their role. In the intercultural negotiations, role information was provided in English for the U.S. participants and in Japanese and English for the U.S. participants and in Japanese and English for the Japanese participants. In the intracultural negotiations, role information was provided in each participant's own language. Everyone was given a same-role partner and one hour to prepare for the negotiation. Japanese participants in the intercultural negotiation were told they might prepare in the Japanese language, although the negotiations would be conducted in English. Participants in the Japanese-Japanese teams prepared and negotiated in Japanese. During the one-hour preparation time, the researchers (one of whom is bilingual in Japanese and English) circulated to answer questions. We had prepared standard answers to questions in advance and consulted with each other before answering any question that had not been anticipated. At the end of the hour, the preparation partners were split up, and each was assigned a negotiation partner. Negotiations were all one-on-one. Negotiation assignments were made so that buyer preparation partners were not assigned to seller preparation partners. Thus, no two buyer-seller negotiation dyads consisted of preparation partners. Participants were given one and one-half hours to negotiate. At the end of the negotiation, they completed a form describing their agreement, if any, and a questionnaire with biographical questions and questions about what they did during the preparation and negotiation, their goals, and the other party's priorities. All questionnaires were provided in English and in Japanese, as appropriate. All Japanese materials were translated and retranslated by two native-speaking, bilingual Japanese nationals. After all data had been collected, results were shown to the group, and the exercise and the negotiation experiences were discussed.

Measures

Dependent variable. The primary dependent variable was joint gains. Joint gains were calculated as follows: Negotiators' net revenue was calculated by subtracting their BATNA value from the gross revenue accruing to them from the agreement they had negotiated. Joint gains were calculated by adding the buyer's net to the seller's net. Appendixes A and B provide examples of net revenue calculations for a buyer and a seller. Only one group failed to reach an agreement. That group was not included in the data set. Maximum possible joint gains were $5.08 million.

Data also were collected on the elements of the agreement: the price paid for the cartoon, the number of runs, whether or not there were financing terms, and whether *Strums* was included in the agreement. It was also possible for negotiators to reach a contingent agreement based on the ratings that the cartoon generated in syndication.

Independent variables. Independent variables were type of negotiation (intercultural versus intracultural) and culture (U.S. or Japan).

Cultural values. We measured cultural values prior to preparation and negotiation using items from Schwartz's (1994) survey of values. This survey, although perhaps not so well known as Hofstede's (1980) work, is superior in several ways. It is based on a conceptualization of values: it was developed with systematic sampling, measurement, and analysis techniques: and perhaps most important, its normative data are recent, collected in the late 1980s and early 1990s.

Individualism versus collectivism was measured using seven items from Schwartz's (1994) survey of values. Items included choosing own goals (selecting own purposes), capable (competent, effective, efficient), successful (achieving goals), intelligent (logical, thinking), self-respect (belief in one's own worth), ambitious (hardworking, aspiring), and independent (self-reliant, self-sufficient). A high score indicated individualism (α = .80).

Hierarchy versus egalitarianism was measured with six items from Schwartz's (1994) survey of values. Items included social power (control over others, dominance), authority (the right to lead or command), preserving my public image (protecting my "face"), wealth (material possessions, money), social recognition (respect, approval by others), and influential (having an impact on people and events). A high score indicated hierarchy (α = .77).

Negotiation schemas and scripts. Negotiation schemas were conceptualized as perceptual sets or cognitive predispositions. They were measured by questions asked prior to the preparation and negotiation. Participants answered a series of questions framed by the words "What is appropriate behavior in negotiation?" Forty-five items measured on five-point Likert-style response formats anchored by "strongly disagree" and "strongly agree" factored into three dimensions. We used the scales formed from summing the items loading on these dimensions as measurements of three negotiation schemas: self-interest, power, and information. The items composing the self-interest scale did not hold up during reliability analysis, so the scale was truncated into a single item: "It's appropriate to satisfy your own needs." The distributive tactics scale, a measurement of power, contained five items, including asking for sympathy, making the first offer, making counteroffers, avoiding public disputes, and compromising (α = .61). The information-sharing scale contained five items, including sharing information with the other party, collaborating with the other party, engaging in a give-and-take exchange, sharing information when the other party shares, and trying to build a relationship with the other party (α = .76).

In another measurement of schemas, we assessed expectations about factors affecting the outcome of a negotiation. We asked how strongly participants agreed or disagreed (five-point scale) with the statement that the outcome of a negotiation was a function of (1) how thoroughly the parties shared information, (2) how powerful the parties' companies were, (3) the parties' roles (buyer, seller), and (4) the parties' alternatives to negotiating with each other (BATNA; Fisher, Ury, & Patton, 1991).

Immediately after the negotiation, before participants had shared their results, they answered a series of questions focusing on their preparation. These were framed by the following: "During the preparation session, how much did you think about . . . ?" ("a lot," "some," "a little," "not much at all"). These items factored into two dimensions that we used as further measures of power and information schemas. Four items were summed into a power scale (α = .82), and 12 items were summed into an information-planning scale (α = .80). These items are presented in Appendix C.

In the postnegotiation questionnaire, we asked negotiators to rank the issues in the negotiation with respect to their importance to the other party. These data were used as indicators of negotiators' scripts. Negotiators were given a list of issues in the order in which they were discussed in the case: price, runs, financing, *Strums*, and other issues (for example, contingent arrangements). Our interest was in the ranking of runs and financing, the integrative issues, and *Strums*, the compatible issue. As can be seen in Table 1, runs were of greater value to the buyer than the seller, since the buyer wanted the right to show the cartoon as frequently as possible, thereby gaining greater advertising revenue. Table 1 also shows that financing was of greater value to the seller than the buyer. The seller preferred to be paid up front.

Each issue received a rank between 1 and 6. We assigned a 6 if an issue was not ranked by a participant. Categories were collapsed for the purpose of data analysis. For runs and financing, we collapsed rankings of 1 and 2 into one category and rankings of 3–6 into another category. This coding was based on the importance of issues as presented in Table 1. Sellers, for example, should have rated runs as the first or second most important issue to buyers, along with price, and buyers should have rated runs as the third, fourth, or fifth most important issue to sellers. The coding for *Strums* was 1 if it received a rank of 1–4 and 0 if it received a rank of 5 or was not ranked. By collapsing categories, we were able to reduce the "ipsative" problem of ranked data, whereby the ranks of the later-ranked items are dependent on those of the earlier-ranked items. All issues had more than one opportunity to be placed in a rank. Collapsing categories was also consistent with the nature of the exercise, in which there was one important distributive issue. Negotiators would not necessarily place their opponent's trade-off issue ahead of the distributive issue.

Measures for ruling out alternative explanations. We asked participants to describe what went on during the negotiations by rating 24 items on five-point Likert scales ranging from "strongly disagree" to "strongly agree." These items factored into two dimensions. We labeled the first dimension "frustration." Eight items loaded on this dimension (α = .81; see Appendix C). We labeled the second dimension "cooperation/reciprocity." Six items loaded on this dimension (α = .80; see Appendix C).

Analysis

The unit of analysis for testing our hypotheses about the relationships between cultural group, cultural values, and negotiation schemas was the individual. We used analysis of variance (ANOVA) to conduct a sampling check to determine that Japanese participants were less individualistic and more hierarchical than U.S. participants. ANOVA was also used to test for differences between U.S. and Japanese negotiators with respect to the self-interest schema and the power schema. We used correlations to test Hypotheses 1 and 2, which are about the relationships between cultural values and negotiation schemas. Chi-squares were used to test Hypotheses 3 and 4, which concern the relative accuracy of inter- and intracultural negotiators' knowledge about the importance of issues.

The unit of analysis for testing the joint gains hypothesis (Hypothesis 5) was the dyad. Multivariate analysis of variance (MANOVA) was used to test differences between intra- and intercultural outcomes.

To test Hypothesis 6, concerning joint gains and the incompatibility of intercultural negotiators' cultural values and negotiation schemas, we used the dyad as the unit of analysis. To measure incompatibility, we did the following: For each variable that distinguished between Japanese and U.S. negotiators, we divided participants into three groups based on the variable's grand mean in the total sample of U.S. and Japanese participants. The groups were (1) more than half a standard deviation above the grand mean, (2) within half a standard deviation of the grand mean, and (3) more than half a standard deviation below the grand mean. We categorized dyads instead of computing difference scores in order to distinguish among dyads with high compatibility, low compatibility, and moderate compatibility, for which different joint gains might be anticipated. (For example, one might anticipate high joint gains from U.S. dyads that have high compatibility on self-interest, but not from U.S. dyads that have low compatibility on self-interest.) We then ran an ANOVA with six groups and joint gains as the dependent variable. The unit of analysis was intercultural dyads.

RESULTS

Cultural Group, Cultural Values, and Negotiation Schemas

The samples of U.S. and Japanese negotiators had cultural values similar to those that prior research has shown to be characteristic of those cultures. U.S. negotiators ($\bar{X}$ = 39.45, s.d. = 4.80) were significantly more individualistic than Japanese negotiators ($\bar{X}$ = 35.86, s.d. = 6.40, $F_{1, 176}$ = 17.15, $p \leq .01$). Japanese negotiators ($\bar{X}$ = 23.87, s.d. = 7.39) were significantly more hierarchical than U.S. negotiators ($\bar{X}$ = 21.01, s.d. = 6.58, $F_{1, 175}$ = 7.03, $p < .01$).

These cultural group differences extended to the self-interest and power negotiation schemas. U.S. negotiators ($\bar{X}$ = 4.16, s.d. = 0.72) were significantly more likely than Japanese negotiators ($\bar{X}$ = 3.53, s.d. = 0.82) to espouse a self-interest negotiation schema ($F_{1, 183}$ = 29.35, $p < .01$). The Japanese embraced a power schema with respect to distributive tactics ($\bar{X}_J$ = 18.86, s.d. = 2.51;l $\bar{X}_{U.S.}$ = 15.27, s.d. = 2.66, $F_{1, 178}$ = 77.43, $p \leq .01$) measured in the prenegotiation questionnaire. The Japanese also focused more on power in their preparation sessions than U.S. negotiators did ($\bar{X}_J = 10.69$, s.d. = 2.68; $x_{U.S.} = 9.31$, s.d. = 2.98, $F_{1, 172} = 9.39$, $p \leq .01$). As anticipated, U.S. negotiators embraced the concept of BATNA as power in the negotiation more strongly than the Japanese ($\bar{X}_J = 3.82$, s.d. = 0.61; $x_{U.S.} = 4.26$, s.d. = 0.75; $F_{1, 160} = 10.91$, $p \leq .01$). However, there were no differences between U.S. and Japanese negotiators with respect to their views as to the importance of status in the form of either buyer or seller role in the negotiation or the status of the company. There were no differences between U.S. and Japanese negotiators with respect to schemas for information, whether measured prior to the preparation session, as a norm for information sharing or as importance to the outcome, or after the negotiation, in terms of what was discussed during the preparation session.

Cultural Values and Negotiation Schemas

Table 2 presents the correlations between cultural group, cultural values, and measures of self-interest, power, and information schemas for negotiation. These correlations confirm Hypothesis 1: individualists endorsed self-interest in negotiations. The correlations also confirm Hypothesis 2: negotiators with hierarchical values endorsed distributive tactics and reported spending significant time discussing power in the preparation session.

We used regression analysis to test whether the relationship between cultural group and schemas were mediated by cultural values. These analyses showed that the cultural value of individualism versus collectivism partially accounted for the relationship between cultural group and a self-interest schema. Adjusted R^2s for the models containing different combinations of variables were as follows: individualism/collectivism with self-interest, .05; culture with self-interest, .13; individualism/collectivism and culture with self-interest, .17. The cultural value of hierarchy versus egalitarianism partially accounted for the relationship between distributive tactics and cultural group, with R^2s as follows: hierarchy/egalitarianism with distributive tactics, .04; culture with distributive tactics, .30; hierarchy/egalitarianism and culture, .30. Hierarchy versus egalitarianism also partially accounted for the relationship between power planning and cultural group: hierarchy/egalitarianism with power planning, .05; culture with power planning, .04; hierarchy/egalitarianism and culture with power planning, .08. All of these relationships were significant, indicating that at least some of the relationship between cultural group and negotiation schema could be accounted for by cultural values. However, in all cases, the cultural group-negotiation schema relationship was substantially greater than what could be accounted for by a cultural value, suggesting that negotiation schemas are likely to be multidetermined.

Information in Inter- and Intracultural Negotiations

The results suggest that U.S. and Japanese negotiators may use different scripts for information sharing in negotiations. Hypotheses 3 and 4 focus on perceptions of the importance to the other party of the integrative issues, runs and financing, and the compatible issue, *Strums*. The buyers should have understood that financing was more important to the sellers than runs, and the sellers should have understood that runs were more important than financing to the buyers. To test these predictions, we first broke the sample into buyers and sellers. Then, we compared U.S. inter- and intracultural negotiators and Japanese inter- and intracultural negotiators, so as to be able to identify asymmetries in information exchange if such occurred. The pattern proposed in Hypothesis 3 appeared clearly and significantly with

TABLE 2
Correlations between Culture and Negotiation Schemas

Variable	1	2	3	4	5	6	7	8	9	10	11
1. Culture											
2. Individualism/collectivism	−.30**										
3. Hierarchy/egalitarianism	.20**	.31**									
4. Self-interest	−.37**	.22**	−.14								
5. Distributive tactics	.55**	−.18*	.20**	−.13							
6. Power planning	.22**	.06	.23**	−.08	.06						
7. BATNA[a]	−.25**	.11	−.04	.28**	.04	.04					
8. Company power	−.10	.10	.06	.15	.02	.29**	.21**				
9. Role power	.10	−.18*	−.08	.11	.14	.09	.10	.30**			
10. Information sharing	.07	.00	.05	.15*	.28**	−.06	.31**	.03	.04		
11. Information planning	.05	.15*	.04	.04	.01	.21**	−.13	−.08	−.08	−.06	
12. Information power	.09	.07	.09	−.04	.02	−.02	.05	.07	−.03	.35**	−.05

[a]Best alternative to a negotiated agreement.
* $p \leq .05$
** $p \leq .01$

respect to U.S. sellers. Forty-one percent of the U.S. sellers engaged in intercultural negotiations ranked runs as the first or second most important issue to the buyer, compared to 74 percent of the U.S. sellers in intracultural negotiations ($\chi^2_1 = 5.36$, $p \le .02$). A result not supporting the asymmetric prediction of Hypothesis 4 was that Japanese sellers understood the importance of runs to the buyer whether they were negotiating intraculturally with Japanese buyers or interculturally with U.S. buyers. These data indicate a clear asymmetry in the information conveyed from Japanese buyer to U.S. seller in the intercultural negotiations. Additional significant evidence supporting Hypothesis 3 is the finding that 41 percent of the U.S. sellers in intercultural negotiations ranked financing as the issue with lower value to buyers (ranked 3–5), compared with 72 percent of the U.S. sellers in intracultural negotiations ($\chi^2_1 = 4.74$, $p \le .03$). Again, there were no significant differences in the proportions of Japanese intra- and intercultural sellers who ranked financing as of low value to buyers.

As predicted by Hypothesis 3, U.s. buyers in intercultural negotiations had a tendency to misjudge the importance of runs to the Japanese sellers. Forty-three percent of the U.S. buyers considered the issue ranked first or second by the sellers, compared with 33 percent of the U.S. buyers in intracultural negotiations. This pattern was in the expected direction but was not significant. However, U.S. buyers in intercultural negotiations were as aware of the importance of financing to sellers as U.S. buyers in intracultural negotiations.

The pattern of findings with respect to the integrative issues is consistent with the prediction of Hypothesis 3 but inconsistent with the prediction of Hypothesis 4. Full information seemed to go from the U.S. negotiator to the Japanese negotiator, but less information went in the opposite direction. U.S. negotiators were learning less about integrative issues in inter- than in intracultural negotiations. Japanese negotiators were learning as much about the integrative issues in inter- as in intracultural negotiations.

There were no differences in the proportions of U.S. buyers and sellers in intracultural negotiations ranking runs and financing high and low and in the proportions

of Japanese buyers and sellers in intracultural negotiations making these rankings. This pattern suggests that information exchange was similar in U.S. and Japanese intracultural negotiations.

However, a different pattern emerged with respect to the compatible issue—the second cartoon, Strums. Both U.S. and Japanese negotiators in the intercultural negotiation failed to understand the value of Strums, confirming both Hypothesis 3 and Hypothesis 4. Sixty-three percent of the U.S. intercultural negotiators, compared to 88 percent of the U.S. intracultural negotiators, ranked Strums as one of the top four issues in the negotiation ($\chi^2_1 = 8.69$, $p \le .01$). Likewise, 53 percent of the Japanese intercultural negotiators, compared with 92 percent of the Japanese intracultural negotiators, ranked Strums as one of the top four issues in the negotiation ($\chi^2_1 = 10.55$, $p \le .01$). The proportions of U.S. and Japanese intercultural negotiators ranking Strums as one of the top four issues in the negotiation were not significantly different. This pattern of data suggests that, with regard to Strums, there does not seem to be an asymmetry in perception between intercultural U.S. and Japanese negotiators, simply too little understanding of the importance of this issue.

Intercultural Negotiation and Joint Gains

Intercultural U.S.-Japanese negotiations resulted in lower joint gains than intracultural U.S. and Japanese negotiations, confirming Hypothesis 5. Table 3 shows that intercultural dyads averaged about $3.47 million in joint gains, compared with $4.32 million for intracultural negotiators ($F_{1, 93} = 17.61$, $p \le .01$). There were no significant differences in joint gains between the U.S.-U.S. intracultural negotiators, who averaged $4.33 million in joint gains (s.d. = $0.81 million), and the Japanese-Japanese intracultural negotiators, who averaged $4.29 million in joint gains (s.d. = $0.80 million). Controlling for age showed the following: age, which was correlated with joint gains ($r = .22$, $p \le .05$), accounted for 5 percent of the variance in joint gains; type of negotiation (inter versus intra) accounted for 16 percent of the variance in joint gains; and together, age and type of negotiation accounted for 16 percent of the variance in joint gains. Thus, age contributed no unique variance to the predic-

TABLE 3
Results of Inter- and Intracultural Negotiations[a]

Issue	Intercultural		Intracultural		$F_{1,93}$	p
	Mean	s.d.	Mean	s.d.		
Joint gains[b]	$3.47	$1.14	$4.32	$0.80	17.61	.01
Price	$49,042	$6,957	$51,685	$9,197	n.s.	
Runs	6.47	1.25	7.47	0.81	20.92	.01
Financing	0.73	0.45	0.68	0.47	n.s.	
Strums	0.57	0.50	0.85	0.36	9.42	.01
Contingent contract	0.17	0.38	0.12	0.33	n.s.	

[a] Multivariate $F_{5,89} = 4.6$, $p \le .01$. For the intercultural negotiations, $n = 30$; for the intracultural negotiations, $n = 65$.
[b] Values are millions of dollars.

tion of joint gains, and it was not correlated with joint gains within the inter- or the intracultural group. Our cooperation and frustration scales, measured after the negotiation, were used to control for stronger in-group/out-group effects in intercultural than intracultural negotiations. These scales were not related to type of negotiation (inter or intra) or to joint gains.

There were several ways to increase joint gains in "Cartoon." Negotiators could make trade-offs between financing and the number of runs per episodes. Parties could increase their joint gains by including *Strums* in the agreement. The MANOVA analysis reported in the lower portion of Table 3 indicates that the difference in joint gains between intercultural and intracultural dyads was due to intracultural dyads' negotiating more runs for the buyer and intracultural dyads' greater likelihood of including the purchase of *Strums* in the package. (Multivariate $F_{5, 89} = 4.60$, $p \leq .01$.) The optimal trade-off between runs and financing was eight runs and zero financing. Our simple dichotomous measure of whether or not there was financing indicated no significant difference between groups. Although there may have been some differences between inter- and intracultural groups in the amount of financing, which would be reflected in the overall difference in joint gains, neither the inter- nor the intracultural negotiators found the optimal trade of no financing with eight runs very often. There were also no differences between inter- and intracultural groups in the price paid for the cartoon or in the inclusion of a contingency clause.

Hypothesis 6 proposes that when intercultural negotiators' schemas are incompatible, low joint gains will ensue. The results of ANOVAs testing this hypothesis were not significant. There were numerous intercultural dyads with incompatible negotiation schemas. However, their joint gains were not significantly lower than, for example, those of the intercultural dyads whose negotiation schemas were compatible. There are several possible explanations for this finding. First, recall that the intercultural dyads negotiated lower joint gains than the intracultural dyads. Thus, within-group variance was restricted. Second, with only 30 intracultural dyads and six types of compatibility, the number of dyads within a type was small, and within-cell variance on the dependent variable was often large.

DISCUSSION

The results of this study suggest that intercultural negotiations between U.S. and Japanese managers are less likely to realize joint gains than intracultural negotiations between Japanese managers or intracultural negotiations between U.S. managers. There are several explanations for this finding that are associated with differences in cultural values and the schemas of U.S. and Japanese negotiators.

Information

The information-processing approach to negotiations articulated by theorists (Bazerman & Neale, 1991; Fisher et al., 1991; Lax & Sebenius, 1986) and demonstrated by empiricists (Neale & Bazerman, 1991; Pinkley et al., 1995; Pruitt, 1981; Weingart et al., 1990) to generate joint gains is not, according to this research, uniquely normative in the U.S. culture. Both Japanese and U.S. managers ascribed to a schema for information sharing. However, the data suggest they were less able to enact information-sharing scripts in intercultural negotiations than in intracultural ones. The data suggest that in the case of the compatible issue, including the cartoon *Strums* in the deal, many intercultural negotiators simply did not realize the issue's value to the other side. Despite its obvious value to their own side, intercultural negotiators did not pursue *Strums* to the extent that intracultural negotiators did. In debriefing, we were given a variety of responses to the question, "Why didn't you include *Strums*?", including this answer from a Japanese participant: "I saw this as the first negotiation in a potential long term-relationship. I left *Strums* for the future." Several U.S. participants said, "I raised it and he didn't seem interested, so I dropped it." Other U.S. and Japanese participants admitted never even discussing *Strums*.

Negotiators who create less value than others typically have less understanding of the other party's priorities (Thompson, 1991). Trends in the data suggest that, with the exception of buyers with respect to financing, either the Japanese negotiators engaged in intercultural negotiations were not communicating their priorities, or their U.S. partners were not listening. In contrast, the Japanese negotiators in intercultural negotiations were able to judge their partners' priorities as well as the U.S. negotiators in intracultural negotiations. However, this knowledge did not seem to translate into joint gains equivalent to those realized in either U.S. or Japanese intracultural negotiations. These findings are consistent with the expectation that Japanese and U.S. negotiators will use different scripts to communicate in negotiations and suggest a major communications hurdle for intercultural negotiators.

Another information-sharing hurdle in intercultural negotiations was premature closure and too narrow a focus. *Strums*, the compatible issue, was more likely to be ignored in intercultural than intracultural negotiations. Since *Strums* was included equally often in the Japanese and U.S. intracultural negotiations, culture per se cannot be an explanation. It appears that it is the interaction of two cultures at the negotiating table that results in premature closure and too narrow a focus. It is possible that negotiating in a second language and with someone using a second language may have contributed to premature closure. However, the intercultural negotiators were not time constrained. Many finished before time was up. All the Japanese negotiators in the intercultural program were fluent English speakers, and neither the Japanese nor the U.S. intercultural negotiators expressed significantly more frustration than the intracultural negotiators.

Consistent with our interpretation of premature closure and too narrow a focus in interpreting the results regarding *Strums* is the evidence regarding the use of information about the integrative issue, financing. Similar proportions of buyers understood the importance of financing to the sellers in the intercultural and intracultural negotiations. However, the intercultural buyers were unable to use that information to create gains. The financing issue was somewhat more complex than the runs issue in that it required more math to see how different alternatives would work out for each party. Thus, to succeed in creating joint gains with the financing issue required some commitment to heuristic trial-and-error evaluation of alternatives. All participants had calculators, and the math was not difficult. But although equal proportions of buyers in the inter- and intracultural negotiations knew of the importance of financing to the seller, and of course all the sellers knew how important financing was to themselves, the intercultural negotiators were not as successful as the intracultural negotiators in creating these gains.

Power

Power was particularly important to the Japanese negotiators, as we predicted on the basis of their expected hierarchical cultural values. The Japanese negotiators indicated paying significantly more attention to power in their negotiation preparation than did the U.S. negotiators. They also ascribed to norms of distributive tactics more strongly than the U.S. negotiators. It is not totally clear from the data exactly what the Japanese negotiators viewed as the basis of the power. We asked four questions in the prenegotiation questionnaire about factors contributing to outcomes in negotiations, expecting the Japanese negotiators to indicate company and role (buyer versus seller) more strongly, as suggested by Graham's research (1983, 1993), and the U.S. negotiators to indicate alternatives, or BATNA, more strongly. The expected difference between the U.S. and Japanese negotiators in their perceptions of the importance of alternatives was significant. There was also a tendency for Japanese negotiators to rate role as a more important factor than the U.S. negotiators. There was a reasonable amount of variance on this item among the Japanese, some of whom told us in the postnegotiation discussion that the norm of deference to buyers had fallen in the face of open markets. Of course, these participants were expatriates who generally produced and/or sold Japanese products in the United States. It is important for future research to collect data on bases of power from Japanese negotiators in Japan (which we were unable to do in this study), as well as from Japanese negotiators in the U.S.

Nevertheless, the data on power suggest that the Japanese may not value BATNA as power in the same way as U.S. negotiators and that, in intercultural negotiations, this difference may contribute to a low level of joint gains. In postnegotiation discussions, we were told that because the Japanese have such a long history of having to sell below cost in intercultural negotiations, BATNA was a point to try to reach, not a point from which to begin negotiations. This suggests that BATNA served as a low anchor for some Japanese negotiating interculturally and therefore contributed to premature closure of discussion of options and the relatively low level of joint gains in the intercultural negotiations as compared with the intracultural negotiations.

Self-Interest

Another factor in the intercultural negotiations between U.S. and Japanese negotiators that appears to have affected the level of joint gains was the difference in the two cultures' focus on self-interest. The U.S. negotiators were much more individualistic and focused on self-interest than the Japanese negotiators. Two individualistic, self-interested negotiators may be able to stimulate each other to achieve high goals. This conclusion is consistent with research on the effects of goals in negotiation (Huber & Neale, 1986, 1987; Pinkley, Neale, & Bennett, 1994). Negotiators with easy or no goals are more likely to reach compromise agreements than integrative ones (Humber & Neale, 1987). However, when self-interest is mismatched, one negotiator's goals are more easily met than the other's. The first negotiator may not be motivated to continue the negotiation once her or his goals have been met, and so the dyad reaches premature closure.

Contributions to Theory

In this study, we suggested that cultures differ with respect to schemas and scripts for negotiating behavior. Further, we suggest that when negotiators' scripts and schemas are incompatible, it may be difficult for them to negotiate joint gains. We developed this theoretical perspective by articulating the implications for negotiations of two cultural values: individualism versus collectivism and hierarchy versus egalitarianism. We proposed that when negotiators from cultures differing on these values meet, their opportunities for joint gains may be limited by informational disutilities, including inefficient information sharing and premature closure of the search for alternatives. Our empirical data suggest that, in addition to experiencing these two disutilities, intercultural negotiators who have information may be unable to use it effectively to generate joint gains. Within the context of the intercultural negotiation studied here, U.S. and Japanese negotiators held different views of power in negotiation. When negotiators cannot agree on who is more powerful, it is extremely difficult for them to reach agreement (Ury, Brett, & Goldberg, 1988). When they don't even agree as to what constitutes power, they may be unable to use power as a basis for reaching agreement.

Finally, in the U.S.-Japanese intercultural negotiation context, it appears that the clash of individualism and hierarchy may be particularly dysfunctional when social interaction requires negotiation. The negotiation scripts or patterns of behavior stimulated by concern for self and concern for social power are fundamentally different, even though both represent distributive negotiation schemas. However, the negotiation scripts generated by hierarchical and individualistic values do not provide a common ground on which intercultural negotiators can meet.

This study contributes to theory at three levels. First, it provides a model for developing culture-specific hypotheses about intercultural negotiations. Second, it identifies basic elements of negotiation—information sharing, premature closure of search, information utilization, and the meaning and use of power—that are potentially problematic in all intercultural negotiations. Third, it suggests that incompatibilities in negotiation scripts and schemas interfere with the creation of joint gains in intercultural negotiations between U.S. and Japanese managers. Although we did not find direct evidence that incompatibility of negotiation schemas and scripts resulted in lower joint gains in intercultural negotiations, we believe that this hypothesis should be tested in future research with larger samples. In addition, it seems likely that the fundamental approaches of U.S. and Japanese negotiators differ in ways that were not reflected in our analysis of the incompatibility of scripts and schemas. The Japanese negotiators' relative emphasis on power and indirect information sharing is very different from the U.S. negotiators' eschewal of power and focus on direct information sharing. In this respect, the study contributes to the theoretical understanding of negotiation scripts that are characteristic of U.S. and Japanese negotiators.

Limitations of the Study and Avenues for Further Research

The results demonstrate a set of associations between cultural group, cultural values, and measures of negotiation schemas. They also demonstrate that intercultural negotiations between U.S. and Japanese negotiators are less likely to generate joint gains than intracultural negotiations in either culture. A series of questions concerning the generalizability and validity of these findings merits further discussion and research.

Will the intercultural results generalize to Japanese-U.S. intercultural negotiations when Japanese negotiators have had little experience working with Westerners? Since the cultural values and normative negotiation schemas of the intercultural Japanese negotiators were not significantly different from those of the intracultural Japanese negotiators, we anticipate equal or greater difficulty in negotiating joint gains in intercultural negotiations in which the Japanese negotiators have less Western experience than those in our intercultural sample.

Will intercultural negotiations always be less likely to generate joint gains than intracultural negotiations? We think this will depend on the fit of the cultures, and determining such fit in turn requires an analysis of cultural differences in negotiation schemas and scripts. Different scripts for the same schema need not always be incompatible. For example, altruists and cooperators from different cultures can work together quite nicely (Messick, 1991). However, this study suggests that convergence with one or the other culture's focus may be necessary if high joint gains are to be negotiated. Our findings in this area are necessarily tentative because of limitations owing to sample size, and they merit further empirical investigation and theoretical reflection. Schemas and scripts appropriate for intracultural negotiations but inappropriate for intercultural negotiations may be impossible to turn on and off at will. If effective intercultural negotiations require a common negotiation script, how should negotiators determine whose script should prevail?

REFERENCES

Bazerman, M. H., & Neale, M. A. 1992. *Negotiating rationally.* New York: Free Press.

Bettenhausen, K., & Murnighan, J. K. 1985. The emergence of norms in competitive decision-making groups. *Administrative Science Quarterly*, 30: 350–372.

Drake, L. E., & Donohue, W. A. 1994. *Issue development as negotiated order in conflict.* Paper presented to the annual meeting of the International Association of Conflict Management, Eugene, OR.

Fisher, R., Ury, W., & Patton, B. 1991. *Getting to yes: Negotiating agreement without giving in.* New York: Penguin Books.

Fiske, S. T., & Taylor, S. E. 1984. *Social cognition.* Reading, MA: Addison-Wesley.

Graham, J. L. 1983. Business negotiations in Japan, Brazil, and the United States. *Journal of International Business Studies*, 14(1): 47–62.

Graham, J. L. 1993. The Japanese negotiation style: Characteristics of a distinct approach. *Negotiation Journal*, 9: 123–140.

Graham, J. L., & Sano, Y. 1989. *Smart bargaining: Doing business with the Japanese.* Cambridge, MA: Ballinger.

Hofstede, G. 1980. *Culture's consequences: International differences in work-related values.* Newbury Park, CA: Sage.

Huber, V. L., & Neale, M. A. 1986. Effects of cognitive heuristics and goals on negotiator performance and subsequent goal setting. *Organizational Behavior and Human Decision Processes*, 38: 342–365.

Huber, V. L., & Neale, M. A. 1987. Effects of self and competitor goals on performance in an interdependent bargaining task. *Journal of Applied Psychology*, 72: 197–203.

Kato, H., & Kato, J. S. 1992. *Understanding and working with the Japanese business world.* Englewood Cliffs, NJ: Prentice-Hall.

Lax, D. A., & Sebenius, J. K. 1986. *The manager as negotiator.* New York: Free Press.

Leung, K. 1997. Negotiation and reward associations across cultures. In P. C. Earley & M. Erez (Eds.), *New Perspectives on international industrial/organizational psychology:* 640–675. San Francisco: Jossey-Bass.

Lewis, J. D. 1990. *Partnerships for profit.* New York: Free Press.

Lytle, A. M., Brett, J. M., Barsness, Z. I., Tinsley, C. H., & Janssens, M. 1995. A paradigm for confirmatory cross-cultural research in organizational behavior. In L. L. Cummings & B. M. Staw (Eds.), *Research in organizational behavior*, vol. 17: 167–214. Greenwich, CT: JAI Press.

March, R. M. 1990. *The Japanese negotiator.* New York: Kodansha International.

Marcus, H. R., & Kitayama, S. 1991. Culture and the self: Implications for cognition, emotion, and motivation. *Psychological Review*, 98: 224–253.

Messick, D. 1991. On the evolution of group-based altruism. In R. Sal-tine (Ed.), *Game equilibrium models I: Evolution and game dynamics:* 304–328. Berlin: Springer-Verlag.

Mifflin, L. 1995. Can the Flintstones fly in Figi? *New York Times,* November 27: D1.

Neale, M. A., & Bazerman, M. H. 1991. *Negotiator cognition and rationality.* New York: Free Press.

Olekalns, M., & Smith, P. L. 1996. *Strategic sequences and outcome optimality in negotiation.* Paper presented at the annual meeting of the Academy of Management, Boston.

Olekalns, M., Smith, P. L., & Walsh, T. 1996. The process of negotiating: Strategies, timing and outcomes. *Organizational Behavior and Human Decision Processes,* 68: 68–77.

Ohbuchi, K., & Takahashi, Y. 1994. Cultural styles of conflict management in Japanese and Americans: Passivity, covertness, and effectiveness of strategies. *Journal of Applied Social Psychology,* 24: 1345–1365.

Pinkley, R. L. 1990. Dimensions of conflict frame: Disputant interpretations of conflict. *Journal of Applied Psychology,* 75: 117–126.

Pinkley, R. L., Griffith, T. L., & Northcraft, G. B. 1995. "Fixed pie" a la mode: Information availability, information processing, and the negotiation of suboptimal agreements. *Organizational Behavior and Human Decision Processes,* 62: 101–112.

Pinkley, R. L., Neale, M. A., & Bennett, R. J. 1994. The impact of alternative to settlement in dyadic negotiation. *Organizational Behavior and Human Decision Processes,* 57: 97–116.

Pinkley, R., & Northcraft, G. B. 1994. Conflict frames of reference: Implications for dispute processes and outcomes. *Academy of Management Journal,* 37: 193–205.

Pruitt, D. G. 1981. *Negotiation behavior.* New York: Academic Press.

Pruitt, D. G., & Carnevale, P. J. 1993. *Negotiation in social conflict.* Pacific Grove, CA: Brooks/Cole.

Pruitt, D. G., & Lewis, S. 1975. Development of integrative solutions in bilateral negotiation. *Journal of Personality and Social Psychology,* 31: 621–633.

Putnam, L., & Holmer, M. 1992. Framing, reframing, and issue development. In L. Putnam & M. Roloff (Ed.), *Communication and negotiation:* 128–155. Newbury Park, CA: Sage.

Raiffa, H. 1982. *The art and science of negotiation.* Cambridge, MA: Harvard University Press.

Schwartz, S. H. 1994. Beyond individualism/collectivism: New cultural dimensions of values. In U. Kim, H. C. Triandis, & G. Yoon (Eds.), *Individualism and collectivism:* 85–117. London: Sage.

Shank, R. C., & Abelson, P. R. 1977. *Scripts, plans, goals and understanding: An inquiry into human knowledge structures.* Hillsdale, NJ: Earlbaum.

Tenbrunsel, A. E., & Bazerman, M. H. 1995. Working women. In J. M. Brett (Ed.), *Dispute Resolution Research Center teaching manual materials.* Evanston, IL: Northwestern University.

Thompson, L. 1991. Information exchange in negotiation. *Journal of Experimental Social Psychology,* 27: 161–179.

Thompson, L. 1997. *The mind and the heart of the negotiator.* Upper Saddle River, NJ: Prentice-Hall.

Thompson, L., & Hastie, R. 1990. Social perception in negotiation. *Organizational Behavior and Human Decision Processes,* 47: 98–123.

Ting-Toomey, S. 1988. Intercultural conflict styles: A face-negotiation theory. In Y. Kim & W. Gudykunst (Eds.), *Theories in intercultural communication:* 213–235. Newbury Park, CA: Sage.

Triandis, H. C. 1972. *The analysis of subjective culture.* New York: Wiley.

Triandis, H. C. 1989. Cross-cultural studies of individualism and collectivism. In J. Berman (Ed.), *Nebraska symposium on motivation:* 41–133. Lincoln: University of Nebraska Press.

Tutzauer, F., & Roloff, M. E. 1988. Communication processes leading to integrative agreements: Three paths to joint benefits. *Communication Research,* 15: 360–380.

Ury, W. L., Brett, J. M., & Goldberg, S. B. 1988. *Getting disputes resolved.* San Francisco: Jossey-Bass.

Weingart, L. R., Bennett, R. J., & Brett, J. M. 1993. The impact of consideration of issues and motivational orientation on group negotiation process and outcome. *Journal of Applied Psychology,* 78: 504–517.

Weingart, L. R., Thompson, L. L., Bazerman, M. H., & Carroll, J. S. 1990. Tactical behavior and negotiation outcomes. *International Journal of Conflict Management,* 1: 7–31.

Yoshimura, N. 1997. Interview with Noboru Yoshimura. *New York Times Magazine,* June 8: 68.

APPENDIX A

Example for the Buyer: Net Value Calculation

Assume that you have reached a tentative agreement for the purchase of *Ultra Rangers* that involves the following terms:

- purchase price: $60,000 per episode
- runs/episode: 7
- financial terms:
  YR 0 80%
  YR 1 10%
  YR 2 20%

The calculation of the net value of this agreement is described below.

1.	**Expected Revenue from the Cartoon** Runs/Episode Adjustment $840,000	**$8,400,000**
	Net Value of the Cartoon	**$9,240,000**
2.	**Price of the Cartoon** Price/Episode × 100 episodes $60,000 × 100 = $6,000,000	**$6,000,000**
3.	**Payment Savings**	**$180,000**

YR	Payment	Savings (%)	Savings ($)
0	.80 * $6M = $4,800,000	0%	$ 0
1	.10 * $6M = $600,000	10%	$ 60,000
2	.10 * $6M = $600,000	20%	$120,000
			Total $180,000

4.	**Net Price of the Cartoon** Price of the Cartoon—Payment Savings $6,000,000 – $180,000 = $5,820,000	**$5,820,000**
5.	**Other Terms of the Agreement**	**$ 0**
6.	**Net Profit of the Cartoon** Net Value – Net Price + Other Terms $9,240,000 – $5,820,000 + $0 = $3,420,000	**$3,420,000**
7.	**Value of the Alternative Deal**	**$3,000,000**
8.	**NET VALUE OF THE BARGAINING AGREEMENT** Net Profit – Alt. Deal $3,420,000 – $3,000,000 = $420,000	**$ 420,000**

APPENDIX B

Example for the Seller: Net Value Calculation

Assume that you have reached an agreement on the sale of *Ultra Rangers* that specifies the following terms:
- purchase price: $50,000
- runs/episode: 5
- financial terms:
  YR 0 50%
  YR 1 30%
  YR 2 20%

The calculation of the net value of this agreement is described below.

1. Program Revenue   **$5,000,000**

Fee/Episode × 100 = $50,000 × 100 = $5,000,000

2. Financing Cost   **$650,000**

YR	Payment	Cost (%)	Cost ($)
0	.5 * $5,000,000 = $2,500,000	0%	$ 0
1	.3 * $5,000,000 = $1,500,000	20%	$300,000
2	.2 * $5,000,000 = $1,000,000	35%	$350,000
			Total $650,000

3. Program Revenue less Financing Cost   **$4,350,000**
$5,000,000 – $650,000 = $4,350,000

4. Runs/Episode Adjustment   **$250,000**

5. Other Pieces of Agreement   **$0**

6. Net Revenue   **$4,600,000**
$4,350,000 + $250,000 + $0 = $4,600,000

7. Value of the Alternative Deal   **$2,500,000**

8. NET VALUE OF THE BARGAINING AGREEMENT   **$2,100,000**
Net Revenue—Value of the Alternative Deal
$4,600,000 – $2,500,000 = $2,100,000

APPENDIX C

Questionnaire Items

Information Planning

During the preparation session, how much did you think about...[a]

What information you would like to get from the other party
What information not to share with the other party
What information to share with the other party
What your priorities were
How the other party might act in the negotiation

Setting an agenda for the negotiation
Opening offer
What arguments you might use to support your position
What you might say to defend your position
The range of settlements you would accept
Multiple options for settlement
The order in which you would make concessions

Power Analysis

During the preparation session, how much did you think about...[a]
How advantageous your negotiating position was
How powerful your company was
How advantageous the other party's position was
How powerful the other party's company was

Frustration

How strongly do you agree or disagree?
During the negotiation...
Silence stimulated concessions
I felt frustrated
I was often silent in the negotiation
I wished I had the services of a mediator or third party
I wished I could consult with my preparation partner
I was confused about what the other party wanted
I had to make too many concessions
The other party was often silent

Cooperation/Reciprocity

How strongly do you agree of disagree?
During the negotiation...
The other party reciprocated information (offered information in return for information)
The other party reciprocated offers (made a counter offer in return for an offer)
The other party cooperated
There was a lot of joint problem solving
I trusted the other party
I had to do all the work in the negotiation (reverse-coded)

[a]Possible responses were "a lot," "some," "a little," and "not much at all."

Jeanne M. Brett (Ph.D., University of Illinois) is the DeWitt W. Buchanan, Jr., Professor of Dispute Resolution and Organizations and the director of the Dispute Resolution Research Center at the J. L. Kellogg Graduate School of Management, Northwestern University. She is currently studying work and family issues and intercultural negotiation processes.

Tetsushi Okumura is an associate professor of management and negotiation in the Faculty of Economics at Shiga University and a vice director of the Japan Institute of Negotiation. He finished a Ph.D. program in management at Waseda University. His current research focuses on cross-cultural negotiations, negotiated social orders in and among organizations, and strategic corporate alliances.

TEAM FRAMES: THE MULTIPLE REALITIES OF THE TEAM

Donald D. Bowen
University of Tulsa

In selecting materials for my organizational behavior classes, I am constantly fighting the battle of so much to teach and so little time in which to teach it. Experiential exercises that address two or more important issues at the same time are, thus, doubly useful.

The exercise described here came into being as I realized that I wanted to discuss the concepts of *framing and reframing* (Bolman & Deal, 1991; Morgan, 1986) in my classes. Because I use ongoing teams in the master of business administration (MBA) core class, I am also interested in introducing the students to concepts like team building, group process, and the skills of managing group process.

I have been aware for some time that most of my students have extensive experience, mostly dismal, in student work groups. Faculty in marketing, finance, management information systems, and management science have been assigning projects to student teams, enthusiastically promoting the value of teamwork as preached by organizational behavior faculty to what we once thought were deaf ears. Students assure me that most of these teams do not go well, however. Stories of social loafing, slacking, and lack of commitment are typical.

I have been convinced (Bowen, 1991; Bowen & Jackson, 1985–1986) that the introduction of team-building activities at the time these student teams are formed can pay two types of dividends:

1. The team will function better in my class.
2. The students will learn that team building can help real-world teams function much more effectively.

As I thought about how to teach the concept of framing, I wanted an experiential approach to the topic so that students would actually experience themselves in the process of exploring a problem from a number of different perspectives. I also wanted the problem they explored to be a real one—not a hypothetical case. Because the real problem facing students at the beginning of the term is how to make their team work

better than those of the past (or suffer the misery of another lousy team project), why not make that the focus for learning about framing?

The exercise in Appendix A is the result of this approach. The exercise consists of an introduction that explains the concepts of team building as well as framing and some of its broader applications. Students are then instructed to explore their own team from a number of frames—those of a task group, a social group, a learning group, and a support group. The teams then report the results of their deliberations to the larger group, thus providing the entire class with a feeling for the range of issues raised by the process of reframing the nature of the team.

The discussions sparked have been lively and seemed to foster a number of new angles and insights on the purpose and utility of the teams. I also require teams to submit a set of team objectives at the beginning of the term. There was a notable difference in the objectives produced by teams after the framing discussion compared to prior classes that had not gone through the exercise. The goals of the teams that had experienced the framing exercise seemed more thoughtful, the teams produced more goals, and the teams generated objectives for areas usually overlooked by teams who are locked in on a task-team frame—goals for social activity and for learning from their experience. In short, the experience seemed to have the intended effect of broadening student horizons about the potential benefits in team learning.

Gallos (1989) has advised that students occasionally have difficulty dealing with the notion that several frames or views of reality can have equal validity. She suggests that such views may reflect a student's lack of tolerance for ambiguity or stage of cognitive development. I have not encountered this problem to this point, probably because my experience has been limited to MBA students. I would not hesitate to use team frames with undergraduates, but I would be alert to symptoms of cognitive stress. Gallos (1989) suggests that if a student exhibits these symptoms, resorting to logical argument will probably only reinforce the resistance. It will be more appropriate to patiently work with the student to help him or her become more comfortable with the notion that reality operates on multiple levels and that each of us has a different perception of that reality.

Author's Note: Correspondence should be sent to Donald D. Bowen, Professor of Management, Department of Management and Marketing, College of Business Administration, University of Tulsa, Tulsa, OK 74104; (phone) 918–631–2586, (fax) 918–631–2142.

From *Journal of Management Education*, February 1998, pp. 95-103. © 1998 by Sage Publications Inc. Reprinted by permission.

The exercise works best where there are movable chairs for small group conversations. The exercise requires from 110 minutes to 125 minutes (depending on whether the introduction has been assigned as preclass reading) for four teams with about 5 minutes more for each additional team. Because teams can lose track of the time elapsed as they become involved in the discussion, it is probably advisable that the instructor provide time prompts to make sure everyone finishes at the same time.

Conclusion

In brief, then, team frames is an exercise designed with the dual purpose of introducing students to the concept of framing while providing a team-building experience. Evidence from lists of team goals suggests that the exercise creates a greatly broadened perspective on the potential benefits and values of team membership and encourages further exploration of aspects usually overlooked in teams preoccupied with task completion.

Appendix A
Team Frames

Objectives:
1. To provide a real-life vehicle for exploring the technique of reframing problems.
2. To provide an opportunity for team building.

Time required: 1 hour, 45 minutes (90 minutes if Introduction assigned as advanced preparation) plus 5 minutes for each team.

Group size: Up to 10 teams of 4 to 9 participants each.

Advance preparation: Read the Introduction before class.

Introduction

Are some people born with a gift for creative problem solving? Are the rest of us stuck if we do not have this magic chromosome? Or can we learn techniques that can help us become more effective problem solvers? Everyone has had the frustrating experience of trying to solve a problem when nothing seems to work. What we need is a new way of looking at the problem—one that generates new and potentially productive ideas and perspectives. One that gets us beyond our own conceptual biases and perceptual blinders. In this activity, you will be practicing an approach for gaining fresh insights—a different slant on matters. This technique is usually referred to as framing or reframing. You might find it helpful to think for a minute about how many meanings you can identify for the verb *to frame*. Notice that each new definition of the term provides an entirely different way of looking at the activity described as framing. If you frame a house, you erect the skeleton of the structure. When you frame a picture, you put a border around the picture. Framing your friend has a much more sinister connotation—it means that you concoct false evidence, which leads someone to suspect your friend of malfeasance. Framing an argument, however, is simply planning what you will say. Similarly, if you frame your response to another person's question, you are probably concerned with couching your statement in terms he or she will find relevant and understandable.

Framing and reframing, then, deal with how we define the situation. As we reframed framing, we completely redefined the perspective we took toward the activity of framing. We

can do the same thing with any problem. The trick is simply to define the problem in different terms. One popular text, Bolman and Deal's (1991) *Reframing Organizations,* is based on the premise that we can be more effective managers if we learn to reframe our organizational problems in terms of the major frames or perspectives of organization and management theory. Bolman and Deal (1991) suggest that there are four essential perspectives one needs to be able to apply:

1. Structural: Structural theories of organization deal primarily with the patterning of activities, communication lines, functions, and assignments of tasks. Structural theories tend to prescribe the formal organization—who reports to whom, who does what, and so forth.
2. Human Resource: The human resource frame focuses on issues of how people and organizations relate; how organizations can better satisfy people's needs, provide more meaningful work, draw on the untapped productivity and creativity of employees, and avoid alienating and frustrating working conditions.
3. Political: Political theories of organizations look at organizations as political systems with shifting bases of power, coalitions, and constituencies, and unending conflicts between different interest groups contending for the allocation of scarce resources.
4. Symbolic: The symbolic frame recasts the organization as a mechanism whereby participants attempt to make sense out of the ambiguity and uncertainty of life—the result of living and operating in an uncertain and turbulent world. Making sense is largely a matter of creating symbols, which make the random and illogical world seem otherwise. The symbols become the culture of the organization—the collection of stories, ceremonies, rites, and artifacts through which the organization expresses and maintains its important symbols.

Consider a manager attempting to resolve a difficult and pressing problem such as declining productivity of his or her workforce. How he or she frames the problem will determine the types of actions they might consider taking. For example, if he or she thinks of the problem in structural terms, they might consider reorganizing to achieve a more rational allocation of tasks and functions. In a human resource frame, he or she might canvas employees to identify what aspects of their jobs are dissatisfying or frustrating. The political frame might lead him or her to adopt a tough stance in bargaining with the union to obtain concessions on work rules and standards. With a symbolic perspective, he or she might attempt to identify the culture of the organization, perhaps by listening for the stories that people tell about working for the company. Do the stories describe a culture that discourages or devalues hard work and achievement? Are the heroes of the stories the people who get away with doing as little as possible?

Note that each frame leads our manager to see the problem from a new perspective and to direct his or her attention to different types of variables in the situation. Which one is correct? Perhaps all of the frames are valid? Perhaps each can help him or her to take actions that will move toward solving the problem. It may be that some frames suggest areas where action is more urgent, but each of the frames has its own validity; each presents a reality that is equally real!

In the exercise that follows, you will be asked to apply this process of reframing the issues to achieve a better understanding of how your team functions and how it might function better. The basic assumption is that teams meet a wide variety of needs and, thus, can be framed in different ways. Members of a team often get caught up in the team's activities (usually the task at hand) and forget that the potential for satisfying other important needs is always present and can be fulfilled if we shift our frame a bit.

Consider a team of workers in a factory. Most of the time, the relevant frame for describing the team would be as a task team performing their assigned duties. However, even while the group works, people talk, joke, plan social events, and otherwise operate as a social group, too. Look even a little more closely and you will see some of the more senior workers teaching new members tricks of the trade (or how to evade obnoxious supervisors or company rules). The group is also a learning group, you conclude. And the response of the group when one of the members is under extraordinary stress suggests that the group also functions as a support group.

That brings us to the second objective of this activity. When belonging to a team becomes a source of satisfaction of many of our more important needs, our attitudes toward the team become increasingly positive. We enjoy team meetings, even when they involve hard work, and we are highly motivated to make the team's efforts successful.

Athletic coaches recognize the value of team building. The arduous hours of practice in both the preseason and regular season hone more than physical skills and timing. The shared ordeal also builds a sense of collective identity and commitment among the players—a commitment that translates into the extra effort required to overcome adversity during the season.

Progressive managers also recognize the need for highly motivated team members in today's competitive business climate. Team-building programs can be very effective in heightening team spirit. Adventure approaches to team building (e.g.,

Outward Bound or Ropes Course programs) build impressive camaraderie—the organizational counterpart to football practice. Other strategies of team building, as this exercise will demonstrate, build group cohesiveness and commitment by breaking down barriers between members and by inducing them to consider options in managing team goals and processes that are often overlooked under the pressure to get the job done (Bowen, 1991). Enjoyable and productive teams are those in which members respect and like each other and in which the team satisfies many important needs of its members.

Procedure

STEP 1

Discuss and assess your team as a task team. Appendix B lists several dimensions and issues bearing on team effectiveness. If your group is to be effective (or more effective) as a task team, how should it operate in terms of the issues in Appendix B? Notice as you discuss these dimensions in this step, as well as subsequent steps, that there are not generic answers for all groups. What makes a particular group effective depends on and varies with the objectives of the group. Make notes about your conclusions; you will need to refer to them in Step 5. (15 minutes)

STEP 2

Discuss and assess your team as a social group. How could this team satisfy member needs for affiliation and friendship? If the group made room for play and enjoyment of each others' company, what effect would these social relationships have on the work of the team? Would they help or hinder? What kind of profile would the team have on the dimensions in Appendix B if it was functioning as a social group? Make notes of your conclusions; you will need to refer to them in Step 5. (15 minutes)

STEP 3

Discuss and assess your team as a learning group. What would the team look like on the dimensions in Appendix B if it was maximizing the learning and growth of each member? To what extent would members be encouraged to experiment with new roles and behaviors? How could you provide useful feedback on members' influence on each other? Make notes of your conclusions; you will need to refer to them in Step 5. (15 minutes)

STEP 4

Discuss and assess your team as a support group. How might your team provide emotional and moral support to its members when they need it? If a member is under stress or on the spot, how should the team respond in terms of the dimensions of Appendix B? Make notes of your conclusion; you will need to refer to them in Step 5. (15 minutes)

STEP 5

Review the notes you have taken. Your task at this point is to design your team so that it is capable of functioning effectively in all four modes. Your analysis has probably identified some things you need to do more effectively or some areas where the group needs to develop itself and its capabilities. Do some of the issues seem to demand more attention than others at this point? Are there some issues that you had not previously considered or issues you had not considered to be of importance? What can you do to develop yourselves and your team to function more effectively? What is likely to be the effect if you overlook them?

Prepare a brief statement summarizing your priorities, integrating your conclusions, and identifying important tasks or actions for the team to undertake to address the major priorities. Appoint a spokesperson to present your conclusions and plans. (20 minutes)

STEP 6

Present the highlights of the document prepared in Step 5 to the rest of the class. (5 minutes per team)

STEP 7

Discuss the activity in terms of the discussion questions. (10 minutes)

Discussion Questions

1. If group members tend to see their group in terms of a single frame or function, how might this inability to see other frames cause a group to be less effective and efficient than it might otherwise be?
2. How can a new team use the idea of reframing to set goals for the team?

Concluding Points

1. Should a team attempt to perform well on all four frames simultaneously or is it better to concentrate on one mode at a time?

Appendix B
Dimensions of Variation in Group Functioning

The first five dimensions are phrased as polar continua. On these dimensions, where should the group be when it is functioning effectively? Items 6 through 9 require qualitative answers.

1. How frequently does the group meet?
   Minimal
   (only when required)
   Maximum
   (members look for opportunities to get together)
2. How long are group meetings?
   Minimal
   (members want to keep them as short as possible)
   Maximum
   (meetings are long because members enjoy the activities and being together?)
3. What kind of commitment on the part of the members is required for this type of group to be effective? How strong should this commitment be?
   Minimal
   (just enough to get by on required tasks)
   Maximum
   (members make the effectiveness of the group and the welfare of its members their highest priority)

4. What kind of openness (sharing of thoughts and feelings, taking risks with one another) does the group need to be effective?
   Low openness
   (share thoughts or ideas only if relevant to the task; little sharing of feelings)
   High openness
   (share deep personal feelings and concerns)
5. To what extent does effectiveness require contributions of members?
   Minimal
   (one or two members can do what is needed)
   Maximum
   (all members must be giving their very best)
6. What does the group produce through its meetings when it is being effective?
7. What must members bring to meetings for the group to be effective? Skills? Attitudes? Contributions? Preparation? Why?
8. What should members get out of meetings? What needs do they seek to fulfill?
9. What are the key issues in how the group functions to be successful as this type of group? What elements of group process are necessary for effectiveness?

References

Bolman, L. G., & Deal, T. E. (1991). *Reframing organizations*. San Francisco: Jossey-Bass.

Bowen, D. D. (1991). Team-building: Some suggestions for redirection. In C. N. Jackson & M. Manning (Eds.), *ASTD OD Annual. Vol. 4: Intervening in client organizations* (pp. 16–24). Alexandria, VA: American Society for Training and Development.

Bowen, D. D., & Jackson, C. N. (1985–1986). Curing those "ol' ohmigod-not-another-group-class" blues. *Organizational Behavior Teaching Review, 10*(4), 21–31.

Gallos, J. V. (1989). Developmental diversity and the OB classroom: Implications for teaching and learning. *Organizational Behavior Teaching Review, 13*(4), 33–47.

Morgan, G. (1986). *Images of organization*. Newbury Park, CA: Sage.

Unit 4

Unit Selections

EXERCISE 4: Organization Structure and Design: The Club Ed Exercise, Cheryl Harvey and Kim Morouney

Key Points to Consider

❖ How has the industrial revolution influenced the development of organizational systems?

❖ Describe some of the factors that are currently influencing the organization.

❖ What will be the role of technology in organizational development?

❖ Discuss performance appraisal in relation to organizational systems.

❖ What is the role of human resources in organizational systems?

❖ Discuss the impact of culture on the organizational system.

 **Links**   **www.dushkin.com/online/**

20. **Center for Organization and Human Resource Effectiveneess**
   http://socrates.berkeley.edu/~iir/cohre/cohre.html
21. **Global Business Network (GBN)**
   http://www.gbn.org/home.html
22. **Human Resources—Corporate Culture**
   http://www.auxillium.com/culture.htm
23. **Organizational Development**
   http://home.navisoft.com/hrmbasics/orgdev.htm

These sites are annotated on pages 4 and 5.

People live in groups, but for groups to be successful and to survive, they must have a purpose. When the earliest tribes first settled in fertile river valleys, one of the objectives of the tribe was to establish the city-state that would provide the members of the tribe with safety from marauding bands of less-civilized people that threatened the city-state. This is a function that is still provided by nations in the form of armies and other defense functions. Religion then became the next large-scale organization and was often a function of the state, but religious leaders learned to distance themselves from the state. The key to the long-term success of religious beliefs was to not tie them too closely to one particular nation, empire, or king.

Christianity became greater than the Roman Empire, and while the Empire contracted, Christianity expanded to the peoples who were bent on the destruction of the Empire. Kings and emperors derived their authority from God, and the Church established the legitimacy of that authority as the representative of God on earth.

Commercial organizations began to rise in power as the industrial revolution began in England in the 1700s. As the production of goods and services moved from craftsmen and cottages to machinery and factories, organizations were formed that could successfully produce goods and services. As organizations grew larger, it became clear that work needed to be divided into various sub-functions. Specialization of labor was the obvious key to efficient production, with individuals performing tasks for which they were the best suited. Early management theorists such as Max Weber, who developed the theory of bureaucracy, which is still the basis for the organization of most corporations, and Henri Fayol, whose 14 points can still be seen in the writings of Peter Drucker, Tom Peters, and W. Edwards Deming, addressed these issues of organization. It is still an issue that faces corporations. Forward-looking organizations are trying to determine "The Shape of the New Corporation." (See article 21.) The problem is that things are moving so fast that it is difficult to determine that shape. It could be that organizations will simply not have even a semipermanent shape, but rather be an ever-changing entity, growing, shrinking, and changing with demand. Corporations must learn to go "Beyond the Org Chart" (see article 22) if they are going to learn how organizations really function in the modern era.

Conditions outside of the corporation are changing very rapidly and the factors that are driving this change are outside the control of the organization. These factors include rapid technological change. There was more technological advancement in the twentieth century than in the entire rest of recorded history. Social changes are also moving at a faster rate than ever before. There is no room for racial prejudice or gender bias. The market is simply too competitive for organizations to indulge in discrimination. In some ways, the future has already happened in that certain trends in the society have become clear and their impact can be predicted. A part of these trends has been the changing of the meaning of work and the workplace. The workplace may be changing to the point where it will no longer be recognizable, as discussed by John Challenger in "There Is No Future for the Workplace."

This, of course, means changes in work design, the way people actually perform their jobs. Computers and simulations are already playing a large role in this function. These changes are addressed by Sylvia Ann Hewlett in "The Feminization of the Workforce." Given all of the various factors that have an impact on organizations and the workforce, how will organizations attract and keep their best employees? This issue is examined by Roger Herman and Joyce Gioia in "Making Work Meaningful: Secrets of the Future-Focused Corporation."

To keep people focused on the tasks before them, it is necessary to guide and reward them appropriately. Performance appraisal, feedback, and rewards are the keys to keeping good people and continuously pointing them in the right direction. To keep the best employees they must be allowed to perform and to be given the appropriate feedback and rewards, as John Luthy has written in "New Keys to Employee Performance and Productivity."

The human resources department has come a long way in its development from an employee welfare office to personnel to human resources. For organizations to be successful they must look upon their employees as an asset. Organizations are demanding more from the human resources function than they have in the past and will demand even more in the future, according to Bill Leonard's article, "What Do CEO's Want from HR?"

Every organization has a system of beliefs, ideas, and goals that are developed by the history of the company, the experiences of the people in the organization, and the guidance and examples provided by senior management. The culture of an organization directly reflects the ideals of that firm and the people who work there. It has a direct impact on their commitment to the company and the ideals of that company. An organization that wants to be successful and effective must engage in "Building Heart and Soul" (see article 29), because people who are committed to an organization are going to be more effective employees. As "Cultural Change Is the Work/Life Solution" (see article 30) explains, the emergence of women and minorities has changed the workplace. The needs and demands of employees will be different, and successful organizations will meet those needs to keep those employees who will be key to the success of the organization.

Organizational Systems

The Shape of the New Corporation

Plug-in workers, globe-hopping executives, and stem-to-stern tech. The 21st-century company is here.

BY JEREMY MAIN

From the moment you step into the new headquarters of SEI Investments, you know you're not in old-fashioned corporate America anymore. Spread out on a rural hillside near Valley Forge, Pennsylvania, the $293 million asset-management company inhabits five industrial-style buildings. Inside, exposed structural steel, pipes, and ducts—painted fuchsia and blue in one building and yellow, gold, and red in another—carry through the factory motif. Most striking, however, are the thick coils of wire hanging from the ceiling—staffers call them "pythons"—containing phone, computer, and electrical wiring. Look closer, and you see that all the office equipment, desks, chairs, computers, and filing cabinets are on wheels.

The design was inspired by SEI's need to change—frequently, quickly, and cheaply. The business began 25 years ago making software for bank trust departments. With accelerating speed, it has added services and products: mutual fund and 401(k) administration, and cash-management programs for investment advisers, to name a few. Of necessity, employees are constantly shifting and recombining to develop new services and products to meet customers' reconstellating needs. CEO Al West says he got tired of paying $2,000 per move per person to relocate furniture and redo wiring under the floors. These days, when teams switch assignments—which may happen once a year or even more often—they just unplug their pythons, wheel their chairs and desks to the next location, plug into a new python, and go to work. SEI can get a new team resettled and working in an hour or two.

The rolling furniture isn't the only thing that's flexible at SEI. A batch of teams organizes and delivers the company's products and services. Tasks not central to business—personnel benefits, and food services, for example—are outsourced. Teams do their own recruiting for new employees and perform all secretarial work themselves, and they definitely get their own coffee. SEI awards annual productivity bonuses to teams, and their

> **Top VeriFone executives only meet face-to-face at quarterly strategy sessions, somewhere in the world.**

Road Warrior
VeriFone

EXECUTIVES AT VERIFONE IN SANTA CLARA, California, could be sitting on their duffs. The company, acquired last year by Hewlett-Packard for $1.2 billion, has 70 percent of the U.S. market for swipe machines, which verify credit cards when you make a purchase. Since its start-up in 1981, however, the company's philosophy has been to keep top executives in the field to listen to customers and push through new contracts.

With the development of electronic payment systems and Internet commerce, going out on the hustings is more important than ever. Robin Abrams, 47, who became CEO this March, says that she spends 60 percent of her time out of the office looking for "face time with the marketplace." Traveling put her in touch with the fact that European customers worry much more about the security of their credit cards than Americans. If she had stayed at home, she says, "I wouldn't have had that input."

Abrams expects her top managers to travel as much as she does. VeriFone's sales chief lives in Paris, and others are scattered around the world, so Abrams, who is based at company headquarters, keeps in touch mostly by phone and e-mail. Top executives only meet face-to-face at quarterly strategy sessions, somewhere in the world. Recent meetings took place in Paris and Taiwan. The mandate to keep on the move has paid off. Using technologies developed by GemPlus, GTE, Mondex International, and others, VeriFone was the first to develop a smart card system for the U.S., which would allow individual consumers to download money onto their cards from computers. Says Will Pape, one of VeriFone's founders, "Getting there first means getting control."

From *Working Woman*, October 1998, pp. 60-63. This article was adapted from *Driving Corporate Change: How the Best Companies are Preparing for the 21st Century*, Free Press, 1998. © 1998 by Jeremy Main. Reprinted by permission.

Spinmeisters
Hughes Electronics

THE FORD MOTOR CO.'s Rouge, Michigan plant, opened in 1908, not only turned out the first Model T's but also operated a steel mill to produce car bodies and a glass factory to manufacture windshields. From the assembly line to the cafeteria line, Oldcorp did it all.

That near-feudal arrangement came under attack in the 1980s, when managers began to spin off work that other companies could do better or more cheaply. The first job to go was payroll, but others soon followed: janitorial services, advertising, property management—in short, anything that might prove distracting from a company's main business, or "core competency."

In recent years, many corporations have gone a step further. They have begun to outsource activities considered to be part of their core. Take Hughes Electronics, the $5 billion telecommunications company owned by GM. You'd think such a high-tech company would never let computers and information services out of its hot hands. But, in 1994 it gave Computer Sciences Corp. in El Segundo, California, an eight-year, $1.5 billion contract to operate them. Hughes turned over to CSC all its information systems, including telephones, networks, and all the platforms, from mainframes to desktops. CSC now owns and maintains the equipment and acquires, manages, and develops software. During start-up, it offered jobs to all the Hughes employees who worked in information systems.

"More than anything else, Hughes desperately needed consistency," says Heidi Trost, the CSC vice president in charge of GM business. Before the contract, Hughes engineers had chosen and configured their own PCs. As a result, it seemed to have "one of everything," she says. Hughes has cut costs, preserved capital for its core business of making electronic products, and gotten all its computer systems to talk to each other.

Globe-zilla
ABB

THERE'S NO COMPANY MORE GLOBAL THAN ABB, AN anonymous-sounding firm based in Zurich with $35 billion in annual sales. The result of a 1988 merger between Asea of Sweden and Brown-Boveri of Switzerland, ABB has an 11-member board of directors from eight nations and 19 nationalities on headquarters staff. But that's not what makes it international. The electrical engineering firm, which builds and manufactures equipment for power plants and transportation systems, is grouped into 37 global divisions that operate local plants. In this flattened organization—headquarters has a staff of only 171—the operating companies decide pretty much on their own how much to invest in new plants and equipment or in research and development, and, more important, how to get business.

Unlike its U.S. competitors, General Electric and Westinghouse, ABB can boast of its production capacity all over the world but particularly in emerging nations in Asia, Australia, Eastern Europe, and Africa, where most new transportation and power systems are under construction. That advantage has allowed ABB to rake in hundreds of millions from contracts in Thailand, Poland, and other developing nations. Given their independence, who needs Zurich? Well, headquarters ties all these companies together with a global information system and acquires—what else?—more of those local operating companies.

Data-Based
Pioneer Hi-Bred Intl

INFORMATION TECHNOLOGY IS THE LAST THING YOU'D ASSOCIATE with 70-year-old Pioneer Hi-Bred International in Des Moines, which uses part-time farmer-salespeople to sell to their neighbors. But it has also been on the scientific cutting edge, developing hybrid seeds to produce plants for the most harvestable yield. Pioneer tests about 110,000 hybrids a year at 125 research centers around the world. Making decisions based on so many tiny bits of information is "like having a map of all the roads in America and navigating a driver from the East to the West Coast by the fastest, most direct path," says corporate vice president Tom Hanigan.

That takes big-time information management. Like most companies, Pioneer had traditionally used computers for routine tasks like accounting. But within the past 10 years, it developed a computer system that would fully integrate all the company's functions from seed production to purchasing. The ability to track data from beginning to end has revolutionized the company. Today, researchers at testing stations enter data on seed characteristics into hand-held computers. Headquarters uses the information to decide which 5,000 hybrids will advance to the next stage: company greenhouses and farm test plots. Pioneer has shaved three years off the time it takes to get seeds to market.

What's more, salespeople can download and print out research reports on the hybrids in production. Instant access to information has given the company command of the market, with earnings of $243 million on sales of $1.7 billion in 1997. Pioneer's market share is 43 percent; its nearest competitor's, about 9 percent.

leaders decide how to split the money. "Working on different teams allows you to be totally outside the box with no physical or emotional barriers," says Alice Lindenauer, a team business manager.

This is a far cry from the traditional corporation, with its soothing stability and command-and-control hierarchy. True, for most of the 20th century, "Oldcorp" was the powerhouse that fueled economic prosperity. But at the threshold of the new millennium, Oldcorp is beginning to show its age. It moves slowly, its rigidity discourages inventiveness, and, in a memorable phrase from General Electric chieftain Jack Welch, it is so wrapped up in itself that it presents its face to the CEO and its ass to the customer.

So now a new corporation is a-borning in America, shaped by a changing business climate—one with increasingly demanding customers, pressure from low-cost rivals, a shrinking globe, and an explosion of information. On the following pages, you'll read about some of the forward-looking measures companies are taking to stay competitive.

The common thread among these 21st-century companies is their flexibility. To use a sports metaphor, Oldcorp is like a football team, a force of armored heavyweights performing complex plays exactly as ordered. Newcorp is more like a soccer team, swift and agile, whose players can slip into one another's roles as they adapt to new situations.

With these changes come new and shifting demands. We may be burying the "organization man" without much regret, but the life of the corporate executive in the new structure poses its own challenges. Oldcorp managers, after all, merely had to make the numbers. Their Newcorp counterparts must meet a less predictable standard. General Electric managers, for example, now have to measure up on two scales: one for traditional performance goals, and a second for adherence to a set of "values," which include vision, team skills, speed, and ability to communicate. Whatever their performance, managers who fail on values get the boot. And forget about family life. To stay competitive in the mobile marketplace, Newcorp managers may have to deliver bedtime stories via e-mail.

Moreover, there are no guarantees that the new corporate shapes and techniques will succeed. In the effort to be lean and mean, corporations may risk losing their strength and solidity. Yet those willing to invest time, money, imagination, thought, and planning in their own redesign, as those here have done, will have a sporting chance to rise to the top and stay there.

JEREMY MAIN *is the co-author of* Driving Corporate Change: How the Best Companies Are Preparing for the 21st Century. *Additional reporting by:* DANIEL PALEY-ELLISON.

Beyond the Org Chart

An organization chart may be the map of your company's chain of command,
but you have to look beyond it to discover who's *really* important.

By Phyllis Gail Doloff

Beyond the org chart lies the real organization. Who talks to whom. Who listens to whom. Who has influence—rather than a title. Who knows the gossip. Who can get things done now—instead of through formal channels and protracted process. Who knows how to accomplish the impossible—even when the formal organization says it can't be done. And who's really making the decisions and moving the work forward.

This is the invisible side of the organization: the informal network that isn't reflected on the org chart. The formal and informal organizations co-exist in the same space and time but are often independent entities, operating at times in concert with each other and at times in spite of each other. Org charts convey the most obvious information (formal reporting relationships and honorific titles) and a secondary level of inferable information (perks, privileges, and obligations implied by title or position in the hierarchy), but while they can effectively show the skeleton of an organization, they don't reveal the more important links, the connective tissue—or personal influence.

Trying to evaluate the interaction of people within an organization has always been the purview of HR and consultants specializing in the "soft stuff." The "stuff" in question is usually the behavior of individuals (wonderful, deplorable, or otherwise noteworthy) and its effect on their performance. The data is difficult to get and even more so to describe. Personal observations are by definition subjective, and they become even less precise when managers cloak their conclusions in politically correct euphe-

misms to avoid offending the individual under review and to guard the organization against liability.

No wonder describing and measuring the interaction of entire groups has been nearly impossible.

The newest cottage industry in the consulting community is the illumination of that shadow organization. Consultants are using a construct called social network mapping (also known as organizational network analysis or organizational network mapping) to provide a clear snapshot of the organization's human and intangible workings. This tool allows companies embarking on new ventures, or looking to better understand the state of their workplace dynamics, to X-ray a chosen segment of their organization and derive tangible, quantifiable findings on who the movers and shakers are.

Here's how social network mapping works: Employees are asked a series of questions about their communications with their colleagues. Questions are tailored to the setting and needs of the organization, but typically focus on three main points:

- whom individual members of the group communicate with;
- the nature of the communication (exchanging information, obtaining approvals, seeking knowledge or assistance, etc.); and
- how often the interaction takes place.

The data is then compiled and analyzed, and presented both visually and statistically. For a sense of the visuals, think of an org chart with additional lines penciled in to connect the boxes of people who exchange information, and a second org chart with pencil lines drawn between seekers and givers of ap-

PHYLLIS GAIL DOLOFF *is a Westfield, N.J.-based HR professional and freelance writer. She wrote "The '90s Woman: Victim or Opportunist?" in the September 1998 issue.*

proval. The statistics further detail the frequency of interaction—how often information is exchanged or how often approval is sought and given. The results leave both managers and employees with confirmation of what they've always intuitively known about their organization but have never been able to articulate—much less document.

The end product is a snapshot of how the surveyed group actually functions. The results can offer an eye-opening portrait: managers who talk to virtually no one (neither subordinates nor peers); seemingly obscure technicians who are widely respected and sought-after as subject experts; and employees in unremarkable positions who hold remarkable sway and influence over peers. Often the data reveals the gatekeepers of unofficial authority and power and uncovers silence between groups and departments where there ought to be (or was thought to be) a steady exchange of information and knowledge.

Managed Knowledge Is Mightier Than Management

Perhaps the most prominent reason social network mapping has gained a toehold in the consulting industry is that there has been a fundamental shift in how companies view themselves and in what they consider their most valuable resources. Certainly a company's product or service is important, as well as the quality of its people, but it has become clear that a knowledge of the organization and the processes and workings that roll it forward has become one of an organization's fundamental resources.

Social network mapping becomes more important as the time frame in which companies must innovate, manufacture, and get new products to market shrinks. Over the past decade, companies have found that wall-to-wall cuts (in which each manager antes up 10 percent of his staff) have often left gaps in an organization's store of tacit and explicit knowledge. Companies are learning that they can no longer afford to slash budgets and staff without calculating the effect of the losses on the organization's knowledge bank.

A company may be hawking the greatest invention since the hula hoop, but if its front-end thinkers, planners, and sales force don't know what's happening in the back rooms of production, it can't market, produce, and distribute its product effectively. It's also becom-

ing increasingly clear that technology alone cannot solve an organization's woes or propel it ahead of its competitors. Technology can be a wonderful tool if the company is organized in a way that allows its employees to make the best use of its benefits. After all, what's the point of hiring the best and the brightest if you accidentally—it might as well be systematically—exclude them from the company's knowledge base? (And if you haven't yet noticed, in today's job market, the hottest in 25 years, employees who feel excluded can—and do—vote with their feet.)

Age, race, and professional diversity can also be invaluable business resources, and many companies spend a great deal of money and time fostering the perfect employee set. But achieving the ideal mix is not the same thing as sustaining or making the most out of the mix you've already mustered. Employees who are invited through the front gates, but then denied access to the inner sanctums of an organization, are little more than poster children. They'll leave (remember that hot job market?), and that means repeated recruiting expense and effort, with little value added for the trouble.

When Would I Ever Use This?

Social network mapping sounds great in theory, but when should a company actually invest time and money in it? Gerry Falkowski, an executive consultant with IBM's Consulting Group, recommends that clients use it to answer the question "now what?" after the usual suspects have been rounded up, interrogated, and summarily shot—and the project is *still* not moving forward. The classic example would be that of the organization that finds itself inexplicably stalled in the implementation phase of a large project, despite exhaustive and exquisite planning efforts. Falkowski also recommends social network mapping for organizations embarking on new ventures.

Joe LeClear was a systems-engineering team leader with Newport News Shipbuilding when his company started a joint venture with Electric Boat to build submarines for the U.S. Navy. Until then, the two companies had been longtime competitors with very different approaches to the shipbuilding business. Over the preceding decade, Electric Boat, while refining its submarine-construction techniques, had moved to the use of teams. Newport News Shipbuilding was working toward a team-oriented approach but basically still operating in a traditional hierarchy, and still enjoying a reputation for low-cost design capabilities.

For the joint venture, the two organizations would exchange information using a common three-dimensional software modeling package. At the same time, Newport News Shipbuilding retained IBM's Falkowski to assist in converting its engineering drawings from a paper to an electronic vault, and its organization from a hierarchical to a team-based model. In trying to marry infinite detail, intricate process, and inexorable change, the question became, as LeClear says, "How are we going to build a ship together?"

The two companies started by mapping the process of physically building a boat together. To determine whether Newport News' organization was functioning optimally, Falkowski proposed using a social network map of the company's information-exchange and communication paths. He asked three basic questions of the participants, who ranged in profession from welders to attorneys to purchasing agents, in order to answer the who, the how often, and the how. With whom do you interact to keep informed about developments within the company? From whom do you seek feedback and suggestions before making decisions? With whom do you interact to complete assignments?

Participants were supplied with a roster of peers, subordinates, and managers and asked to rank their interaction with each as Low, Moderate, or High for each of the three questions. The answers, says LeClear, identified whom the employees believed they talked to, whom they actually talked to, who actually heard them—and exactly where the gaps in communication were. There were visible "islands" of people who talked to each other but had limited communication outside their island. Clearly, there existed socially isolated units that were critical to Newport News Shipbuilding's new program, which would need to be integrated for the program to succeed. LeClear, who is now manager of document management at AlliedSignal, admits that he wasn't a proponent of the concept until he saw the end result. It changed his mind, he concedes. "I could understand [it then]. I would use it to evaluate where my organization's strengths are."

Other companies have used social network mapping to diagnose the business effectiveness of their diversity efforts. Belinda Ross is a diversity and organizational-effectiveness

The arrival of powerful computer hardware and software has moved social network mapping from academic exercise to commercial product.

consultant at a West Coast high-tech firm who used social network mapping to extend the definition of diversity beyond the traditional categories of age, race, and gender to encompass an array of professions such as engineers, programmers, and non-exempt employees. She wanted to discover which "cultures" dominated her company. Ross views social network mapping as a means of asking, "Where is the intellectual capital in the organization, and how well is it being spread?"

What she found was that some form of glass ceiling existed for all groups. One discovery: Her company's experienced engineers were not sharing information with its new hires. "We were wasting recruitment dollars if we were not educating our newly hired engineers," she says. "From the survey results, we identified successful 'barrier busters' and made them visible, recognized, and available to others as models. We ran brown-bag luncheons to share technology." Ross also plans to use social network mapping at an upcoming meeting to diagnose communication and connection gaps across product lines.

Eric Darr, senior manager of knowledge-based business at Ernst & Young, has used a mapping process in consulting assignments that focus on knowledge-management issues such as product development. In another assignment, Darr studied the transfer of knowledge from a retiring segment of its population to a successor generation and examined the "community" of employees responsible for innovation in the organization.

Where Have You Been All My Life?

The concept of mapping the social interaction of a defined group of people has been around since the 1930s, but until recently, the data was impossible to collect and analyze for anything beyond very small groups, or in a way that was digestible by corporate clients. It was the arrival of powerful and easily accessible computer hardware and software that has moved social network mapping from academic exercise to viable commercial product.

Usable software is the essence of the service's success, and the consultant who seems to have cornered the market so far is Ohio-based innovator Valdis Krebs. Krebs developed the prototype for the software over two weekends in the early '90s. At the time he was installing software as a project manager for TRW and finding that the new systems technology never addressed the "human systems issues," which may be why people resisted it despite its obvious advantages. After meeting with a vendor offering a succession-planning software package, Krebs came up with an idea to create software that visualized an organization's unseen workings. Serendipitously, he was also taking graduate courses in organizational design and artificial intelligence at UCLA, and used his idea for a project that satisfied requirements for both courses. His InFlow software was the result.

Krebs went out on his own shortly afterwards but found that most companies wouldn't begin to understand the concept of networks until the Internet and the World Wide Web exploded in popularity in the mid-'90s. Since then, complexity theory, chaos theory, and fractals have become garden-variety conversational references. "Now people 'get' the idea of networks," he says today. "Until five years ago, companies thought in terms of hierarchy."

Although a number of software products are available, Krebs' InFlow software may prove to be the most user-friendly alternative available on the market today. Darr believes software used in the academic community can be too arcane for the business community. Other commercial applications offer visual information but lack InFlow's statistical eye to detail. Some systems can be used only with a maximum of 50 participants or nodes, but Krebs has used this program successfully with as many as 600 participants.

New Views of the Organization

While consultants readily admit that social network mapping is not the next TQM, they are excited about its prospects. Many predict that social network mapping will be applicable in many settings and circumstances and have the ability to diagnose a wide variety of issues.

When Krebs was being interviewed for this article, he was working with an organization in the midst of a merger. Management was planning to identify the key players in the acquired organization to guarantee that communication efforts would be targeted and executed to the best of their ability. Yet Krebs stresses that social network mapping is not engineering. Instead, he says, it's a "soft" reorganization, intended to make changes in the white space on the org chart—which represents the relationships between people—rather than cutting or moving the boxes that represent the people themselves. These changes are often achieved through informal "fixes" such as assignments to task forces, upgrades to the organization's e-mail system, or even physical moves of individuals or departments to provide more desirable, neighborly access to other work units.

Another Krebs client, Vancho Cirovski, manager of organizational capabilities at Hiram Walker & Sons Ltd., explains that his company identified issues with assimilating recent hires and with the merging of two divisions totaling about 40 employees. Opinion surveys repeatedly indicated that there was a lack of communication between the two divisions. A specially appointed communications team was unable to resolve the issues. The two divisions then decided to examine the state of their communications along project and functional lines, and to determine if an employee's tenure with the company figured into the success or failure of the communication.

The first mapping survey, in late 1995, clearly identified instances of relative isolation in higher levels of management. Communication within each functional unit was satisfactory, but not between functional units and between related units that were physically located in separate buildings. An employee's longevity with the company turned out to be insignificant in determining successful communications with the rest of the organization. By late 1996, a follow-up survey confirmed the existence of some of the same problems—still centered around the issue of physical distance—as well as an improvement in the units' orientation toward their internal customer. Since then, Hiram Walker & Sons has physically moved employees to create the geographic access necessary to foster good communications between the related units.

Social network mapping is an inherently benign process, but if the collected data is mishandled, results could be disastrous. Consultants stress that the results should be made available to all participants—just as any survey's results should be—but both clients and consultants agree that information unearthed could be used as a weapon to damage reputations and careers. While companies can acquire the skills to perform the mapping themselves, consultants caution that the data—and what managers do with the findings—is potential dynamite in unskilled hands. IBM's Falkowski cautions, "Children shouldn't try this at home. This should never be used as the justification to reorganize people out of a job or to fire them." Once participants understand that their company might use the data against them, the organization will lose its chances of ever obtaining valid responses again.

An Elegant Opportunity

Even with the risks, social network mapping has proven that its utility outweighs its potential harm. Cirovski has seen senior managers do an about-face and reverse long-held biases against individuals as data has revealed their value in the organization.

Companies have realized that hierarchies—illustrated through the org chart—allow for only incremental change. On the other hand, networks, because of their informal nature, facilitate rapid change. The conclusion is simple and elegant: By identifying and sanctioning naturally occurring networks, companies can provide new, low-cost ways to maximize an organization's productivity and profitability as well as provide an opportunity to cultivate and capitalize on organizational coincidences.

Social network mapping has finally asked and answered the question that has been in the air throughout the downsizing and outsourcing of the '90s: *Who is really important to the organization?* It may be that people with enough history in and across the organization to understand how and why it functions are its most invaluable resource. (It goes without saying that a trove of history is valuable only if it is accompanied by the capacity to interpret and use it intelligently. Anyone who has hard-earned knowledge and no ability to apply it to new circumstances is still just a yutz.) It may be that anyone—whether a recent hire or a veteran—with a talent for effectively developing and exploiting a network of relationships is worth his weight in gold.

The Future That Has Already Happened

By Peter Drucker

I n human affairs—political, social, economic, and business—it is pointless to try to predict the future, let alone attempt to look ahead 75 years. But it is possible—and fruitful—to identify major events that have already happened, irrevocably, and that therefore will have predictable effects in the next decade or two. It is possible, in other words, to identify and prepare for the future *that has already happened.*

The dominant factor for business in the next two decades—absent war, pestilence, or collision with a comet—is not going to be economics or technology. It will be demographics. The key factor for business will not be the *over*population of the world, of which we have been warned these last 40 years. It will be the increasing *under*population of the developed countries—Japan and those in Europe and in North America.

The developed world is in the process of committing collective national suicide. Its citizens are not producing enough babies to reproduce themselves, and the cause is quite clear. Its younger people are no longer able to bear the increasing burden of supporting a growing population of older, nonworking people. They can only offset that rising burden by cutting back at the other end of the dependence spectrum, which means having fewer or no children.

Of course, birthrates may go up again, though so far there is not the slightest sign of a new baby boom

> Managers face two converging trends: the declining work force and the ascent of knowledge work.

in any developed country. But even if birthrates increased overnight to the three-plus figure of the U.S. baby boom of 50 years ago, it would take 25 years before those new babies would become fully educated and productive adults. For the next 25 years, in other words, the underpopulation of the developed countries is accomplished fact and thus has the following implications for their societies and economics:

• **Actual retirement age**—the age at which people stop working—will go up in all developed countries to 75 for healthy people, who are the great majority. That rise in retirement age will occur well before the year 2010.

• **Economic growth** can no longer come from either putting more people to work—that is, from more resource input, as much of it has come in the past—or from greater consumer demand. It can come only from a very sharp and continuing increase in the productivity of the one resource in which the developed countries still have an edge (and which they are likely to maintain for

a few more decades): the productivity of knowledge work and of knowledge workers.

• **There will be no single dominant world economic power**, because no developed country has the population base to support such a role. There can be no long-term competitive advantage for any country, industry, or company, because neither money nor technology can, for any length of time, offset the growing imbalances in labor resources. The training methodologies developed during the two world wars—mostly in the United States—now make it possible to raise the productivity of a preindustrial and unskilled manual labor force to worldclass levels in virtually no time, as Korea demonstrated 30 years ago and Thailand is demonstrating now. Technology—brand-new technology—is available, as a rule, quite cheaply on the open market. The only comparative advantage of the developed countries is in the supply of knowledge workers. It is not a qualitative advantage; the educated people in emerging countries are every whit as knowledgeable as their counterparts in the developed world. But quantitatively, the developed countries have an enormous lead. To convert this quantitative into a qualitative lead is one—and perhaps the only—way for the developed countries to maintain their competitive position in the world economy. This means continual, systematic work on the productivity of knowledge and knowledge workers, which is still neglected and abysmally low.

Implications of Knowledge As a Resource

Knowledge is different from all other resources. It makes itself constantly obsolete, so that today's advanced knowledge is tomorrow's ignorance. And the knowledge that matters is subject to rapid and abrupt shifts—from pharmacology to genetics in the health-care industry, for example, or from PCs to the Internet in the computer industry.

The productivity of knowledge and knowledge workers will not be the only competitive factor in the world economy. It is, however, likely to become the decisive factor, at least for most industries in the developed countries. The likelihood of this prediction holds implications for businesses and for executives.

The first—and overarching—implication is that the world economy will continue to be highly turbulent and highly competitive, prone to abrupt shifts as both the nature and the content of relevant knowledge continually and unpredictably change.

The information needs of businesses and of executives are likely to change rapidly. We have concentrated these past years on improving traditional information, which is almost exclusively information about what goes on *inside* an organization. Accounting, the traditional information system and the one on which most executives still depend, records what happens within the firm. All recent changes and improvements in accounting—such as activity-based accounting, the executive scorecard, and economic value analysis—still aim at providing better information about events inside the company. The data produced by most new information systems also have that purpose. In fact, approximately 90%

or more of the data any organization collects is information about inside events.

Increasingly, a winning strategy will demand information about events and conditions *outside* the institution: noncustomers, technologies other than those currently used by the firm and its present competitors, markets not presently served, and so on. Only with this information can a business decide how to allocate its knowledge resources to produce the highest yield. Only with such information can a business also prepare for new changes and challenges arising from sudden shifts in the world economy and in the nature and the content of knowledge itself. The development of rigorous methods for gathering and analyzing outside information will increasingly become a major challenge for businesses and for information experts.

Knowledge makes resources mobile. Knowledge workers, unlike manual workers in manufacturing, own the means of production: They carry that knowledge in their heads and can therefore take it with them. At the same time, the knowledge needs of organizations are likely to change continually. As a result, in developed countries more and more of the critical work force—and the most highly paid part of it—will increasingly consist of people who cannot be "managed" in the traditional sense of the word. In many cases, they will not even be employees of the organizations for which they work, but rather contractors, experts, consultants, part-timers, joint-venture partners, and so on. An increasing number of these people will identify themselves by their own knowledge rather than by the organization that pays them.

Implicit in all this is a change in the very meaning of *organization*. For more than a century—from J.P. Mor-

gan and John D. Rockefeller in the United States to George Siemens in Germany, to Henri Fayol in France, through Alfred Sloan at GM, and up to the present infatuation with teams—we have been searching for the one *right* organization for our companies. There can no longer be any such thing. There will be only "organizations," as different from one another as a petroleum refinery, a cathedral, and a suburban bungalow are, even though all three are "buildings." Each organization in the developed countries (and not only businesses) will have to be designed for a specific task, time, and place (or culture).

There are also implicaitons for the art and science of management. Management will increasingly extend beyond business enterprises, where it originated some 125 years ago as an attempt to organize the production of *things*. The most important area for developing new concepts, methods, and practices will be in the management of society's *knowledge resources*—specifically, education and health care, both of which are today overadministered and undermanaged.

Predictions? No. These are the implications of a future *that has already happened.*

About the Author
Peter Druker is the founder of the Drucker Foundation for Non-Profit Management and the author of many books on the study and practice of management. He may be contacted through Harvard Business School Press, 60 Harvard Way, Boston, Massachusetts 02163.

This article is reprinted with permission from his latest book, Peter Drucker on the Profession of Management, which is available from Harvard Business School Press (telephone 1–888–500–1016; Web site www.hbsp. harvard.edu) or from the Futurist Bookstore for $29.95 ($26.95 for Society members), cat. no. B–2147.

There Is No Future for the Workplace

As fast-moving technology allows more employees to work at home, what will become of the traditional workplace? Already, some strange things are happening as downsized companies scramble to hire out-placed workers.

By John A. Challenger

If you want a snapshot of tomorrow's workplace, bring your camera to Fremd High School in Palatine, Illinois. There you will see Motorola engineers working closely with students to solve real engineering problems. You might also take a picture of the billboards in central Florida, where Walt Disney World advertises for help.

Teens working on real-world engineering projects and billboards advertising jobs give an accurate picture of today's labor shortage. Companies like Motorola are working with high schools to attract more students to the engineering profession and to their companies, while Disney and many other firms are creatively advertising their need for help.

The impact of this shortage on tomorrow's workplace is not clear. If it continues, how will it affect the way we work in the future?

I think two key factors—population and technology—will determine the landscape of tomorrow's workplace. As I discuss how these factors can affect the next generation of workers, I exclude the impact of economic policies that can alter the trends in these areas.

A Continuing Shortage of Workers

I see a future economy with continued worker shortages created by consumer demand, coupled with an employment population too small to meet it. The next generation of workers will continue to be a scarce commodity for employers.

The traditional want ad will be replaced with "situation wanted" ads: Workers will place these ads on the Internet or other media and wait for companies to call them. They will have good reason to expect a call

back. The U.S. Bureau of Labor Statistics projects 151 million jobs by 2006 and 141 million people employed. As often happens today, many of those workers will be working two jobs.

To attract new workers, companies will need to offer different kinds of perks and benefits. Money alone is not going to be the deciding factor. Businesses will need to create benefits to address the specific needs of workers.

For example, a worker who needs day care for two young children may be attracted to an employer willing to make that service part of the compensation and benefits package. Another employee who may need substantial help with retirement financing may get special payroll deductions that can be directly deposited into a personal mutual fund or investment portfolio. Companies will provide free financial counseling.

Originally published in the October 1998 issue of *The Futurist,* pp. 16-18. © 1998 by the World Future Society, 7910 Woodmont Avenue, Bethesda, MD 20814; http://www.wfs.org/wfs. Reprinted by permission.

Companies will no longer view benefits as a company-wide provision. Instead, they may want to allocate a budget for benefits and authorize hiring managers to provide funds to employees within the limits of that budgeted amount. Such a change could affect many companies that currently provide benefit services, including major medical care.

The employer of tomorrow may wish to find alternate ways to help employees fund medical insurance. Because of the nature of this kind of expenditure, I see major medical insurance becoming a shared expense between employer, employee, and private or publicly funded assistance.

The need to tailor benefits will become more crucial as the demographics of the work force change. I expect those changes to come from two diverse groups: teens and those over 50.

The teen population is on the rise. The U.S. Education Department reports that high-school enrollment will jump 13% over the next 10 years, adding another 1.9 million students by 2007.

Another important trend is that many older workers are retiring later in life. The U.S. Bureau of Labor Statistics reports that the number of workers aged 65 and older increased 31% (3.8 million people) between 1985 and 1995. As the over-50 population increases, I suspect there will be even more workers in their 60s and even 70s.

The so-called Generation X'ers will probably become the minority age group in the workplace of tomorrow, sandwiched between the teens and the over-50 workers. Employers could face two scenarios: The two groups could form a strong connection or they could become polarized. Employers will need to avoid the polarization between teens and the over-50 workers and develop policies that will bring them together.

I like to use the grandparent/ grandchild model. Take a close look

PHOTOS:©PHOTODISC, INC.

The workplace as we know it will disappear, says employment expert John Challenger. But employers will have to ensure that self-directed workers and telecommuters do not lose touch with the organization.

at families with strong relationships: If the grandparents are still around, you are likely to see a very intimate bond between them and the teen-aged grandchildren. That bond usually develops when the grandchild is very young and continues through the child's adult years.

Employers will need to find ways to bring that relationship to the workplace. One way is to let the over-50 workers know they are expected to mentor the younger employees. Pairing teens and over-50 workers on specific assignments will help build those connections. Remember, most people in these two age groups will have grandparents or grandchildren at home and should easily relate to this relationship model.

Of course employers should not forget the problems of the generation in between. Generation X has the potential to see itself as a separate tribe needing defense from the other two groups. For that reason, companies will rely more and more

on the maturity and level-headedness of the over-50 worker to maintain a good balance among all employees.

The Impacts of Technology

The other major trend changing tomorrow's workplace will be technology, which has already made it possible for American business to become more productive. Computers and robots are now doing the work of two or three people, helping to keep total wages in check and hold down inflation. These are the most obvious results of technology.

Less noticeable and more interesting is the impact that technology will have on the nature of leadership.

The Bureau of Labor Statistics reports that 27% of the civilian labor force worked flexible schedules last year. That is an increase of almost 83% from 1991, when only 15% of workers had flexible hours. These figures show that when a person

A mother works at home. Technology is enabling more employees to adopt flexible hours instead of a traditional nine-to-five schedule.

does his or her job is becoming less important than meeting deadlines.

Add to that the increasing number of telecommuters who work at home or in their cars, and it becomes obvious that employees need not always be at a predetermined location to get the job done. As long as the brain is working, the employee is working, or at least potentially.

That word "potentially" is a critical one. How will companies direct and manage a work force that can be almost anywhere?

Before the infusion of technology in our lives, people reported to work at a specific time of day and went home at a set time, too. There was a supervisor or manager who assigned work and directed employee activity. It was understood that from 8:00 a.m. to 5:00 p.m. the employee was dedicated to the job.

In our high-tech society, the worker might be taking a shower, watching Oprah, or having lunch with his or her daughter between 8:00 a.m. and 5:00 p.m. While the supervisor is watching the evening news, the employee might be put-

ting the finishing touches on a report needed for the presentation tomorrow morning.

Technology has shown employers that it does not matter how the employee spends his or her time as long as the job gets done to everyone's satisfaction. That makes for a significant change in the way we function. Even workers on the assembly line are experiencing a change in workplace organization. The structure we identify as a workplace is disappearing.

Most management layers have been downsized out of American corporations during the 1990s. Today, there are fewer managers to report to and fewer decisions that require their input. The concept of empowering workers has left an indelible mark, not only on the work force, but on the marketplace as well. Consumers are expecting and getting better service from companies, and businesses are doing more to improve the service they give.

As technology helps companies deliver greater satisfaction to their customers, it also changes the work

force. Workers of tomorrow can no longer rely on brawn to get them a job. The days of unskilled, manual labor are fading into the past.

Today's factories are becoming laboratories of technology. There are technical jobs in manufacturing that did not exist 10 years ago. Computers have even made an impact in the repair and maintenance field: Your auto mechanic, for instance, is just as likely to hook your car up to a computer terminal as he or she is to remove your carburetor.

The result of such technological development is that new opportunities have been created for women in fields that have traditionally been dominated by men. The most recent figures compiled by the Bureau of Labor Statistics show that in 1996 almost 61% of U.S. technicians, engineers, sales engineers, and technical sales support staff were women. This trend is likely to continue as demand for engineering and technical jobs exceeds the supply.

Although industry leaders are attempting to attract young talent into technical areas—Motorola maintains a partnership with Fremd High School—fewer students are graduating with appropriate college degrees. Education Department figures for 1995 show a drop in the number of students completing college-level programs in computer and electrical engineering since 1990. Yet, the Commerce Department estimates demand for information technology workers alone will reach a million by 2005.

Factories may be hit the hardest by the lack of competent workers: In a National Association of Manufacturers survey, 88% of respondents reported a shortage of skilled help in at least one job category. More than half reported employee shortcomings in basic math, writing, and comprehension skills.

Training will become the next boom industry as employers are forced to take on the responsibility of educating unskilled workers. The new economy will not allow American industry to wait for the politicians to fund public education. Employers will need to become the public schools of the next generation.

These results point to what we can expect over the next 25 years. Workers will be more independent and self-directed and companies will need to form partnerships with educators to prepare young people for the high-tech workplace.

Turning Managers into Leaders

But what about leadership? How will tomorrow's managers and supervisors lead self-directed teams whose members are spread out over multiple states? Is it even possible to lead such a group? Employers will need to prepare for this new kind of management now.

Employees work out in company exercise room. Some organizations offer recreational facilities to reduce workers' stress and to attract skilled people.

Today's job descriptions are outdated the moment they are written. Most people would probably admit that their job descriptions are not accurate. So why do we keep them?

An alternative to the traditional job description might be to write job goals. Goals focus on accomplishments, which the company leadership can track; job descriptions focus on tasks, which are untraceable and often unimportant.

I use the term "company leadership" instead of "manager" for a reason: Supervision of tomorrow's workers will not require managers. Managers want to control tasks in the hope of predicting outcomes. Leaders want to plant seeds in the hope of harvesting unprecedented

Stress Reduction
An Expanding Employee Benefit

Stress in the workplace has become a significant problem for workers in the 1990s. Many employees are struggling to balance work and family life and to cope with job insecurity created by waves of mergers and acquisitions, according to John Challenger, an expert on employment issues.

The National Safety Council estimates that 1 million people are absent from work on any given day due to stress. The American Institute of Stress reports that 40% of employee turnover is related to job tension. Companies are responding to the problem by offering their workers a variety of ways to reduce tension:

- Gerber Technology has added a fully equipped exercise room to its existing volleyball and basketball facilities, encouraging employees to work out during lunch and breaks.

- Leo Burnett Company, a Chicago advertising agency, has contracted a massage therapist to help employees relax and relieve tension.

- Maxtor Corporation allows workers to bring their children to work on special "Kids' Days."

- Ben & Jerry's organizes an annual "Dog Days of Summer" party where workers at headquarters are allowed to bring their dogs to the office.

- National Semiconductor in Santa Clara, California, offers an on-site fitness center with classes in yoga, karate, and general health. It also helps employees quit smoking.

As the work force shrinks, companies may increase stress-reduction perks to attract skilled people, help reduce absenteeism, and boost employee morale. Concierge services, for example, could be expanded to include shopping, housekeeping, and even snow removal. Other benefits could include child care, elder care, and pet sitting.

"These services help reduce stress because they relieve employees from the minutia of daily life. In an age when worker retention and attendance are critical to a company's success, anything that reduces stress is a good investment," says Challenger.

Source: Challenger, Gray & Christmas.

crops. Leaders operate in the mercurial world of the poet: They are the dreamers of corporations.

The only job a leader has is to inspire greatness, then get out of the way. To do that today requires some personal contact. I do not believe, for example, that we can fully appreciate someone's leadership qualities simply by reading his or her words. We would gain so much more by seeing and hearing that person utter the words. A leader's communication style and sincerity would make a greater impression on us, perhaps a lasting one.

But in the high-tech world of tomorrow, leaders will have fewer opportunities to talk to people in person. They will need to rely on electronic devices to express their ideas. Perhaps the CEO will make a multimedia CD that employees can explore at their leisure. Would that communication be a good substitute for personal contact?

A shop superintendent can quickly communicate with the president of the firm simply by sending an e-mail. A decision can be made quickly and implemented in a third of the time it used to take. But what if the president wants to convey how crucial this particular decision is to the success of the company? Can the executive do it with e-mail?

These are the demands that will be placed on tomorrow's business leaders. Their ability to convey ideas to teams composed of people working in different parts of the country will be a major challenge.

One problem the new leader faces is the isolation of self-directed workers. With so many people working from their homes and cars at all hours, it is difficult to maintain a sense of belonging. People can lose touch with their organization and begin to miss the normal camaraderie of the traditional workplace.

It is critical that business leaders provide opportunities for the next generation of workers to get together periodically. This will allow employees to see each other and make direct connections. It will also give the leaders of the company an opportunity to communicate one-on-one.

I believe this sense of isolation will be serious enough to create a new job category: the director of socialization, who will be responsible for helping workers connect with each other while giving them an opportunity to express themselves to someone other than the boss.

The need for people to feel a part of a human organization is crucial to achievement. People want to connect with other individuals, not just electronic message pads or laptop computers. That will be just as true in 2020 as it is today.

Working for the Customer

My world exists on the edge of job creation and job destruction. My firm works with companies struggling to find the right balance between workers and need.

This is no easy task, and many companies fail to do it correctly. However, the workers they shed are quickly absorbed by other firms eager to satisfy their need for growth. The result is a "just-in-time" employment system that will continue well into the next millennium. This system will force the American worker and employer to rethink ideas of loyalty and commitment. Few employers will guarantee jobs to everyone, and few workers can afford to rely on employers to develop their skills and careers.

The workplace will become an environment dedicated to fulfilling customer demand. The needs of employers and employees will be subordinate to the need to satisfy customers.

Perhaps the New Economy is really nothing more than a consumer economy. Economic growth may rely less on government and more on companies, large and small, successfully satisfying an unrelenting consumer who wants more products and services, faster and at a better price.

Our worker populations will need to be better prepared for this kind of demand. Only those adequately educated can handle the ever-changing technology designed to help us compete effectively in this market of world consumers.

The current trends in population and technology challenge us to rethink our goals for education and work. We cannot hope to sustain our economic health over the next 25 years unless we ensure that every able-bodied person can effectively participate in that growth.

As in most projections for the future, mine ends with a warning: Invest in education or suffer the consequences.

We need to commit more than money, however. We need to create education standards that prepare the next generation to build a future. As business and professional people, we need to invest ourselves and participate in the development of those standards. We need to make them relevant to the marketplace. Only then will our investment in education bring solid returns for everyone: employers, workers, and consumers.

About the Author

John A. Challenger is executive vice president of Challenger, Gray & Christmas, Inc., a firm that pioneered outplacement as an employer-paid benefit in the late 1960s. His address is Challenger, Gray & Christmas, Inc., 150 South Wacker Drive, Chicago, Illinois 60606. Telephone 1-312-332-5790.

This article is based on his presentation at the World Future Society's 1998 Annual Meeting in Chicago.

The Feminization of the Workforce

SYLVIA ANN HEWLETT *is author of the controversial book,* A Lesser Life, *and professor of economics at Sarah Lawrence College. In the following article, Hewlett argues that the demographic realities of women's increasing workforce participation will force employers to become more responsive to family needs.*

The massive structural shifts of the last two decades have made our economy much more dependent on working mothers. In fact, of the 17 million jobs created in the United States during the 1980s, two-thirds were filled by women, and the fastest growing segment of the workforce is now mothers with preschool children.

Not surprisingly, issues of family support policy have become central to the lives of modern women. Whether one is talking about private-sector initiatives to provide on-site day care or public initiatives that provide universal access to pre-natal care or parental leave, these policies are capable of decreasing the strain in the lives of working women and of enhancing their earning power. In the absence of family support policies, the birth of a child reduces the average woman's future earning capability by 19 percent. Job-protected parental leave and subsidized child care can narrow the wage gap between men and women significantly.

A 1989 *New York Times* poll found that 83 percent of working women were torn by the conflicting demands of their jobs and the desire to do a better job with their children. When asked to name the most important problem faced by women today, the tensions between work and family won the number one slot—issues such as abortion rights were much less important to them.

The reason why this issue is so critical to women is simple: Working mothers continue to bear the main physical burden of running the home and raising the children. In addition, in divorced and never-married situations, women shoulder the lion's share of the financial bur-

> when asked to name the most important problem faced by women today, the tensions between work and family won the number one slot—issues such as abortion rights were much less important to them.

den—and it now costs $192,000 to raise a child to 18.

THE LOGIC OF THE BOTTOM LINE Since women workers have become critically important to the functioning of the economy, it is increasingly in the self-interest of employers to provide benefits and services that ease the burdens of their female employees. Between 1982 and 1988, the number of employers offering systematic child care or parental assistance as part of their benefits package rose from 600 to 3,500.

Even traditional firms have been caught up in the new enthusiasm for family supports. On the face of it, Corning is not an obvious candidate for avant-garde personnel policies. It is a traditional, blue-collar firm that has dominated the small town of Corning, New York, for generations. Until recently, its workforce was almost exclusively male. However, along with most American corporations, Corning has ex-

perienced a steady expansion in the ranks of its women workers. The number of women executives tripled between 1978 and 1988, while the number of women in technical, administrative and manufacturing jobs almost doubled.

This increasing dependence on women workers brought with it one major problem—an attrition rate of female employees that was twice as high as among male workers. This worried top management a good deal—it was bad for image and morale, but it was also bad for business. The Corning managers did some calculations and found that it cost $40,000—including search costs and on-the-job training costs—to replace each worker they lost.

Because management suspected that family burdens had a lot to do with the high turnover rate among women, they conducted a survey to find out what kinds of services and benefits would most help their workers deal with the new tensions between work and family life. By the end of 1988, Corning had in place a package of family support policies that included parental leave, part-time work, flexible work schedules, job sharing, flexible spending accounts for child care, and a parent resource center that was conducted in collaboration with the public school system.

Until very recently, the list of companies that developed family support policies for their employees was quite short: Merck, American Can, Campbell Soup, AT&T, Polaroid, Control Data, IBM, Johnson & Johnson and Eastman Kodak are famous for their on-site child care, flexible benefit plans and generous parental-leave policies. But as Corning Glass demonstrates, firms need not be progressive or even public spirited to have such policies; all they need do is consult their bottom line. Family support policy is fast becoming a win-win proposition: good for the working parent, good for the company. The needs of the American work place and the needs of American women may be merging for the first time in recent history.

From *New Perspectives Quarterly*, Vol. 15, No. 3, pp. 66-69. © 1998 by Blackwell Publishers. Reprinted by permission.

> **family support policy is fast becoming a win-win proposition: good for the working parent, good for the company.**

A WIN-WIN PROPOSITION

Much of the new employment is in the service sector, where high levels of general education, adaptability, and the ability to tolerate a low wage rate are at a premium. Women are more likely to be interested in these jobs and more likely to do well at them. The economy is now operating at low levels of unemployment, and those men who remain out of work often lack the education, attitudes or skills necessary to qualify for the available jobs.

As we look into the future, the pressure is building on corporations to get into the business of family support. The structural facts that conspired to turn family policy into a win-win proposition in the late 1980S are only becoming more urgent as we enter the 1990s. The baby-boom generation is aging and most firms face an extremely tight labor market. According to the Bureau of Labor Statistics, the workforce grew at 10 percent between 1980 and 1985, but will only grow five percent between 1990 and 1995. By 1993, there will be 23 million unfilled jobs slots in our economy. In this labor-scarce world, corporations will find child care and parental leave important weapons in the battle to attract and keep new employees—three-quarters of whom will be women with dependent children.

If the profitability of firms is now tied up with their ability to create a pro-family workplace, there is also a collective logic that underscores a new and urgent need for our public policies to do a better job by our children. America's family problems now threaten the social and economic fabric of the nation. Anyone who has looked at the data recently cannot help but be impressed by the severity of the situation:

■ 21 percent of all children are growing up in poverty.

■ 28 percent of our teenagers leave high school without graduating, marginally literate and virtually unemployable.

■ 49 percent of divorced men neither see nor support their children in the wake of divorce.

Oddly enough, one of the best statements of what we should do about these massive problems has come out of the business community. In 1987, the Committee for Economic Development (CED), a group of 200 CEOs and business executives, published a study entitled *Children in Need*. The primary focus of this study was that 30 percent of American children are facing major risk of educational failure and lifelong dependency. The arguments put forward by the CED are compelling:

Poverty-ridden, neglected children grow into problem-ridden youngsters who are extremely difficult to educate and absorb successfully into the workforce. Not only does this increase welfare and prison costs, it also seriously undermines the economic strength of our nation. The US is moving into an era of intense competition. In the 1990s, maintaining our domestic and international markets in the face of fierce rivalry from low-cost producers is going to become even more difficult. The prospects for keeping our competitive edge are slim, unless we increase both our rate of productivity growth and the quality of the products we make. Both these goals are critically dependent on the caliber of our future workforce and on our ability to educate and train young people. Schools should do more, but they will continue to fall short of the mark unless we strengthen families. Schools alone cannot compensate for the tasks that burdened parents no longer perform.

The CED study calls for a major new commitment to child-welfare and family supports by the government and the private sector. The report is particularly eloquent in presenting the cost-benefit

> **schools alone cannot compensate for the tasks that burdened parents no longer perform.**

arguments for early intervention in the lives of families. Improving the prospects for mothers and children through prenatal care and early childhood education, for example, is not an expense but an excellent investment—one that can be postponed only at much greater cost to society.

This year's high school dropouts will cost the nation more than $240 billion in lost earnings and foregone taxes over their lifetime, and this does not include the billions more for crime control and welfare expenses. To use the language of the report: "The nation cannot continue to compete and prosper in the

> **woman power will have to be utilized more efficiently if we intend to cope with the looming labor shortages of the 1990s.**

global arena when more than one-fifth of our children live in poverty and a third grow up in ignorance. And if the nation cannot compete, it cannot lead."

In the 1970s, feminism concentrated on pressuring men to share in responsibilities on the home front—with very limited success. Indeed, not only do married men do rather little housework, but divorced and never-married fathers routinely abandon their children.

Feminism in the 1990s should focus some prime energy on sharing the costs and responsibilities of child rearing with the private sector and with government. For the first time, the hard-edged logic of the bottom line is on our side:

The economic facts of life in the 1990s will conspire to make mothers and children scarce and valuable resources, assets that businessmen will be loath to neglect or squander. Woman power will have to be utilized more efficiently if we intend to cope with the looming labor shortages of the 1990s, and children will have to be cared for better if we are going to survive as a competitive economy.

Making Work Meaningful:

Secrets of the Future-Focused Corporation

By Roger E. Herman and Joyce L. Gioia

Workers and managers alike face unfamiliar challenges and new demands in the fast-moving, unforgiving business climate of the twenty-first century. *Survival will depend on teamwork, loyalty, and vision at every level.*

Today's worker is no longer willing to work in an authoritarian and dehumanizing environment. Workers want meaning in their work and balance in their lives. Given the amount of time people spend at work, they want opportunities to contribute and to know how their work contributes to the organization. They also want to be valued as individuals with goals and aspirations, not just replaceable drones in the hive.

Illustrated by Tom Chalkley

The very nature of organizations can make this change difficult. Every organization has reasons for its existence. A corporation is a structured environment with a purpose—a business purpose. It is an environment established to create wealth, not a natural human social environment. The foundation for building human relationships in such an environment is a mutual respect for what employees contribute to the organization and for the individuals themselves. The evolution to this new, meaningful corporate culture will encompass many changes. These will affect not only the design of work and compensation, but quality of life, environmental accountability, social responsibility, and scope for the human spirit.

Creating Meaningful Work

The first step on this evolutionary path is to redefine work. What is work? And how do employees relate to the work they do? Research shows that people want to do more than simply "attend" work.

A recent survey by Response Analysis of Princeton, New Jersey, identified employees' top three most important aspects of work. Of the 1,600 people responding, 52% wanted to be responsible for their work and the results it produced, 42% wanted acknowledgment for their contributions, and 39% wanted their tasks matched to their strengths.

Today, and in the future, companies that hope to attract and motivate enthusiastic and dedicated employees will demonstrate their sensitivity to the level of responsibility workers want. They must design work so that employees can take responsibility and be rewarded appropriately. In doing so, these organizations will take a big step toward making work meaningful. Here are some more key elements for redesigning work:

• **A valued part of the whole.** Repetitive factory routines and office work that simply moves paper from in-box to out-box are mindless tasks that destroy motivation and productivity. Workers want to know that their work is important and how it fits into the corporate strategy. To make this transition smoothly, organizations must share more information with more people than ever before. Employees want to be responsible for results, so they must have access to the information that will enable them to fulfill that responsibility.

People want to do more than simply "attend" work.

• **Making an impact.** Employees need to know not only how the work they do affects others and the organization's strategic goals, but how they—as individuals—can make an impact. Who knows better how to improve the processes and environment than the people involved on a daily basis? Successful organizations understand and appreciate that this ability to improve workplace effectiveness is part of the intellectual capital of their work force, that what employees know can be even more valuable than what they do.

Through their knowledge and experience, workers can provide the organization with a wealth of information that cannot be acquired elsewhere. In order to tap this intellectual capital, the organization must create a culture that encourages and supports collaboration. Employees will contribute their knowledge enthusiastically in a corporate culture that values the individual.

• **Responsibility for outcomes.** Having the responsibility and authority to make decisions increases the meaning of work. Being able to recommend and implement improvements allows individuals to see their impact on the organization. Employees respond positively when they are given clear goals and the authority to make things happen.

This kind of exchange can only survive in a culture built on mutual trust. The organization must trust that employees are capable of making the right decisions. Employees, on the other hand, must trust that it is safe to risk making decisions—even wrong ones. This process doesn't take away accountability. It does, however, focus on objective results, and it creates an environment for continuous feedback and improvement.

• **Measuring results.** For workers to be responsible and find their work meaningful, they need direct and timely feedback. Making changes and improving performance comes from an ongoing evaluation process. When workers gain feedback from the customer (internal or external), they can gauge their influence in making things happen, solving company problems, and making appropriate decisions.

To assure a continuous flow of valuable feedback, tomorrow's most successful corporations will establish systems for customers to evaluate service performance. They will also provide ongoing coaching for every worker and involve employees in their performance rating, encouraging them to take initiative in improving their work and their results.

Every employee's work can be measured in some way. Successful corporations develop those measurements, assure the flow of information needed to assess progress, and facilitate the evaluative process. Working without feedback is like bowling in the dark: You may put out lots of energy but get no sense of return. Tomorrow's employees—and many of today's—won't tolerate that vacuum.

• **Meaningful rewards.** The profitability of a company is directly related to the quality and efforts of its workers. Therefore, a direct relationship between job performance and reward makes work more meaningful.

Future-focused companies are learning that corporate responsibilities extend beyond their own front door.

Compaq Computers enjoys an unusually low turnover rate among its employees. Like many companies in the computer field, Compaq expects its people to work long and hard to achieve big results quickly. In many companies an atmosphere of constant push would inspire people to seek employment with less pressure somewhere else.

Instead, high quality people stay with Compaq. The company's culture emphasizes individual responsibility for results and high respect for individuals—from the top of the organization down. This attitude is shown in all sorts of interactions, including providing access to information, resources, and higher management. Both the company and its employees benefit from creating opportunities for every employee to self-actualize and to be rewarded for achievements. By constantly measuring employee perfor-

mance to assure that contributions are rewarded proportionately, Compaq's empowerment concept achieves its full potential.

• **Team effort.** Even with the focus on individual accomplishment, there is a powerful sense of the team at Compaq Computers. Every employee is expected to support everyone else to serve the customer. The worldwide profit-sharing plan reflects this togetherness: Distribution is based on a balanced formula of customer satisfaction and return on invested capital. All employees benefit from this program.

To remain involved and loyal to an organization, employees should share in the profits they create. Workers are reluctant to give 110% only to see executive salaries skyrocketing while their own incomes barely keep pace with inflation.

Rewards (financial and other) for a job well done acknowledge the

contribution of the individual. Not only are these incentives motivational, they underscore each individual's importance within the organization. Future-focused companies are redesigning compensation to reflect this connection. Performance-based compensation packages can actually help keep payroll costs in line while motivating valuable employees.

The Ritz-Carlton hotel and resort company has always been at the forefront of customer service. After winning the Malcolm Baldrige National Quality Award in 1992, Ritz-Carlton established a pilot project of self-directed work teams that embodied many of the components of meaningful work. The pilot was so successful that, by 1995, more than 30 Ritz-Carlton hotels and resorts were using the same self-directed work team concept. By giving frontline workers control over the process and outcomes of their jobs, management taps into employees' problem-solving skills and reinforces their commitment to high level customer service.

With self-directed work teams of line employees in control of daily activities, managers have time to provide vision and direction. As a result, Ritz-Carlton has experienced an increase in satisfaction from owners, guests, and employees. Additionally, the team environment allows employees to gain experience in a broad range of activities. This experience is valuable for recruiting and retaining good employees, since it enables employees to become more marketable both within the Ritz-Carlton group and to other organizations in the hospitality industry.

Creating a Meaningful Organization

Meaningful work is just part of what it will take for companies to maintain a high-performance work force and remain competitive in tomorrow's marketplace. Future-focused companies are learning that corporate responsibilities extend beyond their own front door.

Increasingly, workers will choose their employers based on how they perceive the organization's aims and values. Their choices will be deliberate, and they will not hesitate to leave employment that they decide isn't "right" for them.

• **Balancing work and family.** Quality of life, on and off the job, is more important to today's workers than ever before. Parents struggle to balance the requirements of the workplace and the needs of their children and extended families. Some workers care for both children and elderly relatives. Even employees without such responsibilities want time to pursue personal interests. Future-focused companies are finding ways to facilitate a balance between the work and personal lives of their employees. By addressing these issues, employers support a motivated, stable, productive work force.

To remain competitive in tomorrow's marketplace, companies must be highly sensitive to employee needs and expectations and be prepared to make a significant investment in the area of personal/professional balance. This makes sense on several levels. Cost/benefit analysis reveals a favorable return on such an investment in companies, large and small. Sensitivity to individual employees' concerns outside the workplace can create a meaningful environment conducive to a stable, productive work force. Those companies that

fail to address these needs and interests will lose their best and brightest to competitors that offer better quality-of-life programs.

• **Personal and professional growth.** Employees also want to develop a meaningful career path that makes them more marketable both internally and externally. To accomplish this, they want opportunities to learn, to increase their responsibility, and to implement solutions. Learning opportunities include both academic and experiential methods and apply to both job training and improving personal skills.

Companies always benefit when workers are actively engaged in improving their skills or knowledge. Professional development adds meaning to work; personal development adds meaning to the individual. Both build self-confidence and self-esteem. Knowledgeable, confident workers are essential for the lean and meaningful companies of the future.

Few workers expect to stay in the same job forever. They want to try new kinds of work and to grow, expand their capabilities, and avoid boredom. People who have no opportunity to try different types of jobs with their current employer are

Seven Skills for Meaningful Workers

Technical and technological skills will take on greater importance. There will be a growing need for people who can understand and fix systems—from computer systems to product distribution systems to plumbing systems.

Visionary skills will be in demand. The ability to gather and absorb a wide range of input, then use that knowledge, understanding, and perspective to guide organizations into the future, will be vital.

Numbers and measurement will be important, of course, but smoothing the flow from month to month, from quarter to quarter will be essential for highly profitable long-term performance. Practically every company will have to move away from today's obsession with looking ahead only as far as the next financial reporting period.

Ability to organize will definitely be important in the corporation of the future. Everywhere there will be a need to organize something: resources, workflow, marketing mix, financial opportunities, and much more. All will demand high levels of organization—and reorganization.

Persuasive skills will be used in many ways by the corporation of the future. The most-effective individuals will be those who know how to present information and ideas so that others can understand and support a particular position. Good salesmanship will be essential in many more interactions than we consider today, especially inside the organization.

Communication skills—careful listening, clear writing, close reading, plain speaking, and accurate description—will be invaluable. In tomorrow's fast-paced business environment there will be precious little time to correct any misunderstandings. Communications breakdown may well become a fatal corporate disease.

Ability to learn will be above everything else in importance—empowering people to grow in effectiveness and help their companies achieve desired objectives. Some of this skill is innate, but many people enhance their ability to learn—and to relate different aspects of learning—through college and university courses. We believe the liberal arts education experience will prove to be the most valuable type of education for tomorrow's leaders.

The top employees of the coming century will be flexible, creative, and motivated toward making a positive difference in the world. They will seek balance, growth, and fulfillment in both their work and home environments. The corporation of the future must respond to these needs and desires; otherwise, they will find themselves hampered by a lack of qualified people to accomplish the organization's work.

—*Roger E. Herman and Joyce L. Gioia*

likelier to leave in search of something new. So, wherever possible, give people a chance to experiment. Cross-training and cross-experience build understanding and expand an employer's capacity to quickly assign people where they're needed most.

Workers may resist changing jobs to try something new if there is no safety net in the event they don't like the new work. Can they say, "no thanks," and return to their former assignments? The Land's End Company, in Dodgeville, Wisconsin, responds to this uncertainty with something they call "job enrolling." Employees can try a new job temporarily without transferring from their current position. If they like the new work, they can request an official transfer.

• **Company/employee relations.** Not only prospective employees, but investors and consumers are also coming to judge companies by how they deal with issues like diversity, harassment, hiring and firing, profit sharing, and other labor/management policies. A number of companies recently in the news know all too well the public impact of internal decisions. To cite just two examples, AT&T lost huge image points when it laid off thousands of workers in a year of profits. And Texaco's failure to handle discrimination within its own ranks will remain in the public consciousness for years to come.

Prospective employees are reluctant to join a company that has a history of treating its people badly, and current employees are easily lured away to companies with better track records. Investors are also watching companies carefully because the connections between employee re-

How a company is perceived by society will have an impact on its ability to find good employees.

tention and profitability have been made quite clear.

Diversity is a major concern in corporate America, and it will remain so for years to come. Much more than a racial issue, the emphasis is now on celebrating differences among people and making active use of the varied perspectives that workers from different backgrounds bring to the job.

The Hearst Corporation celebrates the unique talents and contributions of all its employees, whether they are high-profile reporters, secretaries, or little-seen printing press operators. When someone at Hearst does something worthy of recognition, flowers are sent—to the employee's spouse. Really special contributions call for a small gift from Tiffany's. Receiving the gifts at home brings the family into the celebration and helps connect the worlds of homelife and work experience.

• **Corporate social responsibility.** Employees also want to know that they are working for an ethical company with a mission and a clear set of values they can believe in. Younger workers today are typically more interested in the mission of a company than the price of its stock. Older employees, who have put in their time under the pressures of the old system and weathered the overwhelming changes of the last two decades, are now more cynical and less inclined to give their all to a company they instinctively mistrust.

To win these valuable workers over, companies that look toward the future will need to live up to their mission statements. Employees and customers are aware of what organizations give back to the community. In a tight labor market, prospective employees will include a company's social report card in their decision process. Thus, how a com-

pany is perceived by society will have an impact on its ability to find and keep good employees.

Customers, shareholders, and other stakeholders are also looking for more than just profit. Companies are being held increasingly accountable for being good corporate citizens. Whether shopping for consumer goods or investing in stock, the general public is becoming more aware of a company's policies and standards, and people are voting with their pocketbooks.

• **The company and the environment.** Environmental awareness will play a role in any future corporation's image. Whether a company applies environmental considerations at every stage of its operations or ignores these issues unless it gets caught can make a major difference in employee loyalty and market acceptance. A company that takes an active role in protecting the environment, both in its own products and through community involvement, will have a stronger position in tomorrow's marketplace.

• **Spirituality in the workplace.** The human spirit, where hopes, dreams, and aspirations lie, has long been banished from the workplace. Yet there can be no meaning in either work or life when this aspect of human existence is ignored. To be their best, people must be able to express their values, to share their hopes, to tap into their creativity in the workplace. A future-focused corporate culture will make a place for such spiritual expression, which may take many different forms, resulting in

benefits ranging from better internal communication to new product design.

Putting It All Together

Evolving into a meaningful organization presents some big challenges. Some changes will be easy for companies to adopt; others will be less comfortable. The key will be the *motivation* behind the shift. Sensitivity to the human spirit—in the work environment—will drive

The core relationship is between a company and its employees.

the most sincere, longest lasting, and most effective movements into true meaningfulness.

Successful future organizations must be mindful of all their relationships and act with integrity at all times. But the core relationship is between a company and its employees. The ability to build strong, collaborative relationships with employees will determine whether a business evolves through time or is lost along the way.

With the imperative to find and keep good employees in a shrinking labor market, the efforts made to positively change the relationship of employees, their work, and the organization will be the defining factor in the successful corporation of the future.

About the Authors

Roger E. Herman and Joyce L. Gioia are strategic business futurists and Certified Management Consultants. Their address is The Herman Group, 3400 Willow Grove Court, Greensboro, North Carolina 27410. Telephone 1-336-282-9370; Web site www.herman.net.

This article draws from their book *Lean and Meaningful: A New Culture for Corporate America*, which is available from the Futurist Bookstore for $27.95 ($25.50 for WFS members), cat. no. B-2184.

New Keys to

Employee Performance and Productivity

John Luthy

Almost 20 years have passed since public managers began recognizing that traditional performance measurement and employee evaluation systems were inadequate for a rapidly evolving workplace. Even with this realization, however, more than 80 percent of surveyed government organizations still use outdated performance evaluation processes that are insufficient to motivate, encourage, or recognize employees. To say the least, progress has been slow.

Thirty years ago, the work of Frederick Hertzberg and others demonstrated that money alone does not motivate employee performance; nor does it reinforce loyalty or devotion to various organizational initiatives. Rather, it is a "satisfier" that enables an employee to satisfy personal and family needs and, to some degree, to reflect his or her status in the workplace. Even with the information provided by these early studies and by many studies since, public organizations have floundered among simplistic approaches to employee performance evaluation and correspondingly weak attempts to link performance with pay.

This mix has produced a variety of systems that encourage "bracket creep," badly skewing pay systems while discouraging personal initiative, performance, efficiency, dedication, and productivity. Longevity continues to drive far too many compensation decisions, encouraging almost an implosive survivalist mentality rather than collaboration, lateral movement, personal growth, skill transfer, and continuous improvement.

Work over the past two decades has consistently indicated that individual contributions must be based on clear direction, personal planning, individual and team assignments, and well-articulated knowledge, skills, and personal attributes. Without such clarity, employees have no expectations to meet; nor are they able to follow patterns that constitute standard performance ideals in the organization. Only when time is taken to develop a job model for each employee, with detailed assignments and an opportunity for peer review, will

> **The process of employee performance evaluation has assumed an expanded meaning over the past decade. No longer can it be merely an annual exercise to justify compensation decisions. It is a critical management tool that must become one of the central initiatives within every public agency.**

From *Public Management*, March 1998, pp. 4-8. © 1998 by John F. Luthy, President, The Futures Corporation, Executive Management Development Institute, Boise, Idaho. Reprinted by permission.

evaluation be worthwhile and provide a sensible basis for personal and professional development, career advancement, and merit compensation.

Employee Contribution And Development Planning

After reviewing dozens of evaluation systems, this author believes that there must be an approach that allows clear evaluation based on desired attributes, necessary technical knowledge and skills, and accomplishment toward established objectives. Formal and informal research consistently reveals that employees desperately want to be judged on their accomplishments and to seek new opportunities based on their own abilities to perform. They certainly don't want to be put into a categorical box or compared with fellow employees as the central means of evaluation. Rather, they want to be recognized and rewarded for their unique contributions as they relate to specific job duties, professional capabilities, and overall performance in the organization.

Here are some important questions now being debated more openly by public managers: How can we deal with employees who work hard for two or three years, receive healthy pay increases and even promotions, then begin coasting? When money is tight, are there alternative means of rewarding employees for making consistent and meaningful contributions? What is a logical method of linking employee and/or team performance with compensation? What kinds of compensation are there, and how is each type calculated? What should the relationship be among strategic planning, performance budgeting, and employee evaluation? And, ultimately, how can the evaluation process contribute to teamwork, morale, productivity, initiative, creativity, efficiency, and workplace harmony?

To achieve desired outcomes, performance must be reviewed based on annual or quarterly goals, objectives, and assignments. Clarity is imperative if supervisors are to judge contribution accurately and to assess the question of who deserves merit increases. Public managers are being asked to do more with less, and this trend will continue. How, then, can a manager thoughtfully guide an operation in a manner that encourages high productivity, accurately depicts who is actually performing, and establishes a nonintrusive system that monitors and documents true employee contribution?

Supervisor/Employee Cooperation

In an evolved system, supervisors and employees work together to create an employee contribution and development plan that is specific to the employee and his or her position. A review of the essential knowledge, skills, behaviors, attributes, job tasks, and desired outcomes that constitute high-quality performance becomes the foundation for guiding professional growth and development, as well as for assessing performance. Careful attention during the initial plan development ensures that the plan accurately profiles a particular position, its inherent responsibilities, and the qualifications essential for employee success.

Developed and used properly, this plan will determine progress toward annual objectives, the achievement of important professional development goals, and the successful implementation of agreed-upon actions. Each element will help evaluate overall employee contribution and performance for the purpose of merit increases or special cash awards that do not add to base pay (tools that seem to be gaining in popularity). Quarterly or semiannual progress updates, plus an annual review, also provide excellent opportunities to promote ongoing communication between employees and supervisors. Updates and employee reviews alike, however, must be based on well-defined plan content, that is, essentially on a customized model for a particular position (not to be confused with a job description).

Perhaps most important here is a new pro-

New Training Package!

International City/County Management Association's *Employee Performance: Appraisal and Management* will make it easy for you or anyone on your staff to facilitate supervisory training in performance appraisal and management!

For more information, call ICMA's fax-on-demand line at 703/531-0915, select "3" for resource information and follow the prompts.

---

cess that removes much of the subjectivity from performance evaluation and replaces it with objective criteria derived directly from established job responsibilities. Performance discussions can thus be based on objectives and actions required by the job, as defined in advance by both supervisor and employee. Removing the subjective aspect of employee evaluations is in itself a major advance from most systems being used today.

A key success factor, of course, is cooperation between employees and supervisors, which requires supervisors to actually teach, mentor, and plan with employees. This is a critical point because it is estimated that fewer than 40 percent of supervisors are genuinely good at supervising! What we normally see is old-style foremanship, which causes an environment of ordinate/subordinate relationships that are counterproductive in trying to build and maintain a cohesive, collaborative, and highly efficient team.

Seven Dimensions of Continuous Improvement And Development

There are seven types of input, or "dimensions," critical to fostering continuous improvement and individual team development. Dimensions 1 through 4 form the basis for thoughtful and accurate evaluation. They involve criteria identified jointly by the employee and the supervisor, and they clarify what is expected on that specific job in a finite period of time.

To fashion the kind of public workplace that we all know is successful, employees must believe that the organization is willing to invest in their personal and professional development. Therefore, dimension 5, career management, also is required because this step in the process gives the employee a regular chance to work on his or her personal and professional development.

Dimension 6 offers an opportunity to use corollary peer and customer reviews as parts of employee evaluations. Dimension 7 is a special employee-to-supervisor feedback system that encourages communication and provides growth opportunities for managers. These last two dimensions are optional but are recommended as part of the comprehensive performance management process.

The following overview describes the type of input and/or the process needed to complete each particular step in a performance evaluation.

Dimension 1

Core/Job-Specific Attributes. This dimension involves those qualities and behaviors common to successful, performing employees at all levels throughout the organization. Think of these as traits considered important for all employees to exhibit to foster and maintain the kind of culture that is desired.

Dimension 2

Technical Knowledge and Skills. This step relates to a person's understanding and ability to use the technical information methods, procedures, and equipment needed to perform the functions of a particular job. This section of the performance evaluation sets forth in clear detail the technical KSAs (knowledge, skills, and abilities) necessary for success in a specific job.

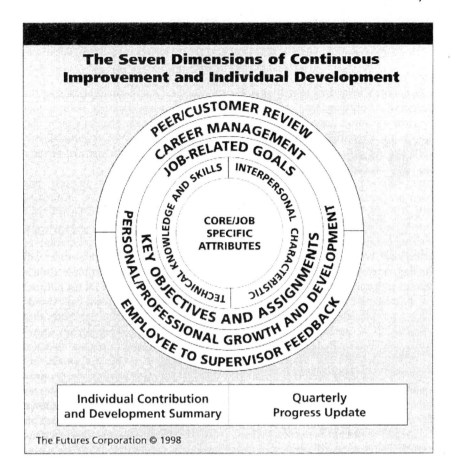

The Seven Dimensions of Continuous Improvement and Individual Development

PEER/CUSTOMER REVIEW
CAREER MANAGEMENT
JOB-RELATED GOALS

KNOWLEDGE AND SKILLS | INTERPERSONAL
PERSONAL/PROFESSIONAL
KEY OBJECTIVES AND ASSIGNMENTS
TECHNICAL KNOWLEDGE | CHARACTERISTIC
GROWTH AND DEVELOPMENT
EMPLOYEE TO SUPERVISOR FEEDBACK

CORE/JOB SPECIFIC ATTRIBUTES

Individual Contribution and Development Summary	Quarterly Progress Update

The Futures Corporation © 1998

Dimension 6

Peer/Customer Review. This optional but recommended step invites insight and input from coworkers and from internal (or external) customers. Most evaluations neglect the people with whom the employees interact, when it is these very people who could best describe and verify behavior, efficiencies, or outcomes unnoticed by a supervisor.

Dimension 7

Employee-to-Supervisor Feedback. In this dimension, employees are allowed to give helpful suggestions and feedback to supervisors in a positive manner that permits both parties to achieve greater success. Few supervisors or managers naturally solicit feedback on how they could do a better job for their employees.

This dimension provides that opportunity but does so in a way that forms part of the general improvement effort, instead of standing as an isolated incident or session to deal with a perceived problem. While optional, this step is highly recommended because it helps identify supervisors who need training and development and introduces a nonsensitive method of discussing how work groups can make consistent improvements in communication and cooperation.

With the growing popularity of "360-degree reviews," dimensions 6 and 7 provide a means of review that will become quite common over the next three to five years. If completed as part of the overall performance plan, however, these dimensions are softened without compromising their value.

Dimension 3

Interpersonal Characteristics and Skills. These are the traits and qualities that facilitate communication, cooperation, and collaboration among team members and with others. This section of the evaluation lists the characteristics needed to foster good working relationships among people in and outside the organization, while reflecting the leadership qualities needed in lead persons, supervisors, and managers.

This is a key area often neglected in performance planning and only addressed when serious interpersonal problems exist. This dimension openly establishes those characteristics that an organization expects of its employees and provides another basis for annual review. *Interpersonal communication and conduct represent the one area that, if not addressed, leads to the most internal problems and the greatest frustrations noted by managers at all levels.*

Dimension 4

Job-Related Goals, Key Objectives, and Assignments. This critical dimension allows for performance contracting as part of an overall professional and organizational development process. This section of the evaluation identifies goals, objectives, assignments, responsibilities, and special projects that relate specifically to the employee's job and for which the person will be held accountable. It is short, concise, and specific, so that clarity exists as to what outcomes are expected. This dimension is one of the key factors in annual deliberations over merit pay.

Dimension 5

Career Management, Personal and Professional Growth and Development. At this point, areas of personal and professional development are identified by each employee and perhaps by the supervisor, as part of the overall professional improvement and career planning efforts. This is another important aspect of a system that promotes organizational improvement through employee development.

Employees consistently raise concerns over their own options for development, often leaving when they feel stifled. The approach described in this article blends improvement and development with career planning, allowing the employee and the supervisor to chart a course that benefits both the employee and the organization.

This aspect of the process receives a great response among staff because it demonstrates a respect for and commitment to personnel, who often feel isolated and powerless to advance or improve their lot in life.

A Total System

Each of the seven dimensions stands alone. The entire process can be established on-line so that hard copies can be downloaded as necessary, and if alterations are needed, these can be accomplished with minimal effort. The only printing required is that of the initial folder in which each employee's individual plan is filed, and this, too, can be optional if funds are short. The process has been developed to set clear boundaries regarding what the organization expects, what the job requires, what outcomes need to be achieved, and what areas of growth and development will prove beneficial.

At first glance, the process appears time-consuming. Actually, if done properly, it takes no more time than traditional, simplistic processes. Yet it pays significant dividends both to employees and to the organization. Most time is accrued when each employee's initial plan is developed and while supervisors and employees learn the process. After that, most aspects of the plan (such as core attributes, technical skills, and interpersonal skills) will change little over time, and amendments can be made easily during quarterly and annual reviews.

Remember, part of the process is the responsibility of the employee, with general guidance and support from the supervisor. It is a collaborative process allowing supervisor and employee to work together to plan, then jointly to assess contribution (performance) according to the criteria they already have established. This type of "performance contracting" has been around for many years and has been successful when properly implemented.

Supervisor Training and Employee Orientation

As with any new system or approach, implementation must be thoughtful and well planned. Supervisor training and orientation of all employees is critical in departing from a process that has been around for decades. Particularly for those supervisors who have used a checkoff or mark-the-box system to evaluate employees, moving to a new process that seeks collaboration and interaction can be quite a shock. Some are threatened, others argue they have no time, while others see the value of working cooperatively on performance management and organizational development.

A supervisors' handbook and training guide can help with the initial training, then serve as a desk reference. During training—which can be done in large groups in half-day sessions—supervisors and managers should receive a brief refresher course on management theory, organization development, motivation, communication, and planning. It also is an opportunity to discuss internal problems and frustrations that will be addressed by this new approach to performance management.

A Meaningful Contribution

The seven dimensions reviewed in this article encompass every element considered critical to employee and organization development, performance review, career planning, and continuous improvement. Once supervisors and employees have used the system, they will begin to see the value of collaboration, joint planning, and internal improvement.

The process positively changes the work environment and alleviates the ordinate/subordinate relationships that destroy teamwork and initiative. While initial training and orientation are critical, real progress toward full implementation only is made once the process is being used throughout each agency.

Linkage Between Strategic Planning and Performance Budgeting

Because a primary emphasis has been placed on strategic planning for public agencies, it has become increasingly apparent that, to have meaning, performance planning and evaluation *must* be tied to strategic plans. This linkage is accomplished through individual and team performance plans, which include many of the objectives and actions/strategies described in an agency's strategic plan.

Written properly, plan actions and strategies will identify accountable parties who can be evaluated on whether and how well the agency's goals, objectives, and/or recommended actions have been accomplished. Similarly, because properly executed strategic plans drive performance budgets, there will be a direct relationship among plans, budgets, and both agency and individual performance.

Moving Forward

Systems involving employee contribution and development planning represent a major leap forward from most systems currently used in public agencies. Developed over the past 12 years and based on the best practices found in the public and private sectors, employee contribution and development planning will foster internal efficiency, quality, continuous improvement, and new levels of collaboration. Taking only a short time to learn, it will involve a new approach for many old-school supervisors, quite a number of whom have failed to invest in their employees. The approach can be easily customized to meet the needs of individual agencies or managers, however, and it will allow each organization to include clear performance expectations based on its own unique circumstances.

By clarifying expectations, goals, and assignments, plus describing the knowledge and skills required for success, an organization can build an enduring foundation for employee performance measurement and for consistent process improvement. As public agencies move into the next decade, it will become even more important for them to maximize employee effectiveness, experience, and productivity.

For public administrators to be successful, they must begin changing their perspectives and begin practicing an entirely new style of performance management. If they fail to do so, public organizations face the prospect of being unable to fully mobilize potent but often latent human resources to match the enormous velocity of change and meet the increasingly difficult challenges of the twenty-first century.

John Luthy is president of The Futures Corporation and founder of the Executive Management Development Institute, Boise, Idaho. All rights to this article are reserved to John F. Luthy, 1998.

What Do CEOs Want from HR?

*CEOs agree on HR's increasingly important role.
Here's how they say HR can fulfill it.*

BY BILL LEONARD

What do chief executive officers really think of the human resource profession? And how do CEOs think HR should change to meet the growing needs of their organizations? To find out, *HRMagazine* recently interviewed five CEOs who represent a broad spectrum of industries, company sizes and geographic locations. One CEO spent many years working in HR; the others have less experience with human resource management.

Despite these varied backgrounds, the comments from all five CEOs reveal common themes—and common areas where HR can stand to improve.

A UNIQUE RELATIONSHIP

As HR professionals increasingly strive to become strategic partners with top management, their relationship with CEOs takes on new significance. All the CEOs interviewed for this article agree that—of all the members of their management teams—their relationship with the top HR professional may be the most important.

The amount of time CEOs spend with HR executives underlines the importance of this relationship.

"I'm probably speaking with our senior v.p. of human resources about 40 percent of my time at work," says Robert McDonald, CEO of the North American division of Standard Chartered Bank in New York. "It seems that I am always talking to her and seeking her advice and input."

Reprinted with the permission from *HR Magazine,* November 1998, pp. 80-86. © 1998 by the Society for Human Resource Management, Alexandria, VA.

Likewise, Mike R. Bowlin, chairman and CEO of ARCO, the Los Angeles-based oil and energy giant, constantly consults his top HR executive.

"I believe that I spend as much time with John Kelly (senior vice president of HR) as anyone else who works for me," he says. "There is no major decision that takes place in the company that John is not involved with, and I fully expect him to have an opinion on business decisions. As CEO, I use John as a personal consultant and sounding board for ideas and problem solving. Many times, he and I go to lunch and just bounce ideas off each other, which works well for us."

All five CEOs say that as HR has gained more access to their offices, the head of HR has assumed a unique relationship with the CEO. But how can HR make sure that relationship remains solid?

"The key to a good relationship between the CEO and the head of HR is honesty," believes Craig Sturken, chief executive officer of Farmer Jack Supermarkets in Detroit. "For the relationship to really work well, there has to be a trust, closeness and almost intuitive understanding between the CEO and the head of HR. The last thing that you want to do as CEO is stifle that relationship; it's crucial to the success of your business."

Girard Miller, president and CEO of ICMA Retirement Corp. in Washington, D.C. says HR must relate well to both employees and top management. "It's a hard role to play, I believe. A good HR professional must have the ability to thoroughly develop a trusting relationship with the employees, while at the same time be something of a collaborator and serve as a confidant to the CEO."

Miller adds that HR must work closely with CEOs. "I'm a firm believer that the HR function must be a direct report to the CEO," he says. "I think that there are just too many opportunities for mischief, if it is not."

**T. Michael Goodrich
President and
Chief Executive Officer
BE&K Inc., Birmingham, Ala.**

Goodrich became president of BE&K in 1989 and was named CEO in 1995. He began working for BE&K in 1972 as assistant secretary and general counsel.

BE&K is one of the largest privately owned engineering and construction companies in the United States. Last year, the company had nearly $1 billion in sales and currently has a workforce of nearly 8,000.

THE STRATEGIC ROLE OF HR

Why do these CEOs place such emphasis on the strategic role of HR in their organizations? The answer lies in the evolving and strategic role of the profession.

"HR has become a very important component in our strategic planning processes," says Mike Goodrich, president and CEO of BE&K Inc., an engineering and construction company based in Birmingham, Ala. "We need to anticipate where our company is going to be five to six years down the road, and HR is crucial to understanding the changing demographics and expectations of our workforce."

The other CEOs agree that HR executives must understand and embrace their evolving strategic role, which includes helping track the skills of the workforce and matching them up with the organization's needs.

"HR management is one of the critical resources that we have to carry on our business plan," says Bowlin. "Our people are what will truly build a sustainable competitive advantage. In the long run, everyone has the same access to capital and technology, so a company's human resources is what makes the difference and makes it successful. It is the key resource."

McDonald fully expects "HR to be the guardian of information as to where your best people are in the organization and what their talents are."

Miller adds that "HR needs to know how the personnel talent of the organization can make a difference to the short-term business plans as well as the long-term strategy."

THE BOTTOM-LINE APPROACH

As HR's role as a strategic partner has evolved, the focus and knowledge necessary to be a successful HR executive have also changed. For example, the CEOs interviewed for this article emphasized that—although HR has improved its understanding of financial issues—more work needs to be done.

"When it comes to the bottom line, I would say that HR generally has been a bit out to lunch," says McDonald. "But their understanding of the bottom line has improved over the past few years, and I do believe most HR executives are striving to better understand how their decisions and actions can truly affect the bottom line."

Miller goes so far as to characterize HR's comprehension of financial issues as "soft." "HR professionals are not as far along as I, as a CEO, would like to see them," he says. "I believe they get the idea when it comes to their own budget but have a tough time understanding concepts such as variable costs versus fixed costs."

Miller says this is true with his current vice president of HR but adds that she has been a willing student. "And her willingness to learn is really the key here and clearly shows that she is interested and committed to improving the bottom line of this organization," he adds.

Sturken's experience mirrors that of McDonald and Miller; a solid financial orientation has not been a strength of most of the HR professionals he has worked with.

"I believe there has been a lack of concentration on the bottom line among many of the HR people I have known," Sturken says. But, like Miller, he sees improvement.

"I will hand it to my current vice president of HR," he says. "She is trying hard to learn and improve her knowledge and skills, and I believe that her efforts will pay off for both her and our company in the long run."

Sturken encourages HR professionals to strengthen their financial knowledge by taking advantage of educational opportunities. "I always advise my HR staff to take courses in business finance and financial planning," he says. "There are a lot of seminars and workshops on the fundamentals in accounting for nonfinancial manag-

**Robert P. McDonald
Chief Executive Officer
North America
Standard Chartered Bank,
New York**

McDonald began working for Standard Chartered Bank in 1992, when First Interstate Bank was acquired by Standard Chartered. Prior to 1991, McDonald worked for 20 years with Chase Manhattan Bank in London and New York.

Standard Chartered is an international bank, which focuses most of its activities on Asia, Africa, the Middle East and Latin America. The bank has more than 26,000 employees worldwide, with nearly 600 in the United States.

ers. I have had managers come back from these courses and give suggestions and ideas to our accounting department on streamlining and improving some systems."

OTHER SKILLS

Besides a strong bottom-line orientation, several of the CEOs say their HR executives and managers need to be more aggressive and work on their powers of persuasion.

"At my company, we have a saying that you need to push the envelope," says Goodrich. "And HR has never really pushed the envelope with me. I have no problem saying 'no' if I think it's too

**Mike R. Bowlin
Chairman and
Chief Executive Officer
ARCO, Los Angeles**

Bowlin was appointed president and CEO of ARCO in July 1994 and was named chairman of the ARCO board of directors one year later.

Bowlin began his career with ARCO in 1969 as an HR representative and moved steadily up the ranks, holding positions such as manager of HR of ARCO's Alaska operations, vice president of human resources for ARCO Oil and Gas Co. and senior vice president of ARCO Resources.

ARCO, an acronym for the Atlantic Richfield Co., is the seventh largest oil company in the United States. The Fortune 100 company has 24,000 employees worldwide and annual sales of more than $18.6 billion.

"The people who acquiesce too quickly are usually gone quickly," he says. "But then if you have someone who tries to be too controlling, that's not good either. What we want is a team player who is knowledgeable, bright and aggressive and has good consulting skills," Bowlin says.

Part of being a good consultant, says Bowlin, is being persuasive. "This is a skill that HR needs to work on, I believe," he says. "To succeed, you must have the ability to be persuasive and move the organization forward and to influence key business decisions."

To be more persuasive, however, many HR professionals need more education in business fundamentals.

"Clearly, HR professionals today are better trained than I was when I began my career 30 years ago [in HR]. But they do need sufficient and fundamental business training to participate and contribute to the company."

Miller goes a step further, saying that HR managers seem to lack some business training that is necessary to perform in today's workplace.

"I find generally that many HR professionals' business math skills and dimensions are fairly weak," Miller says. "I believe that the skill level is slowly improving and that's largely due, in part, to the fact that it is changing from the personnel function to the HR function."

Miller also believes that HR professionals have a "lack of vision" when it comes to the big picture of the organization.

"HR professionals have been getting by focusing on the day-to-day. They need to develop a broader and farther-reaching vision and understand where their organization is headed and how they can help steer the company in that direction," Miller adds.

McDonald says that HR is "being a bit insular." He says that one of the major problems with HR is that the profession's executives and managers have tended to focus solely on their HR departments.

"Their primary focus was HR, and the company was secondary to that. All the company did was provide them a paycheck, and that was the prevailing attitude 20 years ago," says McDonald. "It has improved, but I think because of that attitude, HR's reputation among other departments was a bit tainted. That reputation has improved vastly in recent years, but there's always room for improvement."

McDonald believes that improvement comes when HR sees itself as an internal consultant. "It really makes my job easier if I'm working with someone who sees themself as working with internal clients rather than seeing themself as just a part of the HR group," says McDonald. "Those

much. I have said 'no' plenty of times to our information technology department. But HR has never pushed hard enough or far enough for me to say 'no' yet."

Bowlin says that HR has moved into the role of internal consultants at ARCO, but he is quick to point out that the term "consultants" does not mean he wants a bunch of "yes men or women" on his staff. He wants people who will challenge and question decisions that they believe are flawed.

who think outside the four dots and believe that they are serving internal clients get my vote."

BEYOND SKILLS

The CEOs interviewed for this article tend to agree that the best and most successful HR professionals have a real passion for their jobs.

"The better HR professionals that I have worked with have been compassionate and have deep feelings for our employees," says Goodrich. "They have a burning desire to see our employees succeed and build better lives for themselves. It's a trait that I have truly admired among most of the really good and successful HR professionals that I have known."

Bowlin agrees that true success comes from a passion for your job. "To really truly succeed, you have to be passionate about your work. You have to feel that you can make a difference," he says. "And if you are really good and passionate about your job, and you work in HR, you can really make one of the most positive impacts of any group within a company."

THE FUTURE OF HR

All five of the CEOs have to think strategically about the short- and long-term issues that confront their organizations. Two of the key issues they identified for their organizations—and, consequently, for HR—are recruiting and diversity.

Sturken says that the primary problem his company faces is a drastic labor shortage. The tight labor market has made recruiting and retention top priorities at his company.

"Retail is really tough right now," Sturken says. "It's a quality of life issue. The question that we face is, How can we improve our employees' lifestyle? People don't want to work weekends and evenings, and that's the lifeblood of retail. None of the old rules work when it comes to recruiting and hiring people. HR has to be very creative and market and merchandize our company and the advantages of working here. It's a very different ball game now."

Goodrich agrees that the labor market's rules have changed but attributes many of the changes to a dramatic shift in demographics.

"We really have been paying close attention to the changing demographics of our workforce," Goodrich says. "We have more women and more Latinos working in the construction industry today, and we must be prepared to respond to these changes."

He adds that the aging of the workforce will present some interesting challenges to the workplace. That is a trend that will also profoundly affect Miller's organization, which manages retirement funds for local governments.

"As the baby boom generation ages, we will have a powerful growth curve over the next five to six years in this organization," Miller says. "The demand for more retirement benefits and retiree medical care will be tremendous and will affect all businesses. We have to begin considering how we are going to pay for those benefits."

Bowlin believes that effectively managing multicultural diversity is the primary challenge that faces HR and corporate America.

"ARCO has to design HR systems that recognize cultural differences and help the company be more effective in those cultures. It's a high priority for us," Bowlin says. "As this company becomes more global, how we manage diversity will be key to our success."

The workplace challenges of multicultural diversity only emphasize the importance of developing a global focus when dealing with HR issues, according to McDonald.

"The challenge of HR is cross-cultural. It is a huge job to make that cultural bridge," he says. "HR professionals can prepare to meet these challenges by making themselves available for international assignments, and by that I mean living outside the country for three to four years. International mobility is key. Today's economy is a global economy, and HR has to be ready to accept the roles and challenges that the global marketplace brings."

Bill Leonard is senior writer for HRMagazine. *Patrick Mirza, managing editor of* HRMagazine, *contributed to this article.*

Building Heart and Soul

More than 80 percent of Americans say they would like to run their own business, according to Eric Klein and John Izzo, authors of *Awakening Corporate Soul* (Fair Winds Press, 1998). Perhaps that's because most feel that no employer will ever treat them as well as they want to be treated—a message corporate America seems to be taking note of.

And so a new trend is developing in which employees are being valued and treated in new ways. Call it the new "corporate spiritualism," where businesses are just as concerned about nurturing employees' well-being as they are about the bottom line. Just a look at lists like *Fortune* magazine's *100 Best Companies to Work For,* and the kinds of cultures these organizations have cultivated, gives you an idea of what "doing the right thing" in a company today can do for its success.

While much of creating a spiritual workplace is about a new mind-set and a "way of doing business," there is no set protocol. Each business must develop the culture that works best for that business and industry.

CHANGE UNDERFOOT

A confluence of factors are involved in this new trend, including a shrinking pool of talented workers, a demanding Baby Boom generation and, most notably, the switch in focus from yesterday's "hard" assets such as property, plants and equipment to today's "soft" assets such as patents, processes, creativity and customer satisfaction. The numbers tell the story: According to a Brookings Institute report, as little as one-third to one-half of most companies' stock mar-

ket value is accounted for by traditionally labeled "hard" assets.

"Previously, our work world revolved around manufacturing, which was an orderly, engineered process that permitted surveillance of pre-planned activity," explains organizational psychologist Harvey Hornstein, Ph.D., Columbia University professor and author of *Brutal Bosses* (Riverhead. 1997). "It was an environment that was hospitable for command-and-control-type management. All you needed was obedience to get the work done. It excluded all concern regarding people's lives, values, interests and needs," he adds.

FROM ALIENATION TO AFFILIATION

Then came the computer, the growth of the knowledge industry and the need for business to rapidly adapt to change. "Today the premium is on innovation and creativity, and one cannot legislate innovation and creativity," notes Hornstein. "If you create an environment in which people feel alienated and only do what is required of them, then you won't get commitment and loyalty. Commitment and loyalty are nurtured by affiliation, which is a product of the progressive management approaches that we are associating with when we talk about attention to spirituality."

If there is a downside to this new emphasis on values and culture, it's that people's expectations can be raised too high. Says Hornstein, "Employees hear so much about being valued that they may have unrealistic expectations that the employer will always be there for them and help them in ways that are not feasible or acceptable."

To help discern between policies, programs and cultures that are merely "nice to have," and those that actually have a positive effect on business, more and more companies are routinely conducting attitude, productivity, and employee

and customer satisfaction surveys. According to the *Wall Street Journal,* employee satisfaction surveys are on the rise, especially among the multinationals.

For example, in an elaborate 800-store study, Sears Roebuck found that employees' attitudes about their workload, treatment by bosses and eight other such matters have a measurable effect on customer satisfaction and revenue. Sears discovered that if employees' attitudes on 10 essential counts improves by 5 percent, customer satisfaction will jump 1.3 percent, driving a one-half point rise in revenue.

Employee attitudes that affect profit vary by company—ranging from feelings about communication to feelings toward management—but experts agree that one cultural element that consistently comes into play in successful companies is valuing the work/life balance. "Workers frustrated over not having a life outside work aren't very effective," points out Palmer Morrel-Samuels of Employee Motivation & Performance Assessment of Chelsea, Mich.

Behemoth **Johnson & Johnson** got its balancing act together early. A decade ago, J&J introduced its Balancing Work and Family Program. "The components of the Work/Family program are a tool for recruiting and, even more so, retaining good people," says John McKeegan, a company spokesperson, "because people know that J&J is a company that will help people balance these competing demands."

The help J&J offers employees is expansive—benefits include onsite gyms, smoking cessation programs, six onsite childcare centers, adoption programs, financial support, eldercare assistance, and helping spouses of relocated employees find employment.

"We have a philosophy, our credo, that says that our first responsibility is to our customers, our second is to our employees, our third is to the communities we live in and the last is to our

DOES YOUR BUSINESS HAVE A SOUL?

Here's what today's trend toward "corporate spiritualism" means, according to leadership consultants, organizational psychologists, authors and practitioners:

➤ Getting rid of managers who are stuck on the old command-and-control style of doing business. Putting in place managers committed to the notion of creating relationships at work as a way of increasing profitability.

➤ Conducting regular (at least annual) employee satisfaction surveys. Ask employees what they want most. Then give them those benefits and work systems that will both make them happy and make good business sense.

➤ Creating an environment where employees feel nurtured and affiliated, then reciprocating with commitment and loyalty.

➤ Providing training that specifically targets employee interest and talent.

➤ Offering "hard" work-family benefits such as onsite childcare centers, onsite gyms or substantial financial support for such care, and "soft" benefits such as flexible work hours and consultative or supportive services for family needs.

➤ Involving employees in the larger strategies of the business and connecting them to the products delivered.

➤ Creating systems with fewer levels of employee review but allowing just as much accountability.

stockholders. If we serve the first three groups, then the stockholders will be served," says McKeegan. Every two years J&J surveys its employees about what it calls the "Credo Values" to find out how employees feel the company is doing. "If we see that we're deficient in an area, we try to improve," McKeegan continues. "As a matter of fact, the Balancing Work and Family Program came out of a Credo Values survey we conducted back in 1988."

SENSITIVITY AFFECTS PROFIT

Johnson & Johnson was onto something that many companies are just now beginning to realize: It's virtually impossible to run a productive and profitable workplace and not value the personal lives of employees. In fact, Harvard Business School accounting professor Robert Kaplan compared employer sensitivity to work-life matters with corporate quality initiatives in a recent *Wall Street Journal* article. "If you're out of control on [work-life matters], it's going to hurt performance. Then, you don't

even get a chance to implement your strategy because key people leave," says Kaplan.

If employees' lives outside work need to be valued, then the relationships at work need to be valued even more. Daniel Hanson, who heads a $250 million division of **Land O'Lakes**, is a leading voice for creating a workforce community that relies on relationships at work to maintain organizational strength, productivity and sanity. Author of *Cultivating Common Ground: Releasing the Power of Relationships at Work* (Butterworth-Heinemann, 1997), Hanson has successfully implemented change at Land O'Lakes by fostering open communications, offering a meaningful profit-sharing system and implementing a variety of "community at work" programs.

According to Hanson, "community at work" is a way of doing business. It requires employees to care about people who aren't so lovable. Hanson says building community at work is a "nittygritty" process that resolves conflict and differences and builds trust and caring. Community at work comes from such things as self-managed, cross-functional

teams. For example, one team at Land O'Lakes decided to get rid of cubicles altogether. Others have implemented mentoring programs. Hanson has also tried what he calls "participation leadership," treating everyone as an equal by eliminating the sales meeting and replacing it with an all-division meeting so that everyone, not just the sales staff, could be recognized for their contributions. For diligent organizations, Hanson suggests benchmarking employee sentiment to gauge long-term satisfaction with work.

Sound like utopia? Even Hanson admits it's not all hearts and flowers. "You can run into resistance from your people at a very high level—people who are wedded to the old command-and-control system," he explains. "We had one HR director who we had to let go because they could not adjust to the change."

Hanson has also encountered the problem of unrealistic employee expectations, but managed to find a solution. "We realized we had to cultivate change through understanding that employees' expectations were too high. Once we learned to define 'community at work' so people wouldn't be disappointed, we saw results."

THE WAVE OF THE FUTURE?

This new movement of corporate caring faces its challenges, but it seems to be taking hold in an increasing number of successful organizations. Will it last?

"You can't package enthusiasm and you can't package 'spiritualism,' " says consultant Stephen F. Boehlke, of Stephen F. Boehlke & Associates and SpiritLead Inc. Boehlke prefers the term "meaning" to "spiritualism," and breaks it down into simple terms. People need to feel more connected to the outcome of their work and the larger strategies of the corporation, he explains. If that works for business, it sounds like a win-win proposition.

JOANNE COLE is a business writer and president of Cole Communications & PR Marketing in New York.

Cultural Change Is the Work/Life Solution

Even the most progressive approach to work/life balance will fail without strong commitment from management and a culture that supports it.

By Ann Vincola

Work/life strategies have not only hit the corporate mainstream—they've become drivers toward competitive advantage.

The ever-changing values of tomorrow's workforce have created unprecedented demands for flexible, diverse benefits and policies. To be leaders and employers of choice, organizations are increasingly focusing on managing human capital.

A study conducted in April 1997 by Hewitt Associates in Lincolnshire, Illinois, indicates that over the past five years, there have been increases in every category of work/life initiatives. Of the 1,050 employers polled in 1996, 68 percent offered flexible scheduling, 86 percent offered child care, 30 percent provided elder care, 23 percent had adoption benefits and 85 percent

Ann Vincola is senior vice president of Work/Life Benefits, heading its consulting division and Boston office. E-mail anfusod@workforcemag.com to comment.

made employment assistance programs available.

The 1996 "Mercer Work/Life & Diversity Initiatives Benchmarking Survey" conducted by New York City-based William M. Mercer revealed the same trends. Of 800 employers questioned, an astounding 94 percent instituted flexible scheduling policies. Particularly, 79 percent had written policies allowing part-time employment and another 2 percent were considering them. Thirty-eight percent offered flex-time and another 11 percent were considering or

developing programs; 34 percent had compressed work weeks, while another 8 percent were considering or developing policies; and 26 percent allowed job sharing, with another 10 percent considering or developing programs.

Given this trend, the critical question that emerges is this: Is the rise in work/life

---

■ **Organizations must stop viewing work/life benefits as an accommodation. Rather, they should look at the benefits as strategic business initiatives.** ■

---

programs seen in theory *and* in practice? According to *Business Week's* 1996 research of balancing of work and family, the answer was "no." While 48 percent of the 8,000 employee respondents to *Business Week's*

"Balancing Work and Family" survey said they could "have a good family life and still get ahead" in their companies, 60 percent reported that management did not, or only somewhat did, take people into account when making decisions. Although many companies offer benefits, this disregard from management is felt because the underlying cultural issues still aren't well addressed.

Business Week's 1997 survey on the same topic indicated that things began to change—at least at the top. At companies that ranked highest overall, it was reported that family-friendliness is ingrained in both culture and business strategy.

However, beyond the top tier, employees indicated that work and family strategies aren't working well. Lacking true business grounding and often at odds with corporate culture, family-friendly programs

• It must be fully integrated with the other aspects of the organization's human resources programs.

The first step of creating a work/life strategy is to gain commitment from senior management and then cascade that commitment throughout the management of the company. Awareness and acceptance of family issues at the top is a good starting point—and companies seem to understand this concept. Fifty-four percent of respondents in the *Business Week* survey reported that top management demonstrates support for family balance.

But the definition of "support" remains vague. Most often support from management is seen as lip service that doesn't translate into action. Yet still, the question remains: How can you make sure that these executives will act on their word?

tent, employers still see work/life benefits as an accommodation, rather than as a strategic business initiative.

However, the Ford Foundation study points out, "Addressing work/family concerns as legitimate and systematic issues for corporations can lead to innovation in work practices that not only help employees, but also improve the bottom-line results for the company."

Despite potential benefits to the company, the study found that making the link between work and work/life issues is difficult. Significant organizational barriers—such as beliefs about what makes a good worker, how productivity is achieved, and how rewards are distributed—strain this connection. In a large percentage of companies, the work/life benefits are designed and administered by HR, but are implemented by line managers. Delineating responsibility along these lines reinforces the belief that business issues are separate from employees' personal lives.

To solidify this link between work and work/life, and to gain support for the program, a critical element of implementing a work/life strategy is to objectively highlight the impact that creating a people-friendly work environment has on the bottom line. Assessing the impact can take a number of directions:

1. Effect on recruitment and retention: Work/life initiatives play a critical role in an organization's recruitment and retention strategies. But placing a quantitative value on their effect will be instrumental in giving credibility to the program by linking its existence directly to the company's bottom line and streamlining it into the overall business strategy. Issues to look at include:

• Cost per hire—a decrease in costs per hire signifies a decrease in recruiting costs, training time and so on.

• Customer defections—a decrease in the number of customers leaving you and going to your competition means an increase in customer satisfaction. Keep in mind that customer defections can be a result of many factors, including lack of resources, errors or inability to commit to promises. You need to delve into why customers are going elsewhere so that these issues can be remedied.

• Lost intellectual capital—turnover rates in excess of 10 percent and low retention rates indicate the organization isn't properly managing needed knowledge, skills and behavior.

2. Impact on productivity: It's also advantageous to look at the impact of work/life programs on the productivity of the workforce. But what's the payoff for helping a parent put in a productive day at work, knowing an ill child is well cared for? Or how do you assess the benefit of providing an employee with a referral to a

---

■ Gain commitment from senior management and then cascade that commitment throughout the management of the company. ■

---

are viewed by employees as add-ons and concessions primarily targeted at women with kids—even though that group accounted for less than a quarter of survey respondents.

To truly impact the work and personal lives of employees, organizations must stop viewing work/life benefits as an accommodation. Rather, they should look at the benefits as strategic business initiatives that drive culture change throughout the organization. A work/life strategy will be successful only when it's embedded in the culture of the company—it must be integrated into work practices and must be supported by a commitment from top management and training for managers.

Creating a work/life strategy is a journey.

Designing and implementing an effective work/life strategy can't happen overnight. The change must be approached as a journey that evolves over time, instead of a one-time occurrence. Adopting this vision will enable employers to learn how best to respond to the dilemmas raised by an increasingly diverse workforce. Before embarking on the journey, keep in mind a few key points about strategy development:

• It must be achieved in stages
• It involves long-range planning
• It requires a change in attitudes and management style
• It must relate to corporate goals

One way for senior-level managers to demonstrate their support for the programs is to solicit input from employees at all levels. A 1996 Ford Foundation Study *Relinking Life and Work* found that everyone—line managers, HR staff and front-line staff—brings assumptions to the workplace.

After senior management sets the tone for open commentary, putting work/life concerns on the table as legitimate issues for discussion turns out to be liberating for all who are involved. Employees can examine their own assumptions, and determine which ones support and which ones impede the achievement of both personal and business goals.

Without visible support from the top, work/family efforts can quickly be crippled. CEOs need to commit publicly to supporting the initiatives. Those who do this best are the ones who recite personal values and experiences, like David Olson of Patagonia, Randall Tobias of Eli Lilly, Lew Platt of Hewlett-Packard, or Kurt Landgraf of DuPont. CEOs must also require direct reports to show they are acting and managing sensitively. Those who don't understand this sort of commitment are out.

Look at work/life issues as business issues.

A sure sign that upper managers support work/life initiatives is when they draw the link between the programs and the overall business strategy. But, to a large explumber if a pipe suddenly bursts? Again, to take a more quantitative look, address issues such as:

• Payback—measure the payback of various programs in terms of dollars, such as dependent-care programs, employee time saved, or tardiness. A dollar value can be assigned to improved employee morale and public relations.

• Return on investment—an increase in the return on investment indicates that the program is making a positive contribution to the company's bottom line.

Work/life must become part of the culture.

Commitment from managers and employees alike comes from a culture in which embracing work/life balance is pervasive and consistent. The Ford Foundation study confirmed that the organizational culture, plus the image of what it means to be an ideal employee, gets in the way of using the benefits that are offered.

Programs like part-time work, flextime and telecommuting are there, but the culture often identifies those that take advantage of them as less committed to work. If a person indicates a desire for a part-time job, he or she is seen as no longer interested in professional growth and opportunity.

There are a number of ways to weave a work/life perspective into a corporate culture. At Schaumburg, Illinois-based Motorola Inc., a work/life vision statement is reinforced by regular training for supervisors and seminars for the front-line staff, and by 50 professionals responsible for guiding the direction and implementation of these programs worldwide. It's translated into benefits offered to workers companywide that reflect the company's values and business goals.

Newark, Delaware-based credit-card issuer MBNA Corp.'s universal top-down culture reinforces the notion of respect for employees at literally every turn. Execs and rank-and-file workers mutually carry, and quote from, a laminated card printed with the company's core precepts, reading "MBNA is a company of people who expect to be treated fairly."

In last year's *Business Week* survey of work and family strategies, 78 percent of MBNA employees indicated they didn't have to sacrifice career progress for life balance. The reason is in part because they see the company's top officers confronting family issues of their own. Vice-Chairman David W Spartin, for example, sends his children to the same onsite daycare facility as do other employees.

Companies that truly entrench the initiatives into the corporate culture integrate family support into the business itself. At Palo Alto, California-based Hewlett Packard Co., CEO Lew Platt demands that every business unit identify work-family issues and propose action plans as part of their annual business reviews. So, when HP's printer group, facing higher consumer demand, had to increase the number of shifts its manufacturing department worked, it also investigated options for round-the-clock child care. Financial managers won approval of a plan to get work done more efficiently by rescheduling activities causing peak-period bottlenecks, avoiding staffing gaps and providing technology to allow work from home.

Platt says, "I sincerely believe employers who find the answers to the questions [surrounding work/life] are going to be leading employers in the future. These leaders will attract and retain the very best people in the future. This is the competitive advantage."

Putting it all together.

The journey to creating a people-friendly work environment will be filled with twists and turns. As the workforce becomes increasingly diverse and organizations strive to be employers of choice, the work/life strategy will take center stage. But even the most progressive approach will fail without commitment from management and a culture that supports a people-friendly environment. These two factors form the basis of any work/life strategy.

"In the work/life equation, attitude is far more important than any particular policy or program," says Paul Allaire, Xerox chairman and CEO in his address to the 1997 CEO Summit on Relinking Life and Work. "We must nurture an attitude, a corporate culture, that respects differences among people, an attitude that assumes people want to do the right thing, an attitude that values empowerment so people can get the job done."

ORGANIZATION STRUCTURE AND DESIGN: THE CLUB ED EXERCISE

Cheryl Harvey
Kim Morouney
Wilfrid Laurier University

The structuring and design of organizations is often a topic that students find too abstract and theoretical. They experience a great deal of difficulty understanding the impact that particular organizational structures and specific reward, control, measurement, and information systems have on individual behavior and on organizational performance. Using cases and news reports about Club Med's evolution in organization design and structure as prototypes, we have developed an exercise that involves students in the design and redesign of an organization as it is transformed from a simple, single-site enterprise to a complex, multinational business.

Suitable for both undergraduate and graduate students, the exercise requires students to work in small groups to design the structure and systems of a resort business as it grows from one location to more than 100 different sites over a period of almost 40 years. Students grope with discovering the solutions to the problems of differentiation and integration, of control, of operating in a variety of cultural rather than national contexts, and of responding with strategic and organization design changes to shifts in the competitive environment. The five-stage exercise can be done in one quick-paced 3-hour session or extended over two or more shorter class periods to explore all of these issues in as complex a fashion as the instructor desires. Instructors may also choose to modify the suggested times and discussion questions to deal in greater detail with the concerns related to a particular type of structure or a stage in organization evolution.

When we use this exercise with undergraduates, the students begin to translate their abstract textbook knowledge into a simple, concrete example to which the class can refer again and again. We find the exercise as effective with graduate students. Here, the teaching focus is on bringing students with a wide variety of experiences working inside organization structures

to a common conceptual understanding of the contingencies of structure and design.

The steps in the exercise (see the appendix) follow the evolution of the resort as it grows from 1 to 2 to 5 then to 80 and to more than 100 different locations spread all over the globe. At each stage, students are given a brief description of the business and questions that help them focus their efforts as they work in small groups to design the organization. Groups present their plans to the rest of the class and discuss the organizational issues and problems that their designs address. We usually assign chapters from a text; classic articles, such as those by Duncan (1979), Greiner (1972), or Lawler (1988), could also be included. Before beginning the exercise, instructors might read the case titled *Club Mediterranée* (Horovitz, 1981).

In the first step, the establishment of the initial resort, students typically draw a simple functional organization with a president/chief executive officer; vice presidents of marketing, human resources, customer services, finance, and operations; a managerial layer; and line staff. A detailed discussion of what functions should be included is often beneficial because students tend to underestimate the number of different functions that an organization of this type needs. We usually ask students who have visited a resort to describe their experiences and spend some time brainstorming jobs and tasks. At this first stage, students usually omit a board of directors, which can lead to a brief exploration of governance/ownership/stakeholder issues, but the discussion generally focuses on the functional approach to organizational structure and its advantages. Although we have included some discussion questions in our instructions at each step to focus students' attention on issues to explore, these can be amended or replaced with questions more suited to your purposes. For example, we commonly ask the following at each stage: What type of structure have you drawn? Why is it appropriate? What problems are you trying to address with this structure (system)? How does this structure (system) relate to your strategy?

At the second stage, the addition of a second resort, we usually ask one group to present its design and then ask if

Author's Note: Correspondence should be addressed to the authors, School of Business and Economics, Wilfrid Laurier University, Waterloo, Ontario, Canada N2L 3C5; (phone) 519–884–0710, ext. 2557 (Harvey) or 2485 (Morouney), (fax) 519–884–0201, (e-mail) charvey@wlu.ca or kmoroune@wlu.ca.

From *Journal of Management Education*, June 1998, pp. 425-429. © 1998 by Sage Publications Inc. Reprinted by permission.

anyone did it differently. Students typically replicate the existing structure and add to the hierarchy by creating a supervisory layer at each of the two locations. Whereas most also replicate the existing strategy, some change the focus of the second club by locating it in a different climate or targeting different clientele. Have they made corresponding changes in the clubs' respective designs? A discussion of the issues of centralization versus decentralization and of strategy as a determinant of structure can begin at this stage.

Students either extend the structure of the previous stage in the third stage of development as the number of resorts expands to five or they begin to differentiate a corporate and a geographic structure, centralizing some functions such as finance, human resources, and marketing. They spend time discussing the club's strategy and its customer focus. The discussion of this step can explore centralization/decentralization; differentiation/integration; organization culture and structure; the role of human resource systems, control, and information systems in organization design; and size as a structural determinant.

In response to the organization's evolution 20 years later in the fourth stage, students usually identify the following issues: duplication of functions, centralization/decentralization, differentiation/integration, and information needs. They usually move toward a hybrid or a matrix structure to meet the needs of geographic diversity and/or market segmentation. Discus-

sion focuses on control versus autonomy, training and culture as adjuncts to structure, and the strategy-structure link.

With the last step, as the business copes with significant changes in its circumstances, the emphasis is on the generation of issues and on the relationship of structure to strategy, size, environment, culture, job design, and systems design. A discussion on the evolution of organization design based on Greiner (1972), Duncan (1979), Lawler (1988), Miles and Snow (1994), and Galbraith (1995) concludes and summarizes the exercise.

Instructors can make the exercise more or less complex by focusing only on structural transformations and ignoring systems design, examining questions related to running businesses in diverse cultures, emphasizing strategic decisions and their structure and design implications, and exploring their own particular views of the most relevant determinants of structure and design.

Students invariably enjoy the exercise, and their group discussions are vigorous. For both those students who have not had very much working experience and for those who have, the exercise serves to clarify the theoretical material they have read as they try to understand the logic of their own structuring decisions. Students with work experience use the exercise as an opportunity to vividly describe the influences of structure on their own organizational behavior, and these personal stories contribute to an understanding of some of the trade-offs of organization design.

Appendix
Organization Structure and Design: The Club Ed Exercise

Objectives

This exercise gives students an overview of the issues involved in designing organizations. Students explore the structural alternatives and organizational systems options that are available as they design and redesign a changing organization to resolve issues resulting from growth, internationalization, and environmental shifts.

Time Required

Approximately 3 to 4 hours, either all at once or distributed over two or more sessions.

Group Size

Any number of groups of three to five persons.

Materials

Five overhead transparency blanks and markers for each group of students. Hole-punch the transparency blanks if the exercise will carry over several classes.

The Steps

Step 1: 20 minutes

Determined never to shovel snow again, you are establishing a new resort business on a small Caribbean island. The building of the resort is under way and it is scheduled to open a year from now. You decide it is time to draw up an organizational chart for this new venture, Club Ed. What jobs do you need to have covered? What tasks need to be done? What services will you provide? Work in small groups to draw your organization chart and be prepared to present your design and to answer the following questions: What should it include? and Why should it look like this?

Step 2: 20 to 30 minutes

Your instructor will select one or two groups to present their designs and lead the class discussion.

Step 3: 15 minutes

You are into your 3rd year of operation, and the club is wildly successful. You begin to think of expanding with a second club. Where would you locate this second resort? Should it be just like the first? How would you manage running the two? Work out your ideas on paper, drawing up an organization chart that includes two clubs.

Step 4: 15 minutes

Group presentation and class discussion.

Step 5: 20 to 30 minutes

Five more years go by, and you would not recognize a snow shovel if you saw one. You now own five Club Eds. Where have you expanded to, and how do you keep in touch with it all? What are your biggest problems to date? Have you dealt with them in your structure? How have your human resource, control, and information systems developed? Draw an up-to-date organizational chart and prepare to explain your rationale to your classmates.

Step 6: 20 to 30 minutes

Two group presentations and discussion in the whole class.

Step 7: 20 to 30 minutes

Twenty years later, you and your partners own 80 Club Eds, spread in a variety of South American, Central and North American, Caribbean, and South Pacific locations. What are the current issues and problems that have to be dealt with through Club Ed's organizational structure? What should the structure be?

Step 8: 20 to 30 minutes

Group presentations and class discussion.

Step 9: 20 to 30 minutes

Ten years pass. The Club is now in 112 locations and operates 3 cruise ships. A recent customer profile shows that almost 50% of its customers are repeat business and are older than 40 years old. The three "S's" (sun, sand or snow, and sex) marketing theme is out of date in a world where AIDS and fears of skin cancer are all too real. Reservations have been down over the past several seasons as the recession recovery sputters repeatedly. How does Club Ed restructure to adapt?

Step 10: 20 to 30 minutes

Group presentations and class discussion.

Discussion Questions

1. How does the nature of an organization's technology influence organization design?
2. How can we measure the effectiveness of Club Ed? How does feedback on effectiveness influence organization design?
3. How can Club Ed structure itself as an adaptive organization? Does it always have to react to environmental changes or are there some ways it can be proactive?

References

Duncan, R. (1979, winter). What is the right organizational structure? *Organizational Dynamics*, pp. 59–80.

Galbraith, J. R. (1995). *Designing organizations.* San Francisco: Jossey-Bass.

Greiner, L. E. (1972). Evolution and revolution as organizations grow. *Harvard Business Review, 50*, 37–46.

Horovitz, J. (1981). *Club Mediterranée.* Lausanne, Switzerland: IMEDE.

Lawler, E. E. (1988). Substitutes for hierarchy. *Organizational Dynamics, 17*(1), 5–15.

Miles, R. E., & Snow, C. C. (1994). *Fit, failure and the hall of fame.* New York: Free Press.

Unit 5

Key Points to Consider

❖ How can organizations change to meet the continuing changes in the environment?

❖ What impact will the international economy have on organizations?

❖ Name the ways that corporate mergers across international borders effect organizations.

❖ How does change affect members of organizations? What is the impact of stress?

❖ Why is synergy sought by organizations?

 **Links**

www.dushkin.com/online/

These sites are annotated on pages 4 and 5.

Organizations must change and develop to meet the changing environment in which they exist. Two things are certain: (1) the environment will change, and (2) the organization will change. The question is how the organization can change to successfully meet the changes in the environment. History is full of once highly successful organizations that have ended on the ash heap of history. In 1920, the Pennsylvania Railroad was the third largest corporation in the United States. Today, there is no Pennsylvania Railroad. This is not to say that the functions and tasks that it once performed have ceased; they continue to be performed by Amtrak and Conrail. What it does say is that the Pennsylvania Railroad, at the height of its success, did not do what it needed to do to survive. Conditions changed and alternative means of transportation for both freight and passengers became available; including an interstate highway system. The Pennsylvania Railroad remained a railroad and the company declined into bankruptcy.

Today, organizations are constantly trying to change in an effort to meet a changing environment. Corporations merge, divest, privatize, go public, in what seems to be endless machination of buyouts and takeovers with little or no thought given to what the long-term consequences will be down the road. Just because a merger is hailed by Wall Street does not mean it will be successful in the long run. Chrysler Corporation's purchase of American Motors a few years ago looks like a great success for Chrysler, but it remains to be seen if the more recent merger with Daimler-Benz will pay dividends. It is, perhaps, one of the great ironies of multinational corporations that the Jeep, the most successful and identifiably American product to come out of World War II, is now owned, produced, and marketed by a German company.

To prosper, organizations must change, especially in a highly sophisticated and technologically advanced society. Because of this rapid change, it is necessary for companies to become learning organizations. How to do that is discussed by Swee Goh in "Toward a Learning Organization: The Strategic Building Blocks." These changes can be implemented in organizations, but to do so requires a real commitment to change.

Perhaps the biggest single challenge to organizations is the international economy that exists today. This segment of the economy has grown significantly over the past 30 years. In the early 1970s and late 1960s international trade represented less than 10 percent of the gross national product (GNP), while, today, it accounts for over 30 percent. Multinational organizations do not view the world as ending at the national border of their home country. They view it as a global economy where resources, competition, and personnel come from all over the globe. General Motors competes in a worldwide market. It is no accident that Toyota has factories in the United States, because the United States is the largest

automobile market in the world, just as it is no accident that Ford Motor Company has had production facilities in Germany since before World War II.

Multinational organizations must learn that "Building Teams across Borders" (see article 33), is going to be one of their primary activities in the years ahead. For multinational corporations to be truly successful in taking advantage of all of their assets in this highly competitive world, they must avail themselves of all of the talents of all of their employees. Multinationals are faced with the problem of "Integrating Corporate Culture from International M&As." (See article 32.) That cultures in different countries are different is a given in the global economy. Being able to successfully deal with those differences will be a factor that will lead to success. The employees will, of course, have to adapt to the organization and, to a certain extent, the organization will have to adapt to the employees.

One of the consequences that all of this change leads to is emotional stress. Change causes stress, and stress is one of the major health concerns for individuals in an organization. Dealing with stress will no doubt continue into the twenty-first century. Some organizations are trying to help their employees to deal with stress better and, as a result, to become more productive, as Gail Dutton writes in "Cutting-Edge Stressbusters."

One of the things that stress can lead to is burnout. Burnout has many symptoms, among them a lack of enthusiasm for the job, depression, and a general dread of what is going to happen next. Today, burnout is big business with many professional and health care workers involved in this aspect of medicine.

Organizations continue to seek to become more than what they really are. They are constantly seeking advantages over their competition in an effort to become more successful and more profitable. The only way that they can do this is to become greater than just the sum of the parts, and this they must do through their people. In an era where all the major players in an industry have essentially the same equipment, financial resources, and access to the same raw materials, the only way to build a lasting competitive advantage is by having the best people do the job, and the way to maximize those efforts is to create synergy in an organization. Corporations are "Desperately Seeking Synergy" (see article 35) in an effort to become increasingly more competitive. This does not mean that all attempts at seeking synergy are successful, because they are not. But, it does mean that organizations will continue to attempt to create situations where the whole is greater than the sum of the parts. Companies need to continue to attempt to create synergy if they want to be successful, because it is only through the maximum use of their human assets that they can hope to achieve competitive advantage and prosper in the coming millennium.

Toward a Learning Organization: The Strategic Building Blocks

Swee C. Goh, *Faculty of Administration, University of Ottawa*

The literature on organizational learning has been elusive in providing practical guidelines or managerial actions that practicing managers can implement to develop a learning organization. Some of the questions raised by managers about the concept of a learning organization are as follows: What is a learning organization? What are the payoffs of becoming a learning organization? What should I do to encourage organizational learning? How do I know if my company is a learning organization? What are the characteristics of a learning organization and how do I sustain one? Is there an implementation strategy? Clearly a discussion with a managerial perspective on how to build a learning organization is lacking in the literature.

To answer the first and most frequently asked question, "What is a learning organization?", we need a definition. The following definition best reflects the conceptual approach of this paper:

> *A learning organization is an organization skilled at creating, acquiring and transferring knowledge, and at modifying its behavior to reflect new knowledge and insights (Garvin, 1993).*

This working definition is only a starting point. More important is the need to explain how to become a learning organization, not what it is. This paper will develop an organizational archetype of a learning organization to focus on some of the details of how to build one.

Before getting to this, we need to answer a second frequently asked question which is, Can a learning organization improve my bottom line results? A manager promoting the concept should be ready to answer this question. One approach is to ask whether the organization is looking for a short-term or long-term results. Organizational learning is a long-term activity that will build competitive advantage over time and requires sustained management attention, commitment, and effort. A list of companies frequently cited as learning organizations confirms this fact. These companies include Motorola, Wal-Mart, British Petroleum (BP), Xerox, Shell, Analog Devices, GE, 3M, Honda, Sony, Nortel, Harley-Davidson, Corning, Kodak, and Chaparral Steel. Not only have these organizations maximized their competitive positions in good times, they have been carefully nurtured in turbulent times. As a result, these companies are envied by their competitors (de Geus, 1988; McGill, Slocum & Lei, 1993; Leonard-Barton, 1992).

Studies have shown that long-term investments in these companies would have given an investor spectacular returns. More to the point, these companies were built to last and have been managed effectively since their founding (Collins & Porras, 1994).

To address the other questions mentioned about how to build learning organizations, over 80 published articles and books on the learning organizations were reviewed. My involvement with nine different organizations in helping them measure and build their learning capability has also provided additional insights (Goh & Richards, 1997). Information from interviews, discussions with senior managers, and focus groups with employees were also part of this review process.

From *SAM Advanced Management Journal*, Vol. 63, No. 2, Spring 1998, pp. 15-22. © 1998 by the Society for Advancement of Management, Texas A&M University Corpus Christi, College of Business, 6300 Ocean Drive, FC111, Corpus Christi, TX 78412.

The objective of this paper is similar to the tradition of human resources practices research, that is, to identify a bundle of managerial practices and organizational processes that differentiate these learning companies. Current research shows that identifiable bundles of human resource management practices are linked to organizational performance (Pfeffer, 1994). Selected literature from this area was also reviewed to provide further insights about managerial practices in a learning organization.

A Matter of Perspective?

A premise of our approach is that all organizations can learn. Some learn better than others and survive, while the more successful learners thrive. Those that fail to learn will eventually disappear (Nevis, Dibella & Gold, 1995). The role of leaders in organizations is to set the necessary conditions for the organization to develop an effective learning capability. That is, managers need to take strategic action and make specific interventions to ensure that learning can occur (Shaw & Perkins, 1991). For example, introducing mechanisms to facilitate the transfer of knowledge between work teams and developing a widely shared vision supported by employees can influence the learning capability of an organization.

This normative perspective suggests that a set of internal conditions is required for an organization to become a learning organization. This paper will describe a set of managerial practices or strategic building blocks of a learning organization. In addition, the paper will discuss the supportive organization design needed and the required competencies of employees as key foundation building blocks of a learning organization.

Strategic Architecture of a Learning Organization

David Garvin (1994) suggests that it is time to move away from high aspirations and mystical advice to managers and move on to clearer guidelines for practices and operational advice. He argues that we need to inform managers how they can build a learning organization. Successful learning companies like Honda, Corning, and GE have managed their learning capability to ensure that it occurs by design rather than by chance. These companies have implemented unique policies and managerial practices that have made them successful learning organizations.

In essence, being a learning organization requires an understanding of the strategic internal drivers needed to build a learning capability (Stata, 1989). This paper synthesizes the description of management practices and policies alluded to in the literature about learning organizations. Only those mentioned repeatedly by many writers were considered as differentiating management practices of an effective learning organization. From this review, it is argued that learning organizations have the following core strategic building blocks:

1. **Mission and Vision**—Clarity and employee support of the mission, strategy, and espoused values of the organization.
2. **Leadership**—Leadership that is perceived as empowering employees, encouraging an experimenting culture, and showing strong commitment to the organization.
3. **Experimentation**—A strong culture of experimentation that is rewarded and supported at all levels in the organization.
4. **Transfer of Knowledge**—The ability of an organization to transfer knowledge within and from outside the organization and to learn from failures.
5. **Teamwork and Cooperation**—An emphasis on teamwork and group problem-solving as the mode of operation and for developing innovative ideas.

Although presented as separate dimensions, these building blocks are interdependent and mutually supportive conditions in a learning organization. It is further argued that an "organic" organization structure, where job formalization is low, as well as the acquisition of appropriate skills and knowledge by employees are also essential additional building blocks. These additional elements are the supporting foundation for the achievement of the core building blocks in the list. Figure 1 illustrates the new organizational archetype and the strategic and foundation building blocks of a learning organization. Each one of these strategic building blocks is now discussed in more detail.

1. Clarity and Support for Mission and Vision

A learning organization is one where employees are empowered to act based on the relevant knowledge and skills they have acquired and information about the priorities of the organization. According to Senge (1990), information about the mission of an organization is critical to empowering employees and developing innovative organizations. Without this, people will not extend themselves to take responsibilities or apply their creative energies.

Having a clear mission that is supported by employees is, therefore, a critical strategic building block of a learning organization. If this is widely shared and understood by employees they will feel more capable of taking initiatives. A clear understanding will mean actions that are aligned with the organization's goals and mission. GE and Motorola are good examples of companies where senior managers and the CEO

Figure 1: THE NEW ORGANIZATIONAL ARCHETYPE

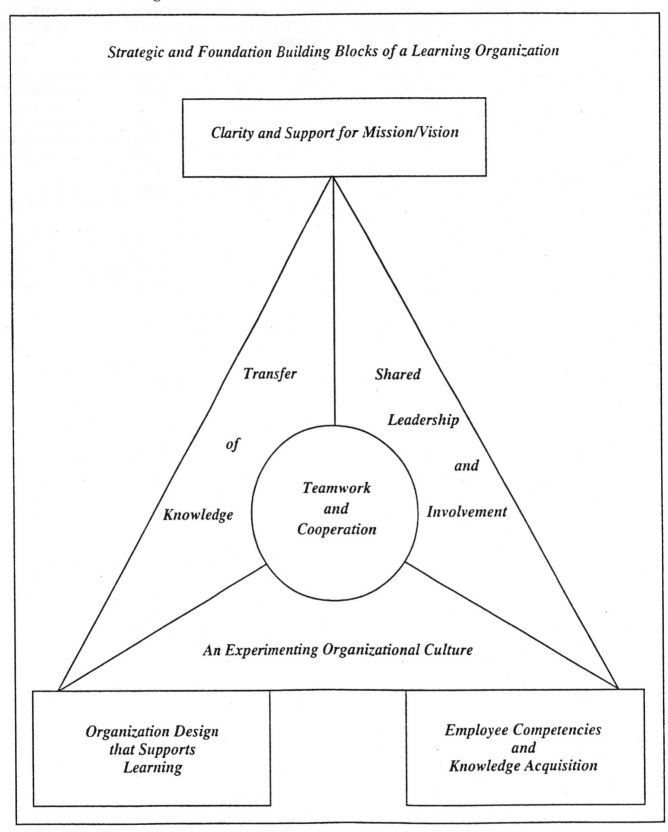

spend considerable time articulating a vision and creating employee commitment to achieving it.

2. Shared Leadership and Involvement

In a highly competitive environment, employees are encouraged to take calculated risks, to deal with uncertainty, and to innovate. Such an environment requires a shared leadership style in a nonhierarchical organization. Managers are seen as coaches, not controllers; level or rank is not as important as the ability of the individual to contribute to the organization's performance. Leaders need the skills to facilitate change. Leaders should also be able to provide useful feedback to employees and teams to help them identify problems and opportunities. Leadership in a learning organization means involving employees in decision-making. Leaders should also be willing to accept criticism without being overly defensive and to learn from it.

Nortel has frequent training sessions and workshops that include all levels of employees. The sponsoring senior manager for the workshop is always present. These managers will participate fully in the workshop, interacting with employees during activities in the session and soliciting ideas and input from them. This sends a powerful signal to employees of the nonhierarchical and shared participative leadership being practiced at Nortel. It also creates a common experience and the development of shared mental models about problems and issues in the organization (Senge, 1990).

3. A Culture that Encourages Experimentation

An important if not essential part of a learning organization is its ability to create new knowledge and to use it to capitalize on new opportunities open to the organization. This requires questioning the current status quo and how things are done, which allows employees to bring new ideas into the organization. Managers should also be willing to encourage individuals and teams to continuously improve work processes and try new ideas. Obviously a system should be in place to reward innovative ideas that work.

The notion of "skunk works," where time and resources are set aside for employees to engage in creative pet projects are all part of management practice to encourage an experimenting culture. Hewlett-Packard and 3M are excellent examples of organizations with an experimenting culture. At 3M, experimentation is not only encouraged but is built into the activities of individual employees in the organization. Such activities include allowing a percentage of work time for employees to pursue an unusual personal project. In the case of Hewlett-Packard, time-activated obsolescence of products is a strategy used to ensure continuous experimentation, product improvement, and the development of innovative new products.

4. Ability to Transfer Knowledge Across Organizational Boundaries

Skill and knowledge acquisition are obviously useless unless they can be transferred to the immediate job by the employee. It is even better if this knowledge can also be transferred to other parts of the organization to solve problems and energize creative new ideas. Learning from past failures and talking to other staff members about successful practices or experiences are all part of the transfer of knowledge. Learning organizations not only encourage these practices but also have mechanisms or systems that allow them to happen. Part of this knowledge transfer involves learning successful practices from other organizations and competitors as well.

Xerox and AT&T have developed benchmarking processes that are good examples of encouraging knowledge transfer. Both companies have programs that benchmark the managerial practices of the best companies in an industry and their competitors. This encourages the transfer of knowledge about what competitors and other companies are doing that could be applied or emulated at Xerox or AT&T. Such benchmarking activities guarantee that they are always learning to improve their management processes, and their products or services.

5. Teamwork and Cooperation

Without doubt a key strategic building block for a learning organization is an emphasis on teamwork. By working in teams, employees bring their collective skills and knowledge to bear on problems and to develop innovative ideas for the organization. To be effective, teams should be formed with employees from a variety of functional areas. A cross-functional teamwork environment breaks down the stovepipe syndrome, especially if employees are frequently rotated among different teams as part of a deliberate career development program and human resource management policy.

Honda is the best example of a learning company with a strong focus on teamwork and cooperation. Employees are cross-trained for many activities so that they can be rotated to different teams. At the Honda plant in Alliston, a human resources associate can also work on the assembly line if needed. Problems and work-related issues are shared by members of each team every morning to encourage a group problem-solving approach.

Supporting Foundations

The five strategic building blocks require two major supporting foundations. First, there has to be an effective organization design that is aligned with and supports these building blocks. Second, appropriate employee skills and competencies are needed for the tasks and roles described in the strategic building blocks.

• *Organizational Design*

The organization structure of learning organizations has been described in the literature as organic, flat, and decentralized, with a minimum of formalized procedures in the work environment. Some research has supported this finding: organizations with a strong learning capability tend to have low scores on formalization in their organization structure. These research results clearly show a negative relationship between formalization and learning capability (Goh & Richards, 1997).

Other researchers (Mohrman and Mohrman, Jr., 1995) have also found that learning organizations generally have fewer controls on employees and have a flat organization structure that places work teams close to the ultimate decision-makers. The implication is that the five strategic building blocks can only operate effectively when the organization has a flat, non-hierarchical structure with minimal formalized controls over employee work processes.

• *Employee Skills and Competencies*

The literature on learning organizations frequently asserts that these organizations strongly emphasize the training and skill development of their employees. However, the training is not in the traditional mode of individual job-focused skills. Learning organizations invest in training experiences that develop entire teams or whole work units. The training also emphasizes the development of a common experience, framework, or theory of action for the team or work unit (Mohrman & Mohrman, Jr., 1995).

To build a learning capability, all five of the strategic building blocks require specific skill sets for employees and managers. Skill competencies also need to match some of the behavioral skill sets required in a learning organization, such as shared leadership, coaching behaviors, and providing feedback. Learning organizations also start their training of employees more toward behavioral skills and less toward technical skills that have a short shelf-life (Kiernan, 1993).

Xerox is a good example of this. It implemented a group training program for all employees at all levels in the organization called "Leadership Through Quality." The training was focused on learning how to work in teams and on a problem-solving process that is applied throughout Xerox. Increases in employee skills and competencies in these two areas have had an enormous impact and have produced gains for Xerox in product quality and customer service.

Measurement and Intervention

Building a learning organization requires an organization to focus on and implement these five major strategic building blocks and to ensure that the two supporting foundations are aligned to facilitate learning. As described, this requires a shift in the cognitive and behavioral skills of managers and employees. Deliberate interventions in the organization design and an appropriate training and skill development program should also be implemented to reinforce employee learning.

To move in the direction of this new organizational archetype, a measurement process is needed to diagnose the current learning capability of the organization against these five yardsticks. A survey measure has been developed that can assess organizations on these five building blocks and supporting foundations (Goh & Richards, 1997). Such an instrument can be used as the starting point for determining the existing learning capability of an organization. Results from the survey can also identify the weak strategic building blocks for change intervention.

The current organization design and the skill development program also need to be assessed and evaluated to ensure that they are aligned and provide support to the strategic building blocks. Following these assessments, the organization can then design a series of intervention strategies to increase the overall strength of these building blocks, so it can move closer to the archetype described in this paper. Obviously, the intervention strategies should be tailored to the circumstances and constraints facing the organization and to the assessment results. An example would be the introduction of Lotus Notes to share best practices as an intervention to improve knowledge transfer in an organization.

Lastly, managers should track and measure the organization's performance improvement after the interventions have taken place. There should be measurable improvements in service delivery, successful innovation of new products, product quality, and other tangible gains (Garvin, 1994). The organization should be remeasured as well to determine whether overall learning capability has also improved.

Conclusion

In summary, the paper suggests that these five strategic building blocks and the supporting foundations are the key factors in this new organizational archetype called a learning organization. These building blocks and supporting foundations need to be present or to be implemented to have a learning capability. However, if this idea of a learning organization is to take hold in organizations and gain credence and support by practicing managers, it must also have an impact on organizational performance.

The archetype presented in this paper describes the specific strategic and foundation building blocks and measurement and intervention processes that are required to become a learning organization. This should allow managers to take practical actions, initiatives, and interventions needed to build a learning organization and to measure their success in achieving this outcome. Building a strong learning capability is crucial for knowledge-intensive organizations and for companies operating in a highly competitive environment. As stated by Stata (1989), the rate at which individuals and organizations learn may become the only sustainable competitive advantage in the future.

Dr. Goh focuses on the measurement and implementation of organizational learning in public and private sector organizations and also on the management of large-scale organizational transformations; he has published in several journals, including the Academy of Management Journal and International Journal of Management.

REFERENCES

Collins, J., & Porras, J. (1994). *Built to last: Successful habits of visionary companies.* New York: Harper Collins.

de Geus, A. P. (1988, March–April). Planning as learning. *Harvard Business Review,* 70–74.

Garvin, D. (1993, July–August). Building learning organizations. *Harvard Business Review,* 78–91.

Goh, S. C., & Richards, G. (in press). Benchmarking the learning capability of organizations. *European Management Journal.*

Kiernan, M. (1993). The new strategic architecture: Learning to compete in the twenty-first century. *The Academy of Management Executive,* 7–21.

Leonard-Barton, D. (1992, Fall). The factory as a learning laboratory. *Sloan Management Review,* 23–38.

McGill, M., Slocum, Jr., J., & Lei, D. (1993, Autumn). Management practices in learning organizations. *Organizational Dynamics,* 67–79.

Mohrman, S., & Mohrman, Jr., A. (1995). Organizational change and learning. In I. Galbraith and E. Lawler (eds.), *Organizing for the future: The new logic for managing complex organizations* (pp. 87–109). Jossey-Bass Publishers.

Nevis, E. C., Dibella, A., & Gould, Jr. (1995, Winter). Understanding organizations as learning systems. *Sloan Management Review,* 73–85.

Pfeffer, J. (1994). *Competitive advantage through people.* Boston: Harvard University Press.

Senge, P. (1990, Fall). The leader's new work: Building learning organizations. *Sloan Management Review,* 7–23.

Shaw, R., & Perkins, D. (1991, Winter). Teaching organizations to learn. *Organization Development Journal,* 1–12.

Stata, R. (1989, Spring). Organizational learning—The key to management innovation. *Sloan Management Review,* 63–74.

Integrating Corporate Culture from International M&As

There are many positive outcomes from a business merger or acquisition: reducing costs by eliminating expenditures for redundant resources; cost efficiencies derived from increased buying power; increased revenue by cross-selling products to each other's customers; and combining product lines to provide more comprehensive offerings and capture greater market share. It's also no secret that in exchange, there are numerous human resources, technology, financial, legal and marketing issues related to integration that need to be resolved.

But if you're venturing into the international arena, a whole new set of challenges await you, and these issues demand special treatment and attention. Many international companies, such as Citicorp, Merrill Lynch, Bank of Montreal, Johnson & Johnson, Motorola, Inc. and Chase Manhattan can attest to that fact as they deal with their own international M&A. The fundamental challenges are often rooted in differences in culture. At such times, HR executives are confronted with situations that, due to a "totally different way of doing things," are seemingly impossible to surmount. Without proper intervention, there are feelings of loss of identity and the overwhelming experience of learning new "rules" for doing business and relating with coworkers from sometimes vastly different cultures.

The amount of organizational integration in a merger or acquisition falls along a continuum. At one end of the spectrum is a complete integration of one organization's systems and processes into the other, and the adoption of the acquiring organization's name and identity. At the other end exists an almost virtual segregation of the two organizations. Which model is most appropriate for a given situation depends on factors such as the similarity of the organizations, their financial status,

OPERATIONAL STRATEGIES & TACTICS FOR SUCCESSFUL INTEGRATION

EXECUTIVE SPONSORSHIP

✔ Elevate and profile initiative

✔ Inspire desired behaviors by actions supporting the initiative

✔ Structure leadership incentives for senior managers

✔ Ensure accountability for results among senior managers

✔ Appoint project manager; endorse project leadership team

PROJECT MANAGER

✔ Create, articulate and execute project vision, strategy and tactics

✔ Ensure cross-functional alignment with project strategy

✔ Deliver and execute project implementation plan

✔ Structure communications and planning process for the initiative

PROJECT LEADERSHIP TEAM

✔ Establish a leadership team (i.e., core project team) composed of senior representatives from product areas, market research, market development, finance, marketing communications, regulatory, etc.

✔ Deliver a consistent, "one company" image to the market

✔ Tap resources and expertise as needed

✔ Ensure accountability for results in their area of responsibility

✔ Inspire desired behaviors supporting initiatives within their area of responsibility

markets, competitors, core values, management practices and policies. What works for one M&A could spell disaster for another, as failure to integrate the different entities can lead to organizational splintering, service duplication, overall inefficiency in resource utilization, and failure to retain key players.

A U.S.-based financial services company, in the throes of pursuing worldwide markets through an aggressive acquisition campaign, recognized the need to develop a very structured process to ensure timely and effective acquisition integration. Evaluation of its culture revealed the following potential problem areas:

➤ **Insufficient clarity regarding roles and responsibilities.** This led to turf wars and service duplication. Managers, receiving unclear definitions of tasks to be completed, were left to operate under old dictates and guidelines. Department heads noted repetition and "competition" in services provided due to a lack of communication.

➤ **Lack of a common vision and purpose.** The acquiring company had been guided by the vision of a local, highly personal service organization. Upon "marrying" the new companies, this vision had to be adapted to include a global, more sophisticated and consistent approach without jeopardizing local responsiveness.

➤ **No new detailed business strategies.** Lack of clear direction left the acquired companies in a semi-holding pattern, creating unnecessary anxiety for both staff and customers.

➤ **No documented linkage to core systems.** This prohibited a smooth transition and modification of existing systems in acquired companies. For example, customer databases needed to be combined under one system and structure.

➤ **No expectations of acquisition's outcomes.** Grapevines surfaced that staff of the acquired companies would be labeled "extraneous" and be left without jobs with the newly formed entity. Immediate intervention was required to correct this misconception.

FOUR STEPS TO SUCCESSFUL INTEGRATION

1 ESTABLISH THE PURPOSE, GOAL AND FOCUS OF THE MERGER. This is the time to develop a new corporate mission, vision and strategic objectives where appropriate. In addition, it is imperative to integrate communications, human resources, information materials and other critical operating systems.

2 ADOPT A PROJECT MANAGEMENT ORIENTATION. The new company must develop mechanisms to identify the most appropriate organizational structures and management roles.

3 ESTABLISH THE FIRM NOTION OF SPONSORSHIP AND MEMBERSHIP. The sponsor is the ultimate client who has initiated the project and has ultimate control over the internal resources required to get things done. Members are involved directly or indirectly and must include representatives from key constituent groups that have a stake in the project outcome. (See sidebar for additional strategies and tactics.)

4 CONSIDER THE MANAGEMENT OF COMMUNICATIONS AND EXPECTATIONS. In the absence of specific communication, grapevines will prevail. Employees will assume the worst in the face of ambiguity. A project management orientation facilitates communication between departments and individual interests, discouraging such grapevines from taking root. Specialists (e.g., HR, legal, regulatory, marketing, etc.) remain responsible in their respective areas, but are encouraged to integrate with other departments. They are required to think through the ramifications of their actions with respect to the other "pieces of the puzzle" and to examine their own functional orientation. Systematic steps to manage communications and expectations are:

➤ Identify the people who need to be aware of, can support, or will participate with your efforts. Team leaders can oversee facets of each department, allowing the project manager to work on a macro level, gathering information from several members simultaneously.

➤ Anticipate their situations, styles and reactions, and formulate plans for "bringing them on board," using an approach which allows stake holders an opportunity for input and involvement. Make sure verbal or written confirmation is provided any time an exchange includes future actions, as to what the actions are, and who will perform them.

➤ Set specific target dates or deadlines for any follow-up or actions the parties have agreed to take. Develop a system for efficiently keeping the involved parties informed of progress. Newsletters, inter- and intradepartmental memos and informal lunch meetings were vehicles used to facilitate the communication of vital updates. Find ways to give recognition, thanks or credit for assistance or contributions.

MAINTAINING CONTROL

In even the smoothest of M&A transitions, speed bumps are bound to surface. It is essential during these times to monitor and maintain control of the cultural integration process. Due to the very

> **Even in the smoothest M&A transitions, speed bumps are bound to surface.**

nature of M&As, competing agendas are likely to exist. Some straightforward tactics can help you manage these conflicts with ease.

Explain the situation in a descriptive, non-evaluative manner. Keep the facts in front of all audiences. Schedule regular update meetings and open forums, supplemented by newsletters and memos, to keep rumors to a minimum. Emphasize the common goals, objectives and desired outcomes. Management at all levels plays a key role in creating dialogue about new goals and individual accountabilities in achieving them. Focusing on a shared future minimizes fear and anxiety. Finally, acknowledge other agendas and concerns. Honestly confronting questions of job loss and change-related anxiety to keep positive momentum.

The tasks laid before HR management in times of international M&As are monumental. Companies all over the world are finding out firsthand that there is more to an international merger or acquisition than just sharing resources and capturing greater market share. Differences in workplace cultures sometimes temporarily overshadow the overall goal of long-term success of the newly formed entity. With the proper management framework and execution, successful integration of cultures is not only possible, but the most preferable paradigm in which to operate. It is the role of the sponsors and managers to keep sight of the necessity to create, maintain and support the notion of a united front. It is only when this assimilation has occurred that an international merger or acquisition can truly be labeled a success.

RITA E. NUMEROF is president and *MICHAEL N. ABRAMS* is vice president of Numerof Associates in St. Louis, Mo.

Building Teams Across Borders

Today your organization may have the technology to make global teams a reality. But all the wiring in the world won't be enough if you haven't started with a solid foundation.

By Charlene Marmer Solomon

Admit it. If you think about it, global teams are probably one of the toughest games around, with little chance to succeed. And if you're really honest about it, you'd confess that it's astounding when intercultural teams have any success at all. Luckily, they do. And the credit, in no small measure, goes to the managers—both HR and line—who realize what a complex task awaits the global team. They improve the odds by providing tools to help team members make their groups work.

Global teams come in various configurations. Generally, they fall into one of two categories: *intercultural teams,* in which people from different cultures meet face-to-face to work on a project, and *virtual global teams,* in which individuals remain in their separate locations around the world and conduct meetings via different forms of technology. Obviously, both kinds are fraught with enormous challenges.

Given the communications and cultural obstacles, what do companies gain from these units? Teams help global companies, preventing them from needing to reinvent the game with each new project. They enable organizations to realize 24-hour productivity via the latest in technology. They allow cross-pollination between cultures as well as business units, adding depth of knowledge and experience to the endeavor.

But effective global teams are not simple to create or maintain. With myriad challenges—from time and space logistics, to cultural assumptions that no one articulates because each individual believes them to be so universal—teams must continually overcome considerable obstacles. While you may be eager to capitalize on the expertise of individuals from around the world, and even have the technology to do so, it's important to remember that global teams must master the basics, understand the rules, learn to harness both cultural and functional group diversity and become adroit at communication and leadership.

Mastering the basics and understanding the rules.

"Everybody wants to know what's happening at the edge and the next wave of things to come, but we still

---

Charlene Marmer Solomon is a contributing editor for GLOBAL WORKFORCE. *E-mail charsol@aol.com to comment.*

find people who don't do the basics very well," says Mary O'Hara-Devereaux, coauthor with Robert Johansen of *Global Work: Bridging Distance, Culture and Time* (Jossey-Bass Inc., 1994). "People need some understanding of what a team is—the variations of the team's work and the variety of cultures that are on it, ways to communicate effectively, and how to work with distributed leadership so that everyone on the team has leadership roles."

Covering the basics means ensuring everyone associated with the venture appreciates the difficulties involved with participating in a global team. There should be solid business reasons for forming one. And it's important that team members and associated managers understand the following considerations:

• The team champion should have the mandate to choose the people with the right skills for the job.

• The team should have measurable goals that participants have had the opportunity to discuss and agree with.

• Meetings must have clearly established objectives and predetermined agendas.

• Team members must make time to discuss the lines of communication. What methods will members use to communicate? Does everyone have equal access to the communication? (See "Make the Most of Teleconferencing" and "Develop an E-mail Protocol.")

• Participants should recognize the role of language difficulties and manner of speaking in cross-border teams. For example, individuals from various English-speaking countries will speak in different dialects that may be troublesome for some members. Allow time for group members to acclimate to each other.

• Members must realize that people need to understand each other's differences before they can effectively come together as a group. Teambuilding sessions and cross-cultural training can help with this.

Of course there's a lot more to creating a team than a simple list of do's and don'ts. Clear expectations, defined responsibilities and an appreciation of cultural differences are among the basics to be accomplished by each team at the outset. Every member must know and comprehend the business objectives, understand the timetables and agree to follow a set of team rules. These are basic elements to success, but they require time and careful consideration if the team is going to consent and abide by them.

Fairfax, Virginia-based Mobil Corp. knows this lesson first-hand. About 10 years ago, Mobil undertook a companywide study and determined that it had to change significantly if it was going to be able to remain a profitable oil company in a volatile marketplace. Its assessment initiated global teams. The company realized that these work groups maximize an individual's knowledge by sharing it throughout the company with others via natural work teams, as well as transferring best practices within the company. In other words, the best practices from one group would be carried to another via team members.

With more than 43,000 employees—only 16,500 of whom are in the United States—and with operations in more than 140 countries, most natural work teams have representation from all over the world, such as the Speed-Pass™ program initiated by Mobil in the United States.

Working with Texas Instruments, Mobil developed electronic transaction payment systems for service stations. These are like bank debit cards that are customer-activated at pay-at-the-pump terminals. Mobil first tested Speed-Pass™ in the States with excellent results. The next step was to form a global team to lob that learning from one country to another.

"A project champion, who was the individual who had implemented SpeedPass™ in the U.S., was in charge of creating the team with others from the Fuels Advisory Council who nominated individuals to participate," recalls Bill Cummings, who represented Japan on the team and is currently Mobil's media relations advisor at the U.S. headquarters. Desiring cross-pollination, Mobil charged the individual who had successfully implemented Speed-

Make the Most of Teleconferencing

Teleconferences are so much a part of conducting everyday business that it's easy to forget the basics of making these communications work effectively. Here are some ideas for intercultural teams.

• Obtain the best equipment within budget. The quality of sound varies tremendously.

• Be sure all locations have equal access to communications links.

• Allow individuals ample opportunity to learn to use the technology.

• The group should choose a conference leader and rotate that leadership. The leader should make sure the group works as a team and isn't at the mercy of the most vocal individuals.

• Written agendas should be distributed to everyone before the meeting.

• The group should decide ahead of time what the length of the phone conference will be.

• The conference leader should recap the goals of the discussion before starting. He or she should review updates since the last meeting.

• The leader should encourage everyone to participate. If someone is quiet, the leader should try to draw out the individual—or encourage the individual later with a phone call or e-mail.

• The group should be sensitive to time zones. Naturally, someone will be inconvenienced, so it's important to rotate the times meetings are held.

• Someone should write a brief recap of the main points of the conference and distribute it after the call.

—*CMS*

Develop an E-mail Protocol

While e-mail is necessary and beneficial, it's important to recognize that it's a medium that uses only text and offers no visual or nonverbal clues. It's wise to develop an e-mail protocol among global group members, minimizing the chances for misunderstandings when using this tool. Cornelius Grove, partner at Brooklyn-based Cornelius Grove & Associates LLC, offers the following list of considerations as you develop your guidelines.

Topics. Which topics are appropriate for e-mail and which are not? Which topics should be addressed in person or over the phone instead?

Frequency. How frequently should members use e-mail?

Urgency. What constitutes urgency? Is it possible to define the terms "ASAP" and "urgent"?

Participation. Who should participate? Does every team member need to be a recipient of every e-mail?

Showing respect. How can team members demonstrate respect for each other? (This is important with hierarchical cultures.) Are titles necessary?

Time of day. Should there be "blackout" periods when e-mails are not sent or received?

Jokes, profanity, intimacies. What kinds of guidelines should exist regarding topics, language or personal relationships?

Communication guidelines. Should there be guidelines for handling situations that arise in e-mail, but dictate voice-to-voice communication?

—CMS

Pass™ in the U.S. with the project leadership. Not only did this individual choose the team representatives, but he communicated to them that their global expertise was critical to the success of the project. He encouraged them to express their different viewpoints.

For example, it was clear that it had taken 20 years for Americans to move from full-serve to mini-serve to self-serve to pay-at-the-pump. Countries like Japan were still accustomed to full-service. Other countries were at different points along the same journey. Only people who had first-hand knowledge of the cultures of countries such as Japan, Australia and Singapore could help take this U.S. best practice and transplant it successfully overseas.

"The concept of taking lessons learned and applying them across as many different countries, cultures and experiences as possible is a fundamental part of Mobil's corporate culture," says Cummings. "Clearly, individuals from the different regions would bring their cultural know-how and business perspectives to the team effort. It was their job to evaluate whether or not it was possible to transplant the lessons learned into other cultures."

Harnessing group diversity.

Even though almost all of the dozen individuals in the group already had been on other global teams, they first gathered face-to-face in Los Angeles. Mobil generally has its team members huddle in one location at the launch of a new effort so they can begin to build relationships with each other and clearly understand the team's business mission.

This initial meeting was also the occasion in which team members began to understand their roles, confirmed their commitments and decided the rules by which the team would operate. This particular team consisted of marketing and line managers, technology specialists, information technology experts and retail specialists. There were individuals from Texas Instruments present, as well, creating a global virtual team across two companies.

Mobil gave the team members ample time (five days) to get acquainted with the product so they could understand it thoroughly and begin to contribute their ideas for marketing it in their respective regions. This face-time together is when the team leader typically solidifies the group and guides it toward working jointly. Again, several points should be established clearly at this stage: specific team objectives, how to accomplish them, who is responsible for what and when, and general project timetables.

Cross-cultural training is a basic prerequisite for these meetings. Says O'Hara-Devereaux, "I think we haven't done it very well, so we like to pretend that we are through with it now, and everybody did it." She continues, "I do think, however, people have grown acclimated and accustomed to working with people who are different than they are. They go into teams expecting things to be a little bumpier. But they've done it enough times now that there is a whole set of new expectations and experience and awareness that people bring different elements to the team. They're comfortable with the relationships that are formed."

Communicating across the field.

Once the basics are addressed and cultural differences acknowledged, communication takes center field. But communication is achieved through experience, not necessarily through rigid training. "We saw that the workforce was becoming global, so we decided to teach people how to use technology and be sensitive in global teams," says Santa Clara, California-based 3Com's Debra Engel, currently executive advisor, and for the past 15 years senior vice president of corporate services. That personal experience accelerates the learning immensely. Says Engel, "It's amazing how quickly it has switched from a world in which you so rarely had contact with others outside your

Try These Books and Articles for More Information

Try the following list of resources as you conduct additional research. Many relate details about teams in general. Others discuss global teams.

ARTICLES
You can find the following articles in the WORKFORCE ONLINE archives. Go to *www.workforceonline.com,* where you can click on "Research Center." Scroll down to the Topic Index, and select the designated categories.

1. Global Teams: The Ultimate Collaboration
Index Category: Global HR
Subcategory: Global HR
Work teams already have become an established institution in the American workplace. But what happens when a company such as Maxus or Intel transplants the concept abroad? Many of the same rules apply, but you must also help global teams cope with different cultures, languages, locations and time zones. This article was written by Charlene Marmer Solomon and published in the September 1995 issue of PERSONNEL JOURNAL.

2. Motorola's HR Learns the Value of Teams Firsthand
Index Category: HR Trends and Strategies
Subcategory: Teams
After training many business functions to work in teams, HR staff members realized that they must do the same. Two HR departments at Motorola have learned to practice what they preach. This article was written by Kate Ludeman and published in the June 1995 issue of PERSONNEL JOURNAL.

3. Self-directed Skills Building Drives Quality
Index Category: HR Trends and Strategies
Subcategory: Teams
By Instituting a TQM process that supports employee empowerment, Granite Rock Co. gained an edge over its competition. For this, it won the 1994 Personnel Journal Optimas Award for Competitive Advantage. This article was written by Dawn Anfuso and published in the April 1994 issue of PERSONNEL JOURNAL.

4. Team Staffing Requires New HR Role
Index Category: HR Trends and Strategies
Subcategory: Teams
In team-based organizations, staffing can't be handled in a traditional manner. Instead, HR must play an advisory role and allow team members to help make hiring decisions. This article was written by Shari Caudron and published in the May 1994 issue of PERSONNEL JOURNAL.

5. Teamwork Takes Work
Index Category: HR Trends and Strategies
Subcategory: Teams
When rugged individualists are faced with working as part of a well-coordinated group, turmoil often results—but only if they're unprepared. Ongoing training and communication are the keys to unlocking each team's potential as its members learn that their number one priority is to satisfy customers, not management. This article was written by Shari Caudron and published in the February 1994 issue of PERSONNEL JOURNAL.

BOOKS
Each of the following books is available for purchase online through Amazon. Go to *www.amazon.com* and search by title.

1. Capitalizing on the Global Workforce: A Strategic Guide for Expatriate Management
Written by Michael S. Schell and Charlene Marmer Solomon
Published by Irwin Professional Publishing
November 1996
ISBN: 0786308958

2. Cross Cultural Team Building: Guidelines for More Effective Communication and Negotiation
Edited by Mel Berger
Published by McGraw-Hill Book Co. Ltd.
June 1996
ISBN: 0077079191

3. Global Work: Bridging Distance, Culture and Time
Written by Mary O'Hara-Devereaux and Robert Johansen
Published by Jossey-Bass Publishers
May 1994
ISBN: 1555426026

4. International Human Resource Management
Written by Dennis R. Briscoe
Published by Prentice Hall Press
April 1995
ISBN: 0131910086

5. Teams at the Top: Unleashing the Potential of Both Teams and Individual Leaders
Written by Jon R. Katzenbach
Published by Harvard Business School Press
November 1997
ISBN: 0875847897

6. Virtual Teams: Reaching Across Space, Time and Organizations With Technology
Written by Jessica Lipnack and Jeffrey Stamps
Published by John Wiley & Sons
May 1997
ISBN: 0471165530

7. The Wisdom of Teams: Creating the High-Performance Organization
Written by Jon R. Katzenbach and Douglas K. Smith
Published by Harper Business
March 1994
ISBN: 0887306764

—CMS

own work to one where the customer base and marketplace segmentation is disappearing and groups need to communicate all the time."

3Com distinguishes itself through its use of technology. The company, a networking giant, naturally attracts people who want to push the edge of technology as part of their work. Interestingly, though you might expect 3Com to use whiz-bang high-tech gymnastics in its teamwork, the organization has created a different mentality in the way

people operate. With 5,000 employees in its offices in London, Dublin, Tel Aviv, San Diego and Boston, it pursues the ultimate in the virtual office. 3Com's work with global teams concentrates on obtaining peak performance from solid use of the traditionals: voice, e-mail and teleconferencing.

In fact, phone conferencing handles a huge percentage of the real time interaction. If there is a need for visuals in teleconferences, the team members receive e-mailed documentation. They'll look at the document on their individual computers while participating in the teleconference. This offers better resolution and clarity than video, and people also have the opportunity to make changes in the document right there on the screen.

Indeed, while the company is so technologically progressive that all 3Com employees have the ability to watch the chairman's address via live video at their desks, it also knows how to use technology effectively, rather than randomly. It has actually moved away somewhat from videoconferencing. "It wasn't as productive as telephones when you take into account the time to get to the video-conference facility," says Engel. "We also found that some of the video is actually distracting—the delay and extraneous visual effects detracted from the information."

3Com's global team members (about 80 percent of whom are senior managers) have also become more experienced and efficient with teleconferencing. They have learned the behaviors that make teleconferencing more productive: speaking louder and more clearly, having extensions of the phone speakers, being adept at describing the materials they're discussing, and making sure they ask for people's opinions—whether they're physically present or not.

"People get better and better at teleconferencing and they develop new habits," says Engel. Even when a large percentage of the team is present at the meeting location and others are teleconferencing in, speakers will not project their visuals. Instead, they hand them out, making it easier for them to remember what to describe since some of their audience isn't in the room. "If you're projecting the visuals, you tend to take verbal shortcuts. But if you don't have them projected, you describe them to the people in the room the same way as the people on the phone," she explains.

Most team members simply call one of the conferencing systems and enter the meeting via a telephone from an office, home or a cellular phone anywhere in the world. These are not mere squawk-boxes that distort sound and cause callers to scream every time they can't hear. Sophisticated teleconferencing technology allows several callers to join the conversation in a very natural way, and even listen to prior minutes of the meeting so they can hear what they've missed. 3Com uses a system called Meeting Place, with which the caller uses a series of codes. One code allows access to minutes of the meeting, and another allows immediate entry to the meeting.

Because people are distributed globally, one of the biggest challenges is the timing of the meetings. If you have people in the United States and Europe, you just choose an early morning Pacific time; if you have conferences that include Europe, the Americas and Asia, you should rotate the time so that the same group isn't inconvenienced on every occasion.

Cultivating distributed leadership.

With the fundamentals considered, and communication tackled, the teams must next grapple with leadership issues. This is especially important because work in the late 1990s has become more fragmented. Global teams can be severely penalized if leadership isn't adequate.

And it's important that there isn't just one leader. Instead, each team member should have a shared leadership role. One major barrier to global teams is that most people have multiple job responsibilities. Since they have several roles throughout the organization, it's difficult for everyone to respond in a timely, effective manner. You can imagine this becomes exacerbated when one supervisor is in the States and another is the team leader 10,000 miles away. Individuals will frequently report that their managers require them to perform tasks that interfere with their global teamwork. "People have more roles than they used to," says O'Hara-Devereaux. "Creating a sense of leadership for everyone so it's their job to manage other competing demands is important. It needs to be pushed deeper down into the organization."

Some people may be on four, five or six teams, so they must have a sense of ownership of the processes. This establishes not only division of leadership, but rotation of the overall leadership role, as well. Different people take responsibility for convening and running remote meetings, and measuring progress.

Consequently, global leadership training is another skill that must be developed. People should be selected for team participation with leadership in mind, and they must also be trained, supported and monitored.

In the beginning of the team building, however, there typically is a more traditional team leader who helps define the leadership role, as well as the goals and responsibilities for each person on the team. This individual must ensure everyone has explicit enough information so they can clearly visualize what they'll be doing and where they'll be going.

Finally, people need to provide solutions to the team. They can't be shy about offering their ideas. In many business situations, groups come together to work out solutions from the bottom upward. But most global teams don't have that luxury. Part of the leadership function is to be responsible for coming up with solutions that fit into the overall context of the team's goals.

Challenged from all fronts, successful global teams need guidance to overcome the substantial barriers they encounter. When you think about the tasks your global teams must accomplish—and you consider the language obstacles, the cultural barriers, the business challenges—it becomes apparent that your role as global HR manager is equally complex. You can help your organization's cross-border teams enormously by offering cultural preparation and training on successful teamwork, and by providing ongoing assistance with the maintenance of the team.

Cutting Edge Stressbusters

In a 1996 poll released by Marketdata Enterprises, 5 percent of the 1,000 professionals responding said they experienced 'great stress' on a daily basis, with one-third indicating that this occurred more than twice a week," says Paul J. Rosch, M.D., F.A.C.P., president of the American Institute of Stress at the New York Medical College in Yonkers. In addition, mental stress absences accounted for 11 percent of workers' absences in 1996, double the rate of the previous year, according to Dr. Rosch. These statistics are obvious signals to reduce workplace stress before it reduces your workforce.

HR managers now recognize undue stress as a real factor in the onset of illness as well as turnover, job dissatisfaction, decreased productivity and other workplace ills. And corporations are beginning not only to notice, but to try to do something about it.

THE PROBLEM

"The new corporate expectation is to do everything better, faster and cheaper . . . and it's being felt," says David Stum, Ph.D., president of the Loyalty Institute at Aon Consulting in Ann Arbor, Mich. Employees increasingly are feeling stressed, according to Stum, and he notes that days lost from work because of stress increased 36 percent between 1995 and 1998, from 1.1 days to 1.5 days.

The cost for U.S. employers " . . . is estimated between $200 and $300 billion annually, as assessed by absenteeism, employee turnover, direct medical costs, workers' compensation and other legal costs, diminished productivity, accidents, etc.," says American Institute of Stress's Rosch, "and is spread throughout the corporation, from the mailroom to the executive suite."

Despite demographics, the causes are largely the same. Janet Cahill, Ph.D., professor of psychiatry at Rowan University in Glassboro, N.J., cites the three biggest factors affecting stress as: the degree of control over work; demands on employees (neither too few nor too many are healthy); and lack of support from supervisors and coworkers.

CORPORATE ATTENTION

In response, stress-busting seminars are forming in companies nationwide. But every stress reduction program should begin with a workshop, Cahill says, because "they help organizations focus on the scope and scale of the problem" so that they can better tailor the programs to employee needs.

If companies initiate the effort, they can

then pass it along to a committee of employees to determine how best to address the issue. For example, if the real stressor is the increasing demand of a hectic job and family life magnified by a frustrating commute, the answer may be a wellness center with options like yoga, basketball, weight training and aerobics—the kinds of activities that provide a bit of breathing space between work and home. If on the other hand the key problem boils down to the corporate environment—unresponsive managers, poor training for the job, unreliable equipment, etc.—then the committee can focus on ways to change the environment and thus reduce associated stress that way.

Training is helpful, but must include follow-up. "Providing employee training in individual coping techniques as a preventive measure without also correcting negative stressful working environments is short-sighted and may be viewed by some as blaming the victim for the problems of the corporation," explains Ernesto Randolfi, Ph.D., associate professor of health education and promotion at Montana State University in Billings.

A good stress reduction program should include several options, such as flexibility, strength training and various relaxation techniques to actually change the way one perceives stress, says James Campbell Quick., Ph.D., professor of organization behavior at the University of Texas. "Teaching one skill isn't enough."

WHO'S DOING WHAT?

The Adolph Coors Co. recognized the negative effect of undue stress early, and opened the Wellness Center in 1982. This comprehensive center offers everything from massage therapy and acupuncture to EKG stress testing and "mind/body medicine" classes "to receive greater nourishment through the five senses from the environment." Stress Busters is another class that consists of four, one-hour lectures to first assess individual perceptions of stress and then address those particular needs by directing employees to classes within the wellness program.

Reebok International Ltd., in Stoughton, Mass., offers a similar program. Its fitness center offers massage therapy, yoga, mind strengthening and traditional fitness activities. According to Ronnie Barthiewicz, the company's health promotion manager, "Massage therapy started about seven years ago. It wasn't big until people realized they could use it for stress reduction and athletic injuries." The program has grown from one masseuse for 25 hours per week to two people, available 10 hours per day. Priced at $40 per hour, sessions are 75 percent booked, he says. The yoga classes, Barthiewicz says, generally have five to 10 students, and meet once each week, from 1:00 to 1:45 p.m.

ALTERNATIVES

A dedicated fitness or wellness center isn't mandatory. Employees at San Francisco's **Pacific Exchange** (a stock and options exchange) are finding relief with classes on meditation, conflict resolution, new technologies and the business of the Exchange itself. "The idea is to enhance people's skills . . . to help them develop better coping mechanisms," says Viola Lucero, vice president of human resources. The classes, which started in 1998, have been filled to capacity so far, and more classes have been added for the overflow.

Stress reduction workshops have been combined with a variety of other programs at **St. Joseph Baptist Health System,** in Tampa, Fla., to offer something for everyone. Jeri Binder, manager of clinical education, launched a Benefits of Laughter to reap such medically-proven benefits as increased disease resistance and decreased levels of the stress-inducing hormone epinephrine. Less formally, the hospital has given away sand-filled balloons to squeeze, and placed gelatin in a baggie to roll around the cafeteria tables.

Meditation classes were one of the highlights of this year's program. The classes were free for the hospital's educators, who each left with a meditation tape that, Binder says, they use at least once or twice a month.

Meditation or "mind strengthening" classes generally are one component of stress reduction programs. "The best," according to David Gamow, founder, Clarity Seminars, Mountain View, Calif., "teach clinically-proven techniques to reduce stress." American Medical Association studies have proven that meditation is as effective as prescription drugs in lowering blood pressure.

His classes teach breathing and meditation techniques and help participants understand that stress is caused not by a situation, but by how individuals perceive that situation. "Meditation is martial arts for the mind. There's always something we don't know about a situation, so . . . look," he says.

AVAILABILITY

Onsite programs offer a maximum benefit. "It's not possible to spend seven hours at work and have seven hours of productivity," Dr. Randolfi says. "There's no privacy to close your eyes and analyze a problem." An onsite stress reduction center provides that opportunity by allowing a place for a lunchtime game of basketball or an aerobics class, an opportunity to leave the office midday, change one's perspective and then return to work refreshed.

The Coors wellness center is available from 5:30 a.m. to 7:30 p.m. Monday through Thursday, with reduced hours Friday and Saturday. Membership is free for all 6,000 Coors full- or part-time employees, their spouses and dependents. Temporary workers may join the facility for $10 per month.

At Reebok, employees who want to join the fitness center pay $4 per week, and about half the 1,600 employees in the area have signed up. Reebok's fitness center is available five days per week 6 a.m. to 8 p.m. Monday through Thursday, and closes at 6 p.m. on Friday.

The Pacific Exchange considers its classes as training, and requires its employees to take a certain amount of training time each year.

ROI

Although most firms haven't formally tracked results, employees are reporting fewer medical visits, increased productivity and greater well-being. When Coors Brewing Co. researched the issue, it found a return on investment ranging from $1.24 to $8.33 for every dollar it invested in its wellness program.

Coors is one of the few companies to conduct a cost/benefit analysis of its wellness program. Analysis of Coor's computer model, run most recently in 1988, indicated, "Annual incremental costs associated with poor employee health can be estimated to range from $1,342 to $6,316 per employee, and that total costs to the company range from $1,990,805 to $23,029,000."

"We don't track return on investment anymore because soft data is easy to criticize," Gerstler explains. Instead, Coors is beginning to work with the University of Michigan to construct a database for health costs for those who participate in the wellness center.

Reebok's statistics are based upon a recent employee survey, in which 98 percent of respondents who used the fitness center said that it helped reduce work-related stress; 92 percent said it increased alertness and motivation; 83 percent said it reduced the need for medical care; and 66 percent said it enabled them to stay at work longer.

If you haven't considered the effect of stress reduction on your firm's bottom line, add it to your to-do list. Corporations are learning that stress reduction has some very real benefits that are well worth the effort.

GAIL DUTTON is a business writer based in California, and a frequent contributor to HRfocus.

MAJOR STRESSORS

- Responsibility without authority
- Inability to voice complaints
- Prejudice because of age, gender, race or religion
- Poor working conditions
- Inability to work with others because of basic differences in goals and values
- Inadequate recognition
- Inability to use personal talents to their full potential
- Lack of a clear job description or chain of command
- Fear, uncertainty and doubt

—American Institute of Stress

A healthy dose of skepticism can help executives distinguish real opportunities from mirages.

Desperately Seeking Synergy

BY MICHAEL GOOLD AND ANDREW CAMPBELL

THE PURSUIT OF SYNERGY pervades the management of most large companies. Meetings and retreats are held to brainstorm about ways to collaborate more effectively. Cross-business teams are set up to develop key account plans, coordinate product development, and disseminate best practices. Incentives for sharing knowledge, leads, and customers are built into complex compensation schemes. Processes and procedures are standardized. Organizational structures are reshuffled to accommodate new, cross-unit managerial positions.

What emerges from all this activity? In our years of research into corporate synergy, we have found that synergy initiatives often fall short of management's expectations. Some never get beyond a few perfunctory meetings. Others generate a quick burst of activity and then slowly peter out. Others become permanent corporate fixtures without ever fulfilling their original goals. If the only drawbacks to such efforts were frustration and embarrassment, they might be viewed benignly as "learning experiences." But the pursuit of synergy often represents a major opportunity cost as well. It distracts managers' attention from the nuts and bolts of their businesses, and it crowds out other initiatives that might generate real benefits. Sometimes, the synergy programs actually backfire, eroding customer relationships, damaging brands,

Michael Goold and Andrew Campbell are directors of the Ashridge Strategic Management Centre in London, England. They are the authors of The Collaborative Enterprise: Why Links Between Business Units Fail and How to Make Them Work *(Perseus Books, 1999). They also wrote, with Marcus Alexander,* Corporate-Level Strategy: Creating Value in the Multibusiness Company *(John Wiley & Sons, 1994).*

or undermining employee morale. Simply put, many synergy efforts end up destroying value rather than creating it.

The pursuit of synergy often distracts managers' attention from the nuts and bolts of their businesses.

Avoiding such failures is possible, but it requires a whole new way of looking at and thinking about synergy. Rather than assuming that synergy exists, can be achieved, and will be beneficial, corporate executives need to take a more balanced, even skeptical view. They need to counter synergy's natural allure by subjecting their instincts to rigorous evaluation. Such an approach will help executives avoid wasting precious resources on synergy programs that are unlikely to succeed. Perhaps even more important, it will enable them to better understand where the true synergy opportunities lie in their organizations. (See the insert "What Is Synergy?")

We believe that synergy can provide a big boost to the bottom line of most large companies. The challenge is to separate the real opportunities from the illusions. With a more disciplined approach, executives can realize greater value from synergy—even while pursuing fewer initiatives.

Four Managerial Biases

When a synergy program founders, it is usually the business units that take the blame. Corporate executives chalk the failure up to line managers' recalcitrance or incompetence. We have found, however, that the blame is frequently misplaced. The true cause more often lies in the thinking of the corporate executives themselves.

Because executives view the achievement of synergy as central to their jobs, they are prone to four biases that distort their thinking. First comes the *synergy bias,* which leads them to overestimate the benefits and underestimate the costs of synergy. Then comes the *parenting bias,* a belief that synergy will only be captured by cajoling or compelling the business units to cooperate. The parenting bias is usually accompanied by the *skills bias*—the assumption that whatever know-how is required to achieve synergy will be available within the organization. Finally, executives fall victim to the *upside bias,* which causes them to

concentrate so hard on the potential benefits of synergy that they overlook the downsides. In combination, these four biases make synergy seem more attractive and more easily achievable than it truly is.

Synergy Bias. Most corporate executives, whether or not they have any special insight into synergy opportunities or aptitude for nurturing collaboration, feel they *ought* to be creating synergy. The achievement of synergy among their businesses is inextricably linked to their sense of their work and their worth. In part, the synergy bias reflects executives' need to justify the existence of their corporation, particularly to investors. "If we can't find opportunities for synergy, there's no point to the group," one chief executive explained to us. In part, it reflects their desire to make the different businesses feel that they are part of a single family. "My job is to create a family—a group of managers who see themselves as members of one team," commented another CEO. Perhaps most fundamentally, it reflects executives' real fear that they would be left without a role if they were not able to promote coordination, standardization, and other links among the various businesses they control.

The synergy bias becomes an obsession for some executives. Desperately seeking synergy, they make unwise decisions and investments. In one international food company that we studied—we'll call it Worldwide Foods—a newly appointed chief executive fell victim to such an obsession. Seeing that the company's various national units operated autonomously, sharing few ideas across borders, he became convinced that the key to higher corporate profits—and a higher stock price—lay in greater interunit cooperation. The creation of synergy became his top priority, and he quickly appointed global category managers to coordinate each of Worldwide Foods' main product lines. Their brief was to promote collaboration and standardization across countries in order to "leverage the company's brands internationally."

Pressured by the CEO, the category managers launched a succession of high-profile synergy initiatives. The results were dismal. A leading U.K. cookie brand was launched with considerable expense in the United States. It promptly flopped. A pasta promotion that had worked well in Germany was rolled out in Italy and Spain. It backfired, eroding both margins and market shares. An attempt was made to standardize ingredients across Europe for some confectionery products in order to achieve economies of scale in purchasing and manufac-

What Is Synergy?

The word synergy is derived from the Greek word *synergos,* which means "working together." In business usage, synergy refers to the ability of two or more units or companies to generate greater value working together than they would working apart. We've found that most business synergies take one of six forms.

Shared Know-How

Units often benefit from sharing knowledge or skills. They may, for example, improve their results by pooling their insights into a particular process, function, or geographic area. The know-how they share may be written in manuals or in policy-and-procedure statements, but very often it exists tacitly, without formal documentation. Value can be created simply by exposing one set of people to another who have a different way of getting things done. The emphasis that many companies place on leveraging core competencies and sharing best practices reflects the importance attributed to shared know-how.

Shared Tangible Resources

Units can sometimes save a lot of money by sharing physical assets or resources. By using a common manufacturing facility or research laboratory, for example, they may gain economies of scale and avoid duplicated effort. Companies often justify acquisitions of related businesses by pointing to the synergies to be gained from sharing resources.

Pooled Negotiating Power

By combining their purchases, different units can gain greater leverage over suppliers, reducing the cost or even improving the quality of the goods they buy. Companies can also gain similar benefits by negotiating jointly with other stakeholders, such as customers, governments, or universities. The gains from pooled negotiating power can be dramatic.

Coordinated Strategies

It sometimes works to a company's advantage to align the strategies of two or more of its businesses. Divvying up markets among units may, for instance, reduce interunit competition. And coordinating responses to shared competitors may be a powerful and effective way to counter competitive threats. Although coordinated strategies can in principle be an important source of synergy, they're tough to achieve. Striking the right balance between corporate intervention and business-unit autonomy is not easy.

Vertical Integration

Coordinating the flow of products or services from one unit to another can reduce inventory costs, speed product development, increase capacity utilization, and improve market access. In process industries such as petrochemicals and forest products, well-managed vertical integration can yield particularly large benefits.

Combined Business Creation

The creation of new businesses can be facilitated by combining know-how from different units, by extracting discrete activities from various units and combining them in a new unit, or by establishing internal joint ventures or alliances. As a result of the business world's increased concern for corporate regeneration and growth, several companies have placed added emphasis on this type of synergy.

turing. Consumers balked at buying the reformulated products.

Rather than encouraging interunit cooperation, the initiatives ended up discouraging it. As the failures mounted, the management teams in each country became more convinced than ever that their local markets were unique, requiring different products and marketing programs. After a year of largely fruitless efforts, with few tangible benefits and a significant deterioration in the relationship between the corporate center and the units, the chief executive began to retreat, curtailing the synergy initiatives.

A similar problem arose in a professional services firm. Created through a series of acquisitions, this firm had three consulting practices—organization development, employee benefits, and corporate strategy—as well as an executive search business. The chief executive believed that in order to justify the acquisitions, he needed to impose a "one-firm" policy on the four units. The centerpiece of this policy was the adoption of a coordinated approach to key accounts. A client-service manager was assigned to each major client and given responsibility for managing the overall relationship and for cross-selling the firm's various services.

The approach proved disastrous. The chief executive's enthusiasm for the one-firm policy blinded him to the realities of the marketplace. Most of the big clients resented the imposition of a gatekeeper between themselves and the actual providers of the specialist services they were buying. Indeed, many of them began to turn to the firm's competitors. Far from creating value, the synergy effort damaged the firm's profitability, not to mention some of its most important client relationships. Faced with an uproar from the consulting staff, the CEO was forced to eliminate the client-manager positions.

For both these chief executives, synergy had become an emotional imperative rather than a rational one. Spurred by a desire to find and express the logic that held their portfolio of businesses together, they simply assumed that synergies did exist and could be achieved. Like wanderers in a desert who see oases where there is only sand, they became so entranced by the idea of synergy that they led their companies to pursue mirages.

If business-unit managers choose not to cooperate in a synergy initiative, they usually have good reasons.

Parenting Bias. Corporate managers afflicted with the synergy bias are prone to other biases as well. If they believe that opportunities for synergy exist, they feel compelled to get involved themselves. They assume that the unit managers, overly focused on their own businesses and overly protective of their own authority, disregard or undervalue opportunities to collaborate with one another. As one exasperated CEO told us, "There's the I'm-too-busy syndrome, the not-invented-here syndrome, and the don't-interfere-you-don't-understand-my-business syndrome. If I didn't continually bang their heads together, I believe they would never talk to one another."

Assuming that unit managers are naturally resistant to cooperation, executives conclude that synergy can be achieved only through the intervention of the parent. (The parent, in our terminology, can be a holding company, a corporate center, a division, or any other body that oversees more than one business unit.) In most cases, however, both the assumption and the conclusion are wrong. Business managers have every reason to forge links with other units when those links will make their own business more successful. After all, they regularly team up with outside organizations—suppliers, customers, or joint venture partners—and they'll even cooperate with direct

competitors if it's in their interest. In the music industry, to take just one example, the four leading companies will often share the same CD-manufacturing plant in countries with insufficient sales to support four separate plants.

If business-unit managers choose not to cooperate, they usually have good reasons. Either they don't believe there are any benefits to be gained or they believe the costs, including the opportunity costs, outweigh the benefits. The fact that unit managers do not always share their bosses' enthusiasm for a proposed linkage is not evidence that they suffer from the not-invented-here syndrome or some other attitudinal ailment. It may simply be they've concluded that no real gains will come of the effort.

At Worldwide Foods, for example, one of the corporate category managers attempted to create an advertising campaign that could be used throughout Europe. The single campaign seemed logical: It would promote a unified brand and would be cheaper to produce than a series of country-specific campaigns. And, because the campaign would be funded at the corporate level, the category manager presumed it would be attractive to the local managers, who would not have to dip into their own budgets. But several local managers resoundingly rejected the corporate advertisements, in many cases choosing to produce their own ads with their own money. The category manager, regarding the rejection as evidence of local-manager intransigence, asked the chief executive to impose the corporate advertising as a matter of policy. "How parochial can you get?" he complained. "They're even willing to pay out good money for their own ads rather than go along with the ones produced by my department."

But discussions with the local managers revealed that their rejection of the corporate campaign was neither reactionary nor irrational. They believed that the corporate campaign ignored real differences in local markets, cultures, and customs. The pan-European advertising campaign would simply not have worked in countries such as Germany, Sweden, and Denmark. "I'd have been delighted to get my advertising for free from corporate," stated the German product manager. "But I'd have paid much more heavily in terms of lost market share if I'd used their campaign. We had to go our own way because the corporate campaign wasn't appropriate for our distribution channels or target customers."

Because the parenting bias encourages corporate executives to discount unit managers' objections, it often leads them to interfere excessively, doing more harm than good. If, for example, unit managers believe that the opportunity costs of a synergy program outweigh its benefits, forcing them to cooperate will make them even more skeptical of synergy. If two unit managers have a bad working relationship, pushing ahead with a coordination committee will simply waste everyone's time. Although headquarters sometimes needs to push units to cooperate—when, for instance, some units are unaware of promising technical or operational innovations in another unit—it should consider intervention a last resort, not a first priority.

Skills Bias. Corporate executives who believe they should intervene are also likely to assume that they have the skills to intervene effectively. All too often, however, they don't. The members of the management team may lack the operating knowledge, personal relationships, or facilitative skills required to achieve meaningful collaboration, or they may simply lack the patience and force of character needed to follow through. In combination with the parenting bias, the skills bias dooms many synergy programs.

In one large retailing group, the chief executive was convinced, rightly, that there were big benefits to be had from improving and sharing logistics skills across the company. Knowing that competitors were gaining advantages from faster, cheaper distribution, he felt, again rightly, that his businesses were not giving this function sufficient attention. He therefore set up a cross-business team to develop, as he put it, "a core corporate competence in logistics." As there was no obvious corporate candidate to lead the team, the chief executive decided to appoint the supply chain manager from the company's biggest business unit, in the belief that he would grow into the role. As it turned out, the manager's lack of state-of-the-art logistics know-how, combined with his poor communication skills, undermined the team's efforts. The whole initiative quickly fell apart. The skills bias is a natural corollary to the parenting bias. If you are convinced that you need to intervene to make synergies happen, you are likely to overlook skills gaps—or at least assume that they can be filled when necessary. Professional pride, moreover, can make it difficult for senior managers to recognize that they and their colleagues lack certain capabilities. But a lack of the right skills can fatally undermine the implementation of any synergy initiative, however big the opportunity. What's more, learning new skills is not easy, especially for senior managers with ingrained ways of doing things. If new and unfamiliar skills are called for, it's a serious error to

underestimate the difficulty of building them. It may be better to pass the opportunity by than to embark on an intervention that can't be successfully implemented.

Upside Bias. Whether or not the intended benefits of a synergy initiative materialize, the initiative can have other, often unforeseen consequences—what we call *knock-on effects*. Knock-on effects can be either beneficial or harmful, and they can take many forms. A corporate-led synergy program may, for example, help or harm an effort to instill employees with greater personal accountability for business performance. It may reinforce or impede an organizational change. It may increase or reduce employee motivation and innovation. Or it may alter the way unit managers think about their businesses and their roles, for better or for worse.

> *The downsides of synergy are every bit as real as the upsides; they are just not seen as clearly.*

In evaluating the potential for synergy, corporate executives tend to focus too much on positive knock-on effects while overlooking the downsides. In large part, this upside bias is a natural accompaniment to the synergy bias: if parent managers are inclined to think the best of synergy, they will look for evidence that backs up their position while avoiding evidence to the contrary. The upside bias is also reinforced by the general belief that cooperation, sharing, and teamwork are intrinsically good for organizations.

In fact, collaboration is not always good for organizations. Sometimes, it's downright bad. In one consulting company, for example, two business units decided to form a joint team to market and deliver a new service for a client. One of the business units did information technology consulting, the other did strategy consulting. One evening, when the team was working late, the strategy consultants suggested that they order in some pizza and charge it to the client. The IT consultants were surprised, since their terms of employment did not allow them to charge such items to client accounts. The conversation then turned to terms and conditions more generally, and soon the IT consultants discovered that the strategy consultants were being paid as much as 50% more and had better fringe benefits. Yet here they were working together doing similar kinds of tasks.

The discovery of the different billing and compensation practices—what became known in the firm as the "pizza problem"—caused dissatisfaction among the IT consultants and friction between the two businesses. An attempt to resolve the problem by moving some IT consultants into the strategy business only made matters worse. Few of the IT consultants achieved high ratings under the strategy unit's evaluation criteria; consequently, many of the firm's best IT consultants ended up quitting.

Clarifying the objectives and benefits of a potential synergy initiative is the first and most important discipline in making sound decisions on synergy.

As the pizza problem shows, viewing cooperation as an unalloyed good often blinds corporate executives to the negative knock-on effects that may arise from synergy programs. They rush to promote cooperative efforts as examples to be emulated throughout the company. Rarely, though, do they kill an otherwise promising initiative for fear that it might erode a unit's morale or distort its culture. Synergy's downsides are every bit as real as its upsides; they're just not seen as clearly.

The best antidotes for these four biases, as for all biases, are awareness and discipline. Simply by acknowledging the tendency to overstate the benefits and feasibility of synergy, executives can better spot distortions in their thinking. They can then put their ideas to the test, posing hard questions to themselves and to their colleagues: What exactly are we trying to achieve, and how big is the benefit? Is there anything to be gained by intervening at the corporate level? What are the possible downsides? The answers to these questions tell them whether and how to act.

Sizing the Prize

The goals of synergy programs tend to be expressed in broad, vague terms: "sharing best practices," "coordinating customer relationships," "cross-fertilizing ideas." In addition to cutting off debate—who, after all, wants to argue against sharing?—such fuzzy language obscures rather than clarifies the real costs and benefits of the

programs. It also tends to undermine implementation, leading to scattershot, unfocused efforts as different parties impose their own views about what needs to be done to reach the imprecisely stated goals.

Clarifying the real objectives and benefits of a potential synergy initiative—"sizing the prize," as we term it—is the first and most important discipline in making sound decisions on synergy. Executives should strive to be as precise as possible about both the type of synergy being sought and its ultimate payoff for the company. Overarching goals should be disaggregated into discrete, well-defined benefits, and then each benefit should be subjected to hard-nosed financial analysis.

At Worldwide Foods, for example, one of the newly appointed category managers found that her initial efforts were being frustrated by the imprecision of the CEO's goal. "Leveraging international brands" covered such a wide range of possible objectives, from standardizing brand positioning, to sharing marketing programs, to coordinating product rollouts, that she found it difficult to reach agreement about tasks and priorities with the various local managers.

During a visit to the company's Argentinean subsidiary, for example, she tried to persuade the local product manager to use a marketing campaign that had been successful in other countries. Dismissing the idea, he tried to shift the discussion. "That campaign wouldn't work in Argentina," he said. "What I would like is advice on new-product-development processes.

"I don't think you understand," the category manager countered. "I'm trying to create an international brand, and that means standardizing marketing across countries."

"No," said the local manager. "If we want to leverage our brands, we need to focus on product development."

Everywhere she went, the category manager found herself mired in similarly fruitless debates. All the local managers defined "leveraging international brands" to mean what they wanted it to mean. There was no common ground on which to build.

Finally, the category manager stepped back and tried to think more clearly about the synergy opportunities. She saw that the broad goal—leveraging international brands—could be broken down into three separate components: making the brand recognizable across borders, reducing duplicated effort, and increasing the flow of market-

Disaggregating a Synergy Program

All too often, executives set overly broad goals for their synergy programs – goals that make good slogans but provide little guidance to managers in the field. By disaggregating a broad goal into more precisely defined objectives, managers will be better able to evaluate costs and benefits and, when appropriate, create concrete implementation plans. Here we see how one broad and ill-defined goal – "leveraging international brands" – was systematically broken down into meaningful components that could be addressed individually.

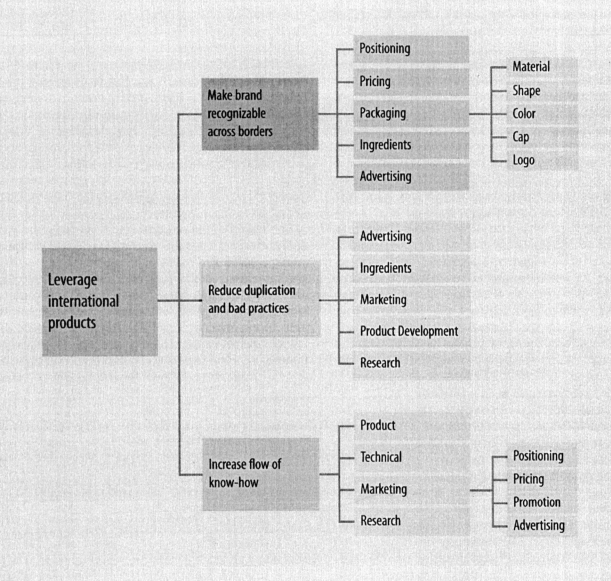

ing know-how. Each of these components could, in turn, be disaggregated further. Making the brand recognizable, for instance, might involve a number of different efforts affecting such areas as brand positioning, pricing, packaging, ingredients, and advertising. Each of these efforts could then be evaluated separately on its own merits. (See the exhibit "Disaggregating a Synergy Program.")

The exercise proved extremely useful. The category manager was able to go back to the local managers and systematically discuss each possible synergy effort, identifying in precise terms its ramifications for each local unit. In some cases, she found she had to take the disaggregation even further. In examining the possibility of standardizing one product's packaging, for example, she found there were local issues about the type and color of the cap; the material used for the bottle; the size, shape, and color of the bottle; and the size of the label. Each item required a separate evaluation of costs and benefits. The type of cap, for example, had a big impact on manufacturing costs—and thus was an attractive candidate for standardization—but some local managers argued that changes in cap design could hinder their marketing efforts. Customers in different countries preferred different cap mechanisms. By carefully balancing the cost savings from economies of scale in manufacturing against the possible loss of sales, the category manager and the local managers were able to reach a consensus on how much to reduce cap variety.

By disaggregating the objectives, the category manager was also able to gain a better understanding of how each effort should be implemented. Standardizing bottle shapes across countries, for example, would require a corporate policy. Otherwise, many of the local managers would go their own way, and economies of scale would be lost. Increasing the flow of technical know-how, by contrast, would be best achieved simply by creating better lines of communication among the technicians in each country. More heavy-handed, top-down initiatives would risk making technical managers resentful and could end up dampening rather than promoting efforts to share expertise.

Even when a synergy prize is found to be sizable, corporate executives should not necessarily rush in.

Once the overall synergy goal has been broken down into its main components, the next step should be to estimate the size of the net benefit in each area. Uncertainties about both the costs and the benefits, however, often lead executives to avoid this obvious task. But without some concrete sense of the payoff, the decision maker will be forced to act on instinct rather than reason. That does not mean that an exhaustive financial analysis has to be performed before anything gets done. In most cases, order-of-magnitude estimates will do. Is the program likely to deliver $1 million, $10 million, or

$100 million in added profits? Is the impact on return on sales likely to be half a percentage point, or one percentage point, or five? This is back-of-the-envelope stuff, but we have found that even such rough estimates promote the kind of objective thinking that counters the biases.

The estimated financial benefits don't always tell the whole story, though. They rarely take into full account the opportunity costs of a synergy program, particularly the costs that result from not focusing management's time and effort elsewhere. The difficulty lies in knowing when the opportunity costs are likely to be greater than the benefits. At one consumer-products company, for example, the corporate center was spearheading an initiative to take a product that had been successful in one country and roll it out in a number of other countries. The local managers resisted the idea. They argued that the program would incur considerable opportunity costs, forcing them to divert marketing funds and management time from other local brands. The key to resolving the dispute lay in determining the strategic importance of the planned rollout.

If the rollout was strategically important, either to the units involved or to the overall corporation, then the benefits would likely outweigh the opportunity costs. But if some other more strategically important initiative was likely to be delayed in order to implement the rollout, then the opportunity costs would be greater. After some soul-searching by the units and by corporate marketing, it was agreed that the rollout had low strategic importance, except in three units. Headquarters scaled back the initiative. It would give advice and support to those units that wanted to go ahead with the product launch, but it would not impose a rollout on the other units.

Sizing the prize provides a counterweight to the synergy bias, forcing corporate managers to substantiate their assumptions that the synergy initiatives they propose will create big net benefits. It also helps counter the parenting bias, as the careful analysis of opportunity costs can help corporate managers better understand the source of any unit manager's resistance. And, by leading to the disaggregation of broad initiatives into discrete, well-defined programs, sizing the prize can set the stage for a focused, successful implementation.

Pinpointing the Parenting Opportunity

Even when a synergy prize is found to be sizable, corporate executives should not necessarily rush in. We would in general urge a cautious approach unless the need for corporate intervention is clear and compelling. Corporate executives should start with the assumption that when it makes good commercial sense, the business-unit managers will usually cooperate without the need for corporate involvement.

When is intervention by the corporate parent justified? Only when corporate executives can, first, point to a specific problem that is preventing the unit managers from working together; second, show why their involvement would solve the problem; and third, confirm that they have the skills required to get the job done. In those circumstances, there is what we call a *parenting opportunity*. We have found that genuine parenting opportunities tend to take four forms:

Perception opportunities arise when businesses are unaware of the potential benefits of synergy. The oversight may be caused by a lack of interest, a lack of information, or a lack of personal contacts. The parent can help fill the perception gap by, for example, disseminating important information or by introducing aggressive performance targets that encourage units to look to other units for better ways to operate.

In general, the greater the number of business units in a company, the more likely it is that perception opportunities will arise. ABB, for example, has 5,000 profit centers organized into a number of business areas. In its power transformer area alone, there are more than 30 units. It is clearly impractical for every unit head to know what is going on in each of the other 29 units. The cost of scanning is too high. The area head, therefore, plays an important role in facilitating the information flow, passing on best-practice ideas and introducing managers to one another. In addition, the area head regularly publishes financial and operating information about each business, enabling cross-unit comparisons and helping each business identify units from which it can learn useful lessons.

Evaluation opportunities arise when the businesses fail to assess correctly the costs and benefits of a potential synergy. The businesses' judgments may be biased by previous experiences with similar initiatives, distorted by shortcomings in the processes or methods they use to assess cost-benefit trade-offs, or skewed by their own strategic priorities. In such cases, the parent should play a role in correcting the units' thinking.

The German subsidiary of one multinational company, for example, was fiercely protective of a new product it had developed. It was not only reluctant to help other units develop similar products, it even refused visits from unit and corporate-center technicians. The reason? The German managers did not trust their French and Italian colleagues to price the new product appropriately. They feared those units would not position it as a premium product and, as a result, would undermine price levels throughout Europe, reducing the exceptional profits being generated in the German market. The Germans' fear of the possible downsides clouded their view of the very real upsides. The standoff was resolved only when corporate executives walked the German managers through the cost-benefit calculations step by step and guaranteed that prices would be kept above a certain minimum in all countries.

Any decision for parental intervention should also take account of the skills of the managers involved.

Motivation opportunities, which derive from a simple lack of enthusiasm by one or more units, can stop collaboration dead in its tracks. Disincentives come in a number of forms. Unit managers may, for example, believe that the personal costs of cooperating are too high—that their personal empires or bonuses may be put at risk. Or transfer-pricing mechanisms may, in effect, penalize one unit for cooperating with another. Or two unit managers may simply dislike each other, preventing them from working together constructively. Identifying and removing motivational roadblocks, whether they reside in measurement and reward systems or in interpersonal relations, can be one of the toughest, but most valuable, roles for the corporate executive.

In one company, the CEO tried for five years to get the managers responsible for North American and European operations to cooperate. The North American business was run by a headstrong young woman with a strong belief in an open management style. Europe was run by a reserved, traditional Englishman who preferred to operate through formal, hierarchical structures. Both managers privately aspired to run the entire global business, but publicly they argued that there were few overlaps between their businesses that would merit collaboration. After a series of failed attempts to get the businesses to work together, each of which ended in bitter rows and recriminations, the CEO finally lost patience and fired both managers. In their places, he appointed more compatible managers who were able to work together with a great deal of success.

Implementation opportunities open up when unit managers understand and commit to a synergy program but, through a lack of skills, people, or other resources, can't make it happen. The business heads of a European chemical company, for example, agreed that it would be valuable to pool their resources when setting up an Asia-Pacific office in Singapore. Their aim was to improve the effectiveness of their sales efforts in markets that were unfamiliar to all of them. The initiative failed because none of the businesses had a suitable candidate to head the office; the individual appointed was not well connected in the region and lacked the skills needed to open new accounts. If the parent had intervened, by providing a suitable manager from its central staff or training and by coaching the man appointed, the chances of success would have increased greatly.

> *When executives manage synergy well, it can be a boon, creating additional value with existing resources.*

Thinking through the nature of the parenting opportunity, and hence the role that the parent needs to play, helps corporate executives pinpoint which type of intervention, if any, makes sense. But any decision to intervene should also take account of the skills of the managers involved. Appointing a purchasing specialist to advise the businesses on gaining leverage by pooling their purchases may be an excellent idea, but if the parent does not have the right person to do the job, the new appointment will end up irritating and alienating the businesses. A lack of the right skills can thwart even the best of intentions.

The discipline of pinpointing the parenting opportunity is probably the most valuable contribution that we have to offer to corporate executives in search of synergy. Thinking clearly about why parental intervention is needed can help managers avoid mirages and select suitable interventions. Unless a parenting opportunity can be pinpointed, our advice is not to intervene at all.

Bringing Downsides to Light

The synergy is attractive; the parenting opportunity is clear; the skills are in place. Is it time to act? Not necessarily. A final discipline is in order: looking carefully for any collateral damage that may occur from the synergy program. Because the pursuit of synergy affects the relationship among business units and the relationship between the units and the corporate center—two of the most sensitive relationships in any big company—it can have far-reaching consequences for a company's organization and strategy. If corporate executives overlook the negative knock-on effects, they risk great harm.

Some synergy efforts send the wrong signals to line managers and employees, clouding their understanding of corporate priorities and damaging the credibility of headquarters. When one company set up a coordination committee to seek marketing synergies among its businesses, the unit managers thought the CEO was abandoning his much-communicated goal of promoting stronger accountability at the individual unit level. They saw the corporate committee as a sign of a return to more centralized control. In fact, the shift of accountability to the units remained a core strategic thrust—the synergy initiative was simply a tactical effort intended to save money. In another company, an initiative to coordinate back-office functions distracted employees from the corporation's fundamental strategic goal of becoming more focused on the customer. They began looking inward rather than outward.

Top-down synergy efforts can also undermine employee motivation and innovation. One consumer-goods company, for example, launched an effort to coordinate research and development across its European units. Although the effort appeared to be highly attractive, offering substantial productivity gains, it backfired. A key source of innovation in the company had been the internal competition between the U.K. and the Continental businesses. By establishing a combined research unit, headquarters ended the competition—and the creativity. The effort succeeded in eliminating duplicated effort and achieving economies of scale, but these gains were overshadowed by the unanticipated downsides.

In other cases, cooperation can distort the way unit managers think about their business, leading to wrongheaded decisions. Consider the experience of a diversified retailing company that tried to encourage greater cooperation between its two appliance-retailing businesses. One of the businesses,

A Disciplined Approach to Synergy

By taking a more disciplined approach to achieving synergy, an executive can gain its rewards while avoiding its frustrations. The first step is to evaluate the costs and benefits – to "size the prize." If the net benefit is unclear, more exploration is needed. If it appears to be small, the executive should not pursue the synergy unless the risks of corporate intervention are low. If it seems large, the executive should determine whether an intervention by the corporate parent makes sense. If the parenting opportunity is unclear, the intervention should be restricted to facilitating further exploration. If no parenting opportunity exists, the executive should resist any urge to intervene. If a clear parenting opportunity exists, the executive should tailor the intervention to fit the opportunity while minimizing any downside risks.

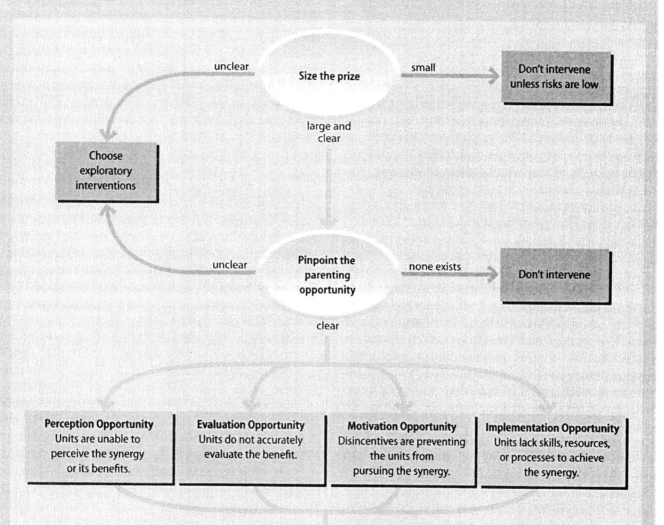

- **Size the prize**
  - unclear → **Choose exploratory interventions**
  - small → **Don't intervene unless risks are low**
  - large and clear → **Pinpoint the parenting opportunity**
    - unclear → Choose exploratory interventions
    - none exists → **Don't intervene**
    - clear →
      - **Perception Opportunity** — Units are unable to perceive the synergy or its benefits.
      - **Evaluation Opportunity** — Units do not accurately evaluate the benefit.
      - **Motivation Opportunity** — Disincentives are preventing the units from pursuing the synergy.
      - **Implementation Opportunity** — Units lack skills, resources, or processes to achieve the synergy.
  - **Select an intervention that will fit the parenting opportunity, will be easy to implement, and will avoid downside risks.**

which focused on selling top-quality appliances at premium prices, was highly profitable. The other, which pursued a pile-it-high, sell-it-cheap strategy, was barely breaking even. The group CEO recognized the differences between the businesses, but he felt certain that synergy could be achieved, particularly in purchasing. To encourage greater cooperation, he put the head of the profitable business in charge of both operations.

The new leader of the two business units initially looked for areas where purchases could be pooled to gain greater leverage over suppliers. But although some small cost reductions were quickly realized, the program soon ran into difficulty: the two businesses were buying different kinds of products, with different price points and different proportions of store-branded items. It was clear that big savings could only be achieved if the two businesses bought identical products. The managers of the struggling unit initially resisted this course, but as they learned more about the product and pricing strategies of their more successful partner, their thinking began to change. Entranced by the wide margins available from selling premium goods, they began shifting their strategy. They bought better-quality products, boosted service levels, and raised prices.

The result was calamitous. The unit's traditional, price-conscious customers went elsewhere for their bargains, while upmarket purchasers stuck with their traditional suppliers. In emulating its sister company, the unit had undermined its business. It had tried to take its product mix upscale without taking account of its competitive positioning. The new strategy was soon reversed, but it took more than a year to remove the inappropriate products from the supply chain. The unit suffered big losses and major write-offs.

It is never possible to predict all the unintended consequences that can flow from a synergy initiative (or, for that matter, from any management action). But by simply being aware that business-unit collaboration can have big downsides, managers will be able to take a more objective, rigorous view of potential synergy efforts. In some cases, they will be able to structure the effort to avoid many of the potential downsides. In other cases, they will be able to kill proposals that would have created more problems than they solved.

First, Do No Harm

Managers have sometimes accused us of being too skeptical about synergy. They argue that the dis-

ciplined approach we recommend—clarifying the real benefits to be gained, examining the potential for parental involvement, taking into account the possible downsides—will mean that fewer initiatives will be launched. And they are right. We believe that corporate managers should be more selective in their synergy interventions. In all too many companies, synergy programs are considered no-brainers. Cooperation and sharing are viewed as ideals that are beyond debate. As we've seen, such assumptions often lead to failed initiatives that waste time and money and, sometimes, severely damage businesses. Real synergy opportunities exist in most large companies, but they are rarely as plentiful as executives assume. The challenge is to distinguish the valid opportunities from the mirages. (See the exhibit "A Disciplined Approach to Synergy.")

In some cases, the analysis of synergy opportunities will raise questions that will be hard to answer. The size of the prize may be uncertain: Will a joint Internet marketing group help or hinder our businesses as they move into electronic commerce? The parenting opportunity may be unclear: Is the German product manager resisting the corporate marketing campaign out of chauvinistic stubbornness, or is the German market really different? The needed skills may be unproven: Will our technical manager be able to lead a coordination committee on production planning? The risks may be hard to pin down: Will a cross-Asian product-development group undermine innovation?

When uncertainty is high, we recommend that corporate executives proceed cautiously. Rather than intervene decisively, they should encourage further exploration. The mechanisms for exploration may be similar to those for implementation—pilot projects, fact-finding visits, temporary assignments and task forces, forums for sharing ideas—but they are very different in intent. An exploratory mechanism is designed simply to collect facts. The end result is a better-informed decision maker. In implementation mode, by contrast, the intention is to change the way managers are working or thinking.

Sometimes, the best course will be to do nothing. The opportunity may be too small to justify the expenditure of management time, there may be no clear reason for the parent to intervene, or the risks may be too high. The thought of doing nothing will, of course, make many executives distinctly uncomfortable. After all, it goes against the grain of the most basic managerial instincts: to take action, to get things done, to create a whole greater than the sum of the parts. Yet executives who are not prepared to countenance a do-nothing outcome should ask themselves whether they are in the throes of biased thinking.

If convinced that the benefit is sizable and the parenting opportunity real, executives can then search for the best kind of corporate intervention. There are usually several possible choices, all with different advantages and drawbacks. Synergies from combined purchasing power, for example, might be achieved by centralizing purchasing, by setting up a purchasing coordination committee, by establishing a corporate advisory center, by creating a cross-unit database on purchases, or by setting corporate standards for terms and conditions. The decision on how to intervene should depend on the nature of the benefit and the parenting opportunity. But it should also take into

account the available skills in the organization and the ease with which implementation is likely to take place. And it should seek to minimize the downside risks. Carefully selected interventions are the best way to release truly valuable synergy.

When synergy is well managed, it can be a boon, creating additional value with existing resources. But when it's poorly managed, it can undermine an organization's confidence and erode the trust among business units as well as between the units and the corporate center. Synergy's upsides are real, but so are its downsides. And the only way for managers to avoid the downsides is to rid themselves of the biases that cloud their thinking. When it comes to synergy, executives would be wise to heed the physicians' creed: First, do no harm.

DECISIVE DECISION MAKING: AN EXERCISE USING ETHICAL FRAMEWORKS

Mark Mallinger
Pepperdine University

For the past several years, ethics has become an increasingly important topic in the literature. Issues related to favoritism, discrimination, and the improper use of information systems are just a few examples of workplace behaviors under study.

Frameworks provide a way of analyzing ethical dilemmas. Pagano (1987) has developed a set of frameworks based on ethical principles. The five frameworks consist of the following:

- utilitarianism,
- self-interest,
- categorical imperative,
- legality, and
- light of day.

The purpose of this article is to present an exercise dealing with ethical behavior and demonstrate the application of the ethical frameworks just described. In the discussion that follows, a definition of the frameworks is provided and alternative classroom pedagogies are offered. The theoretical foundation of the frameworks presented here is a summary of the work of Dahl, Mandell, and Barton (1987).

Frameworks Defined

Utilitarianism can be described as the practical, pragmatic position, that which provides "the greatest good for the greatest number" (Barry, 1986; DeGeorge, 1986; McPherson, 1970).

Self-interest or ethical egoism, based on principles associated with the belief that humans act rationally and with good judgment, proposes that acting in accordance with reason and one's own self-interest results in the greatest good (Barry, 1986; Matthews, Goodpaster, & Nash, 1984; Rachels, 1993). In fact, some philosophers question whether we ever act unselfishly (Rachels, 1993). If that is the case, then self-interest would be the only explanation for behavior.

Both utilitarianism and self-interest recognize cost-benefit in the determination of ethical behavior. In the case of utilitarianism, the benefits to the group are weighed against the costs. The ethical behavior that follows should be in line with the outcome of the analysis; that is, if benefits outweigh costs, then the action is moral. The self-interest and utilitarian framework both focus on the ethical consequences of behavior. However, self-interest relies on benefits to the individual, rather than the group, as the determining factor in the moral analysis.

Categorical imperative or deontology examines behavior based on that which is considered morally right or wrong regardless of its consequences. The deontologist evaluates morality of an action on whether that action conforms to the moral "law." Moral action, therefore, is purely a matter of principle. To be ethical, behavior should be consistent and have universal application (DeGeorge, 1986).

The *legality* framework states that what is ethical is considered to be that which conforms to written law or institutional policy (Pagano, 1987).

The *light of day* framework refers to the reaction one would have if one's behavior were known by others, especially associates, friends, and/or family. If one could be comfortable having these valued others aware of the behavior, then it would be considered ethical to engage in that action (Steiner & Steiner, 1985).

Overview

The exercise in the appendix asks students to arrive at a decision that could have significant societal consequences. Students are required to take the role of a seismologist who has developed a method for predicting earthquakes. The scientist has finalized a study that concludes that a major quake will hit the Los Angeles area within 48 hours. Students are asked to decide what they would do with the information. My objectives are for students to become actively involved in their learning, to share multiple perspectives in assessing ethical behavior, to recognize the value of using frameworks to assist them in the decision process, and to have them take responsibility for their educational development.

Author's Note: The author thanks Russ Gough for his insightful recommendations and comments along with the two anonymous reviewers for their suggestions. Requests for reprints should be sent to Mark Mallinger, Graziadio School of Business, Pepperdine University, Malibu, CA 90263.

Application of Frameworks

Each of the five alternatives in the appendix represents one of the ethical frameworks. Alternative (a) describes the light of day approach. In this case, the scientist is conferring with his or her associates to assist in the decision. The inference is that the seismologist would not likely take action that would be out of line with that of colleagues. Alternative (b) is the categorical imperative response. One could argue the moral obligation of the scientist is to inform the public. Alternative (c) represents the legality framework. Organizational policy is the best judge of what is appropriate. Alternative (d) portrays self-interest. Given the consequences of undesired behavior being potentially greater than the value of preparation, the seismologist's reputation becomes the issue in question. He or she may be the person who is held responsible. Finally, Alternative (e) represents the utilitarian approach. Reliance on a cost-benefit analysis will dictate the greatest good for the greatest number. The difference between Alternatives (d) and (e) is the unit of analysis. That is, the self-interest choice focuses on an individual cost-benefit, whereas the utilitarian approach uses societal gains and losses.

Pedagogy

At the beginning of class, I distribute the exercise and have students individually rank order the choices. Then I ask them to form teams. I tell students that the purpose of the exercise is to explore multiple approaches and that although they may reach a consensus, having dissenting positions within the group is acceptable. After allowing them 15 to 20 minutes for intragroup discussion, I then ask the groups to share their recommendations. I do not lead the discussion; the intergroup dialogue is student operated. In cases where the discussion loses momentum, however, I try to assist in raising the energy level by asking questions of the class or of a specific team. At an appropriate time, I intervene to summarize and wrap up. Because I employ a collaborative learning approach (Mallinger & Elden, 1987; Michaelsen, 1992), having students responsible for group discussion is part of the ongoing classroom climate. Faculty who do not rely on

teams may want to have more control of the discussion once the initial group interaction has ended.

I conclude the exercise by defining the ethical frameworks and describing the value and limitations of each of the strategies. In addition, I share the results of previous organizational behavior classes. The comparisons are useful in that students frequently are interested in where they stand in relation to peers, and the results provide the opportunity for them to assess their actions in regard to similar others (light of day).

Results

I have used the exercise with both American and German students. Although at this time the sample size is relatively small, the results demonstrated that utilitarianism (Alternative [e]) was the most selected choice among the American MBAs, whereas light of day (Alternative [a]) was the favorite of the German students. It is interesting to note that both groups rated self-interest (Alternative [d]) as the least attractive behavior. The German students completed the exercise after the Americans, and when told of the results of the group from the United States, they affirmed that cultural differences could be at work to explain the variance. They said that Americans rely on scientific models more so than do Germans; estimating the value of human life is not the German way of assessing choices (utilitarianism was ranked second lowest among the German group). In addition, risk avoidance was discussed as a reason explaining light of day as the highest rated item. It is generally accepted that Germans (see Hofstede, 1993) tend to be lower risk takers than some other cultures, particularly Americans. Light of day tends to spread the risk by incorporating the impressions of others in the decision process. Therefore, an unintended but intriguing outcome of the exercise was the opportunity to include cultural differences as part of the discussion phrase of the exercise.

I would appreciate hearing from those readers who use the exercise. It might be interesting to compare results to those of other organizational behavior faculty, particularly those who teach in cross-cultural domains.

Appendix
Decisive Decision Making: An Exercise Using Ethical Frameworks

Objectives:

To understand ethical frameworks
To value different perspectives
To recognize the value of frameworks in decision making
To raise awareness of one's own ethical agendas

Time required: 1 hour

Group size: 4 to 5 members

Students needed: 8 to 30 students

Procedures

STEP 1 (10 minutes)
Read the exercise and rank order choices.

Ethical Decision Making
You are the chief seismologist at one of the leading research facilities in North America. You hold a Ph.D. from the most prestigious university in the country specializing in this field.

For a number of years, you have been working on perfecting a method for predicting major earthquakes on the West Coast. you report to the director of the research center. The organization is dependent on government agency funds in the form of research grants along with funding from corporate interests.

Recently, you have developed a sophisticated technique that you believe is able to forecast, within 80%, the likelihood of the occurrence of an earthquake during a 48-hour period. The results of a rigorous study that you have just completed indicate that a 7.3-magnitude quake will hit one of four fault lines in Southern California within the next 2 days. Three of the faults are in less populated areas where major damage will be relatively low. However, the fourth fault is the San Andreas, which, if affected, would result in significant damage to structures and a considerable amount of casualties. What is your ethical responsibility regarding the sharing of this information?

Listed below are five alternative strategies. Indicate the action you would take by selecting the most appropriate item, and then rank order the remaining choices. That is, record your first choice by writing the letter of the item, followed by your second choice, and continuing until you have listed all five options.

(a) Without discussing your findings, hypothetically ask colleagues in your field what they would do in a similar situation. Seek the advice of experts like yourself to confirm your decision; avoid actions that are not supported by your peers.

(b) You must share the information with the media. After informing the research director, it is your responsibility to make sure the news of this potential disaster is released to the public. Notifying the director and other government officials is not sufficient; important information may be withheld. You must be sure the truth is known.

(c) Refer to the procedures and policies manual published by the research institution. If the organization has a policy regarding the responsibility for the disclosure of information, you should follow these procedures.

(d) You must be very careful about the dissemination of your research findings. There is a 20% probability that the quake will not occur, and even if the quake does occur sharing information could be harmful. You will likely be held responsible for the chaos and panic that may result. Your career is at stake; you cannot afford to be wrong.

(e) You need to calculate the expected costs associated with the quake. That is, you must compare the value of sharing the information openly to that of maintaining silence. Given the probability of the occurrence of the quake, assign estimated values for injuries sustained, resources needed for cleanup, buildings/structures destroyed, and loss of life. Compare these calculations to estimated value related to releasing information. The amount should include an assessment of the reduction of injuries and deaths but should be offset by the costs of preparation and the pandemonium that is likely to result if prior information is known. (Assume you have a computer program that contains the financial estimates; you need only to enter probability.) If releasing information to the public has a higher expected value than remaining silent, then you must divulge your data.

STEP 2 (15 minutes)

Form groups of four to five students each. Discuss the issues and reach a group consensus, if possible. That is, try to find agreement regarding the rank order of the five choices.

STEP 3 (20 minutes)

Interact with other groups regarding choices. Discussion should focus on explaining reasons for selections.

References

Barry, V. (1986). *Moral issues in business* (3rd ed.). Belmont, CA: Wadsworth.

Dahl, J., Mandell, M., & Barton, M. (1987, March). *Ethics and the undergraduate business student.* Paper presented at the annual meeting of the Western Academy of Management, Big Sky, MT.

DeGeorge, R. T. (1986). *Business ethics* (2nd ed.). New York: Macmillan.

Hofstede, G. (1993). Cultural constraints in management theories. *Academy of Management Executive, 7,* 81–94.

Mallinger, M., & Elden, M. (1987). Improving the quality of worklife in the classroom: QWL as self-managed learning, *Organizational Behavior Teaching Review, 11,* 43–56.

Matthews, J. B., Goodpaster, K. E., & Nash, L. L. (1984). *Policies and persons.* New York: McGraw-Hill.

McPherson, T. (1970). *Social philosophy.* New York: Van Nostrand Reinhold.

Michaelsen, L. (1992). Team learning: A comprehensive approach for harnessing the power of small groups in higher education. In D. Wuluff & J. Nyquist (Eds.), *To improve the academy* (pp. 89–112). Stillwater, OK: New Forums.

Pagano, A. M. (1987, August). *Criteria for ethical decision making.* Paper presented at the annual meeting of the Academy of Management, New Orleans, LA.

Rachels, J. (1993). *The elements of moral philosophy* (2nd ed.). New York: McGraw-Hill.

Steiner, G. A., & Steiner, J. F. (1985). *Business government and society* (4th ed.). New York: Random House.

Q

Quint, David, 60, 62

R

racial issues. *See* diversity
Randolfi, Ernesto, 207, 208
reaction, recognition programs and, 63
recognition programs, 63
recruiting: diversity and, 51–52, 56; family/work issues and, 187
Reebok International Ltd., 207–208
reengineering, 19, 20–23, 28
reframing, teams and, 146–149
reinforced organizational rules, communication of, 103–104
relationship management, 92–93
"rent an employee," 24–25
resilience, chaos theory and, 15–16
restructuring, 16
results, recognition programs and, 63
retention: diversity and, 50–51; family/work issues and, 187
retirement age, increase in, 160
Reynolds, Craig, 11–12
reward systems, 25
Ritz-Carlton, 171
Rockefeller, John D., 161
Rosch, Paul J., 207
Rosenthal, Jim, 21
Ross, Belinda, 157
rules, communication of organizational, 94–106

S

Sanchez, Carol M., 22–23
Sante Fe Institute, 18
Sara Lee, 23
Schein, Edgar, 25
Schick, Allen G., 22–23
Scott Paper, 23
Sears Roebuck, 184
SEI Investments, 152
self-awareness, emotional intelligence and, 108–110
self-estrangement, employee alienation and, 44
self-interest: ethics and, 222, 223; negotiation and, 142
self-navigation subculture, 24
self-organizing entity, chaos as, 11–13
self-regulation, emotional intelligence and, 109, 110–112
sensitivity training movement, 19
sexual harassment, 59
Sharkey, Art, 34

Shell Oil Company, 194
Shepherd, Herb, 26
Shieber, Sylvester, 33
Siemens, George, 161
Simmons, Annette, 129, 130
Sinclair, Mary Jane, 53
Skandia, 14
skills bias, synergy and, 210, 213
skills set training, workplace diversity and, 57
Sloan, Alfred, 161
social contract, between employers and employees, 24–25, 28
social isolation, employee alienation and, 44
social network mapping, 155–159
social process, of coalition formation, 119
social responsibility, corporate, 174
social skills, emotional intelligence and, 109, 114–115
societal/institutional focus, cynicism and, 38, 39
Socrates, 38
Sony, 12–13, 15, 194
speed, chaos theory and, 10
spirituality, in the workplace, 174, 184–185
Stacey, Ralph, 11
Standard Chartered Bank, 179–183
Stiebel, David, 129
Stiglitz, Joseph, 21
St. Joseph Baptist Health System, 208
strategic planning, 178
stress, workplace, 165, 207–208
structural theories, of organizations, 147
structure, organizational, 189–191
Stum, David L., 32–33, 207
Sturken, Craig, 179–183
Sunbeam, 23
symbolic theories, of organizations, 147
synergy, collaboration and, 209–221
systems changes, workplace diversity and, 57, 58

T

Taylor, Frederick, 20
team frames, 146–149
teamwork: chaos theory and, 14; in future-focused corporations, 169–174; learning organizations and, 195–197
technology, 21, 23, 162–166, 173, 176, 177, 200–206; chaos theory and, 9
teleconferencing, 203, 205–206
telecommuting, 164

Texas Instruments, 203, 204
3 Com, 204–205
3M, 14, 194, 197
Trost, Heidi, 153
Tobias, Randall, 187
Toffler, Alvin, 16
total quality management (TQM) 19, 22
transitions, managing chaos theory and, 15
trust, 26, 28, 35–36; employee cynicism and, 42–43, 44
Tucson, AZ, clique analysis of health and human services networks in, 82–91
Tulgan, Bruce, 32

U

upside bias, synergy and, 210, 213–214
utilitarianism, 222

V

values, 15, 21, 92–93, 97
VeriFone, 152
vertical integration, synergy and, 211
VISA, 12, 13
virtual global teams, 202–206
vision: in future-focused corporations, 169–174; learning organizations and, 195–197
"voting with your feet" technique, participation and, 46–47

W

Wade, Judy, 21
Walker, Chip, 24
Wal-Mart, 194
Weingarten, Lisa, 53
Welch, Jack, 154
Wendt, Henry, 28
Westinghouse, 153
Wheatley, Margaret, 12
Willis-Johnson, Lisa, 51
Wilson, Judy, 50
women, working, 56, 167–168
work ethic, motivation and, 64–65
Workforce Commitment Index, 31, 32
work redesign, 20
written organizational rules, communication of, 103–104

X

Xerox, 188, 194, 197, 198

AE Article Review

NAME: DATE:

TITLE AND NUMBER OF ARTICLE:

BRIEFLY STATE THE MAIN IDEA OF THIS ARTICLE:

LIST THREE IMPORTANT FACTS THAT THE AUTHOR USES TO SUPPORT THE MAIN IDEA:

WHAT INFORMATION OR IDEAS DISCUSSED IN THIS ARTICLE ARE ALSO DISCUSSED IN YOUR TEXTBOOK OR OTHER READINGS THAT YOU HAVE DONE? LIST THE TEXTBOOK CHAPTERS AND PAGE NUMBERS:

LIST ANY EXAMPLES OF BIAS OR FAULTY REASONING THAT YOU FOUND IN THE ARTICLE:

LIST ANY NEW TERMS/CONCEPTS THAT WERE DISCUSSED IN THE ARTICLE, AND WRITE A SHORT DEFINITION:

ANNUAL EDITIONS revisions depend on two major opinion sources: one is our Advisory Board, listed in the front of this volume, which works with us in scanning the thousands of articles published in the public press each year; the other is you—the person actually using the book. Please help us and the users of the next edition by completing the prepaid article rating form on this page and returning it to us. Thank you for your help!

ANNUAL EDITIONS: Organizational Behavior 00/01

ARTICLE RATING FORM

Here is an opportunity for you to have direct input into the next revision of this volume. We would like you to rate each of the 35 articles listed below, using the following scale:

1. Excellent: should definitely be retained
2. Above average: should probably be retained
3. Below average: should probably be deleted
4. Poor: should definitely be deleted

Your ratings will play a vital part in the next revision. So please mail this prepaid form to us just as soon as you complete it. Thanks for your help!

RATING

ARTICLE

1. Shifting Paradigms: From Newton to Chaos
2. The New Agenda for Organization Development
3. The New Loyalty: Grasp It. Earn It. Keep It.
4. *Trust,* an Asset in Any Field
5. Organizational Cynicism
6. Building a Rainbow, One Stripe at a Time
7. Why Diversity Matters
8. Walking the Tightrope, Balancing Risks and Gains
9. Measuring the Effectiveness of Recognition Programs
10. Motivation: The Value of the Work Ethic
11. Guide Lines
12. Will Your Culture Support KM?
13. Managing Oneself
14. Networks within Networks: Service Link Overlap, Organizational Cliques, and Network Effectiveness
15. Managing Staff Relationships
16. Organizational Rules on Communicating: How Employees Are—and Are Not—Learning the Ropes
17. What Makes a Leader?
18. Interest Alignment and Coalitions in Multiparty Negotiations

RATING

ARTICLE

19. Keeping Team Conflict Alive
20. Inter- and Intracultural Negotiations: U.S. and Japanese Negotiators
21. The Shape of the New Corporation
22. Beyond the Org Chart
23. The Future That Has Already Happened
24. There Is No Future for the Workplace
25. The Feminization of the Workforce
26. Making Work Meaningful: Secrets of the Future-Focused Corporation
27. New Keys to Employee Performance and Productivity
28. What Do CEO's Want from HR?
29. Building Heart and Soul
30. Cultural Change Is the Work/Life Solution
31. Toward a Learning Organization: The Strategic Building Blocks
32. Integrating Corporate Culture from International M&As
33. Building Teams across Borders
34. Cutting-Edge Stressbusters
35. Desperately Seeking Synergy

(Continued on next page)

AL EDITIONS: Organizational Behavior 00/01

NO POSTAGE
NECESSARY
IF MAILED
IN THE
UNITED STATES

BUSINESS REPLY MAIL
FIRST-CLASS MAIL   PERMIT NO. 84 GUILFORD CT

POSTAGE WILL BE PAID BY ADDRESSEE

Dushkin/McGraw-Hill
Sluice Dock
Guilford, CT 06437-9989

ABOUT YOU

Name _____   Date _____

Are you a teacher? ☐ A student? ☐
Your school's name
_____

Department
_____

Address _____ City _____ State ____ Zip ____

School telephone #
_____

YOUR COMMENTS ARE IMPORTANT TO US !

Please fill in the following information:
For which course did you use this book?
_____

Did you use a text with this *ANNUAL EDITION*? ☐ yes ☐ no
What was the title of the text?
_____

What are your general reactions to the *Annual Editions* concept?
_____

Have you read any particular articles recently that you think should be included in the next edition?
_____

Are there any articles you feel should be replaced in the next edition? Why?
_____

Are there any World Wide Web sites you feel should be included in the next edition? Please annotate.
_____

May we contact you for editorial input? ☐ yes ☐ no
May we quote your comments? ☐ yes ☐ no